ENCYCLOPAEDIA
OF
CARD TRICKS

Revised and Edited by
JEAN HUGARD

Associate Editor:
JOHN J. CRIMMINS, JR.

faber and faber
LONDON · BOSTON

First published in 1961
by Faber and Faber Limited
3 Queen Square London WC1N 3AU
First published in Faber Paperbacks 1964
Reprinted 1967, 1971, 1975 and 1981
Reissued 1989

Printed in Great Britain by
Richard Clay Ltd, Bungay, Suffolk
All rights reserved

ISBN 0 571 07017 5

Introduction

By FRANCIS WHITE

President of The Magic Circle

Jean Hugard was known and revered throughout the world of magic as a practical performer, inventor and author; and, until his recent death, he was in close consultation with my American colleagues on current magical subjects.

This new revised edition of his *Encyclopaedia of Card Tricks* is one of the most complete works on card miracles, and will be welcomed by professional and amateur conjurers, for it is a leading textbook on a specialized branch of magic. The masters of magic, drawn from all parts of the world, contributed many of their finest effects to this book, and their generosity has been rewarded by this new production of the *Encyclopaedia*.

Much patience and time was spent by Hugard in assuring himself that each of the many effects described was practical in performance, and that the explanations of each effect would be readily assimilated by the student.

It is therefore possible for the reader of this book, even if untrained in the subtleties required by a skilled magician, to follow the early examples and, with a minimum of practice, to acquire sufficient knowledge to present an exhibition of simple tricks. An experienced performer with a profound knowledge of card magic will possess, in Hugard's work, a brilliant book of reference which will enable him to revive many splendid tricks, the details of which he may have forgotten.

Magic is an intriguing hobby and, for some, a remunerative profession, but the basic principles are limited and new tricks are rare.

However, I continually witness demonstrations which include what appear to be miracles hitherto unseen but which, after they have been explained, I find are new compositions on old themes. Here lies the secret of the repeated joy magicians obtain from their art, for by the exercise of their wits and ingenuity they are able to originate a trick which may baffle their fellow magicians, even if the basic moves are known to the profession.

It is by reason of this ability that members of The Magic Circle are happy to meet weekly and exhibit before an experienced audience their latest creations, and exchange ideas. The *Encyclopaedia* will be of general assistance to all as an attractive work of reference and I warmly commend it as an addition to the library shelves of students and trained exponents, to study in earnest or to refer to in leisure.

Contents

CHAPTER 1

Miscellaneous Impromptu Card Tricks

CHAPTER 2

Spelling Effects in Card Magic

Contents

CHAPTER 3

'You' Do As 'I' Do Card Mysteries

CHAPTER 4

Card Subtleties Utilizing Key Cards

Contents

CHAPTER 5

'Slick' Principles in Card Magic

CHAPTER 6

Card Mysteries Employing Diachylon

CHAPTER 7

Double-Back Principles in Card Magic

CHAPTER 8

Magic Utilizing Double-Faced Cards

Contents

CHAPTER 9

Card Mysteries Using a One-Way Back Design

CHAPTER 10

Mysteries Using Reversed 'Ordinary' Cards

Contents

CHAPTER 11

Calculation Tricks With Ordinary Cards

CHAPTER 12

Mysteries of a Prearranged Ordinary Pack of Cards

Contents

CHAPTER 13

Magic With a Svengali Pack of Cards

CHAPTER 14

Magic With a Mene-Tekel Pack of Cards

CHAPTER 15

Magic With a Stripper Pack of Cards

Contents

CHAPTER 16

Magical Mysteries With Special Packs, etc.

Contents

CHAPTER 17

The Use of Short Cards in Magical Effects

CHAPTER 18

More Miscellaneous Tricks

Contents

CHAPTER 19

Indispensable Sleights

CHAPTER 20

The Nikola Card System

1

Miscellaneous Impromptu Card Tricks

TWIN SOULS   Al Baker

This effective trick can be done with any pack of cards. Begin by having the pack shuffled by a spectator. In taking it back sight the bottom card, make an overhand shuffle, bringing it to the top and note also the bottom card at the end of the shuffle. Go to a lady and say you will make a prediction foretelling exactly what she is about to do. Write on a slip of paper, 'The gentleman will get the........of........' filling in with the name of the top card of the pack. Fold the slip and put it on the table under a glass or some other object. Hand the pack to the lady and ask her to think of a number, then when your back is turned, to deal that number of cards face down on the table, turn the top card of those dealt, note what it is, replace the packet on the pack and make one complete cut burying the chosen card in the middle. Turn away while the lady does this.

When she is ready, turn again and take the pack. Go to a gentleman and under pretence of fixing on a suitable card to impress on his mind, run over the faces of the cards, find the former bottom card and cut at that point. Note the card thus brought to the top. On a second slip write, 'The lady will get the........of........' fill in the name of this top card. Fold the slip and put it with the first. Ask the lady to whisper the number she chose to the gentleman. Hand the pack to him and tell him to deal the cards face down and note the card at that number. This done, reassemble the pack and shuffle it as you build up the effect by recapitulating what has been done. Hand out the slips in the reverse order to that in which you wrote them. Have the two cards named, then have the slips opened and read, proving that you predicted the choice of those very cards.

THE MAGIC BREATH

This is a good example of how the presentation can be made to transform a simple trick into a striking effect. The trick is that in which a card is sent to any number chosen by the spectator, the first time the cards are counted a wrong card appears but on a second count the right one turns up. The method is simplicity itself. The card is on the top so that the first count brings it to the number required so when the packet is replaced on the pack and again counted it is found at the correct number. In the older method the cards were replaced on the pretext of a miscount, a very weak procedure.

A card having been freely chosen, noted, replaced and brought to the top, execute several shuffles keeping it there. Addressing the spectator you say, 'Have you a magic breath? Well I will show you how to find out. If you have you can send your card to whatever position you please merely by breathing gently on the cards. Will you choose a number? Nine? Then just blow on the pack and think intently of that number as you blow.' Spectator blows, turn your head away with a slight grimace. 'Your breath does not seem to be very magical, but I may be mistaken. Will you take the pack and count down to your number?'

He does this and turns a wrong card. Take the pack, put the packet counted on top and execute a false shuffle; take the card he turned up and push it in somewhere amongst the top eight cards. 'I knew you would fail,' you say, 'instead of thinking while blowing, you blew while thinking, not the same thing at all. Let me show you a real magic breath. See, just a gentle zephyr, but it has sent your card to the number required. What was it you chose? Nine?' Deal eight cards, have the spectator name his card and turn the ninth.

The testing of the spectator's breath can be done delicately or broadly according to the type of audience.

REVERSED COURT CARD   Jordan

Effect. Four cards are placed in a row, faces up. While performer's back is turned a card is turned end for end. He finds the one that has been reversed.

Method. This is a development of the very old trick which was done by using cards the white margins of which were a little wider on one side than the other. In this method pick out of a pack of Bicycle cards the K

Q and J of S. Note the small white spades used in the body of the design. The J has five small spades pointing up or down according to the way the card is turned. The Q has seven pointing to left or right and in the centre of the K design the large jewel is shaded at one end only.

Lay these cards in a row face up noting the way the designs point and invite a spectator to place any other Court card down with them. Turn your back while the spectator turns one card end for end. If he turns one of the S you recognize it by the changed position of the design, but if these are unchanged then you know that the fourth card must have been turned.

THE SAGACIOUS JOKER   Gibson

Using any pack, the Joker is first placed face up and a spectator is asked to shuffle the cards, then take out any face-down card and without looking at it put it in his inside coat pocket with its back outwards. This done he passes the pack to a second person who does the same thing. The process is repeated with a third and fourth person. Thus four cards have been selected at random and even the spectators who have them in their pockets do not know what cards they are. You take the pack, remove the Joker and touching it to each person's pocket you call the names of the cards correctly.

To do this take the face-down pack, spread it to find the face-up Joker, cut to bring it to the top. Make a double lift taking the next face down card with the Joker and holding the two as one. Keep the Joker with its face squarely to the front and as you go to the first spectator sight the index of the card behind the Joker. Touch the Joker to his pocket and slowly tell the value of the card just sighted, then to get the suit insert the Joker in his pocket, drop the card from behind it and pick up in its place the card that was in the pocket. Take care to get it squarely behind before removing the Joker. Now name the suit. Spectator takes the card from his pocket and shows it. You sight the index of the new card behind the Joker and repeat the process. Always name either the suit or the colour before inserting the Joker in the pocket.

No. 2. In this method the rather awkward business of changing the cards in the pocket is avoided. After taking the pack to remove the Joker, run over the cards till you reach it, then reverse it and apparently take it out and put it face down on the table, really draw out the card next to it which may be any card at all. Cut the pack to bring the Joker to the top and keep the pack in your left hand. Pick up the card from the table sighting it. Insert it in the first person's pocket, calling its name and leave it there, bringing out the card originally placed in the pocket. Proceed in exactly the same way with all the others. Finally as the cards are being verified you have ample opportunity to put the last card left in your hand on the bottom of the pack and take off the Joker which you throw face up on the table.

No. 3. This is an adaptation of 'The Whispering Queen' (p. 27).

Using any pack that has a Joker, have it shuffled by a spectator. Take it and in removing the Joker sight and memorize the second, third, and fourth cards from the bottom. Invite a spectator to cut about the middle, put the packets on the table and place his hands on top of them. Tell him to lift one hand. If he lifts the hand from the original bottom half of the pack you say, 'You want to use this packet? Very well.' Hand it to him and put the other aside. But if he raises the other hand simply remove that packet and let him retain the one under his hand. Give any plausible reason that occurs to you and have him count the cards face down. Whatever the number may be you say, 'That's fine. I think we'll succeed.' Tell him to take off the top card and put it in the middle, do the same with the bottom card, and put the next card in his pocket without looking at it. The next two cards are put in the pockets of two other persons, also without being looked. Now since these three cards are the ones you memorized you have no difficulty in naming them, pretending, of course, to get the information from the Joker which you insert in the pockets and study carefully each time.

No. 4. In this method four cards are freely selected and placed in spectator's pocket without being looked at as in the first method, but in putting the pack aside you must note the bottom card and really take the Joker only in your hand. Suppose the bottom card is the 7S. Advance to the first person, touch the Joker to the outside of his pocket and slowly name the colour and value of the bottom card of the pack, in this case the 7S. To get the shape of the pips you say direct contact must be made. Insert the Joker, drop it and seize the card already in the pocket. Now name the suit, S, and bring out the card holding it face down. Tell the spectator to leave his card as it is till you come back to him. As you go to the second person tilt the card in your hand a little and sight the outer index. Go through exactly the same process, naming the card in your hand and exchanging it for the one in the pocket. Same with the third and fourth spectators. You will have to remember these cards and their order.

Finally, put the supposed Joker, really the card from the fourth person's pocket, face down on the table and have the first person take out his card without looking at it and put it face down on the supposed Joker. Drop the rest of the pack on top. Lift the pack with your left hand by the sides as you say, 'Yours was the only card I am doubtful about.' Bend your head down pretending to listen, then say, 'Yes I was right it is the 7S.' With the tip of the left third finger draw back the bottom card and with the right hand pull out the next, the Joker, throwing it face up on the table, and next the 7S. Pick up the Joker and with it touch the spectators' pockets, again name the three cards. They are taken out and verified.

THE TRIO   Elliott

Allow a spectator to shuffle the cards (any pack). Take them back and under pretence of removing the Joker, memorize the three cards below the top card. Riffle shuffle, retaining the four top cards in the same position. Put the pack on the table and ask the spectator to cut it into two packets. Say that you will 'take' one packet and invite him to touch one. If he touches the original lower portion of the pack, take it and put it aside: if he touches the original top portion tell him to take it. In any case that is the packet he must get.

Instruct him to take the top card of this packet and push it into the middle, the same with the bottom card, then to take the top card and put it face down on the table and hand the second and third cards to two other spectators. Now proceed to reveal the cards by mind reading, pulse reading or any other way that pleases your fancy.

CARDS OF CHANCE

In this trick a special move is necessary that is not at all difficult. It is to apparently show the faces of all the cards but to keep one hidden. You have the card on the top, turn pack face outwards and run the cards off one by one from the left hand into the right. When you are about two-thirds through separate the hands for a moment and spread the cards remaining in the left hand to show the indices at the same time pushing the lowest card, the top card of the pack and the one to be concealed, a little forward behind the others. Bring the hands together and as you take off the face card of the left-hand packet pull off the top card behind those in the right hand with the right fingers. Then show all the rest of the cards.

You have a pack shuffled by a spectator and in taking it back sight the bottom card, then overhand shuffle it to the top. Suppose it is the 10S. Cut, bringing it to the middle, keeping the tip of the little finger on the 10S. On a slip of paper write 10S and put it face down on the table without showing what you have written. Ask a spectator to point to a card and contrive to have the 10S in position as he points. Take the card out and put it face down on the table. Ask him to call the name of any card. Suppose he names the 2D. Hand him a slip of paper and have him write that and put the slip on the table. As he does so find the 2D and slip it to the top. Run over the faces of the cards and show the card is not in the pack. Go to a second person and force the 2D just as you forced the 10S. He names, we will say, the AH. Put the 2D down and as he writes AH on a third slip find that card, slip it to the top and show it is not in the pack, using the move explained. Finally force the AH on a third person and place it on the table opposite your first slip, calling it the 10S. Have the pack examined, the three cards named are not in it. Gather up the three cards, mixing them, then match them with the three slips.

PUSH Farelli

Any pack is shuffled by a spectator and returned to you. With the blunt end of a pencil push out a packet of cards from the middle. Invite a spectator to note the top card of the projecting portion by lifting a corner and noting the index. You note the index of the bottom card of the top packet as you turn the cards edgewise to push the projecting packet flush with the pack. By running through the pack and noting the card below this one you learn what card the spectator looked at. Reveal it in as striking a manner as you can. There is little danger of the two cards being separated if you allow the spectator to make a short overhand shuffle. This strengthens the effect greatly.

CARD DETECTIVES Gravatt

With any pack, after it has been well shuffled, secretly sight the two top cards. Riffle shuffle retaining these cards on the top. Put the pack down and have a spectator cut it at about the middle. Invite him to touch one packet. Whichever he touches interpret his choice so that he gets the one with the two cards you know on top. Tell him to do just as you do.

Take the bottom card and put it in the centre of your heap. He does the same. Put the top card in your right-hand pocket. He does the same. Put the bottom card in the middle and the top card in your left-hand pocket. He does the same. Lastly put the top and bottom cards in the middle. He follows suit.

'It is a most peculiar thing,' you say, 'but through some strange sympathy that exists amongst the cards, the one in my right-hand pocket will indicate to me what the card in your right-hand pocket is, and the one in my left pocket will tell me what the one in your left-hand pocket happens to be.'

Take out the card from your right pocket, show it and then deducing from it any plausible or fanciful reason, name the card in his right-hand pocket. Do the same with the other cards. The putting of the cards from the bottom to the middle is merely to confuse and misdirect the spectator.

THE 'EASY' CARD IN WALLET

This method has several good points. The wallet is not prepared and the hand taking it from the pocket is empty.

Use a wallet that opens lengthwise and slip a heavy rubber band around one side. Open it so that the covers touch, back to back, and hang it over the edge of your inside coat pocket, the rubber band side in the pocket, the other side hanging out.

From any shuffled pack have a card freely selected, marked, returned, and bring it to the top. (Chap. 19.) Place both hands with the pack behind your back. Take the marked card in your left hand, reach up under your coat at the back and push the card under your right armpit, retaining it with a slight pressure of the arm against the body. Bring the pack forward and throw out a card, any card, as you say, 'Your card?' The answer will be 'No.'

Place the pack on the table, casually letting it be noted that your hands are empty. Take hold of the right edge of your coat with your right hand. With the left take the card from under your arm, slip it into the wallet, lift this from the pocket, flipping it over and closing it, and bring it out with the band side to the front. Put the right fingers under the band and pull it off as if it really encircled the wallet, open this and invite a spectator to take out the marked card.

Miscellaneous Impromptu Card Tricks

PREDICTION

You have any pack freely shuffled by a spectator. Take it back face up and mentally note the face card. Secretly reverse the lowest card, as the pack lies and remember it also. Put the pack on the table, reversed card face down, pack face up. Invite a spectator to cut about two-thirds of the cards and put them face down beside the remainder of the pack. As he is doing this you write a prediction (the names of the two sighted cards), on a slip of paper and hand it to a second spectator.

Now have the spectator cut the second pile about the middle and put the cut face up alongside. You now have three piles in a row, the middle one face down, the two outside ones face up. Place the first pile (reversed card at bottom) on top of the middle pile and both of these on the third pile. Invite the spectator to remove the face-down section from the middle, put it on the table and cut it into two parts. Have your prediction slip placed on the top portion and the lower packet placed crosswise on that. The slip is thus between the two cards whose names you wrote on it. This way of placing the cut confuses the spectator into thinking the slip is placed at the place at which he cut.

A SMART LOCATION

Allow a spectator to make a free selection of a card from a freely shuffled pack. Let him replace it anywhere as you ruffle the outer ends of the pack. By keeping a tight hold of the inner ends you prevent the card from going right home. Tap the inner ends quite even and then give the protruding end of the selected card a sharp tap. This will send it through the pack and its inner end will protrude about the 1/8 of an inch. With the right thumb on the inner end of the pack split the pack for a riffle shuffle at this protruding card but pick up one more card below it. The chosen card will thus be the second card from the bottom of the portion in the right hand. Riffle the two parts of the pack together but let the two bottom cards of the right-hand part drop first then complete a genuine riffle. You can show the top and the bottom cards after the shuffle and then, with an overhand shuffle, bring the card from next the bottom to any desired position.

THE WHISPERING QUEEN
Ladson Butler

Any pack, borrowed if possible, may be used. Have the cards thoroughly shuffled by one or more spectators. Take it back and run through it to find and remove the QC, the most gossipy of all the Queens. In doing this spread the four top cards so that you can see and memorize their indices. Read the values to yourself thus for instance 47–36 (forty-seven–thirty-six) and then the suits, say C, D, H, S. After a little practice four cards can be memorized in this way at a glance. Have a spectator deal the cards into four face-down heaps. Push the QC face up below any chosen heap for a moment, then put the card to your ear. She whispers the name to you? and you call it. Repeat with the bottom cards of the other heaps.

THE CARD DOCTOR
Annemann

Effect. Using a borrowed pack, if so desired, the performer has a spectator call any number from one to twelve. Dealing fairly to this number the card is show.1 and initialled by the spectator. Stating that the card is to represent a man who has met with an accident necessitating the removal of one leg, the performer tears a corner from the card and hands it to the spectator to hold. As the story goes, the man has a terrible dream in which he sees himself in many pieces. As he tells this, the performer tears the card into a number of pieces with the face of the card towards the audience. Then into the dream comes a great doctor who covers him with a white sheet, but before anything else can happen, the man wakes up and finds himself still in the hospital, perfectly well except for the missing leg. The corner is then matched to the card by the spectator who identifies his initials.

Method. Before starting take the 6, 7 and 8 spots of each suit and put them on the top in any order. Thus the selection must be from one of these cards. Take the card out and, while the spectator initials it, pick up the pack and the cards dealt, pick out a card of the same suit and put it on the bottom. If the chosen card is a 6, you pick a 7; if it is a 7, pick a 6; and if an 8, take a 7. Suppose the 7C is the card selected, put the 6C on the face of the pack and cut same into two parts. Take back the 7C, pick up the original bottom half of the pack and put the 7C at the bottom, i.e. over the 6C, then slide the two cards together about an inch over the end of the pack that is opposite the odd spot of the 7C.

27

Hold the pack now with its face to the audience, the protruding card seemingly the 7C only. Place the remaining half of the pack in front, timing the patter about the man going into the hospital. Holding the pack firmly, deliberately tear off the index corner of both cards as one. Push out the 7 corner with the thumb and hand it to the spectator, then drop the other corner in your pocket as you take out a rubber band.

Turn the pack face down and apparently withdraw the 7C but with the left forefinger push this card back flush with the pack and draw out the 6C face down and put it on the table. Put the rubber band round the pack and hand it to the spectator. Pick up the card with the fingers covering the missing spot and index corner. As you continue relating the dream, tear it in half, placing the torn corner half in front. Now very openly tear the card several times. It is only necessary to vanish the pieces and the sheet in the dream is represented by your handkerchief which has a dummy packet in one corner. Throw the handkerchief over the pieces and give them to the spectator to hold. Really he gets the dummy packet and you pocket the pieces. Tell the ending of the dream, shake out the handkerchief, the pieces have gone. Riffle the pack at the corner, with the band still round it, stopping at the break and have the spectator remove the restored and marked card from the hospital for identification of the initials and the matching of the corner.

STAMPEDO   Jordan

Effect. A postage stamp is stuck to the face of a card to identify it. Ten cards are placed aside and the chosen card put amongst them. A spectator holds the rest of the pack. Chosen card returns to the pack, leaving ten cards only.

Method. Beforehand moisten one end of a stamp and stick it over an end spot of the 3C, the end of the stamp adhering to the card near its end. Put this card on the bottom and the AC at the top. Begin by forcing the AC, cut and bring the 3C back to the bottom and put the pack on the table. Take the chosen card back, face down, show another stamp, moisten it and, at the same time, the tip of the right middle finger; reach under the AC and stick the stamp to its face in exactly the same position as the stamp on the 3C. Show the face of the card to the audience but do not look at it yourself, put it face down on the table and put pack on top of it.

Deal ten cards in a packet to one side from the top of the pack. Draw back the AC on the bottom and draw out the 3C. Drop it on the packet of ten cards. Cut the pack and hand it to be held. Pick up the packet, take the 3C and push it into the middle far enough to hide the end spot, then raise the hands and show the face of the card, it appears to be the stamped AC. As you push it home wet the free end of the stamp and press it back, this will cause the card to stick to the card next above it so that the packet can again be counted as ten and be shown or fanned with impunity.

The A is found in the pack by the spectator.

COLOUR DIVINATION   Jordan

Effect. From a face-up borrowed pack a spectator deals the red cards face down on your left hand, the black cards face up on your right hand. Putting the black cards face up on the table, hand him the red ones to shuffle. Write something on a piece of paper, fold it and lay it down. The spectator picks any red card, face down, without looking at it and puts it in the pile of black cards. Fan the black pile and show the card, it is the card whose name you wrote on the slip. The card is replaced in the red packet and the feat is repeated.

Method. Count the red cards as they are dealt on your left hand, the twenty-sixth is the one whose name you write on the slip, and as you receive it, slip the tip of your left third finger under it. As you turn to the left to put the black cards on the table, straighten the left fingers, levering the top card upwards, glimpse it, and slide it under the face-up black packet as the hands pass: put that packet down, the added card at the bottom and hand the red cards to be shuffled. Write the name of the card you sighted, fold the slip and lay it down. Turn the black heap face down. The spectator pushes any red card into the black packet, face down without looking at it, as you fan the cards. Make the pass, bringing it to the top, then fan the cards. In the middle will be the card you secretly transferred, whose name is on the slip, but the spectator naturally believes it to be the one he just pushed in. Have the slip read, take the card out and replace it in the red packet. The feat can then be repeated.

THE VANISHING PAIR   Jordan

In taking a pack from its case quickly note the top two cards and let them slip back into the case as you take out the remainder. On a slip of paper write the names of these two cards, fold it and hand it to someone to hold. Have the pack shuffled, then cut into two parts and one part handed to you. Pick up the case and slide this chosen packet into it: by making a break with the thumb at one corner and pushing this corner into the case first, the two cards in the case will be forced into its middle.

From the remaining packet deal four cards in a row face down. Look at the first, call its name as you deal it and give the spectators a glimpse of it; miscall the next two as the two cards you wrote on the slip and don't let their faces be seen as you deal them; name the last one correctly and again give the audience a glimpse of it as you lay it down. Allow a choice of the inside pair or the outside pair. Interpret reply that the inside cards are to be used and thrust them into the packet. Give it to be held. Order the two cards to fly to the packet in the case. The packets are examined and the deed has been done.

THE UNKNOWN LEAPER
Jordan

Any pack, shuffled by anyone may be used. Take it and pass the cards with their faces towards a spectator slowly, one at a time from the left hand to the right, counting them aloud and putting the second under the first so that the same order is retained. The person notes any card mentally and remembers its number from the top. A card must be selected before you reach the middle of the pack. This done, while the cards are upright, pull the top card of the right-hand lot on top of those in the left hand, square the pack and cut it as nearly as possible in half. Again run the faces of the cards in the top half before the spectator's eyes so that he can be sure his card is still in it. It is there, but unknown to him, it lies one card higher than he thinks owing to your having pushed off one card from his packet.

Hand the top packet to the spectator, you take the lower one. Deal one card face down on the table, the spectator deals his top card on yours, counting one; deal a second on this and he deals his second card on top, counting 'Two' continue thus, dealing alternately until he arrives at one number less than the depth of his card in his packet. At this point pick up the pile of dealt cards (the top card is the selected card) with the right hand and as you ask him to name his card and deal it face down on the table, place the right-hand packet over the cards in your left hand as if to square them but hold them upright and with the left thumb pull the top card of the right-hand packet on the top of left-hand pile. Put the right-hand packet down, then deal the top card, the card just transferred, face down on the table. He names the card he thought of and turns his card, it is another card altogether: you turn yours, it is his card.

SELF CONTROL
Leroy

Effect. A spectator shuffles a pack of cards, which can be his own, and then spreads the cards face down on a table. He points to any card he pleases, and that card is removed from the pack and kept in full view. Next he is asked to think of a card. He names it and that card is missing from the pack. He himself turns over the card he pointed out, it is the card he thought of.

Secret. The trick is hardly as good as its sales talk but can be made effective. When the spectator points out a card you pick it up and place it in your outside coat pocket at the top, allowing about half the card to protrude, 'in order to keep it in sight the whole time,' as you say. As soon as he names the card he has mentally selected, pick up the pack, run through the faces quickly and on coming to that card transfer it to the top. Say that you cannot find it and ask the spectator to go through the pack to verify the fact that the card is missing. Palm the top card in your right hand and give him the pack. He also fails to find the 'thought' card. With your right hand apparently take the card from your coat pocket and put it face down on the table, it is the card. What you really do is to push the card in the pocket right down out of sight and insert the palmed card, bringing it out in place of the other.

The following description of the effect of a trick by Robert Houdin in his book *Les Secrets*, published in 1868 will be found interesting. 'To place the first card that comes to hand on a table and to predict that whatever may be the card another spectator may please to think of such card shall be identical in suit and value with the card previously removed.'

The modern inventor puts the card in his pocket instead of on the table and calls it a new trick.

IN HIS POCKET

Prepare for the trick by slipping two cards into your right-hand trouser pocket. When ready to do the trick, you can show the pocket empty by pushing the cards to the top inner corner as you pull out the pocket. Have the pack shuffled, take it back and deal the three top cards face up. Memorize the values, ask a spectator to think of one of the three.

Put them in your trousers pocket. Bring out the two previously hidden cards one by one and put them face down on the pack without showing the faces. Now have the card mentally selected and, remembering the values of the cards still in your pocket, and the order in which you placed them, you have no difficulty in bringing out the right card. It must be produced without hesitation or fumbling.

FIND THE QUEEN Annemann

The effect is that four Aces and one Queen are sealed in separate envelopes. These are mixed thoroughly, yet when they are handed to you one by one you tell which contains the Queen.

The secret is very simple. The Aces are placed in the envelopes on their sides, while the Queen is stood upright. Of course this is not done openly. Place the Queen in the envelope in exactly the same way as the others but under cover of the flap turn it upright.

By not announcing what you are going to do the Queen envelope may be handed to you first of all. In which case you say you 'willed' the spectator to do that and open the envelope to see if you are right, turning the card lengthwise before bringing it out. The same effect can be obtained if the Queen envelope is handed to you last. In all other cases simply place the envelope to your forehead and announce which one holds the Queen. Camouflage the fact that you get your information by feel.

SUPER CARD PREDICTION Vernon

The trick depends upon a special move. Take any pack, hold it firmly at the inner left corner between the thumb and first and second fingers. Press downward to the left forcibly with the thumb and the pack will break cleanly at some point. Close the pack and repeat the action, the pack will break at the same point. If the pack breaks at more than one spot, use greater pressure.

To apply this principle to a trick: borrow a pack after having had it well shuffled. Ask the spectator to take out a pencil and paper and under cover of his doing this, test the pack for the break as above; cut if necessary, to bring it at a point about one-third of the way from the top, after glimpsing the index of the card at the bottom of the portion that slides. Write this card on the paper, fold the slip and hand it to the spectator. Give him the top card and, holding the pack in position for the sliding move, call attention to its being squared perfectly and show all sides. Tell the spectator to thrust the card into the pack, face up, anywhere he pleases, but you take care it goes in under the natural break. Now move the inserted card so that it protrudes diagonally from the corner opposite your left thumb. Raise the pack with the left hand till it is upright, make the 'slide' motion, pushing the upper portion an inch to the right, at the same moment seize this packet and the inserted card with the right hand and draw them away. The bottom card of the packet is shown and your prediction read, they coincide.

THE FINGER POINTS   Baker

Any complete pack is handed to a spectator to shuffle: instruct him to merely think of a card as he shuffles. Take the pack and spread it widely on the table with the faces up. Tell the spectator to hold his right hand over the cards, with his forefinger pointing downwards, and move it slowly from one end of the row to the other and back again. When he comes to the card he thought of tell him he is to say mentally, 'That's it,' but on no account to hesitate or stop. Before he does this take up your position a little distance away from the table.

It is a psychological fact that if the spectator carries out your instructions he will hesitate for a fraction of a second when he comes to his card. If you stood close to him this could not be detected but from a little distance it becomes quite noticeable and you learn the approximate position of the card, within five or six cards at the very most. Return to the table, glance at this group memorizing them, cut the pack to bring them to the top and put the pack behind your back. In memorizing the cards, disregard the suits and remember the values as you would a telephone number, thus 48–762. Ask the number of spots on the card and bring forward the correct one, putting it face down. The suit is named and you turn the card.

THE FIVE CARD MENTAL FORCE   Vernon

The following five cards are placed face up in an even row on the table, KH, 7C, AD, 4H and 9D. The performer addresses a spectator, somewhat as follows: 'I have picked out five cards at random and I want you to mentally select just one. You have an unrestricted choice and you must not think that I am trying to influence you in any way.

For instance, here is an ace, occupying the central position; you may think of it, and again you may not. Perhaps you think I had a motive in placing just one black card among the cards. This might influence your choice, or again it might not. At any rate look over the five cards carefully, as long as you wish, but rest assured that whatever card you definitely decide upon I shall presently place face down upon your hand and, when you yourself are holding the card, I shall ask you to name your card. It will be your card. Even when the card is on your hand you have the privilege of changing your mind, still the card will be the one thought of.'

When the spectator has made his mental choice, pick up the five cards, mix them, draw out the 4H and put it on his hand face down. He names his card, it is almost inevitably the 4H. The trick is a purely psychological one. The spectator rejects the Ace and the King as being too conspicuous, the 7C is the one black card and anyway 7 has become an overworked number in such tricks, the 9D is never chosen, being widely considered an unlucky card, and this reasoning leaves one card only, the 4H. Your patter must be directed towards making the spectator consider each card and form a reason for rejecting or choosing it; if you allow a snap choice the trick is almost certain to fail.

Until you have had some experience with the effect instead of putting the 4H on the spectator's hand, simply lay five cards in a pile with the 4H on the top and KH at the bottom. Then if the KH is named simply turn the packet over.

'JUST THINK' MENTAL MYSTERY

Ask someone to just think of a card as he shuffles the pack. He may change his mind as often as he pleases but, having fixed on one card he must keep to it. Next take a blank card about the size of a playing card, draw four lines across it, making five spaces, the first, third and fifth spaces somewhat larger than the second and fourth. Hand this with a pencil to the spectator asking him to fill in the spaces with the names of four indifferent cards and his card in any order he pleases. You address him somewhat after this manner: 'You may write the cards in any order. Your mentally selected card can be written in any space you see fit. You may write your card in the first space, or the last or again in the middle, but don't let me influence your choice of space as this is entirely up to you.' Almost invariably the thought card will be written in the second space, or, if not there, in the third space. However, you have a second string to your bow by watching his manner of writing. You should stand at some little distance from him since you need only watch his hand. There will always be a little hesitation in the writing of the four cards but, when he writes the name of his mentally selected card he writes it in rapidly.

This having been done, take back the pack and the list, glance at the name of the card in the space you have decided on and throw the list face down on the table. Run through the pack, take out the card and put it face down on the table. Give the spectator the list asking him to cross out the indifferent cards, then turn the card you put out. With very little experiences with the feat you should get the card every time. The impression left on the spectator's mind is that you picked the card from the whole pack.

MATCHING THE ACES   Lubrent

This is another trick of the psychological order, the mind of the spectator being influenced to follow your suggestions.

Take two sets of aces, hand one to the spectator and take the other yourself. Place the AH face down on the table without showing it and say to the person, 'I want you to select any one of your four aces and put it face down on mine. You may pick any ace you please, for instance the AS but don't let me influence your mind or choice. Just put your card down here.' Presuming you have chosen a man for the feat it is practically certain he will pick the AH, since he will eliminate the AS through your having named it. If you are dealing with a lady mention the AC and the probability is she will put down the AD.

Continue then by having the person deal the other three aces face up and you put your corresponding ace on each one. Finally turn the two face-down aces showing they match.

If you have a magician to deal with always put down the AC as your first card. He will ignore the AH and the AD since they play an important part in mental selections of cards. Of the two black Aces he will choose the AC as being less prominent. Finish as above. Tricks like these are not certain to succeed but they are very interesting and, if presented as feats of mind reading, you lose no prestige in case of failure and score when successful.

35

SURPASSO
Gibson

Any full pack and its case may be used. Allow a spectator to shuffle the cards, retaining one and hand the remainder to you. Square these carefully and insert them in the case. The spectator having noted his card, turn your back and hold out the case, open end towards him, asking him to insert his card somewhere in the middle. By pressing on the end of the case with your finger and thumb the card will be prevented from going exactly flush with the rest. Have the flap pushed in.

Keeping your back turned while the spectator writes the name of his card, quickly open the case, grip the pack tightly and pull all the cards half-way out of the case. Run your thumb lightly over the ends and pull out the one card that protrudes slightly, put it in a vest pocket, sighting it as you do so, close the flap again, turn and toss card case on the table. You not only know the card but you have possession of it and you can finish the trick as you wish.

Keep your elbows pressed closely to your sides as you extract the card from the case so that your movements are not betrayed to the spectators.

NEW CARD DISCOVERY

Using any pack that has been freely shuffled, secretly note and remember the top and bottom cards. Looking through the pack to remove the Joker gives a good opportunity for doing this. Then riffle shuffle letting the last card of the left-hand portion fall first, and the last card of the right-hand packet fall last, so that the two cards remain in position. With little practice the cards can be spotted while riffle shuffling. Have any card selected, have it noted and replaced on the top, under-cut burying it in the middle but really bringing it between the two noted cards. You may let the spectator make a short overhand shuffle without danger of separating the cards, or the cards may be cut as often as you please with complete cuts.

Knowing the position of the card you can locate it by running over the faces and finally reveal it as you please. A better way is to riffle the index corners till you spot the noted cards and cut at that point, but this requires some practice.

THOUGHT CARD FROM POCKET

Any pack having been thoroughly shuffled by a spectator, take it back and casually spread the cards from the top as if to have one drawn, really count fifteen, insert tip of little finger and close the spread. Announce that instead of having a card drawn you will attempt to find one merely thought of. Take off the fifteen cards above the little finger and lay the rest down. Take out of the fifteen any Club, then any Heart, any Spade and lastly any two Diamonds: remember the order C H S D D but take no notice of the values except that of the last D which you must remember. Fan these five cards and ask a spectator to mentally select one. This done, drop the five on top of the pack and throw the other packet of ten on top of them and square the pack. False shuffle and cut if you can, then casually cut some cards off the top, really five exactly, and push them into the middle; do the same with a small number, any number of cards from the bottom. Again cut five exactly off the top, put them in the middle and any small number from the bottom into the middle.

The five cards from which the card was mentally selected are now on the top and several riffle shuffles may be made safely leaving them there. Place the pack in your breast pocket and have the card named. You can then instantly produce it from the pack.

NAMING CARDS IN THE DARK

Using a borrowed pack which has been thoroughly shuffled you have given it to any spectator who may be chosen. The lights are put out and this person places any card in your hand. You at once name it and when the lights are put on again you are seen to have called it correctly. The effect may be repeated.

At any favourable opportunity, for instance in the course of a trick in which you had to turn your back to the spectators with the pack in your hands, take off the top two or three cards, memorize them and slip them into a vest pocket. Before the lights are put out hold your hand near to the spectator who has the pack so that he can place a card on it without fumbling. When the lights are put out and he puts a card on your hand, at once slip into a pocket and take out the first of the cards memorized from your vest pocket. Place it face down on your hand and put your hand out in the same position as before.

37

The trick bears repetition and simple as it is has proved baffling if a little semi-scientific talk is introduced about the development possible with the sense of touch and so on.

THE MAGIC THRUST
Annemann

From any pack which has been shuffled by a spectator, let a card be freely selected and noted. Have it replaced and bring it to the top by whatever method you use, and false shuffle, leaving it in that position. Let a second spectator draw a card, show it and ask if it is the card first chosen. On being assured that it is not, lay it face up on the top of the pack.

Ask the spectator who drew the first card to stand on your left side, facing the audience with you. Tell him he is to hold his hands behind his back and that you will place the cards in his hands, he is then to at once draw off the reversed card from the top and thrust it in the middle of the pack. As you put the pack behind his back, make the Charlier pass bringing the reversed card and the chosen card next to it to the middle, and put the pack in his hands. He takes the top card, which faces the same way as the rest, and pushes it into the middle of the pack where it is simply lost. Let him then bring the pack forward and spread it revealing the reversed card. Tell him to cut at this card and name the one he chose. He turns over the next card and the effect is that he has himself discovered his own card.

The trick is included in this section because the necessary one-hand pass can be done so slowly, the cards being out of sight behind the spectator's back, that no sleight of hand is necessary.

U FIND YOUR CARD
Lu Brent

Using any pack allow a spectator to shuffle the cards, then divide them into two packets and give you one. Tell him that while your back is turned he is to select any card from his packet, note what it is and put it face down on the top of his packet. Turn away and with your elbows pressed to your sides reverse the card on the bottom of your packet and also the second card from the top. When the spectator is ready, turn round, place your packet on top of his and tell him to put the pack behind his back. Next he is to take off the top card and put it at the bottom of the pack, then to turn the present top card over and thrust it into the middle. This done he brings the pack forward and you spread it, revealing one reversed card: divide the pack at this point, have him name his card, turn over the card below the reversed card, it is his card, thus proving that he found it himself.

What really happens is obvious enough: in reversing a card he simply rights the card already reversed by you so that it is lost among the other cards when he inserts it. The other card reversed by you at the bottom of your packet is the one that shows up above, as of course it has to do.

THE CARD AND CRYSTAL BALL

The invention of this trick has been claimed by many but the credit cannot be apportioned with certainty. The effect is that a spectator selects a card from any freely shuffled pack and places it in the performer's hand, held behind his back. Keeping the card in that position the performer gazes into a crystal ball and reads the name of the card correctly.

Place a small crystal ball in the left coat pocket. Hand the pack to a spectator to shuffle, then turn your back and have him put any card face down between your hands. Being face down you know which are the index corners and you quickly tear one off. Hold it between the tips of your left first and second fingers, plunge that hand into your left coat pocket and bring out the crystal with the corner of the card face up underneath it. Now with great apparent mental exertion, and repeated requests for the spectator to concentrate on the card, you get first the colour, then the suit and finally the value. It is good acting here that puts the trick over. Drop the ball plus the corner into you pocket and bring the card forward, covering the torn corner with the fingers. You can drop the card into your right coat pocket and immediately repeat the effect, or at once go into some other trick.

This is a good way of using up old or incomplete packs. If you have, on occasion, to do the trick with a borrowed pack, it is well to have a new pack with you which you present to the owner, asking permission to keep the other pack as a memento of a happy occasion.

The trick may be done by placing the card just inside the sleeve of the hand which holds the crystal. With a little care this can be done quite cleanly. The variation was introduced by Joe Berg.

THE SECRET MATHEMATICIAN   Findley

Effect. From any thoroughly shuffled pack a spectator cuts a packet and shuffles it. This is placed in the performer's inside coat pocket. The remaining cards are also shuffled by a spectator and from them he takes any card and first calls its suit only. Instantly the performer brings out a card of that suit from his pocket. Next the value of the card is called and the performer brings out in rapid succession two or more cards whose spots added together make the same value.

Secret. As with so many good tricks this is simple. It was first sold by Jordan some twenty years ago.

Under cover of searching for the Joker you find and bring to the face of the pack an A, a 2, a 4, and an 8, each of a different suit. These may be in any order, but whatever it is it must be remembered. To avoid this memorizing you may use four set cards, say AC, 2H, 4S, and 8D, and get them to the bottom in that order. Discard the Joker and have a spectator cut a packet from the top and shuffle it. While he does this separate the four special cards at the bottom of the remainder of the pack, and hold the division at the inner end with the right thumb. Take the shuffled packet back in your left hand and bring the right-hand packet over it for a moment as you turn to the left to hand this packet to a spectator to hold. In that moment drop the four separated cards on top of the shuffled packet in the left hand. Quietly and smoothly done, without any snatching motion the action will never be noticed. Hand the right-hand packet to a spectator and put the left-hand packet in your inner breast pocket.

Knowing the suit and value of each of the four top cards you can now match the suit and value with any card called, by bringing out the card of the right suit first, then one, two or three cards to make up the value. If the card brought out to show the suit is needed in the value combination simply count it first and follow with the other card or cards from the pocket.

In a version of the effect by Albright the AS and 2H are put in the right coat pocket, the 4D and 8C in the left pocket. A spectator shuffles and cuts the pack in half, retaining one half. You take the other half and divide it in half, placing one half in each of the two pockets, and immediately removing them together with the cards already in the pockets which are then examined to prove the absence of any apparatus. The trick then proceeds as an example of sensitive finger-tips, the required cards being produced from either pocket as required.

Probably the simplest way to do the trick is to seize an opportunity during a previous trick to get the four necessary cards together. When ready to do the trick you have merely to look through the pack for the Joker and casually cut the cards bringing the four to the bottom. Riffle shuffle several times, always letting four or more cards fall first from the left hand, square the pack and have a spectator cut off about half the cards and retain them. The other packet you place in your pocket and proceed as usual, drawing the cards as required from the bottom.

THE CARD MIRACLE—CERTAIN

The principle upon which the following tricks depend first appeared in print in the *Art of Magic* in 1909 (see p. 152), as set forth therein 'the secret lies in locating the selected card by observing where the spectator breaks the pack.' That is to say, when a spectator cuts the pack you estimate how many cards are in the lower packet. If you have beforehand sighted the bottom card it follows that, no matter how many complete cuts have been made, if you again cut it to bring the sighted card to the bottom, you can divide the pack within a card or two of the spectator's original cut. How close you come to it will depend on the accuracy of your estimate. A few trials will show that the principle is not really difficult, particularly since all that is necessary is to come within a few cards of the right spot.

1. TUCKER'S VERSION

Any pack of cards shuffled by spectator, the bottom card sighted and the pack placed on the table. A spectator cuts freely and notes the bottom card of the packet cut, then replaces the cards, squares the pack and makes as many complete cuts as he pleases. Take the pack, run over the faces and find the key card. Supposing you estimated that there were twenty cards in the bottom heap after the first cut, then cut the pack two cards below the key and place these eighteen cards on the top. Put the next two cards from the bottom on to the top taking a mental note of what cards they are. The two shifts of the eighteen cards and the two cards from the bottom to the top are done under cover of the movements of running the cards fanwise as you pretend to search for the chosen card. Finally palm the bottom six cards in your left hand (Erdnase, p. 95).

You now control eight cards, two known cards on the top of the pack and six cards palmed in the left hand. The chosen card is named: If it is the top card turn it over; if the second make a double lift and show it. If neither of these is the correct card you say, 'Why, that card has been in my pocket all evening,' and reach into your inside coat pocket with the left hand to produce the card. Turn your right side a little to the front with the right hand assisting by holding open the coat, and under cover of this action spread the six palmed cards so that you can retain the one named and let the others fall into the pocket. It would be a very poor estimate that failed to get within eight cards of the original cut.

2. ABBOTT'S VERSION. 'THE CERTAIN CARD TRICK'

For this version only forty-eight cards are used. Ask a spectator to shuffle and then cut the pack. Performer meanwhile has an opportunity of glancing at the card on the bottom of the pack. Spectator is asked to hold the pack and peek at one card. Performer merely estimates the number of cards raised. He may lift twelve cards and your guess is thirteen, or again you may guess sixteen. In either case, divide your guess by six; for instance six into thirteen is two and one over, or six into sixteen is two and four over. Discard the number over. Spectator is directed to cut the pack as many times as he wishes, then to lay the cards, one at a time, face up, on the table (dealing from the top of the pack). When he has laid out a row of six cards, from left to right he is directed to lay out another row underneath until he has six rows of eight cards in a row.

Note the key card which is the card that you glimpsed at on the bottom of the pack. Note the row it is in. Suppose the key card is the J of C and it is in the fourth row and the fourth card down, and the number of cards that you guessed was sixteen which as explained above gives you two. Add this two to four which totals six. Spectator is now asked which row his card is in. If his card is in the same row as your key card then his card is the sixth card down from the top. If it is in a row to the right of your key card, then his card is the sixth card down in that row. If his card is in a row to the left of your key card row, add one to six and his card must be the seventh card down. Should your number be more than eight continue the count at the top again.

3. THE NELSON DOWNS ORIGINAL

As worked by Mr. Downs: after locating the original bottom card, he cut the pack one card below it, palmed three cards off the bottom in his left hand and put the next card on top, sighting all five so that when the chosen card was named he knew whether to turn the top card, show the bottom card or pretend to draw the card from his pocket.

The trick can be done without resorting to sleight of hand. Suppose the spectator cuts, as happens most often, within a card or two of the centre. When you take the pack back run through it with the faces towards yourself and find the key card. Cut the cards bringing the key card to the bottom, restoring the pack to the same order as when the spectator made his selection. Count to the twenty-third card from the bottom and shift them to the top. Glance at the indices of the next five cards, the original twenty-fourth, twenty-fifth, twenty-sixth, twenty-seventh and twenty-eighth cards, and memorize them, put one card out on the table face down, and the next two on the top, remembering the positions. Have the card named: if it is the one face down on the table, simply turn it triumphantly; if it is the top card, drop the pack without remark on the table card and turn the top card; if it is second from the top make a double lift; if it is the bottom card, turn the pack over and show it and if it is the one next the bottom simply lift the pack, keeping it face down, draw back the bottom card, and pull out the next one.

A good variation is to sight the top card when laying the pack on the table for the spectator to cut, then when he has cut—looked at card and replaced the cut, let him draw out the bottom card and bury it in the pack. This will eliminate any suspicion that the bottom card is being used as a key, a stratagem that has become rather widely known even amongst laymen.

CUT IN DETECTION   Larsen

Let a spectator shuffle the cards (any pack). Very often you will be able to sight the bottom card at the end of the shuffle, if so remember it as your key card. If not, take the pack from him, sighting the bottom card as you do so and shuffle the cards very thoroughly yourself retaining the sighted card at the bottom: in either case the bottom card is your key card. Put the pack on the table and have the spectator make one complete cut. Watch this and estimate at about what number it lies from the middle of the pack after the completion of the cut. Generally the cut is made very close to the middle. Have him then take any card, note what it is and replace it as near the centre as he can. For example, suppose you estimate that the key lies about eighteen or twenty cards from the top, and the chosen card has been replaced within a card or two of the middle, it will, therefore, be from five to ten cards below the key card. Run through the pack, find the key card and pass the sixth, seventh, eighth, ninth, and tenth cards below it to the top of the pack. Fan them a little and note the values only. Put the pack behind your back and ask how many spots are on the card chosen. Pick out the corresponding card in the five and place it face down on the table. The spectator names his card and you turn it over.

Or you may place two of the five on the top, two on the bottom and reverse the fifth in the middle. Bring the pack forward and have the card named. Reveal it by turning the top card, or making a double lift, showing the bottom card or making the glide and drawing out the next card, or by spreading the cards to reveal the reversed card, as may be necessary.

SLEIGHT OF FOOT
Milton

Effect. Magician never touches the cards; still he finds a selected card in the pack.

Magician asks someone to shuffle a pack of cards, and then to divide the pack into several heaps on the table. A spectator is requested to remove a card from the centre of any heap, note the card, and replace on the top of any heap. The heaps are then replaced one on top of another, and pack may then be cut several times, squared, and placed on floor.

Magician now, with his foot, kicks the pack, and the cards slide apart. He indicates the card just below the point where the pack breaks most prominently, and this card is found to be the chosen card.

Secret. All that is required is a small amount of salt in the waistcoat pocket. After the pack has been divided into three or four piles on the table, performer turns his back and asks a spectator to remove any card from any pile, and replace on any other pile. Meanwhile, performer places first finger into waistcoat pocket and gets a few grains of salt on to the end of finger. Turning around and pointing to piles, he asks spectator on which pile he replaced card. When spectator indicates the pile, performer places finger on that pile; this move will leave a frew grains of salt on top of the selected card, but unnoticed by the spectators. Spectator is now requested to place a pile on top of the one containing the chosen card, then another pile on top of that, until entire pack is assembled. Pack may now be cut, and placed on floor.

With the side of the shoe, strike the side of the pack a sharp blow. The cards will slide apart at the point where the salt is. This break is your cue. Withdraw the card just below it, and you have the chosen card.

2

Spelling Effects in Card Magic

1. SYSTEM FOR ARRANGING CARDS FOR ANY SPELLING COMBINATION

The method, given in the original typescript Encyclopedia, for arranging any desired spelling combination, was very laborious and uncertain: it was simply that of working the combination backwards. The following is a much better and absolutely sure method whereby any arrangement can be worked out quickly and easily. Suppose for example, you desire to get the formula for spelling the cards of one suit from the Ace to the King, one card to be put from the top to the bottom of the packet for each letter, and the card spelt to be turned up following the last letter; take a pencil and paper and mark off thirteen spaces in a row.

— — — — — — — — — — — — —

Spell A-C-E, tapping one space for each letter and mark A in the fourth space: spell T-W-O, and put 2 in the fourth space following: spell T-H-R-E-E and mark 3 in the sixth space farther on, which will bring you to the first space in the row: spell F-O-U-R and mark 4 in the fifth space

3 — — A — — 4 2 — — — — —

farther on: continue in exactly the same way, counting the empty spaces only, ignoring those filled until you finally write in the King, with the result that the formula will read:

3, 8, 7, A, Q, 6, 4, 2, J, K, 10, 9, 5

which will be found to bring about the exact result required.

The same system can be applied to any combination. Another example showing its application to a trick follows—The effect to be brought about is this: from a thoroughly shuffled pack the magician takes all the cards of a selected suit, as they lie after the shuffle and tells the following

45

story, at each word he puts a card under the packet and turns a card whenever its name is mentioned. He says:

'This is the tale of the Jack of Hearts (JH) who stole the tarts, he ate (8) seventy-five (7) (5) and was so sick (6) the King (K) thought he was threatened (3) (10) with appendicitis, but the Queen (Q) at once (A) came to (2) the rescue and by good fortune (4) saved his life; like the cat he had nine (9).'

To arrive at the necessary formula, again mark out thirteen spaces: repeat the story, tapping one space for each word, and insert the card as each one is named. The first round will fill the seventh space with JH and the thirteenth space with the 8: the next round will fill the first space with the 7 and the next with the 5, and the 6 will go in the sixth space, ignoring that already filled by the JH; the next, the K goes into the ninth space, and so on until all the spaces are filled and the complete formula runs:

7, 5, 3, 10, 9, 6, J, A, K, 4, 2, Q, 8

This will be found to bring out the cards correctly.

To work the trick, put any thirteen cards on top of the Heart suit, arranged according to the formula, and place these twenty-six cards on top of the remainder of the pack. You have a card selected, being careful to spread the Hearts only, since a Heart must be drawn, and have it returned to the same position, telling the spectator to remember the suit only. Split the pack at the 8H with the right thumb and riffle shuffle slowly and openly, calling attention to the thorough way the cards are being mixed. Square up and again split the pack for another riffle shuffle, this time being careful to see the 7H fall from the right thumb before dividing the pack. Shuffle slowly and openly again. Everyone will be convinced that the cards are hopelessly mixed; however, the first shuffle merely distributed the Hearts through the lower part of the pack, while the second spread them throughout the whole pack, but in each case the relative positions of the Heart cards remain the same—and when the intervening cards are eliminated their original order remains undisturbed.

Now inquire what the suit of the chosen card was: the answer being 'Hearts', you turn the pack face up and take the Hearts out, as they lie, one by one. This process will reverse their order, so pick up the packet and deal the cards one by one, face down, under pretence of counting them. The double shuffle, the removal from the pack and the counting will have convinced the spectators that the cards must be in haphazard order and the effect when they come out at appropriate times in the telling of the story will be surprising.

As an opening feat for a card routine for small audiences I know of none better. The system and the principle of the double shuffle were devised by me over thirty years ago and they are but little known even yet.

2. SPELLING A CARD (Lawrence Gray—Impromptu)

This trick, which was one of the first and is still one of the best of impromptu spelling tricks, was not included in the original Encyclopaedia although several tricks based on it were.

A card is forced, or sighted, by the magician. It is replaced in the pack which is shuffled by the spectator. Taking the pack, the performer runs through it, face up, to show that the card has not been removed. When he comes to the selected card (say for instance it was the 10C), he begins to spell its name, TEN-OF-CLUBS, passing one card for each letter, and when he arrives at the last letter, S, he inserts the tip of his left little finger above it and holds a break at that point, but keeps right on running through the pack without pausing. He cuts the pack at the break and hands it to the spectator, instructing him to spell the name of his card, dealing one card for each letter and turning up the last card so dealt. The spectator does this and, of course, finds his own card.

Instead of forcing a card, the bottom card of the pack may be sighted and when the pack is divided for the return of the chosen card, this is done by an under cut, so that the sighted card is brought above it. A casual overhand shuffle will not separate the two cards. When running over the faces of the cards the performer has simply to watch for the sighted card and start his spelling on the next. It sometimes happens that the card does not show up until there are not enough cards above it for the spelling, in that case stop when there are only about ten cards to be run over, cut the pack and start again from the face card. The trick bears repetition.

3. DUPLEX COMEDY SPELLER (Larry Gray—Any Pack)

Any pack is thoroughly shuffled y spectator; take it back sighting the bottom card. Spread the cards and allow a free choice. Undercut half the pack for the replacement of the card, thus bringing the key card on top of the chosen one. Cut several times, or a short overhand shuffle may be made with little risk of separating the two cards. To show that the card has not been removed or tampered with, run the cards over before the spectator in an even tempo, telling him to see that his card is still there but not to indicate what or where it is. You watch for the key card, when you reach it, begin to spell its name, starting with it and counting mentally one card for each letter. On reaching the last letter, ask, 'Have you seen your card?' and separate your hands slightly. The answer will be 'Yes.' Bring your hands together reversing the position of the cards they held. The key card is thus set for spelling from the top of the pack, and the chosen card lies under it.

Now illustrate the trick by naming, apparently at random, the key card and spell it, turning it up on the last letter and showing it. The chosen card is now on top of the pack which you hand to the spectator to spell out his card; of course he fails, but in dealing the cards he has put his card in correct position to be spelt. So when you replace the packet on the pack and tell him the mystic word to use, he succeeds in spelling this card.

This is one of the best of the impromptu spelling tricks.

4. FARELLI'S IMPROMPTU SPELLER

(Gray's Speller—Single Card)

Force a card and allow the spectator to replace it in the pack and thoroughly shuffle. Take the pack face upwards in the left hand and deal the cards face down on the table, letting the spectator see the face of each card as you deal. When you reach the forced card spell it in, beginning with the card itself, including the 'of' and on reaching the last letter hesitate and ask the spectator if you have passed his card. The answer is of course 'Yes.' Turn the cards in your left hand face down, pick up the packet from the table and put them on top. If possible use a false shuffle and series of false cuts, then spell out the card turning it up on the last letter.

Instead of forcing a card, the chosen card may be sighted after its return to the pack, or a key card may be used, the card being replaced next to it and so located when the cards are dealt.

5. KNOCK OUT SPELLER

No preparation

Effect. Any pack shuffled freely and spread on the table, a spectator removes any card he wishes, looks at it and replaces it at the spot from which he took it. Magician gathers up the pack, the card is named and he spells it out, dealing a card to each letter, finally turning up the card.

Secret. When the pack is spread on the table it must be done with a wide sweep. The spectator is given a free choice but when he removes a card, count visually to the twelfth card above the spot from which it was removed. When the card is replaced, watch the card to which you counted, and in gathering up the pack hold a break there with the thumb and transfer them to the bottom by cutting the pack. The chosen card will now be the thirteenth card and most cards can be spelled with thirteen letters. If it is necessary to get rid of one or two cards simply take them off the top, fan the pack with them and then put them casually on the bottom. The best way to pick up the cards is to first make the spread from right to left, then when a card has been removed, pick up the cards above the twelfth card beyond it and use them as a scoop to pick up the rest when the card has been returned.

6. A SINGLE SPELLER   Impromptu—4 piles of 13

Any pack shuffled by spectators and dealt into four piles of thirteen cards each.

Any card selected in any heap is noted, and put on top of any one of the piles. Drop one pile on top of this, pick up the two piles and place the remaining two heaps below the packet thus made. The chosen card will, therefore, be the fourteenth card from the top of the pack. It is necessary to run off one card from the top in the false shuffle and spell the selected card with thirteen letters. (See system used in The Double Speller.)

7. SUPERLATIVE SPELLER   (Ben Erens—Impromptu)

Effect. Borrowed pack laid on table and spectator cuts. He chooses either heap, cuts this and looks at the bottom card of the cut. The cut portion is replaced and the pack reassembled. The card looked at is named and the magician spells it out, taking off a card for each letter, and at the end of the spelling shows the card selected.

Secret. When anyone cuts a pack it is usually divided near the centre. The pack having been cut and a pile chosen, invite the spectator to cut that heap and illustrate by cutting the remaining pile about the middle. When he does likewise, make an estimate of the number he cuts off, usually from ten to fifteen. He then looks at the bottom card of his cut and replaces the cards. Pick up this pile and place it on top of the other portion, thus reassembling the pack with the selected card at the number from the top as estimated by you.

False shuffles and cuts may follow according to your ability. Have the card named. Suppose the 4C is the card, and you estimate it is about fourteen cards down. Spell out 'The Four of Clubs' and the card shows up either on the B or the S. In either case act as if that was what you intended. If it doesn't fall at S throw out another card and say 'Four of', and if that is the card say 'Clubs'; but if not, then throw still another card and with it say 'Clubs'. In other words you fit the spelling to the number of cards you estimate the spectator cut. By adding or omitting the 'of' and the final 's' of the suit the spelling can be made flexible enough to fit all cases. With but little practice the number of cards can be estimated to within one or two.

8. YOU SELECTED THE—— (Impromptu)

Have the pack shuffled and ask someone to take out any card, turn it face up and thrust it in the centre of the pack, stressing the word 'centre', and holding the pack yourself. This done, let him look at the card facing the card thrust partly in the pack. Withdraw the face-up card and put it on the top. Spell in the usual way, one card dealt for each letter, YOU SELECTED THE —— at this point ask for the value only of the card sighted. Suppose it is a 10, spell TEN and then ask for the suit. You now make a simple calculation: the card is within a card or two of twenty-six being about the centre of the pack, the phrase spelt has disposed of fourteen cards so you must spell the name of the card in about twelve letters. When the suit is named if it is Diamonds you omit the word 'of'. With the other suits if the card appears on the letter before the final 's' just act as if that is what you intended. If it has not appeared on the final letter turn next one. If it is still not there name the card in full and turn up the next. Only a gross miscalculation will fail to bring the card, but should it so happen use the word 'period' or 'stop' as an excuse for turning one more card.

9. SPELL IT (Buckley—Impromptu)

Remove from the pack the Q, 8, 7, and 3 of Diamonds and the Joker. Shuffle the remainder of the cards and in running them from hand to hand for a spectator to take one, hold an inconspicuous break between the tenth and eleventh cards. A card having been drawn, open the pack at the break and have the card returned at that spot. Follow with false shuffles and cuts.

The card is named and you spell it off, taking a card for each letter and turning up the eleventh card, which is correct. A very simple calculation will indicate the manner in which you must spell and you can turn the card either on the last letter or following the last letter, and you can insert 'of' or omit it as may be necessary. For instance, the A, 2, 6 and 10 of Clubs requires the addition of the word 'of' bringing the total letters to ten and you turn the eleventh card. Again for the 4D, spell 'Diamond, four' and turn the card on the last letter; for the 5S, spell 'Spades, five' and turn the next card. The system will be found to cover every card in the pack except the four discarded ones.

10. IMPROMPTU SPELLER
Impromptu—Card 13th and Spelling varied

Any pack is freely shuffled and any card freely chosen, but in spreading the cards for the spectator, secretly count to and hold a break under the twelfth card. For the replacement of the card, cut at the break and have it put back at that point, drop the packet of twelve cards on top of it and square the cards very openly. False shuffle and make several false cuts leaving the cards on the top in the same position.

Have the chosen card named and spell it according to the following rules:

For Clubs, A, 2, 6, 10, spell THE —— OF CLUBS, turn last card.
    „   4, 5, 9, J, K, spell CLUBS, THE —— turn next card.
    „   3, 7, 8, Q, spell —— of CLUBS turn next card.
Hearts,   A, 2, 6, 10, spell HEARTS, THE —— turn next card.
    „   4, 5, 9, J, K, spell —— OF HEARTS, turn next card.
    „   2, 3, 7, 8, Q, spell —— OF HEARTS turn last card.
Spades,   treat exactly in the same way as Hearts.
Diamonds, A, 2, 6, 10, spell —— OF DIAMONDS, turn last card.
    „   4, 5, 9, J, K, spell DIAMONDS ——, turn next card.
    „   3, 7, 8, Q, spell DIAMONDS ——, turn last card.

The Joker may be spelt THE JOLLY JOKER.

With a very little practice the necessary changes in the spelling become easy to remember.

11. WIZARD SPELLING MASTER (Jordan—Impromptu)

Any pack may be used and it can be thoroughly shuffled by a spectator before the trick. When you take the pack back hold it face up in the left hand and pass the cards one by one into the right hand, as though counting them. As you do this pass all the Diamonds and all the five-letter cards of Hearts and Spades (deuce, three, seven, eight, Queen) behind the first card taken off, and all the other cards on top of it. Turn the pack face down and have the cards dealt alternately into two heaps, face down, by a spectator, who then riffle shuffles the pack. The result will be that the cards which were originally on top, i.e. the D's and five-letter H's and S's will be on the bottom and vice versa. A few cards in the middle will be mixed but they do not matter.

Fan the upper part of the pack and have someone take a few cards, see that he gets nine; do the same with a second person. Fan the lower part of the pack and let the third person get twelve. Each shuffles his own packet. Place the pack remaining on the back of your hand. Let the third party choose a card from his packet, note it and put it on top of the cards on your hand and the balance of his packet on top of that. The other two spectators do the same. Thus there are two nine-card packets at the top, followed by the twelve-card pile.

Any card chosen can be spelled with the same number of letters as there are cards in the heap it was drawn from. Spell the suit first, then the value. For instance, the 7C being named, you say, 'The card is a Club? The seven?' and you spell CLUB-SEVEN. For the 9C you say, 'The suit is Clubs? The nine?' and spell CLUBS-NINE. Again for the 2C you say, 'The suit is Clubs! The two?' and spell CLUBS-TWO and turn the *next card*.

The same system is applied to the card from the twelve-card pile; the suit being spelt first, then the value and the S in Diamonds is used or eliminated as may be necessary.

12. PECULIARITIES OF THE PASTEBOARDS Impromptu

Effect. From a borrowed pack three cards are freely selected, returned and the pack shuffled. Performer spells out a card at random and on the last letter that card appears. Pack is handed to a spectator and he spells the name of his card, it too answers to its name. Second spectator names his card, pack is cut and it appears on the top. The third spectator takes the pack, names his card and it turns itself over face up, amongst the others.

Secret. After borrowed pack has been shuffled, run through it under pretext of removing the Joker, locate any thirteen-letter card (AD, 2D, QH, etc.) and cut the pack so that this card is tenth from the top. Fan the cards face outwards to show they are well mixed, then have three cards taken from anywhere below the top ten cards. Undercut about half the pack and have the first spectator return his card on the original top card. Put the cut on top but hold break with tip of little finger. Go to second spectator, cut at break and have his card returned on top of the first. Do the same with the third person. With the pass, or by a simple cut at the break bring the three cards to the top with the original stock of ten cards below them.

Demonstrate how to spell a card, naming as if at random the card you originally set tenth from the top which will spell out correctly due to the three selected cards now on the top of the stack. In doing this, sight the bottom card of those spelt off, this is the last selected card returned and the first card dealt. If it is a thirteen-letter card all is ready for the pack to be handed to the third spectator. If not take off or add the card or cards necessary to place his card ready for the spelling. Hand the pack to the third spectator and he spells out his card. Put this on top of the cards just spelt off and replace the packet on the top. The three chosen cards are again on top of the pack. Send the top card, that was just spelt to the middle by the Slip Cut (Erdnase, p. 39) leaving the other two on the top.

Dramatically turn up the second spectator's card, the top one, showing that you have magically cut at that very card. Leave it face up, then pick up the two cards as one, by the double lift, turn the pack over in the left hand and bury the card (really two cards) also face up, somewhere in the middle of the pack. As a result of the double lift the first man's card is now reversed in the pack. Hand the pack to him to hold firmly and build up the final climax.

13. THE NEW SPELL   (Hugard—Impromptu)

Any pack shuffled and a card freely chosen. In closing the pack secretly reverse the bottom card. Undercut about half the cards—have chosen card replaced—drop cut on top, and square up very openly. Reversed card is now on top of the chosen card. Overhand shuffle with backs of cards towards you and when the reversed card shows up give it a flick with the left thumb so that it falls to the floor, and drop the cards remaining in right hand under those in left. Chosen card is now on top of the pack. Stoop to pick up the fallen card and reverse the top (chosen) card against your left thigh.

In order to show, as you say, that the spectator's card is not near the top or the bottom of the pack, hold the cards facing the front and run cards off the bottom into your left hand. As you do so, spell mentally the name of the card taking a card for each letter (you know it since it faces you on top of the pack). Pause on the last letter and ask if the card has been seen. At the answer, 'No,' drop the remaining cards from the right hand on the face of those in the left hand, thus bringing them above the reversed chosen card and putting it in position to be spelt out. Run a few more off the bottom in the same way and again ask if the card has been seen, and at the same answer 'No,' put them again on the bottom. Fan off a few from the top to show that it is not anywhere near the top. These cards have been already shown but no one ever notices that.

Hand pack to spectator to be held behind his back. Instruct him to spell the name of his card, bringing forward one card for each letter, being sure to use the 'of'. He does this and nothing happens but when he brings the pack to the front his card lies reversed on the top of the pack staring him in the face.

14. THE AUTOMATIC SPELLER (Mihlon Clayton—Impromptu)

Spectator shuffles his own pack, then turns it and runs over the faces to see that the cards are well mixed. You mentally note the bottom card. Instruct him to deal three piles of six cards face-up on the table. If he deals from the bottom of the face-up pack, dismiss from your mind the card just noted and remember the bottom card of those remaining after the heaps have been dealt. These cards are laid aside face down and the bottom card is the key card. If, however, he turns the pack over and deals from the top then the bottom card already noted becomes the key.

Tell spectator to choose one of the piles while your back is turned, turn them all face downwards, take any card from the pile selected, look at it, and put it on top of any of the other heaps. He is then to shuffle the remaining cards of the pile he chose, and place them on top of his card and, finally, replace the last heap on top of the other two. The resulting pile is placed on top of the remainder of the pack and a complete cut made.

Now if the pack were again cut to bring the key card to the bottom naturally the chosen card will be the twelfth from the top. To bring this about you tell the spectator to deal off some cards face up to show how thoroughly they are mixed. When the key card appears you stop him, as being satisfied he shuffled the pack well, and have him place the cards just dealt at the bottom of the pack. The chosen card is now twelfth card down and as he is to spell it out himself you instruct him how to do it. The majority of the cards spell with eleven or twelve letters, if with eleven he must turn the next card, if with twelve, then on the last letter. For the 3, 7, 8, and Q of Hearts and Spades tell him to spell the suit first, then value. For 3, 7, 8 and Q of Diamonds, spell Diamonds, then value. For the A, 2, 6 and 10 of Clubs tell him to spell 'an' or 'a' as required. In other words as you cannot manipulate the cards you juggle the spelling.

15. SPELLINO   (U. G. Grant—Impromptu)

In this fine trick instead of spelling the name of a card, you spell the spectator's name, his card appearing on the last letter. The trick can be repeated with as many people as you wish.

Any pack may be used and you have a spectator shuffle it. He selects one, remembering at what number it lies from the top. Let us suppose his name is Smith. Take the pack, place it behind your back and place the bottom card on top, then reverse the fifth card from the bottom, there being five letters in the name Smith. Bring the pack forward and inquire what number the selected card was from the top. Suppose the answer is six. Deal off six cards and show that the card is no longer there. It is the next card since you placed an extra card on the top. Replace the cards and cut the pack. Again put the pack behind your back saying that you will reverse a card. Now you get ready for a second name, say it is Sherman, seven letters, so you reverse the seventh card from the bottom. Bring the pack forward, run through it to the first reversed card, being careful not to expose the second reversed card. Divide the pack at the first reversed card and spell SMITH turning the card on the H. It is his card.

Now step up to Sherman and put the pack on the table and have him cut it in two piles, the top we will call A and the bottom B. Let him look at the top card of B, place it on A, and place B on top of A burying his card. Place the pack behind your back to reverse another card. If you intend to repeat the trick with a third person you reverse a card at the same number from the bottom as there are letters in his name. If you finish on the second name, simply bring the pack forward and proceed in exactly the same way as you did for the name Smith, that is cut at the reversed card and spell SHERMAN, turning his card on the N. It will be seen that the trick can be repeated *ad lib.*, but three cards are enough.

16. SPELLINO CLIMAX   (Grant—Impromptu)

Spectator shuffles any pack and hands it to you. Immediately you spell off the names of different cards, turning them up correctly on the last card in each case.

When pack is returned sight the top card—Suppose it is the 10S which spells with twelve letters. Think of any other card which also spells with twelve letters, the AH for instance. By way of explaining what you are going to do name the AH and spell it out a card for each letter without, however, turning the last card. This process places the 10S in position. Make a false cut and then name the 10S: spell it out and turn it up on the last letter. In picking up the packet to replace it on top, sight the bottom card, suppose it is the 6D which spells with thirteen letters. You know it now lies twelfth so you need to have one more card above it. If you can execute a simple false shuffle you do it that way running one card first, if not, simply take any card from the middle without looking at it. Just do it casually without remark. Now spell the 6D. As before note the bottom card in replacing the packet on top. Calculate the number of cards required to spell it and if it is less than thirteen run off the extra card or cards in the shuffle, or simply take them off and put them in the middle. In the latter case you should pretend to study them and make an intricate calculation before naming the card you are about to spell.

The trick can be repeated *ad lib.* and even without the false shuffle will be found effective.

17. HOWARD'S SIMPLEX SPELLER   (Albright—Impromptu)

Shuffle any pack of cards and have one freely chosen. While spectator looks at his card, cut the pack and slightly squeeze the rear end of the lower half, crimping all the cards of that packet. Cut at this crimp and have the card replaced on that packet and drop the upper half on top. Make a series of undercuts throwing them on top and finally cut at the crimp, genuinely and openly, bringing the chosen card to the top. Have the chosen card named.

Spell it by taking off one card for each letter with the right hand. The first card will be the chosen card so you hold the cards low down and parallel with the table top. Take off the second card underneath the first and continue in the same way so that the cards in your right hand keep the same relative order, that is the chosen card is always on the top of the packet being counted off. When this card is well covered by others gradually raise your hands until the cards in both hands are vertical. When you reach the second last letter of the card's name push the chosen card from the back of the packet in your right hand on to the cards in the left hand with your right thumb, the left thumb immediately drawing it back on top of the left-hand packet. At the same moment the right hand takes off another card and then on the last letter the card just slid across is taken and shown.

It will be seen that this is simply an application of the well-known false count, which, if executed with proper tempo, is perfectly illusive.

18. U SPELL YOUR CARD (Impromptu)

From any pack, freely shuffled, a spectator takes any card he pleases. While he looks at it, divide the pack as if about to cut for the replacement of the card, but before separating the hands squeeze the inner end of the bottom packet, bending them to shape U, the outer end remaining straight. Now cut and have the chosen card replaced on top of the lower bridged portion and drop the other packet openly on top. Make a series of run cuts, dropping them on top and finally cut at the bridge, sending the chosen card to the bottom and glimpsing it. Make an overhand shuffle and bring the card to the top.

Now by way of illustrating how you propose to find the chosen card, spell off some other card the name of which spells with the same number of letters. Don't show the last card in this spelling, simply pick up the packet, drop it on top of the pack and spell out the name of the chosen card, which you turn up on the last letter. The trick is not effective unless the pack is given a false shuffle after the packet is dropped on top. It is easy to make a riffle shuffle keeping the packet intact but dropping one card from the left hand on top of it: get rid of this extra card with the slip cut and you will find the effect greatly enhanced.

19. AN EASY SPELLER (Impromptu)

From any pack, freely shuffled, a spectator selects any card he pleases,

Spelling Effects in Card Magic

Have the card replaced, bring it to the top and false shuffle, leaving it there, and sighting it in the process.

Deal cards on the table face down, mentally spelling the name of the chosen card, a card for each letter. When you reach the last letter deal the next card on top of the others a little forward and continue doing the same thing with six or seven more cards, so that there will be a step between the first lot of cards dealt, which spell the name of the card, and the cards following them.

Casually pick up the small packet above the step and drop it on top of the pack, then pick up the remainder and put them on top of all. Hand the pack to a spectator, instruct him how to spell the name of his card and deal a card at each letter. He does this and, of course, turns up his card on the last letter.

PRE-ARRANGED SET UPS

20. THOUGHT SPELLING

Pre-arrange the first eighteen cards of the pack as follows: 10C, AS, 9H, QS, 4D, QD, 2C, 10H, 5S, 3H, KD, 7D, 6C, 2S, KH, 8S, JD, 3D. Put a short card ninth from the bottom of the pack. Have the pack thus arranged in its case. When ready take it out and if possible false shuffle and cut. Take the first six cards, fan them before a spectator asking him to mentally select one card. This done close the packet and put it in his breast pocket, this to prevent any disarrangement of the order. Spread the next six before a second spectator for a mental choice. Close the packet and put it in his pocket. Show the next six to a third person and when his mental choice is made replace the packet on the pack. Take the packet from the second spectator's pocket, putting it on top of the pack in its turn and do the same with the first packet. Spectator makes a complete cut and then you cut at the short card, thus bringing nine cards on top of the pre-arranged eighteen cards.

Ask the first spectator to spell out loud the name of his thought card, as he does so you deal one card for each letter, including 'of' and the last letter 's' of the suit. Place the last card face down on the table. While spectator is turning this over pick up the packet dealt off in spelling, place the top five on the bottom of the pack and the rest on top. Let the first card just spelt remain on the table. Give the pack to the second spectator telling him to spell his mentally selected card in the same way

58

by dealing a card for each letter on to your hand. Hold a break when you have received five cards and as he shows his card is correct, take the pack back, put the five cards on the bottom and the rest on top of the pack. Leave his card on the table also. With the third party you ask him to spell his card to himself in exactly the same way as was done with the other two, and put the card arrived at face down on the table. Call attention to the fact that he was allowed a perfectly free mental choice and so on. Have him name his card and turn it up.

21. QUADRUPLE SPELLING (Thought Card)

Effect. Packets of cards are handed to several people who are requested to think of any card in their respective packets. All the cards are returned to the pack which is shuffled by the performer. The spectators in turn spell their mentally selected cards, letter by letter, the performer, taking off one card for each letter, reveals each card on the last letter of its name.

Secret. Twenty cards are arranged in packets of five, the cards in each packet spelling with eleven, twelve, thirteen, fourteen and fifteen letters, as follows: KC, JH, QS, 4D, 8D—6S, 3C, 7S, JD, 7D—AS, QC, 10D, KD, 9D—AH, KH, 3S, 9D, 3D. These sets are placed on the top of the pack and a false shuffle and cut made before starting the trick. Hand five cards to each of four persons, asking each one to merely think of one card and then turn the packet face down on his hand: this last to prevent the order from being disturbed. The packets may be returned in any order but such order must be remembered: it is best to have the last packet replaced first and so on, the first packet being replaced last of all. Shuffle ten cards on top of the last packet returned and all is set to spell out the first person's card.

After spelling out the first card, replace all the cards on top and in the course of a shuffle run five cards off the top, thus leaving the set-up ready for the spelling of the second mentally selected card. The same procedure follows for the third and fourth cards. With a little calculation you can spell the cards out in any desired order after spelling the first. For instance, suppose number four's card is called for, you shuffle off fifteen cards, that is the first ten indifferent cards and the five cards of the first set now done with.

22. ANOTHER THOUGHT SPELLING (Annemann)

Four sets of four cards are pre-arranged on the top of the pack. The cards in each set must spell with twelve, thirteen, fourteen and fifteen letters respectively. For instance, the first four can be 4H, 7S, 4D and QD, the word 'of' being included with the value and suit of each card. In arranging each packet of four on top of the pack place them in reverse order so that when dealt one card at a time they will be in correct order. At the bottom of the pack have a short.

To work the trick, deal off four piles of four cards: let any pile be chosen and have a spectator mentally select one card in it. Place this packet on top of the pack and the other three packets on top of that; the addition of these twelve cards ensuring the correct spelling of any card of the first packet replaced. Have the pack cut several times and, finally, cutting it yourself at the short card, being careful to carry that card also to the bottom. The thought card will come out automatically after the last letter of its name is spelt.

You, of course, do not know what the card is until it is named. The short card can be dispensed with by noting the bottom card, then after the cutting, fan through the cards and cut or make the pass to bring the bottom card back to its original position.

23. IMPROVED SPELLING TRICK (Kater)

On top of the pack place the following six cards: 10C, 6H, KS, 8H, 9D, 3D—these cards spell with ten, eleven, twelve, thirteen, fourteen and fifteen letters respectively. Put nine indifferent cards on top of these.

Begin by spreading cards face up to prove they are all different and unprepared. False shuffle and cut, leaving the top fifteen cards in position. Fan the pack but expose to the spectator's view the six arranged cards only, requesting him to mentally select one card. This done, close the pack, false shuffle and cut as before, and hand the cards to the spectator. Instruct him to spell out his card, dealing one card for each letter, and turn up the card on the last letter. He does this and finds his card.

Of course any other combination of cards that will spell with the same numbers of letters can be used.

24. THINK IT——SPELL IT   (Eight Card Set-Up)

Arrange the following eight cards in this order: Joker, 2C, 6H, 9S, QS, 9D, QD, 3D. Place these cards on the top and run eight cards on them thus making the Joker the ninth card. Spread the cards for a mental selection of one card by running off the first eight cards quickly, then spreading the next eight slowly. Follow with false shuffles and cuts, being careful not to disarrange the first sixteen cards. The card thought of is named and you spell it out in the usual way, one card dealt out for each letter in the name, the 'of' being used throughout and the card turned on the last letter, except for the Joker and 3D; for these the card following the last letter card is turned up. Any other cards having the same number of letters in their names can be used.

25. IMPROVED CHEVALIER   (Jordan—Set-Up and Riffle)

Arrange the four suits in four piles reading from top to bottom in the following order: 9, 5, 3, A, 8, 7, Q, 6, 4, 2, J, K, 10. Riffle shuffle the Hearts and the Spades together and do the same with the Clubs and the Diamonds. One such shuffle leaves each suit in its original order if the interlying cards of the other suit are disregarded. Put the Spade-Heart packet on top of the Club-Diamond packet, bridging the packets at the division.

To present the trick: cut pack at the bridge and riffle shuffle once. Any suit is called for. Turn the pack face up, the cards appear to be perfectly well mixed. Remove all the cards of the named suit, one at a time, beginning with the first card from the face of the pack and placing them in a face-down pile. That suit will be in the pre-arranged order. Take the pile face down and spell out A C E putting one card for each letter under the pile and turning up the next, the Ace. Then spell D E U C E and turn the Two: continue in the same way up to the King. Special attention should be called to the genuineness of the shuffle.

NOTE (Hugard).—A better and more convincing plan is to arrange the suits as above and assemble the pack with the Clubs on top, followed by Hearts, Spades and Diamonds. Split the pack for the riffle shuffle at the last Heart. Do the shuffle very openly, calling attention to its fairness. Split the pack again at the last Spade and riffle again. The first shuffle spreads each suit into another, the second spreads them throughout the pack but in the same relative order. This makes the trick one of the strongest of all pre-arranged spelling tricks. It can be repeated with any of the three remaining suits.

26. SPELLING ANY CARD CALLED FOR   (Pre-arrangement)

The whole pack must be set-up in the following order: values 2, A, J, K, 3, Q, 5, 6, 7, 8, 9, 10, 4. Suits: C, H, S, D. The key cards for the suits are: for Clubs, 5D; for Hearts, QC; for Spades, QH; for Diamonds, KS. These key cards are either long or wide cards so that any one of them may be found instantly. To spell any card called for cut at the key card for that suit, bring it to the bottom, and spell out the name of the card according to the following table:

Ace, spell ACE then suits, turn card, on last letter.

Two, count off two cards to bottom, spell suit, turn card on last letter.

Three, spell THREE then suit, turn up next card.

Four, spell FOURTH, spell card, suit, then SUIT and turn last card.

Five, spell THE FIVE OF, spell suit, turn last card.

Six, spell THE SIX OF, spell suit, turn next card.

Seven, spell THE SEVEN OF, spell suit, turn last card.

Eight, spell THE EIGHT OF, spell suit, turn next card.

Nine, count 1 to 9, spell OF, spell suit, turn last card.

Ten, count 1 to 10, spell suit, turn next card.

Jack, spell JACK, spell suit, turn last card.

Queen, spell QUEEN OF, spell suit, turn last card.

King, spell KING, spell suit, turn up next card.

Joker, put in pack at sixth place, spell and throw it out.

Spell all the suits with the final S.

27. THE SHUFFLED SPELLING BEE   (Set-Up)

From a full pack separate the Clubs and Spades. Arrange the Clubs thus: 2, K, 10, Q, 7, 3, 4, 9, 5, A, 6, 8, J, and the Spades thus: 3, 8, 7, A, 6, 4, 2, J, K, 10, 9, 5. The red cards are left in any order, on top of them put the Clubs and below them the Spades, and the Joker somewhere in the middle. You are ready for the trick.

Show the pack and dividing it for a riffle shuffle call attention to the fairness of the shuffle but as a matter of fact it simply spreads the Clubs amongst red cards in the upper half of the pack and the Spades amongst the other red cards in the lower half. Turn the cards face up and remove the Joker, then cut anywhere between the Spades and the Clubs and again riffle shuffle very openly. Here again the shuffle has simply spread the two black suits through the pack but their relative order has not been altered and if the intervening cards are eliminated the two packets will be just as they were set up.

Give a spectator the choice of red or black. Interpret his answer as meaning the blacks are to be used. Take the pack face up and throw out all the black cards one by one in a heap face up; this will reverse their order. Again ask for a choice, this time between Clubs and Spades, separate the Spades and the Clubs throwing them face up, one at a time, in two heaps thus bringing them back to their original order. If Spades are chosen, hand that packet to the spectator, if Clubs are named, take that packet yourself as being the one the trick is to be done with. In any case you must take the Clubs. The set-up is arranged so that you can spell with the Clubs each card dealt by the spectator from the Spades packet. This is a most effective arrangement, the two shuffles will satisfy the most sceptical that there can be no pre-arrangement. After this demonstration the two packets are left in proper order for spelling the cards from the A to the K thus A-C-E and the A turns up on the last letter, and so on. The two packets can be spelt together, you with one, and the spectator with the other one.

28. THE DOUBLE SPELLER   (Eight Cards Arranged)

Effect. The pack is given a genuine shuffle and is handed to a spectator who deals it into four heaps, face down. He looks at a card at the top or bottom of any heap, notes it and replaces it. A second spectator does the same. You reassemble the pack. One of the cards is named and you spell it out, the card appearing on the last letter. Continuing from there you spell out the second card.

Secret. Beforehand remove the 3H, QH, 7S and QS and put them on the top of the pack; then take out the 4, 5, J, and K of D and place them on the bottom. To show the trick, riffle shuffle the pack several times without disturbing the four cards at the top and the bottom. Hand the pack to a spectator and have him deal the cards into four piles one card at a time. This will bring one card of the D group on the top of each pile and one card of the other set at the bottom. Two spectators now look at a card either on the top or the bottom of any heap and replace them in the same position. You have simply to note where the two cards are and remembering that there are thirteen cards in each

63

pile, that the D group spells with fourteen letters and the other with thirteen, reassemble the packets accordingly. For instance, if one spectator has looked at a bottom card, you pick it up first; if the second spectator has looked at a top card put one of the untouched piles on it and take these two next, finally dropping the three packets on the last untouched heap. The two cards will then be in position for spelling. The system is so simple no other illustration is required. As with all these tricks a false shuffle and cuts are necessary to make it impressive.

29. THE WHISPERING SPELLER (Tom Seller)

Remove the following eleven cards from the pack: 2D, 10D, 6 D, AD, QS, 3S, 7S, 8S, 8H, 7H, 3H. Note that all of these cards spell with thirteen letters.

Let the cards be thoroughly shuffled and take them back. Explain that you will ask the top card to whisper the name of another card to you. Make a double lift and note the second card being careful no one else gets a glimpse of it. Replace the two, as one, on top of the packet. Name the card you sighted and spell it off letter by letter, putting one card at the bottom each time. The card will automatically arrive on the last letter. The working will be obvious.

You may have the packet shuffled again and repeat the trick *ad lib*.

30. THE JOKER SPELLING ROUTINE Hull

Arrange thirteen cards from top to bottom: 3, 5, Q, A, 10, 9, Joker, 2, 8, 7, J, 6, 4. Place a King on top of the rest of the pack. Spell out ACE putting one card on the bottom for each letter, turn the A and discard it. Continue with the 2 and the 3 spelling TWO and THREE. Hand packet to spectator to try it. He spells FOUR but turns up the Joker. Put the Joker on the bottom and spell FOUR: the 4 turns up. Spectator tries again FIVE and again gets the Joker. Put the Joker on the bottom and spell FIVE: the 5 turns up. Spectator tries SIX and gets the Joker once more. You place the Joker on the bottom and spell SIX, which turns up. Then say you can spell JOKER and get the correct card. Do so and the 7 turns up. Continue with EIGHT turning up that card.

Spectator now tries NINE and gets the Joker. Put this on the bottom and let someone else try with the same results. This may be done several times. Now put the Joker on the top and tell a spectator to spell JOKER and maybe he'll get the 9. He tries but again the Joker shows up. Replace this on top, and spell NINE: make a double lift and again show the Joker. Look chagrined as you replace the card (really two), then, as a bright thought, remove the Joker, really the 9, and put it in someone's pocket. Tell spectator to try once more as he certainly will not get the Joker this time. He spells NINE and the ubiquitous Joker turns up. The card in the pocket turns out to be the elusive 9. Leave the Joker on the top.

Spell TEN and JACK correctly. Hand the remaining two cards to a spectator to spell QUEEN. As he does so pick up rest of the pack, on top of which is the K. Meantime spectator has again got the Joker. Take the two cards, Joker on top and spell QUEEN putting the card face down on the table. As someone turns it over top change the Joker for the K. Finally hand this to one of your victims telling him to spell JOKER. He passes it from hand to hand as he spells and then turns up ... the King.

31. VARIATION OF JOKER SPELLING

The order of the cards for this one is: Q, 7, 10, A, 5, Joker, J, 2, 9, 6, Joker, 4, 8, 3. Two Jokers are used and you have a K in your trousers pocket. Proceed exactly as in the preceding trick to the point where you spell the FOUR and it turns up.

Spell FIVE and SIX correctly, then let spectator try SEVEN; he gets the Joker. Place it on the bottom and spell SEVEN and turn it up. Do the same for EIGHT and NINE. Have the spectator try TEN; he gets the Joker. Put it on the bottom and spell TEN correctly. Spectator spells JACK and again gets the Joker. Place the Joker on the bottom and spell JACK correctly.

Now tell the spectator that he has had so much trouble with the Joker that you want him to spell it and get it out of the way. He spells JOKER and turns it up. You take it. Tell him that as the Joker is out of the way he will be able to spell the Queen without any trouble. He spells QUEEN correctly. As there would be no sense in spelling the King with only one card in his hand you ask him just to show the card. He does so but again he has the Joker and you show the K in your hand. While he was occupied in spelling Queen you simply changed the Joker he handed to you for the K which you had in your pocket.

32. THE JOKER SPELLER (Tom Seller)

Arrange ten cards of mixed suits thus: 3, 5, A, 7, 9, 2, Joker, 8, 6, 4. Take the packet face down and spell in usual way ACE and turn the A on the last letter; spell TWO and turn the 2 on the last letter; spell THREE in the same way.

Hand the packet to a spectator to try; he spells FOUR and turns the Joker. Take the pack, replace the Joker on top and spell FOUR and turn the 4. Spectator spells FIVE and gets Joker. Take the pack, replace Joker on top and spell FIVE and turn it up. Spectator tries to spell SIX and again gets the Joker. You spell SIX and follow with SEVEN correctly. Spectator tries EIGHT and once more the Joker appears. You spell EIGHT and it turns up.

Spectator tries to spell NINE and gets the Joker—you spell it correctly. Hand the last remaining card to the spectator saying, 'That's just your little joke.' Note that every time the Joker turns up it must be replaced on the top.

33. SURE WINNER SPELLING BEE

Effect. The magician takes eleven cards, A to J inclusive, and holds them face down. He slaps the packet twice and turns up the top card, it is an A. He puts the next card under the others. He turns up the new top card, it is the deuce. Proceeding in the same way, one card dealt face up, the next one placed under the others, the cards come out in order from A to J. Picking up the packet the magician slaps it once and repeats the same deal, but this time only the odd cards come out in rotation. Again he deals as before but without slapping the packet and the cards come out hopelessly mixed. He hands the packet to a spectator and he deals them in the same way but again they are mixed up. Taking the packet once more the magician slaps it twice and deals them as before, one out and one under, and the cards come out in proper rotation from A to J.

Secret. The eleven cards must be arranged thus: A, 9, 2, 7, 3, J, 4, 8, 5, 10, 6. Following the system of dealing one card and placing the next on the bottom this rotation brings the cards out in order, A to J and after three repetitions they are automatically brought back to their original order. Instead of the slap any mystic incantation may be used. The cards should be placed in order secretly at the top of the pack and a false cut made so that they appear to be taken at random.

34. FRANK SQUIRES' SPELLER   (Lloyd Jones, contributor)

The following fifteen cards: 3, 4, 9, 10, J, K, of Spades and Diamonds. the Q and 8 of Hearts and the 7 of Clubs, in any order, are placed in the middle of the pack. One of them is forced, a very simple matter. The selected card has then to be returned to the pack so that it will be the twenty-first card down. A short card may be used to ensure this or a count made as the cards are spread for selection and a break held below the twentieth card. False shuffling before and after will add to the effect.

The card having been returned to the required position, twenty-first, place the pack, well squared, on the table and announce that instead of finding the card you will let it find itself. Ask the following questions, 'Red or black card?' 'What suit?' 'High or low?' 'Odd or even?' 'and the card?' The answer to each question is spelt out, the selected card turning up on the last letter of the last question.

For example: suppose the JD is selected . . .

Q. 'Red or black?' A. 'Red.' (Three cards dealt off.)

Q. 'What suit?' A. 'Diamond.' (Seven cards.)

Q. 'Odd or even?' A. 'Odd.' (Three cards.)

Q. 'High or low?' A. 'High.' (Four cards.)

Q. 'And the card?' A. 'Jack.' (Four cards.)

And the Jack turns up accordingly.

Note that no 's' is used in any of the suits spelled. The effect can be repeated by forcing selection from the part of the set-up not disturbed.

35. GWYNNE'S SPELLER

The pack is arranged with the four A's on the top, followed by the four 2's, then the four 3's, and so on up to the four K's.

Remarking that people often wonder why cards are called Ace, King, Jack, etc., performer deals cards as he spells ACE, a card for each letter turning up an A on the 'E'. Continuing in the same way he spells TWO and turns a 2. All the cards are spelt out the same way to the last card of the pack, which turns up on the 'G' in the word KING.

36. SPELL IT YOURSELF   Annemann

Two packs with same backs are required. From one take two sets of six cards as follows: No. 1—AC, 6H, JS, 8S, 9D, QD; No. 2—10C, AS, KH, 7S, 4D, 8D. Note that the names of the cards in each set spell with from ten to fifteen cards in order. Now place these twelve cards alternately in the pack so that they lie at even numbers from two to twenty-four. Put the pack on the table. Remember that any card from two to twelve belongs to set No. 1, and from fourteen to twenty-four to set No. 2. Call this pack 'A'.

Pack 'B' is set with the same cards in the same order on top, then place any nine cards on top of them. It follows that any card of set No. 1 will spell out from the top of the pack, but to spell any cards of set No. 2 six cards must be cut to the bottom. This pack is placed in the left coat pocket *on its side*.

To do the trick; you say you will have a card selected by a spectator and that you, yourself, will take no part in the test. Hand the pack to someone and ask him to call the first number he thinks of up to twenty-five. If he names an even number tell him to count down to that number and look at that card, but if he chooses an odd number he is to deal off that number of cards and note the next one. Turn your back while he does this. You know that if the number is twelve or less his card is in set No. 1, if over twelve it is in set No. 2. Tell the spectator to put the card back in the pack and shuffle it. Turning to him you take the pack, stressing the fact that the card has been chosen by absolute chance, that no one but himself knows the card and not even he knows where it is in the pack. You tell him he is to put the pack in his pocket, then for the first time name his card and spell it out taking one card from his pocket for each letter in its name. To illustrate what he is to do, drop the pack in your left coat pocket standing it upright so that the cards cannot become mixed with those of the other pack. You name any card, say the 4S, and bring out *six* cards one at a time as you spell FOUR OF ——taking them from the top of pack 'B'. Holding these six cards in your right hand, bring out pack 'B' with your left hand. Now if the chosen card stood at twelve or under in pack 'A', replace these six cards on top and hand the pack to the spectator. If, however, the card was in the second set, that is, a number over twelve, put the six cards on the bottom of the pack.

The spectator puts the pack in his pocket and now for the first time he names his card. Build up the effect by stressing the fact that no one else knew what card he had in mind, that he shuffled the pack himself and that no one can possibly tamper with the cards since they are in his possession. He proceeds to spell the name of his card, bringing out a card for each letter and on the last letter produces his very card.

If the change of packs is carried through in an offhand and natural way, without fumbling, the trick is one of the most effective of all spelling tricks.

37. SELLER'S SPELLER IDEA (Tom Seller)

Effect. Pack is shuffled freely by spectators and returned. Any card is called for, magician places the pack in his pocket and proceeds to spell out the name of the card asked for. The last card he produces proves to be the correct card.

Secret. A duplicate pack of cards. This pack is divided into four packets, one complete suit in each packet, the cards in each packet running from A to K. These four packets are placed, beforehand, one in each of four pockets, for instance, the two outside coat pockets and the two trousers pockets. All you have to do when a card is called for is to place the pack in the pocket in which the corresponding suit of the duplicate pack lies. It is an easy matter to find the required card from the pre-arranged set, at the last letter of the spelling.

The placing of the pack in a pocket should be done as if from an afterthought to make the trick even more difficult.

38. INCOMPREHENDO SPELLER
(Jordan—Set-Up, One-Way Card)

Effect. Spectator selects a card and returns it to the pack. Spelling name of his card and dealing from the top a card for each letter, he turns up card on last letter, it is his card.

Secret. The pack has a one-way pattern. Divide pack in half and at bottom of one half put the 2, 3, 7, 8, Q of H and S and the A, 6, 10 of D, in any order but with patterns all the same way. At the bottom of the other packet put the 4, 5, 9, J, K, of H and S, in any order, patterns the same way. Place the packets together, patterns of set-up cards all the same way and bridge them.

To present the trick: Cut at the bridge, riffle shuffle once, turning one packet so that its cards lie in the opposite direction to the cards of the other. Shuffle as evenly as possible so that all the arranged cards will lie at the bottom after the riffle shuffle. Cut about twelve cards from the top and put at bottom. Fan the cards for selection of one and secretly hold a break at the twelfth card. Spread the middle cards so that spectator is sure to get one of the set-up cards and note, as he takes it, which way the pattern lies so that you know to which group it belongs. If it is one of the group containing Diamonds it will spell with thirteen letters, so you cut at the break, have the card replaced there and drop the twelve cards on top; if from the other group it spells with twelve letters, so you release one card from above the break and cut only eleven cards. Spell DEUCE, THREE, JACK, not Two, Trey, Knave.

39. PERFECT SPELLING TRICK

The pack used consists of four sets of thirteen duplicate cards, that is, the name cards in the same order thus: 3H, 8S, 6D, QS, 7S, AD, 8H, 10D, 7H, QD, QH, 3S, 2H. Each of these cards spells with thirteen letters (spell 2H, 'deuce'; but 2D, 'two').

When a card is drawn by a spectator, cut at that point, and put the lower heap on the top of the pack. When the card has been noted and is returned to the pack, be careful it goes in at a point more than thirteen cards from the top. Since the cut has placed a duplicate of the card drawn exactly thirteen cards from the top, the spelling must bring it out on the last letter.

When spelling the card deal the cards face up which not only shows that all the cards are different but keeps them in correct order. By running through the pack and finding the card that was actually chosen and putting it on top of the pack, the trick can be repeated *ad lib*. The card will be very easily found since it is out of the regular order.

40. CARD SPELLING 'DE LUXE'   Faked Pack

Effect. The performer fans the pack showing the cards to be all different. After having the pack cut several times, a spectator is requested to cut the cards wherever he pleases; while the magician's back is turned, remove the top card, note what it is, insert that card in the middle of the pack and then place the whole pack in the outside pocket of his coat.

This done, performer turns and tells the spectator he will remove cards one by one from spectator's pocket. Simultaneously, the spectator is to spell his card mentally, one letter for each card mentally, one letter for each card so taken, and to think of the word 'Stop', when the last letter is reached. After removing a number of cards from the pocket, performer suddenly says, 'You have just thought of the word "Stop" and the card I am now holding is the very card you are thinking of.' Spectator names the card and the performer displays the card he holds—it is that very one.

Secret. The pack consists of four sets of duplicate cards, twelve cards in each set. The cards are: 5S, KH, QC, 9H, JS, 8C, 3C, QH, 9S, 4H, JH, KH. Now, regardless of where the spectator cuts the pack, if he looks at the top card and replaces it in the middle of the pack, the twelfth card from the top will always be a duplicate of the one at which he looked. Any card he may look at will have exactly twelve letters in its name, therefore all the performer has to do is to stop at the twelfth card, the astounding result follows.

41. LAZYBONES

Put a short card on the bottom of the pack and below it any other card, say for instance, the 2C. Under this again put enough cards to spell its name minus one letter and including 'of,' this is to say, nine cards. After a riffle shuffle by which it is easy to leave these cards undisturbed at the bottom, have a card freely selected from amongst those above. When the card has been noted have it replaced by making an undercut, thus bringing the pre-arranged cards just above it. False shuffle and false cut, then force the card below the short card, i.e. the 2C. Hold a break and have this card replaced in the same place. False shuffle again and then cut at the short card thus bringing it and the stock to the top of the pack.

Turn the top card face up to show that it is not either of the chosen cards. Leaving it face up on the pack, make a double lift, getting the 2C secretly below this card. Hold the two as one in the same position and with the left hand turn the pack over on them to show the bottom card also is an indifferent one. The 2C will now be reversed below the rest of the pack. Cut the pack bringing this card to the middle and turn the pack face down. Hand the pack to the spectator who drew the 2C. He runs through the pack and finds his card face up. Tell him to cut the pack at that card and place the cut aside together with the 2C and spell its name: TWO OF CLUBS, dealing one card for each letter. When he arrives at the 'S' have the chooser of the first card name it. The card is turned up, it is correct.

42. THINK OF A CARD   (Annemann—Set-Up and Short)

Effect. From a long row of cards spread on the table, spectator merely thinks of one. Pack is assembled and cut, spectator spells name of his card, dealing one card for each letter and turns up his card on the last letter.

Secret. Eighteen cards on the top of the pack are arranged in three sets of six thus: AC, 5C, 5H, 7S, 9D, 3D; 2C, 6H, 4S, 8S, 4D, 8D; 10C, 10H, QC, 10D, JD, QD. Each group is composed of cards which spell out with ten, eleven, twelve, thirteen, fourteen and fifteen letters. Note that the first group contains only odd cards, the second only even cards, and the third has cards of value ten or over. The ninth card from the bottom is a short. Begin by laying out the cards in a row from left to right, each card overlapping about half an inch. Eighteen cards will make a long row, so stop at that point and ask a spectator to mentally select one card.

Gather up the cards and replace them on the rest of the pack, false shuffle, then cut at the short thus bringing nine cards on top of the set-up. Have the card named and you at once know to which group it belongs. If in the first, hand the pack to the spectator to spell his card, which will turn up on the last letter. If it is in the second group you must illustrate what the spectator has to do by spelling out, say, FIVE OF —— and stop on the sixth card, asking if he understands. Drop the pack on these six cards and hand all to the spectator. If, however, the card is in the third group twelve cards must be dealt off in the demonstration and the rest dropped on them before spectator begins to spell his card. This is a subtler method than dealing the cards in three groups of six.

43. THE SPELLING BEE   (Cannel—Key Card)

Effect. From a thoroughly shuffled pack, three spectators each choose freely any four cards. Each of them mentally selects one card. Performer, going to one of them and cutting the pack, says, 'Please put your card here,' and he holds out the lower portion of the pack. 'Now drop your other cards on top of it,' he adds. He then openly drops the rest of the pack on top of these. He goes through the same procedure with the other two persons and then shuffles the pack. Asking the last person who replaced his card to name the one he thought of, suppose it is the 6S, the performer spells SIX, taking off a card for each letter and turns the next, it is the 6S. He does the same with the other two. The value only is spelt, the suits are ignored.

Secret. A key card is required, a short, a long or any kind of key card you prefer. When the first spectator replaces his card you have cut the pack including the key card. Drop the cut on top openly and square up. Go to the second person, again cut at and include the key card and have his four cards replaced, thus bringing them on top of the other four. Do the same with the third person. Finally cut at the key as before and shuffle the cards in the right hand on the face of the lower packet, thus bringing the three sets of four cards to the top of the pack. Begin with the third person and ask him to name his card; if it is an A, 2, 6, or 10, spell and take off three cards turning up the fourth; if it is the 4, 5, 9, J, or K, turn the fourth card; if it is a 3, 7, 8, or Q, pull the fourth card back on the pack with the left thumb, take it off again and show it as the fifth card. Hold this card in your hand as you ask the next person to name his card—if it is a three- or four-letter card drop it with the others on the table, but if it happens to be a five-letter card put it back on top, making the spelling correct. Do the same for the remaining card.

3

'You' Do as 'I' Do Card Mysteries . . .

A PECULIAR COINCIDENCE

You have two packs of cards, which may be borrowed, the only condition required is that they are complete packs. With a spectator opposite to you let him choose one pack and shuffle it while you shuffle the other. Put your pack down, take his pack with your thumb on the bottom, fingers on top, in one hand, while with the other hand you take hold of his right hand and place it palm upwards. Place the pack face down on his hand. In directing his attention to the position of his hand you have tilted his pack very slightly and glimpsed the bottom card which you remember. On this the whole trick depends.

Instruct him to take a card from the middle of his pack, note what it is and put it on the top of his pack. Then to reach over, take a card from your pack and place it face down on your left hand. You look at this card and murmur 'Quite a coincidence.' Lay the card on top of your pack.

Tell the spectator to do exactly as you do. Cut your pack and complete the cut. He does the same. Cut again. He also cuts. Square your cards very carefully: he does the same. Hand your pack to him and he takes yours. Tell him to find his card while you find yours and both cards are placed face down on the table. He names his card and turns it over, you turn yours, the cards are the same. 'Quite a coincidence,' you remark again.

When the spectator cut his pack the bottom card which you had previously noted was brought on top of the card he chose. All you have to do is, after changing packs, to find the key card and put out the card that follows it.

As in all the versions of the trick it depends on the fact that the mind

74

cannot think of two things at once while executing a manual operation which requires the use of the eyes and the mind.

YOU DO AS I DO

In this version the two packs are shuffled and exchanged, then both are again shuffled and exchanged but before handing over your pack you sight the top card. The best way to do this is to sight the bottom card when taking the pack from the spectator then with an overhand shuffle bring that card to the top. In this way there is no movement of any kind to arouse any suspicion in the spectator's mind as the cards are exchanged the second time.

Spread your pack on the table, the spectator does the same. Take out a card from your spread look at it and put it on the top. He does the same. Square your pack and cut it and he follows suit. Change packs once more, tell the spectator to take out his card while you take out yours. Really you take no notice of the card you drew, but simply remove the card above the card you sighted on the top of his pack. The two cards are turned and prove to be the same.

Throughout the trick lay great stress on having the spectator work in exact unison with you as if everything depended on that.

IDENTICAL THOUGHT

In this variation when exchanging the packs for the second time you note the bottom card of the spectator's pack. Both packs are placed face down on the table and each pack is cut into two portions. The top card of the lower portion is taken and noted, placed on top of the original upper half and the lower portion put on it, burying the card in the middle. The packs are squared and again exchanged. The spectator finds his card in your pack, you find the card below your key card. They are the same. The same idea of working in unison is carried through.

TWO SOULS WITH A SINGLE THOUGHT

This is probably the first version that was brought out for sale. The two packs used were shuffled and exchanged, the performer sighted the bottom card of his pack as he handed it over. Both packs were then spread, a card taken from each pack and noted and held while the packs were squared up. The cards were then placed on the top and the packs cut once, squared and exchanged. The cards were then found, the performer taking out the card just below the card he sighted. The cards prove to be the same in suit and value.

FOLLOW ME

The only point of difference in this version is the method of having the card chosen. After the usual shuffling and exchange of packs the spectator is told to deal cards face down and stop at any card he pleases. The performer follows suit and stops at the same time. The two cards are then dealt with in the same ways as in the other methods.

Some other small variations may be noted such as presenting the effect more as a game than a trick, the spectator being told to see if he can keep up with the performer and do everything he does in the same way and at the same time. The final effect of the two cards being the same comes as a surprising climax.

Again after the two cards are found and removed performer and spectator stand back to back, insert their cards face up in their packs and exchange the packs once more. The packs are then spread and the cards that are reversed are seen to be the same. By this time the packs have been handed back and forth to such an extent that it is impossible for the spectator to retrace the successive steps.

A CLOSE WORK DISCOVERY   Variation by Farelli

After the usual exchange and shuffling of the packs in the course of which the performer has sighted the top card of the spectator's pack, the spectator is instructed to draw out a small packet of cards from the middle of his pack and note the bottom card of the packet, then put the packet on top of the pack, thus putting the card he notes on top of the key card. The performer also draws out a packet and pretends to note a card, then drops the packet on his pack. Both packs are cut several times and the packs are exchanged. The cards are found and put on the top of the respective packs. Making a double lift the performer shows an indifferent card as being the top card of his pack, then replaces it. He asks the spectator to put his card from the top of his pack face down on his right hand. Then taking his top card he touches the spectator's card with it. The cards are then turned face up. They are the same.

76

It is open to question whether the introduction of this change does not tend to destroy the logical sequence of the effect.

A FOLLOW-UP EFFECT

When the packs are exchanged for the last time note the bottom card as well. When you look for the spectator's card you first find the duplicate for the bottom card that you sighted and put it at the bottom of the pack. Therefore at the conclusion of the trick the bottom cards of both packs are the same. Continue by cutting about half your pack, the spectator doing the same. You count the cards in the lower portion of the pack, the spectator does the same and whatever the numbers you say that they are favourable. You each put out the top cards of the packets. They are turned up and prove to be the same.

COINCIDENCE   Donald Holmes

The principle on which this method is based is entirely different. It is this—if you place a card face down on a stemmed goblet on a fairly high table a little distance away from your audience the card is quite invisible. Of course the spectators must be on one level, from a balcony the card would be in full view.

Two packs are used and from each the same card, say the AS, is removed, each being placed face down on a goblet, one on each side of a table. The packs are shuffled by the spectators and packets are freely cut, one from each pack, and placed face down on the goblets. After a little talk about the marvels sometimes wrought by coincidence, the performer lifts the two packets one in each hand and holds them with the faces to the audience. The bottom cards are the same, each spectator having apparently cut at the AS or whatever card has been chosen for the effect.

LLOYD'S DR. JEKYLL & MR. HYDE

Effect. A card selected by spectator while pack is in his own hands, placed in performer's pack and card selected by performer from his pack, placed in spectator's pack. These two unknown selected cards turn out to be the same card. Unprepared packs.

Requirements. Two ordinary packs, same size, white border; one Red-back pack and one Blue-back pack.

Secret. Hand one pack to spectator. Before handing it to him, palm off any card. This could be in the lower waistcoat pocket or in the act of handing him the pack retain one of his cards on the bottom of the pack you hold. Now have him fan his pack, you fanning yours at the same time. Back up, being careful not to expose the bottom card. Now ask him to thoroughly shuffle his pack while you shuffle yours. Execute the overhand shuffle with the face of your cards toward the spectator. First in overhand shuffle draw off his card you have retained to the back of pack, and remember this card, still executing overhand shuffle, until you reach the same card in your own pack, which is a duplicate of his card. When you reach it stop the shuffle, leaving this card on the bottom. Now draw off this card singly to the back picking up rest of the pack, shuffle off leaving his card again on the bottom. **You should now have his card on the bottom and the same card from your pack on top.** Now ask the spectator to remove any card from his pack which he is holding. Be sure spectator does not see face of this card. Lift or cut your pack about the centre and have spectator place any card from his pack at the point you have cut. In placing upper half of pack on his card, execute the slip or draw the top card of pack off on top of card he has just placed into your pack. Insert little finger on top of this card, placing the two halves together, you are now ready to execute the two-hand pass. Remark to the spectator while you execute the pass, to cut his pack about the centre. This acts as good misdirection for the pass. The two-hand pass automatically brings bottom card to centre and the one he just placed in pack second from top. Lift the two top cards as one, NOT EXPOSING FACE, and place in centre of his pack. His card loses itself in his pack, leaving one opposite colour card in each pack. Upon spectator removing your card from his pack and you removing his card from your pack they prove to be the same card. Both packs can now be examined as there is nothing wrong with them. Even the advanced card man cannot dope the method unless you give it to him.

A VARIATION OF THE ABOVE

Two packs as usual, one red-backed, the other blue. Hold the backs outwards, just over the left hand and leave the top card of the red pack on the face of the blue pack. Hand the red pack to a spectator. Tell him to discard the Joker. You run over the faces of your cards to do the same and also to find the duplicate of the card just stolen, say it is the QH. Bring these two cards to the top, the blue-backed card above the red. Both packs are riffled several times and you tell the spectator to cut and place top half on the table. You cut and put the bottom half down. This is never noticed.

Lift the two top cards of packet in your hand as one and drop the rest of the cards on top of the packet on the table. Spectator does the same. Take the top card at which the spectator cut and put it below the two cards in your hand. The order of these three cards (spectator only knows of two) is blue QH, red QH, indifferent red card. Pull the indifferent card back a little and pull out the red about half-way. With right hand place the projecting red card on the blue pack, then the other two cards, as one, on the red pack. Turning the cards crosswise on top of each pack and giving the packs one complete cut may be done for mystification purposes. Finally the cards are shown to be the same.

ANOTHER DO AS I DO

In this version the performer shuffles both packs and notes secretly the top cards of each one, then puts them down on the table. A spectator is asked to choose mentally any three cards, then from these three to decide on one and concentrate his thoughts on that one card only. Performer says he will do the same. Next, the spectator is asked to select one of the packs, performer takes the other and he removes a card, any card, and puts it face down on the table as his card, the spectator doing the same really finding card thought of. The packs are put face down, each puts his card on top and then cuts the cards, packs are exchanged and the rest follows as in the other methods. The choice of a card by both thinking of one at the same time, is the point to be stressed in the patter.

DO AS I DO IN THE DARK

Effect. Performer and spectator each shuffle a pack of cards in the dark. Performer selects a card from the spectator's pack and vice versa. The cards are laid on the table beside the packs. The lights are put on and the cards are found to be identical.

Method. In his pocket the performer has a forcing pack to match the two packs to be used openly. When the lights are turned off he changes the pack in his hands for the forcing pack and it is from this pack that the spectator draws a card. He then exchanges the card he draws from the spectator's pack for a card from the forcing pack, slips this pack into his pocket and takes out the ordinary pack.

When the lights go on again all there is to be seen is the two ordinary packs and the two similar cards.

DOMINATION OF THOUGHT
S. H. Sharpe

This presentation of the 'Do' As 'I' Do trick appeared in the book *Conjured Up*, and was included in the Gravatt Encyclopedia. It is not only the best presentation of the trick but makes it one of the best in the whole range of intimate magic.

'An experiment called "Domination of Thought". I say experiment because conjuring of this nature is never infallible. It depends on psychological workings and I cannot be sure beforehand how your mind will react to the suggestions I put out. Do you think it is possible for me to influence your mind so that you will think just as I wish you to think, without your being conscious of the fact? Well, though everyone thinks he is free to guide his own thoughts, there are times when one mind can secretly control another. I shall try to prove the truth of this statement by compelling your thoughts to run in the same channel as mine—which can be done under favourable conditions. You doubt my words? You think I exaggerate? To convince you I shall furnish three witnesses. Here are two packs of cards. Now in order to get our minds perfectly attuned will you please go through the exactly same motions as I do?

'First we both mix the cards we hold by the same kind of shuffle. Now we exchange packs so that I hold the pack you shuffled and you hold the pack I shuffled. Again we shuffle—and exchange packs. Next we fan our cards and remove one, any one—but first please look steadily in my eyes for a moment. Ready. Remember your card and place it face down on the table. Now square up your cards and put the chosen one on top of the pack, just as I do with the card I have chosen. Then we each cut our packs to bring the chosen cards to the middle and exchange packs once more.

'Now will you please remove the card you thought of and place it face down on the table with the card I thought of as I do?

'We have each gone through the same actions which included thinking of one card. You think you had a free choice. I am sorry to contradict you. You were compelled by the influence of my mind over yours to think of exactly the same card that I myself was thinking of and which I have placed on the table opposite yours.

'Please do not alter the card in your mind because those two cards on the table are so to speak, two subpoenaed witnesses to your choice. But three are more convincing than two, so I shall provide a third—in black and white this time. (Write card on slip, fold it and put it between the two cards.) For the first time will you name the card you thought of? Please turn up your card as the first witness. Here is my thought, the second witness—turn your card. Finally we will call the third witness. Will you please read aloud what I wrote on the slip? So you see three witnesses prove the truth of my statement that a conjurer can sometimes control other people's thoughts.'

On the second exchange of packs note the bottom card of the pack, this is the key card, the rest follows.

A STRANGE COINCIDENCE

Two packs as usual, one red-backed the other blue, but one pack, let us say the blue one, is pre-arranged in any order you may be familiar with. Spectator is given a choice of packs but must get the red one, which he is invited to shuffle thoroughly as you false shuffle the blue pack. As usual the 'Do As I Do' formula is carried out, each performing the same actions at the same time. The packs are put down and several complete cuts made, then the top cards are taken off, held face down and not looked at, the packs turned face up and the face-down cards thrust in a little below the middle.

When the spectator turned his pack face up the bottom card gives you the name of the card he holds and is about to put in the pack reversed, remember this.

The packs are again cut and again you note the face card which indicates what the top card of the pack is. Tell the spectator to take his pack face down, turn his back, take off the top card, note what it is and then thrust it into the pack face up and you say you will do the same. What you really do is to run rapidly through the pack, find the two cards corresponding to those reversed by the spectator and reverse them in different places in the pack, and turn the indifferent card that you reversed right side up.

This done you both turn around. The packs are spread face up on the table and in each two cards are seen to be reversed. They are pushed out and turned over. Each pair is the same.

COINCIDENCE AGAIN

A prepared card is required. It is very simply made, being merely the gluing of an inch square of tin-foil to the upper left-hand corner of the face of the Joker. Foil which will visibly reflect the index of a card can be obtained at any art store. Two packs are used, the one with the prepared Joker in it is handed to the spectator to shuffle. There is no risk in this as you take the pack back after the shuffle and hand him the other, this he shuffles also. You shuffle your pack each time as well.

Invite the spectator to mentally select a card. Tell him he can think of as many cards as he likes but to finally settle on one and stick to it. Tell him to find his card and put it on the bottom of his pack, carefully keeping the back of the pack towards you. Fan your pack and have the reflector card at about the centre and fully exposed. Hold the fan with the thumb and first finger leaving the other three fingers free. Tell the spectator to concentrate on the colour first, then the suit and under pretence of having him hold his pack a little higher, reach out with your right hand, grasp his wrist with the three fingers and raise it a little. Your fanned pack is thus brought directly opposite to his and the bottom card of his pack is reflected in the faked card. The whole action takes only a moment or two and done casually excites no suspicion.

Knowing the spectator's card you can find the same card in your pack and finish the trick as you please.

SYMPATHETIC SYMPATHY   C. T. Jordan, 1920

One of the earliest versions of the effect.

Two packs, red-backed and blue-backed are used, they may be borrowed since no preparation is necessary, also an opaque envelope.

Show the packs face up one in each hand. Call attention to the envelope and in order to pick it up put the pack in your right hand with the other in your left, face up, on top. Hand the envelope to a spectator to examine. Take the pack back in your right hand, suppose it is the blue-backed one, allowing the top card to remain on the bottom of the other red-backed pack, the left hand at once turning that pack face down. Hand the blue pack to the spectator, take back the envelope and put it down in front of you.

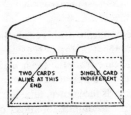

Fan your pack with the faces towards you, find the duplicate of the stolen blue card, put it behind the blue one and put both on top of the pack. Invite the spectator to cut his pack and you cut yours, really you make the first part of the pass, pulling out the bottom portion of the pack and dropping it on the table. Lift off the two top cards, the duplicate red and blue cards, as one, and slip them into the envelope. Take off the top card of the lower part of the spectator's cut, and put it also in the envelope, not showing its face. Slide it to the opposite end of the envelope, take out the duplicates and show them. You can repeat the trick *ad lib.* by noting the index of the card that remains in the envelope. Finally place the blue pack in the envelope and hand both to spectator to examine, everything is thus left clean.

SYNTHETIC SYMPATHY

The red-backed and blue-backed packs used in this feat may be borrowed, no preparation or set-up being necessary. Hand out the packs to be shuffled. Take one pack face up in the left hand, the other in the right hand, thumb and fingers at the ends, backs outwards. Tap the side of the pack in the right hand on the face card of the other and with the left fingers pull off the face card of the right-hand pack, covering the move with a slight turn to the right and turning the left-hand pack face down.

Ask which pack shall be used and interpret the choice to suit your purpose, that is, to spread the right-hand pack face down on the table. Say that you will take one card from your pack, fan the cards facing towards yourself without exposing the back of the card just stolen which

SHOWING HOW CARD "X" IS 'SLIPPED'.

is on the face. Find the duplicate of this card, slide out all the cards between the two and place them on top of the pack. The two cards now at the bottom are first, the card from the other pack, second, its duplicate from your pack. Push the two upward an inch as one card, turn the left hand over bringing the cards face down, take the two as one by the sides between the right fingers and thumb, forefinger on the back, little finger at the inner end. Keep the back to the front.

SHOWING HOW TWO CARDS ARE HELD AS ONE.

Have a spectator push out towards you any one of the other face-down cards. Pick it up without showing its face, put it on the back of the two cards in your right hand, not square but so that about half an inch of the back of the top one of the two shows. Take the protruding ends of these two cards between the finger and thumb of the left hand, push the lower card back against the right little finger and draw the upper card out, leaving the other two cards squared together as one, show the faces of both cards, they are the same.

Drop the single card face up on its pack. With the two other cards held as one, slide them under the cards spread out on the table, scoop them all up together, square the pack and put it face up alongside the other. The two face cards match and both packs may be examined freely.

BACKS UP

Two packs, red-backed and blue-backed, but in this case both have to be prepared beforehand. Remove the court cards from the red pack, mix them, note the bottom one, say it is the JS, put them at the bottom of the pack with a couple of spot cards below them, all the other spot cards will thus be above the court cards. In the blue pack reverse the JS and place it second from the top. Put both packs in their cases.

Introduce the two packs and have one chosen. If blue is named, take it and carry on. If red, toss it to the spectator to hold. In either case take the blue pack from its case. Riffle shuffle it being careful to let the two top cards snap down as one so that the red back is not exposed, cut the pack to bring it to the middle, put a rubber band round, crossing it round the pack sideways and lengthways and toss it to another spectator to put in his pocket.

Ask the first spectator to take the red cards from their case and riffle shuffle them, then turn the cards face up and remove the first court card, reverse it and replace it in the middle. This done tell him to put the pack face down on the table. Now instruct the second spectator to take out the blue pack, take off the rubber band and put the pack also face down on the table.

Build up the effect, the red pack has been shuffled by one man and a court card freely selected without your touching the cards and then reversed, the blue pack being at the time in another spectator's pocket, yet, you say, the sympathy between the cards is such that whatever card was reversed in the red pack will be found reversed in the other. The two packs are spread out and in each the JS is revealed face up.

The feat makes a good introduction for one of the 'Do As I Do'.

MENTAL COINCIDENCE

Any two packs are used, we will refer to one as No. 1 pack, and the other as No. 2. Beforehand take from No. 1 pack any card, noting what it is and put it in your upper right waistcoat pocket just out of sight. From pack No. 2 take the same card and put it seventh from the bottom.

To begin, hand pack No. 1 to a spectator to be thoroughly shuffled. Riffle shuffle pack No. 2 but without disturbing the bottom cards so that the seventh card from the bottom remains in the same position. Both packs are then spread on the table face downwards. Pick out the seventh card from the bottom of your pack and place it face inwards in the spectator's waistcoat pocket, pushing it right in. Ask the spectator to take a card from his pack and push it into your waistcoat pocket in the same way so that the faces of the cards are not seen by anyone.

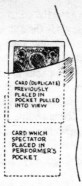

CARD (DUPLICATE)
PREVIOUSLY
PLACED IN
POCKET PULLED
INTO VIEW

CARD WHICH
SPECTATOR
PLACED IN
PERFORMER'S
POCKET

Pull up the card that was already in your waistcoat pocket so that about half its back is in sight. Tell the spectator to do the same with the card in his pocket. Gather the packs and lay them aside. Recapitulate what has been done and patter about mental sympathy, or what you will, to build up the effect. The cards are laid face down on the table, then turned face up, they are the same.

COINCIDENCE

Two packs are required, one red-backed the other blue. The red-backed pack is ordinary but the blue cards must be marked on the backs so that you can readily read them when face downwards, place the 10C on top, 10S on the bottom. In your breast pocket you have a card index with the cards from a duplicate red pack arranged in the usual way, but with two cards to each partition so that it takes up less room.

Thus prepared, invite a spectator to come up to help you. Hand him the red pack to shuffle while you shuffle the blue pack without disturbing the top and bottom cards. This is easily done with a riffle shuffle. Exchange packs with him, put the red pack in your breast pocket while he puts the blue pack in his breast pocket. Note whether he puts the pack with its back outwards or inwards, so that you will know whether the 10C or the 10S is the outside card.

Invite him to take out a card from his pack and hold it face down on his right hand. Tell him to take his time and pick out any card. You do not want him to bring out the outside card, as he would do if hurried. This done, step close to him as you ask if he is sure his choice has not been influenced in any way. This is in order to get an opportunity to read the back of the card in his hand. Step back again, put your hand in your breast pocket and take out the corresponding card from the index and hold it face down on your right hand. The cards are turned over, they are the same in suit and value.

Offer to repeat the experiment but this time you take out a card first. You take from the index either the 10C or the 10S, whichever is the outside card of the pack in his pocket. Tell him to touch the back of your card with the tips of his fingers, then plunge his hand into his pocket and take out a card quickly. He will take the outside card almost infallibly. Show that the two correspond. If he brings out another card simply say he was not quick enough and bring out the correct card yourself.

ANOTHER MARVELLOUS COINCIDENCE

Two packs of cards are used. From No. 1 take any card, say the 10S and from the upper right-hand corner cut off a piece of such size that the missing part can be covered by the ball of the thumb. Put this card on top of the pack. From No. 2 pack take any indifferent card and put it face up on top of a goblet standing on a table that will be a little distance from the spectators. From the front this card will be unnoticeable. Put the 10S from this pack also on the top.

Thus prepared, begin by handing pack No. 2 to a spectator, after having made several false shuffles and cuts. Tell him to hold the pack tightly while he mentally selects any number between one and fifty-two. When you turn your back he is to deal cards to the number chosen, pick up the cards dealt and replace them on the remainder of the pack. This done take the pack and put it face up on the goblet, i.e. on the card that lies on the mouth of the goblet. One card is thus added to the pack and it follows that the 10S the original top card will now be one card farther down in the pack than the number chosen and dealt by the spectator.

Pick up pack No. 1 and shuffle it retaining the mutilated 10S on the top. Tell the spectator you will deal the cards one by one and ask him to call 'Stop' when you have dealt to the number he mentally selected. Apparently you deal fairly, really pull the cards one by one from under the missing corner of the top card, the 10S, which therefore, remains on the top. When the spectator calls 'Stop', pick up the 10S so that the thumb and finger hide the missing corner and hold it face down. Invite the spectator to take pack No. 2 from the goblet, deal cards face down to the number mentally selected and turn the next card. He does this and shows the 10S. You turn the card in your hand and show——the 10S.

A CARD SYMPATHY

Any two packs may be used but they must both be set up in some regular order such as the Si Stebbins or 'Eight Kings, etc.', system. The packs are then replaced in their cases and put ready for use on the table.

Allow a spectator to freely choose either pack, take out the cards and thoroughly shuffle them. Instruct him then to fan out the cards and you take one, pretending to note what it is, and return it to his pack, not letting him see what card it is, and again he is to shuffle his cards. Take the other pack from its case, make several false shuffles and cuts, then spread the cards and invite the spectator to make a free choice of one card. Separate the cards at the point from which he draws a card and hold the hands apart for a moment or two, then put the two packets together but put the right-hand cards under those in your left. A glance at the bottom card will indicate to you the name of the card the spectator has drawn. He replaces the card and you shuffle the pack.

The packs are exchanged, instruct the spectator to take out the card he chose and put it face down on the table, while you do the same. You simply find the duplicate of his card which you know thanks to the system and put it out face down. The two cards are turned face up and they correspond in suit and value.

PARADOX OF PAIRS   (Dr. Jacob Daley)

In this version of 'You Do As I Do', only one pack is used and but a moment of preparation is needed, if it can be called that.

Take any pack and note the two face cards as you hold them facing you. These should be preferably a red and a black card. Run through the pack and pass to the top or back of the pack the two cards of the same value and colour. Thus, for example, the bottom and top cards might be the 4's of C's and S's, and the second card from top and bottom might be the 10's of H's and D's.

Start by dovetail shuffling the pack so as to retain the top and bottom pairs in their respective places. Then place the pack on the table and ask the spectator to cut it into two piles. At this point you pick up each half and shuffle it overhand style and there is a bit of skullduggery in this that is far from being difficult. Pick up the top half first and overhand shuffle, running the two top cards one at a time and shuffling the rest on top. This puts them on bottom in reversed order. Shuffle once more but the fingers (of the hand holding the cards) against the face or bottom card, hold it there while the rest of the under portion is drawn away and shuffled off on top to the last card which is left on top, and this half of pack is replaced on the table. The other half is picked up and given only one shuffle. The fingers of hand holding the cards rest against the face of packet and retain the bottom card while the under portion of packet is drawn away and shuffled off on top to the last card. Replacing this half on the table. Both halves are now apparently well mixed. However, the top card of each packet (if arranged as described before) is a red ten, and the bottom card of each is a black four. Up to this moment everything has been perfectly above-board as the pack was genuinely shuffled to start, then cut by a spectator, and each half shuffled again.

The spectator is asked to pick up a packet and you take the other. Each of you deal a card at a time into a face-down pile together until the spectator wishes to stop. Immediately you prove an unseen force at work by turning each packet face up on the table and showing two red 10's. Now you ask him to count the remainder of his cards on to the table singly in a pile and at the same time you do likewise. If he has the most, he is to place his top card (as pack stands now) face down on the table without looking at it. You turn over your top card (making a two-card turnover), show it, turn it over again with back up and deal it on table. Now he turns his card and it is a black 4. You look surprised and say that to be correct your card should also be a black 4. Turn your card over and it is seen to have changed to match his card. If you had the larger packet in the counting, you merely do your turnover first and lay the card out, asking him to turn over his after and finish the same. If both packets have the same number of cards you call attention to the fact that he cut them himself and that the two packets have a strange attraction for each other. Anyway you have him, the cards match and the number of cards in each pile only serves as the excuse for the counting to reverse the packets and make possible the last part of the trick.

FOLLOW ME
Jean Hugard

(Reprinted from the *Jinx* by kind permission of Theo Annemann the talented editor and proprietor.)

Most of the tricks along this line use only one spectator and the performer. Now it is possible to use two spectators for a double effect. Two ordinary packs are needed. The working will suffice to make clear the effect itself.

Hand one pack to one person and have him shuffle. As he finishes this, hand the second pack to the other person to mix also. While he shuffles, take back the first pack and give it a further mixing while obviously waiting for the second person to finish. You note both the top and bottom cards of your pack. It is easy to merely note the bottom card, shuffle it overhand to the top and note the new bottom card. Now take the pack from the second person and place your 'keyed' pack in his hands. Ask the first person to cut off about half the pack and hold it. At this time, the two spectators each have half a pack and you have a full pack. You know the top card of the first person's cards and the bottom one of the second person's.

Tell them to do exactly as you do. Look at the first person. Take a card from the centre of your pack and look at it. He does the same. Put it on top and cut the pack. He does likewise. Now look at the second person and repeat the procedure. Now have them put the two halves together and cut once more. Take the pack from them and at the same time handing the first man your pack. Tell him to run through it and remove the card he looked at. He does so and hands the rest of the pack to the second person, he looks them over and removes his card too. You fan your pack and remark that at the same time you'll take out the two cards you picked by chance. Lay your pack aside and hold the two cards with the backs out. The first man turns his card so all can see. You turn one of your cards, it is the same. The second man turns his card. Your remaining card matches.

Remembering the two key cards your task has been but a pleasure. When you run through the pack they have looked at and handled, you have only to remove the card to the left (or above) the known top card, which is that looked at by the first person, and the card to the right (or below) the known bottom card. This double bit of business will upset a few at least and make for a much better effect on the whole.

4

Card Subtleties . . . Utilizing Key Cards

A COUPLE OF CARDS GET TOGETHER   Annemann

Make a key card by putting a pencil dot near the upper left corner and the lower right corner. The pack being fanned from left to right with either end outwards, face down, the dot can be seen instantly. When you fan the pack for the selection of a card note where the key card lies and, if necessary cut to bring it to the middle. The card having been noted, fan the pack and break it at the key card, the chosen card being replaced just below it. Close the fan and hand the pack to the spectator asking him to shuffle. Make a gesture with your hands indicating an overhand shuffle. After a short shuffle say, 'Thank you,' and take the pack from him.

Fan the cards again, noting where the key card lies, and have a second card chosen. If necessary, cut to bring the key to the middle. Fan the cards, break the pack at the key and have this second card replaced at that point, thus bringing it on top of the first selected card. Hand the pack to this second person to shuffle in the same way as before, taking it back after a short shuffle. Announce that you will attempt the extraordinary feat of bringing the two cards together, riffle the pack, cut at the key card, sending it to the bottom, and lay the pack down. Have the cards named and turn the two top ones.

Short overhand shuffles will rarely separate the cards, anyway the effect is well worth the risk of occasional failure.

MENTAL VISION   Gravatt

Here again the key card with pencil dot on top left and lower right corners is used. Let the pack be thoroughly shuffled and four cards be freely drawn. Fan the pack to show the cards well mixed, spot the dotted card and split the pack so that the first card is returned under it. Cut the pack several times. Fan and locate the key card and divide the pack one card below it so that the first card returned is at the face of the portion you lift off for the return of the second, tilt this slightly as the second card is returned and so sight the first person's card. Cut the pack again, then locate the dotted card and have the third card replaced under it, cut several times and repeat the operation for the return of the last card.

Put the pack to your forehead and slowly name the card you sighted, the first person's card. Run through the pack, faces towards yourself and remove this card, at the same time memorize the card in front of it, the second card, the one behind it, the third card, and the one behind that, the fourth card. Hand the pack to the second man to shuffle, telling him to concentrate his thoughts on his card: put the pack to your forehead and slowly name it. Do the same with the remaining cards.

PHENOMENAL THOUGHT CARDS

Beforehand take a spot card, a 7 for instance, and with a pin prick the card on the face just near the top index. This will raise a tiny lump on the back of the card which can be felt with the ball of the thumb as you deal the cards. Put this card seventh from the bottom of the pack. To present the trick, shuffle the cards as thoroughly as you are able without disturbing the bottom seven cards. It is easy to manage this with a riffle shuffle.

Turn your back, put the cards behind you and have a card freely chosen from amongst those above the set card. Under cut about half the pack, have the card replaced and put the cut on top. Turn to the table, put the pack down and have a spectator cut it. Have your eyes covered with a blindfold and the pack handed to you. Deal the cards face downwards until you feel the little lump on the back of your key card, the 7. Put it aside face down, hand the pack to a spectator and tell him to turn over the card just put down. It is a 7. He deals cards to that number, finds his card is the seventh.

INDETECTO   Buckley—Key Card and Calculation

A full pack of fifty-two cards is required. Let the pack be freely shuffled: take it back and secretly press the outer index corner of the top card between the nail of the second finger and the ball of the thumb of the right hand. This will cause a slight lump on the back of the card, readily felt by the thumb in dealing. Lay the pack down, ask for a spectator to assist you, first by calling a number, then by dealing cards to that number face downwards on the table. This done tell him to select a card from those remaining in his hands, note what it is, place it face down on the heap of counted cards, shuffle the remainder and put them on top of all, finally to cut the assembled pack as often as he pleases, completing each cut. Next he is to take up the pack and deal two heaps, one card at a time face down alternately, putting the heap on which the last card was dealt on top of the other, square the pack and again cut the pack.

You take the pack and deal slowly till you reach the marked card, you then at once announce the number at which the chosen card now lies. The calculations depend on the number of cards dealt by the spectator on top of which he placed his card. If it is an even number simply divide by two, thus twelve divided by two gives six, his card will lie six cards below the key card. If the number is odd, take the larger half and add to it twenty-six (half the number of cards in the pack), thus the larger half of seventeen is nine which added to twenty-six gives thirty-five, the card will lie at that number.

DETECTED BY FINGERPRINTS

In taking back a pack which has been shuffled by a spectator, note and remember the bottom card. Turn your back and holding the pack behind you invite a spectator to make a free cut, then take off the card on the lower section, look at it and remember it. As he looks at it turn facing him and explain that you propose to find his card by the fingerprints he leaves on it. Meantime quietly slip the bottom card, your key card, to the top of the portion left in your hand after the cut. Turn your back again, spectator replaces his card and then the portion he cut off, and carefully squares the pack. If you care to, let him give a short overhand shuffle, there is small risk of the two cards being separated.

Under pretence of looking for fingerprints, find the key card, the one above it is the selected card.

THE THREE HEAPS

Run through any well-shuffled pack to remove the Joker and, as you do this, note and memorize the three top cards. Hand the pack to a spectator and tell him to deal three heaps face down. After he has dealt several rounds tell him he can deal irregularly, two on one heap, three on another and so on. The three key cards that you memorized have already been dealt and will be the bottom cards of the three heaps, which is all that matters to you. Three persons each take a card from a different pile and look at it, replacing it on the top of the respective heaps. Spectator puts the heaps in a pile and cuts.

To discover the cards you have only to look for the key cards and take out the card just below each one. You can run through the pack and slip the selected cards to the top or bottom and then reveal each one in a different way.

DOUBLE PREDICTION   Jordan

Write two numbers on a slip of paper, six and four for instance, fold the slip and give it to a spectator to hold. Pick up these cards and throw out the top one face up to be used as a locator. Invite a spectator to thrust it into the packet at any point he wishes and then note the card lying above it and the one below. Leaving the locator card in its position between the two noted cards, square the packet, push the top card forward, pull the second card back, the third forward, the fourth back, and so on in the usual way for separating a suit from the rest of the pack. Twist the packets apart, the right hand taking the forward packet and putting it on top of the other cards. Repeat the operation exactly. Spread the cards' faces towards the spectator and have him remove the locator card. Hold a division at that point, one of the cards is now five cards up and the other is five cards down, counting from the division. Your prediction reads six four so you must let one card drop from the upper portion on the lower and then cut at that point, putting the lower cards on top. The sixth card from the top will be one of the noted cards, the fourth from the bottom the other one. By dropping two cards the figures can be made seven, three.

IMPENETRABLE STOP TRICK   Jordan

With any complete pack a spectator, after shuffling it, selects a card by thrusting the Joker into it and noting the card that lies above it. He squares the pack and cuts it as often as he wishes, then deals the cards into the face of the card about half an inch diagonally from the outer index when his card arrives you call 'Stop', that card is turned over, it is his card.

Take out the Joker and hand the pack to the spectator to shuffle. As he does this hold the Joker face up and press your thumb nail sharply into the face of the card about half an inch diagonally from the outer index corner, this makes two lumps on the back of the card instantly found by the ball of the left hand when you hold the cards in the usual position for dealing. When the spectator is satisfied the cards are well mixed, hand him the Joker, tell him to thrust it into the pack anywhere and note the card lying above it. The Joker is then pushed in completely in that position and he cuts the cards as often as he pleases, completing each cut. Now have him deal the cards into two face-down heaps and note the pile that receives the last card, that packet will consist of twenty-seven cards, the other will have twenty-six. Let him give you the heap containing the Joker, you deal the top card face down, he does the same from his heap and the dealing continues thus in unison. If he gave you the twenty-seven heap his card lies at the same depth as the Joker in yours, if you get the twenty-six heap it is one card lower. As you deal you instantly recognize the Joker as you come to it and you give the command 'Stop' as he takes his card to deal it.

MEPHISTO'S PREDICTION   Jordan

Write something on a piece of paper, fold it and hand it to a spectator. He shuffles his own or any complete pack, thrusts the Joker into it and notes the card **below** it, thrusting the Joker right in and squaring the cards into four face-down heaps, a card to each in succession. Assembling the heaps you fan the pack and have the spectator remove the Joker. He takes the pack and cuts where he pleases. Reading your prediction he counts down to the number written and finds his card there.

Suppose you wrote 'Eleven'. When he has selected a card, as above, and has dealt the cards into four heaps, 1, 2, 3, 4, assemble the pack by placing No. 4 on No. 3, these two on No. 2, and the lot on No. 1. Now you know that if the Joker is in No. 2 or No. 3, the selected card will be thirteen cards above it: but if the Joker is in No. 1 or No. 4, it will be fourteen above it. As you fan the pack for the spectator to remove the Joker begin with the top card and count mentally. If the Joker is taken out at any number from fourteen to thirty-nine inclusive, break the pack there, the chosen card is thirteen cards above that point, but as your prediction was eleven you must slide two cards from the upper packet on to the lower and cut the pack there, thus bringing the card eleventh from the bottom.

If, on the other hand, the Joker is taken out at any number from one to thirteen, or from forty to fifty-three inclusive, the card will be fourteen cards above and you must slide three cards from the upper to the lower packet and cut there. Put the pack down and let spectator cut and touch one heap: interpret this so that he gets the lower heap. Pretend that the heap must have a certain number of cards and have him count them. He thus reverses the order and brings his card to the number predicted. Any number up to twelve may be used for the prediction. Avoid thirteen as being too suggestive.

THE SEQUEL   Jordan

This trick follows after Mephisto's prediction.

Use the same pack but discard the card chosen in that feat, leaving fifty-two cards. Have the pack shuffled and the Joker removed. Write a prediction, this time of two numbers. A spectator thrusts the Joker into the pack and notes the card above it and the card below. The same procedure follows as in the previous trick and the cards are found one in each packet at the numbers predicted.

In this case the total of the two numbers you predict must be twenty-six. For instance you write eleven and fifteen. You have the Joker thrust into the shuffled pack and the cards above and below it noted. Proceed in exactly the same way as before, the cards being dealt into four heaps and reassembled in the same way. This time there being fifty-two cards (four times thirteen) the two chosen cards will lie thirteen cards above and thirteen cards below the Joker, therefore, when the Joker is removed and you put the portion of the pack that was below it to the top, one card will be thirteen cards from the top and the other thirteen cards up from the bottom. To bring them to the predicted positions you have merely to divide the pack a card or two above the point at which the Joker lay. In this case you would drop two cards from the upper part on to the lower one before dividing the pack. Under some pretext have the lower part of the spectator's cut counted, thus bringing his card to the lower of the two numbers predicted, eleven, and the other card is already at fifteen from the top. The spectator's cut makes no difference as long as it is somewhere near the middle.

When the Joker is removed and you have dropped the card, or cards, from the upper portion to the lower, separate your hands for a few moments while you recount what has been done, nobody will notice then that in putting the packets together you transpose them.

A COUNT DOWN MYSTERY

Any pack is freely shuffled by a spectator and he is asked to think of any number from one to twenty-six. Take the pack and show the spectator what he is to do, while you turn your back or leave the room. He is to deal cards, you tell him, to the number thought of, look at and note the last card dealt, replace it on that pile, put the rest of the pack on top of it and then give the pack a complete cut. As you actually do all this, by way of illustration, you have ample opportunity to note and remember the top and bottom cards. Suppose, for example, the bottom card is the 10C and the top card is the 7S. You retire and he carries out the instructions.

When you return, pick up the pack and run over the faces until you reach the 7S. Count that card as one and continue to count until you reach the 10C. Stop counting on the card before this one, that will give you the number he thought of and last card counted is the one he noted. It would be a very weak finish to merely announce your knowledge of the card and number right away. For instance you could hold a break at the card and after completing your run through the pack without apparent result, cut at the break, bringing the card to the top. Tell him you will deal cards one by one and at his number he is to think 'Stop'. Do this and stop accordingly. Put these cards on top and tell him to concentrate on his card and deal to his number. He does so and finds his card there.

THE CARD AND NUMBER

Have any pack shuffled by a spectator. Take it and cut off about a dozen cards, noting the bottom card of the packet as you do so. Put the remainder of the pack down. Run the cards off into your left hand, counting them and reversing their order, thus bringing the key card to the top of the packet. Spread the cards in a wide fan and invite a spectator to touch any one, lift the index and remember it. You note the number at which that card lies in the fan. Close the packet and drop it on the table, put the remainder of the pack on top and have the spectator make a complete cut. Deal the cards face up and when the key card appears, you have merely to count to the number noted to find the chosen card. When it falls make a mental note of it but continue the deal without hesitation. Later reveal it as you please.

TONE CONTROL

After having a borrowed pack well shuffled take it back, riffle shuffle it, seizing the opportunity to sight the two bottom cards. Hand the pack to a spectator and have him deal the cards into four heaps a card at a time in rotation. The key card will be on top of piles numbers 3 and 4. Ask him to select two heaps, 1 and 2, or 3 and 4. If he takes 1 and 2 have him put the two packets together, shuffle the cards and select any one and put it on top of either heap 3 or 4, finally putting their heap on top burying the card. If he chooses 3 and 4, do exactly the same but say you will use those two heaps to receive his card.

The chosen card having been buried in packets 3 and 4, let the spectator place the rest of the pack on top and make a complete cut. Turn your back and tell him to deal the cards face up calling their names as he does so. Warn him that no matter how careful he is you will detect his card by his voice when he names it. Since you know the key card immediately before it you have no difficulty in stopping him at his card.

THE MYSTIC SEVEN   L. Widdop

Thoroughly shuffle any pack and, in handing it to a spectator, sight the bottom card by slightly tilting the pack which you hold with your thumb below it. Tell him how to divide the pack into seven packets. 'No need to deal,' you say, 'just cut the pack into seven heaps. From the earliest ages seven has been a mystic number. Now look at the top card of any heap and remember it. Replace it. To avoid all suspicion of any manipulation, I will place three heaps above it and three below it, making it safe from all interference.'

Put the heap which has your key card at the bottom, on the selected card first, then the others above and below. If he looks at the top card of the key heap, let him replace it and then cut that packet once and assemble the others in any order he wishes. In any case the card you glimpsed lies on top of the chosen card. Have the pack cut and lay the cards face upwards in rows. Note the card that follows the key card. Turn away and tell the spectator to pick up his card and hold it, then to have another spectator gather the rest of the cards and put them in his pocket. Continue, 'Put your card face down on the table, place both hands on it and concentrate your thoughts on its name.'

Turn round and slowly get the name in the usual way.

MASTER MENTAL MYSTERY

Any pack may be used: have it thoroughly shuffled by a spectator and in taking it back sight the bottom card. Put the pack on the table after secretly making a mark on the top card with your thumbnail. Instruct the spectators that after you leave the room some of them (any number) are to draw cards from the middle, look at them, put them on top and finally cut the pack *ad lib*. with complete cuts. This done you return, take the pack, run over the faces of the cards, note the previous bottom card and quietly cut it to the bottom, at the same time noting the card next below it which will be the last of the selected cards to be replaced. Take off the top cards one by one, reversing their order, till you come to the card you marked with your nail and this gives you the number of cards chosen. Next miscall the first of these as being the card you noted next your key card. Note what it really is as you put it down, and miscall the next by its name and so on up to the last card.

INFALLIBLE DETECTION

You must know the top card of the pack. A good way to do this and leave the spectator confident that you cannot know any card at all, is to glimpse the bottom card, then shuffle overhand and so bring the bottom card to the top. Hand the spectator the pack to shuffle. If he does a riffle shuffle nine times out of ten the top card will remain there, if not you can see how many cards fall on it. Tell him to think of any number from ten to forty, then when your back is turned, or you leave the room, he is to deal cards face down to the number thought of, look at the card, replace it on the pack and bury it by putting the cards dealt off on top of it. You return and, since his counting has reversed the order of the cards, your key card will lie next above his card. Run through the pack, find the key card and remove the card below it, putting it in your pocket. He runs through the cards, his card is missing, he names it and you bring it out of your pocket.

If his riffle shuffle has added a card or two above your key card you make the necessary allowance for them. If he shuffles overhand you must sight the bottom card after the shuffle and when he counts to his number he must look at the top card of the pile dealt and drop the rest of the pack on top.

FACE-DOWN DETECTION   Larsen

Any pack is thoroughly shuffled by a spectator. Take it back and under cover of a riffle shuffle sight the two top cards. Tell the spectator that after your back is turned he is to deal a row of cards face down, any number he pleases, look at and remember the last card at the right of the row; then he is to deal across the row again, one card at a time, as many times as he pleases and discard the remainder of the pack. He is to pick up starting with that on the right, dropping that on the next one to it, these two on the next and so on, finally cutting the complete packet. This done you turn and take the pack.

To find the card deal the cards face up and watch for the first key card. When it falls begin counting the cards until the second one is dealt. Begin counting again with the next card and when you come to the same number you know that is the card.

DEVILISH CARDS

From any pack, which has been well shuffled, let a spectator select and retain any three cards. Take back the remainder of the cards and quickly memorize the three top cards, false shuffle, keeping them in position. Deal the cards into three piles, a card at a time, until the spectator calls 'Stop', or you may allow him to deal, stopping when he pleases. Put the rest of the cards aside. Tell the spectator to mentally choose one of the three cards he selected, then place one of the three on top of each heap, cutting each heap, assembling them in any order and finally cutting the packet.

Take the packet and cut off about one-third, spreading the cards face up on the table. Now say, 'Your card isn't amongst these, is it?' If the answer is 'No', you are ready to go on, but if the card is there you continue, 'If you are sure of that don't give me any idea of which card it is, don't even look at it, just concentrate your thoughts on it. I will try to get it by the vibrations.' Seeing that one of your key cards is above the selected card you have no difficulty in finding it. If the card is not in the first lot, spread out about half the remaining cards, and if again it has not appeared, you know it must be in the last lot and you can locate it and reveal it in the most dramatic way you can contrive.

COMEDY TWIN CARD PREDICTION

After any pack has been shuffled by a spectator, take it and secretly sight the top card, suppose it is the AC. Write the name of this card on a slip of paper, fold it, and give it to a spectator A. On a second slip scribble some Chinese characters, fold and give it to spectator B. Hand the pack to B and ask him to secretly deal any number of cards one by one, note the last card dealt and replace the cards on the pack. Tell him then to hand the pack to A and whisper the number he dealt, but not the card noted. A deals to the same number and notes the last card, which will be the AC. Tell him to open his folded slip and read it. As he does so, pick up the cards he just dealt and in replacing them on the pack glimpse the bottom card, this will be the card that B looked at. Tell him to take out his slip and read it. Not being able to read Chinese he cannot do it, so you obligingly translate the characters for him by naming his card.

Compare with 'Twin Souls' Miscellaneous Section.

THE NERVOUS CARD   S. H. Sharpe

Shuffle any pack and glimpse the top card. The best way to do this is to note the bottom card as you take the pack from a spectator who has shuffled it, then with an overhand shuffle bring that card to the top. Invite a spectator to cut off about half the cards and spread them face down on the table. You do the same with the remaining cards. Tell him to draw out one card, look at it, put it on top of his packet, square the cards and make one cut. You do the same but you merely pretend to note the card you draw out.

'The card I noted was the........of........,' you say, naming the card you glimpsed. 'What was yours?' He names it. 'I just make a click with my cards and it gives my........of........such a fright that it jumps right over to join your card.' Spread your packet face upwards, the card is not there. The spectator spreads his cards and finds the card you named next to his.

THE NIFTY KEY   Jordan

Take any favourable opportunity, say in gathering the cards after a trick, to note the fifteenth card from the top. Hand the pack to a spectator and tell him to deal off several cards from the top and put them in the middle. Note the number and mentally subtract it from fifteen to give the new position of your key card. Suppose he deals five, your key card will lie tenth from the top. As a blind have him remove a few cards from the bottom and put them in the middle also. Tell him to think of any number between twelve and twenty, then as your back is turned, to count down to the number thought of and note the card that lies there, square the pack and cut it at any point well below his card. You have him tell you the number he thought of, this creates no suspicion since there appears to be no possible way for the knowledge to help you. However, you have simply to subtract your key card number, ten, from the number he thought of, suppose this was fifteen, which gives you the number five. Tell him to further mix the cards by dealing them into five hands, five cards in a row face down, then cards on each in rotation until the pack is exhausted, and collect the heaps in any order he pleases. His card must fall on top of your key card and you can reveal it in any manner you wish. All that has to be done is to have the pack dealt into the number of piles represented by the difference between your key number and the number the spectator thinks of.

UP YOUR SLEEVE

Take any favourable opportunity to place two cards, which you memorize, in your left sleeve , safely out of sight but within easy reach. Have the pack shuffled, turn and hold your hands to receive it behind your back. Instruct the spectator to cut off a packet and count them secretly. When he has done so, turn facing him, keeping your hands behind your back and take the two cards from your sleeve, putting one on the bottom and the other on the top. To gain time for this you tell him to square his packet carefully and when you turn round again to put it back on the top of the pack and make one complete cut so that the cards will be buried in the middle, and square the pack carefully. This is done.

Turn again and bring the pack forward. You have only to run over the faces till you reach the first of your key cards, then count until you come to the second. You can reveal your knowledge of the number in any way you please. For instance by cutting off the same number.

THE QUARTETTE

From any pack freely shuffled have four cards freely selected. As the cards are being noted secretly bend the lower right corner of the bottom card a little upward by pushing it back slightly and bending it with the right thumb. With the right hand pull out the lower half of the pack and have the last card chosen placed on top of the portion in your left hand and slap the right-hand packet on top but insert the tip of your little finger between the packets. Keep the front ends of the cards tightly closed, tap them square and ruffle them. Go to the third person who chose a card, divide the pack at the little finger break and have his card replaced on top of the other one. Repeat the same operations with the remaining two, finally drop the right-hand packet openly on top of the fourth card without inserting the little finger, the bent corner will locate the four cards. If carried through quickly without hesitation the spectators will be satisfied the cards have been replaced in different places at haphazard. To confirm the fact that the cards are really lost in the pack, let a spectator cut the pack freely with complete cuts, then cut at the bent corner card yourself. Deal four piles, a card at a time and the chosen cards will be at the bottom of each pile. Assemble the pack by putting pile No. 1 on No. 2, these two on No. 3, and these three on No. 4. The cards will now lie thirteenth, twenty-sixth, thirty-ninth and fifty-second. Deal the cards face up, telling the third person to think 'Stop' when he sees his card. Mentally note the thirteenth and twenty-sixth card. Deal to the thirty-ninth card and stop, throwing the card out. Replace the dealt cards face down on the remainder. Discover the twenty-sixth card, the second chosen, by reading the spectator's mind. Spell out the first person's card, the thirteenth; any card can be spelt with twelve or thirteen cards by manipulating the words 'the' and 'of'.

Replace the cards dealt and casually display the bottom card so that the fourth person will note it. Turn the pack face down and glide the bottom card back. Tell him that you will deal from the bottom and stop at any card he calls for. Pull out the second card from the bottom and put it face down. Pull out the next one above the pulled-back card, show its face and replace it on the bottom, covering the chosen card and again casually display the pack face outwards. The person will be convinced you have made a mistake and that his card has been put on the table. Turn the pack down, deal the bottom card, letting its face be seen as you put it on the first card dealt. Draw back the next card, the chosen card and retain it, dealing the cards above it one by one until the person tells you to stop. Draw out his card, put it face down apart and place a coin or a pencil on it. You claim that that card is his. Having seen, as he thought, that his card was already dealt, he is bound to say you are wrong. Work this up, then turn the dealt cards face up, his card is not there. Have it named and turn it over.

THINK OF A CARD   Larsen

Have a spectator shuffle the pack, take it and run cards from the left hand into the right, asking him to stop you at any point. When he does so separate the cards at that point and hold the right-hand packet before his eyes, spreading the indices of the last five or six cards and telling him to make a mental choice of one card. In the meantime turn slightly to the left away from him and with the left thumb lift the lower left corner of the top card of the left-hand packet and sight the card.

Square the right-hand packet and drop it on top of the cards in your left hand. Have the pack cut several times with complete cuts. You have only to locate the key card and finish the trick in your favourite way.

DEMON'S DETECTION   Jordan

Effect. Shuffle and cut any pack and leave the room. A spectator then follows the instructions you previously gave him thus—he thinks of a number under ten and deals from the face-down pack cards to that number and notes the last card. He then continues dealing a card at a time on each card already dealt until there are not enough left to cover the row; these cards he places on the last pile, at the bottom of which is the card he noted. He picks up this heap first, places it on the next to the left, these two on the next and so on until the pack is reassembled. He cuts several times and you return. You deal the cards and stop on the noted card.

Card Subtleties . . . Utilizing Key Cards

Method. Secretly note the two top cards of the pack after the shuffle; make a false cut. When the spectator follows your directions the original top card becomes the bottom card of the first heap, and the second card will be at the bottom of the second heap. When you return fan the pack and cut it to bring the second card you noted somewhere near the top of the pack. Turn the pack face down and deal the cards face up. Suppose the original top card was the 7H and the second card the 3C. When the 3C appears start counting and stop at the 7H. This gives you the number of cards dealt in each heap. Divide fifty-two by this number and if there is no remainder then the spectator's card is that number below the 7H. If there is a remainder add it to the number, the total will give the position of the noted card below the original top card.

Example: with the two top cards as above, 7H, 3C. You find the 7H six cards below the 3C. Fifty-two divided by six gives eight and a remainder of four, six added to four equals ten, therefore the chosen card is ten cards below the 7H.

5

'Slick' Principles in Card Magic

The first record of the use of the 'slick' card that I have been able to find is by Robert Houdin in his book *Les Tricheries des Grecs* under the title of 'la carte glissée'. Probably the device had been used by gamblers for many years previously. In an article in the *Sphinx* of Vol. 23, No. 1, p. 2, Mr. Max Holden called the attention of the magical fraternity to the many good uses the slick card can be put to. His method of preparing such a card was to put some paraffin wax on the face, spreading it evenly and polishing the card with the back of a spoon. With an occasional re-polishing such a card will retain its slippery quality for a long time. A later method, that is now generally used, is motor-car Simoniz. Simply coat the card and rub it briskly with a cotton swab, let it dry overnight. Put on a second coat, again rub it with a soft cotton cloth and let it dry thoroughly. It is advisable to polish the face again before using.

Before going into the explanation of tricks based on the use of such a card a short description of the proper method of handling it will be necessary. Insert a slick card about the middle of the pack and square up the cards. Hold the pack in the left hand as if about to deal. Place your right fingers under the pack at the end nearest you and the thumb on top, push forward with the thumb, exerting a little pressure. You will find that the pack will split at the slick card. Cut at this point and that card will be at the bottom.

Again insert the card and shuffle so that you do not know just where-abouts it is. Hold the pack in the left hand and square it. Put your right thumb and fingers in the same position as before but hold the pack upright and push with the thumb just enough to locate the point at which the cards break. Turn the pack down and fan the cards but keep your eye on the break so that you know exactly where the slick card is. Have a card chosen and replaced to the left of the break, that is under the key card, and square up. When you again locate the break and cut at it the selected card will be on the top and the key card at the bottom.

When you know the key card is in the middle, with the right thumb and fingers in the same position as before, push off about a dozen cards and slide them to the bottom. Now with the right thumb again push on the cards but this time exert a little pressure and the cards will break at the key card; take these cards off and put them on the bottom, the key card becoming the bottom card of the pack.

With the pack behind your back the cards can be made to break at the slick card in just the same way, that is by pressure of the right thumb and fingers.

It will be readily recognized that by having a chosen card inserted in the pack, either above or below the slick card and the pack squared up, the chosen card can be brought to the bottom or top of the pack at will by making the break as described and then cutting at that point. As facility in the use of the card is acquired the break can be located by pressure of the left thumb. It must lie flat on the back of the top card, then with the cards very slightly spread, make it press downwards and outwards, the cards will break at the slick card. The push must be made with the thumb flat on the top card, not just the tip, and the cards should be held as flatly as possible.

You may have the slick card on the bottom, then a card having been chosen, undercut for its return, dropping the lower portion on top, thus bringing the slick card immediately above it. Square the pack, locate the break and cut the cards. The chosen card is on the top and the slick card again on the bottom.

Finally, avoid making the break when attention is focused on the pack, do it when the attention is directed elsewhere.

THE HALF MOON LOCATION

With the slick card near the middle of the pack spread the cards on the table face down in a semicircle with one sweep of the hand. Note the position the slick card occupies, which will be just about the point of the semicircle that is nearest the spectator. Invite him to take a card, look at it, replace it in the spread, assemble the pack and cut it several times. In spite of this apparently fair procedure you can easily locate the card.

When the cards are spread in this semicircular, half moon fashion a spectator will almost invariably take a card from a point very near that at which the slick card lies. In such case you ask him to replace it in the same spot and simply note how many cards are between it and the slick card, above or below, as the case may be. After the cards have been gathered up and cut, you have only to locate the key card by the squeeze, make a cut and you know just how many cards from the top or bottom the chosen card lies. If, however, the card is taken from one end or the other, tell the spectator to replace it in the middle of the spread and then make your count from the slick card in the same way.

LOCATION PLUS

This is one of those 'take a card, look at it, put it back, now shuffle, that's your card' things, and on top of that it is not certain to come off. However, the method may be useful on occasion to squelch the obnoxious individual who has the little knowledge that is so dangerous to the magician when coupled with a mean disposition.

The method is simple. After a card has been chosen, as the spectator is noting it, locate the break at the slick card, cut there and have the card returned under it, square the pack openly and hand it to the spectator to be shuffled. It is well to indicate with your hands the action of an overhand shuffle as you give the pack, for with this type of shuffle the odds are in your favour, viz. that the two cards will not be separated are about ten to one. If the spectator insists on a riffle shuffle the chances are not so favourable. I have been assured, however, by performers who make use of the method that they have never failed twice in succession.

EVERYBODY'S CARD

A trick which is comparatively old is that in which after a number of spectators have drawn a card, and returned them to the pack, they are asked to call out the names of the cards selected—and they all call the same card. In the old method the performer had to control the card every time it was replaced in order to force it on the next person, and unless he was an expert in palming he could not allow the spectators to shuffle the cards.

By using the slick card as the force card the trick becomes not only much more effective but much easier to do. You can allow each person to replace the card anywhere in the pack that he pleases and shuffle to his heart's content, yet you can find the card in a moment and have it in readiness to force on the next spectator, An expert in straight forcing will have no difficulty with that part of the trick but for most card workers it is a good plan to use a variety of forces. A reference to Annemann's *202 Ways of Forcing* will be useful in this connection.

Another good finish is to pick out as many cards including the slick card as have been chosen, spread them fanwise and ask if everyone sees his card. They all do, of course. Throw away one card and repeat the question. Continue in the same way until it dawns on them that they all picked the same card from the shuffled pack.

STAGE LOCATION

This trick is a variation of one made famous by Alexander Herrmann and called by him 'The Egyptian Pocket'. There are not very many tricks with cards which are effective on the stage or platform but in good hands this routine cannot fail to be highly entertaining.

The working is greatly simplified by the use of the slick card. With this card at the bottom allow these cards to be freely selected. Shuffle the slick card to the middle and have the first card replaced immediately above it. Square the pack, go to the second person, locate the break and have the card replaced in the same way. Treat the third card in exactly the same way. Finally cut at the slick card and the three chosen cards are thus brought to the bottom.

Inviting the first person to stand up place the pack in his inside breast pocket. Showing your hand empty, plunge it into his pocket and bring out all the cards except the bottom card. Ask him to name his card, then to reach into his pocket and take it out.

Riffle shuffle cards leaving the two bottom cards intact. Go to the second spectator, ask him to stand up. In the meantime you have palmed the bottom card in your right hand. Tell the spectator to take the pack out quickly, and the moment he had done so thrust your hand into his pocket and bring out the palmed card at the finger-tips. Have the card named, turn it over and show that the spectator also succeeded in leaving that one card behind.

With the third card the proceeding is varied a little. Put the pack in the third spectator's pocket with his card on the outside laying the pack on its side and turning his card upwards on end. Tell him to name his card and then quickly reach in his pocket and bring it out. If you impress upon him that he must do it quickly the trick never fails and makes a fitting climax to a very effective routine.

'Slick' Principles in Card Magic

THE MASTER CARD SPELLER

For this feat one of the four cards in the pack that spell with ten letters, A, 2, 6 and 10 of C, must be used as the slick card. Suppose you prepare the AC. Take out five other cards that spell with eleven, twelve, thirteen, fourteen and fifteen letters—for instance, 6H, JS, 8H, 9D, QD. Put the AC on top of the five and place the packet on top of the pack. Riffle shuffle and make several false cuts but leave the top six cards intact.

Deal a row of six cards and invite a spectator to lift any one, look at it and replace it face downwards, then to move all the others slightly so that you cannot get any clue from the positions of the cards. This done, turn around, pick up the cards so that they remain in their original order. AC on the top of the packet, QD on the bottom.

Have the spectator shuffle the remainder of the pack and cut it into two packets. Drop the six cards on top of one pile and put the other on top of all. Invite the spectator to cut several times with complete cuts. Point out that no one can possibly know where any of the cards now are and while talking squeeze the pack locating the AC, and cutting it to the top.

Riffle count nine cards from the bottom and cut, bringing them to the top. Ask the spectator to concentrate on the name of his card and hand the pack to him. Tell him to spell the name of his card and deal one card for each letter. No matter which of the six he selected his card will infallibly turn up on the last letter.

For an exhaustive treatment of the spelling trick see special section devoted to that subject.

COUNTING BY EYE

Have the slick card thirteenth in the pack.

Announce that by constant practice you are able to count the number of cards in a packet instantaneously. As you speak you have squeezed the pack and located the break. Cut off the twelve cards and throw them down, saying that there are just twelve. As a spectator verifies this, thumb count eight more from the bottom and pass them to the top. Take back the twelve and drop them on top of the pack, making twenty cards above the slick card. Square the pack very openly and ask a spectator to call any number between twenty and twenty-five. Squeeze the pack and have the break located giving you twenty cards ready for the cut, so you have merely to take off enough more to make up the number. It is not advisable to carry the effect any further.

ODD OR EVEN

With the slick card thirteenth from the top, make the squeeze, locate the break, cut off the twelve cards and toss them on to the table, calling them even. While a spectator verifies this, thumb about nine or a few more cards of an odd number and pass them to the top above the slick card. Take back the first packet and drop it on top, again make the trick cut taking off all above the slick card, drop them on the table calling odd.

For the third and last effect pass five or seven cards from the bottom to the top, take back the other cards and again square the cards perfectly, tapping the sides and ends on the table. Invite a spectator to say whether the number this time shall be odd or even. You have only to locate the break and take off the packet with or without the slick card to prove that you are infallibly correct in your estimate.

THE MYSTIC CUT

Using the AC prepared for the last trick as your key card, make up a sequence of cards, the values running from 10 down to A and mixing the suits. Place this packet on top of the pack, the 10 being the top card.

Spread the pack and have a card freely selected from anywhere below the group. As the spectator notes the card, cut the pack to bring the set-up packet as near to the middle of the pack as possible. Squeeze the pack, locate the break and cut at the key card. Have the card replaced and drop the cut on top thus bringing the key card above it. A false shuffle at this point will strengthen the effect.

Invite the spectator to cut the pack as near the middle as he can and turn the cut face up on the table. He is then to take off from the lower portion as many cards as are indicated by the value of the face card. On the last figure of the count he names his card and turns up that very card.

So long as the cut is made in the group of arranged cards the feat cannot fail.

'Slick' Principles in Card Magic

A SLICK CARD ROUTINE

Lane

This effective series of tricks makes use of the slick card and a set-up. The slick card may be any card at all but we will suppose it is the 9S. From the top of the pack downwards arrange the following cards: 7S, 9D, KD, AH, 9S, KH, 7D, AD, KC, 9C, AS, 8S, 8D, 9H, 5C, 6C, 10S, KS, 6D, JH, JD, 4D, 6H. Twenty-three cards in all.

These cards must be on the top of the pack, the slick card on the bottom and next above the key card, a seven. When introducing the routine a false shuffle should be executed. For an explanation of the best methods see chapter on 'Indispensable Sleights'.

1. Casually count off five cards, reversing them, and replace them on the top (this is done for a purpose that appears later). Fan the pack and have a card freely selected from below the arranged cards. As the spectator notes his card, undercut, have the card replaced on top and drop the lower portion on it. The slick card is now just above the chosen card. Square the cards very openly. Go to a second person, squeeze the pack, locate the break and force the same card on him. The first spectator is asked to name his card, second spectator shows that is the card he holds. Or, you may simply bring card to the top, palm it off and produce it from your pocket. In either case replace the card in the lower part of the pack.

2. The next effect is one of prediction. In reversing the first five cards at the beginning you brought the top card, 7S to the fifth place. To bring them back to the same order you illustrate what you want a spectator to do. Tell him he is to think of a small number, deal cards (you deal five) place them back on the top (do this with the five cards) pick up and look at the top one (pick it up but don't look at it, you already know that it is the 7S) replace it on top and make one complete cut. (Don't illustrate the cut.)

Before the spectator counts his number, take pencil and paper and write 'Seven of Spades'. Put this under some object on the table writing downwards. Turn away while spectator counts, looks at top card, replaces it and cuts, squaring up the pack. Turn round, take the pack and while asking the spectator to whisper his number to a second person, squeeze the pack, cut at the break and glimpse the top card. This card is the one just noted by the first spectator, so you take the slip of paper and write its name **above** that already written, the 7S. The count has brought the 7S to the position to be found by the second person. Hand the pack to the second person instructing him to deal cards to the number whispered to him; to place the packet on the pack, look at the top

112

card and make one complete cut. This done, call attention to the fact that in each case you wrote a prediction before the cards were looked at. Have the cards named, then have a third person take the slip, open it and read what you wrote. Under cover of the surprise this causes squeeze the pack, cut at the break and you have the cards back in their original order.

3. Have a spectator cut the cards near the middle, put aside the top packet and take up the lower one. Make an overhand shuffle retaining the slick card on the bottom and bringing the 7S to the top. Spread the cards, counting seven and holding a break at that point, and have a card freely chosen and noted. Cut off the seven cards, have the card returned, counting seven cards on top. False shuffle several times then locate the break and cut. Turn the top card, 7S, count off seven cards, ask the spectator to name his card. You turn it up.

4. Take up the other half of the pack and put it on top of the cards in hand. Turn the pack to a spectator, tell him to deal off some cards face up one by one on the table, to stop whenever he likes, replace the packet on the face of the pack, note the card facing him (the last card dealt), then give the pack one complete cut. Turn away as this is done. When he is ready, turn and take the pack, put it behind your back, squeeze and cut to the break, put the slick card on top as well. Announce that you have found the card and have placed it at the same number from the top as he had it from the bottom. The number is named, deal the cards and turn the one at that number, it is the card the spectator noted. Put the rest of the cards on top of those just dealt and the pack is again in the arranged order.

5. Now suggest a game of poker, ask how many hands shall be dealt as if it made no difference to you how many, but you must deal either three or four hands. If three is chosen, deal three hands of five cards each as in a regular game. This is the result:

1st hand: 7, 7, 8, 9, A; discards 7, A, gets a straight.
2nd hand: 9, 9, 9, 8, A; discards 8, A, draws two cards.
3rd hand: K, K, K, 5, A; discards 5, A, draws two J's, full house.
If four is chosen, here is the result:
1st hand: 7, 8, 9, 10, K; discards K, draws J, making a straight.
2nd hand: 9, 9, 9, K, K; stands pat.
3rd hand: 5, 6, 7, 8, K; discards K, gets 4D, a straight.
4th hand: A, A, A, J, 6; discards the 6, draws J, full on aces.

6. Assemble the pack thus: take the remainder of the pack and the discards, shuffle overhand and leave the key on top. Pick up the hands in any order and put them on the top. Cut to the key, hand top half to one

spectator, other half to a second person. Both may shuffle as they please. Second person picks out any card from his packet and pushes it into first spectator's cards, and these cards are then thoroughly shuffled. You find the card.

This is the method: counting the values of the cards (J–eleven, Q–twelve, and K–thirteen) the total of the cards in the four hands is 143. To this add the value of the slick card to get the total before the chosen card is added to the packet. Simply add the values, subtract and you have the card.

7. Shuffle the key to the top. A spectator deals as many cards face down on the table as he pleases, counting them as he does so. He squares up the packet and puts it on top. This while your back is turned. Turn again, take the pack, cut to the key card and you instantly have the cards he counted out. Again deal them one by one to show how much quicker you did it, and also to get the key back on the top.

8. Hand the pack to a spectator to shuffle. It is best to have the shuffle by the overhand method. A riffle shuffle, especially with some people who handle cards roughly, bends the cards and interferes with the manipulation of the slick card. Take pack and have a card freely chosen, noted and replaced under the key card. Square the cards very openly, tapping ends and sides on the table, spread and have a second card freely selected. Again make the break at the key and have the card returned at that spot, thus bringing it on top of the first card. Square up and immediately hand the pack to a spectator for an overhand shuffle. Allow him time for two or three movements, say 'Thank you,' and take the pack back. The odds are almost 100 to 1 against the cards having been separated. Recapitulate what has been done, build up the effect and order the two cards to join one another. Show them.

9. For this effect you require an extra card of the same pack pattern, say an 8 spot which you place reversed above the key card which is on the bottom (the author does not say just how you are to do this without being observed). On top, place the duplicate 8 from the pack. Count off seven cards, not reversing them, and put them on the bottom.

Allow a card to be freely selected and noted. Under cut about half the pack and drop on top of the card as it is replaced. Cut to the key card bringing it to the bottom and the duplicate 8 to the top. Turn this card and show it, dropping it on the table. Cut the pack, take off several cards from the top and show the chosen card is not amongst them, turn the pack face up and show that it is at or near the bottom. Pick up the duplicate 8 spot and put it with the pack behind your back. Slip the duplicate 8 under your belt.

'Slick' Principles in Card Magic

Bring the pack forward, run over the backs till you come to the reversed 8 spot. Count off seven cards and deal the eighth face down. Have the card named and turn it over.

10. Hand the pack out to be shuffled. Take it back and cut to the key card bringing it to the bottom. Allow a card to be freely replaced, drop the lower portion on top, bringing the chosen card below the key card. Let a spectator square the pack perfectly. Take it and put it behind your back. Cut to the key card, take it off the bottom and slip it under your belt. Bring forward the card now on the top, have the chosen card named and turn the card over. Put the pack down and you can bet £1,000 that it is absolutely free from any preparation.

6

Card Mysteries Employing Diachylon

The first use of diachylon in connection with cards that I have been able to trace was by Hofzinser, the great card expert who flourished in Vienna in the middle of the nineteenth century. It seems to have been kept a closely guarded secret until the appearance of Prof. Hoffmann's last book, *Latest Magic*, which was published in 1918. From that time its use became increasingly popular and a number of very good tricks dependent on its use have been devised.

Diachylon, when rubbed on the back of a card, renders it adhesive without altering its appearance and if another card is pressed against the surface so treated, the two adhere, and to all intents and purposes become one card. The two may be handled freely but can be separated with slight pressure. Hoffmann advises that the diachylon in its solid form be rubbed on the card shortly before it is to be used. If used in the paste form, however, it is best to apply a very small amount with the blade of a knife. It is not necessary to treat the whole surface of a card, simply apply it to several of the pips if the face of a card is to be treated, or at the corners and the middle of a card, if the back is to be prepared. The diachylon will spread better and make a thinner film if slightly heated first. The following method of application is recommended by Judge Fricke:

'I have done this by painting the cards with diachylon dissolved in carbon tetrachloride. Due to the variation in batches of diachylon some experimenting will have to be done. Too heavy a solution holds the cards too affectionately. It is so nearly colourless that when applied no one can notice it. Use a cotton swab, let the cards dry thoroughly before re-assembling them and the deed is done. I have doped my Svengali cards this way. Thus prepared they may be given the regular overhand shuffle as well as the riffle and the two cards can be lifted with ease as one. Just sliding off the top (short) card carries with it the regular card below it.'

THE FLYING CARD

Prof. Hoffmann gives two tricks only as illustrations of the use of diachylon. In this, the first, a card box is prepared with a duplicate card, say the 7D, placed in box so that after it has been shown empty, closing it will bring the card into evidence. The top card of the pack has its back prepared and the 7D is forced on a spectator. The pack is cut to bring the diachylon card to the middle and the 7D is returned on the top of it. The performer has then merely to square the cards, squeeze them well together and hand the pack to be shuffled. Taking the pack he orders the card to leave the pack and fly to the box. He counts the cards one by one showing their faces as he puts them on the table. There are fifty-one only, the 7D has disappeared, being safely hidden behind the prepared card. The card box is opened and reveals the 7D.

By replacing this card in the box so that the flap will fall on it and so vanish it, then separating the double card in the pack, the 7D may be made to reappear in the pack. But in any case the trick in this form is rather crude, though it might be made an effective interlude in a more elaborate effect.

THE MISSING CARD

Two complete packs and an extra card, the JD for instance, are required. Pack No. 1 has on top a card with its back prepared with diachylon and its own JD on the bottom. Pack No. 2 is unprepared. The extra JD is in your pocket.

Offer pack No. 2 to be shuffled and while this is being done, palm the JD from your pocket. Take the pack back, adding this card to the top and put the pack down. Pick up pack No. 1, force the JD and receive it back on top of the prepared card which you cut to the middle. Square up the cards, squeeze the pack and hand it out to be shuffled. Ask a spectator to name a small number; suppose seven is called. Announce that you will order the chosen card to leave pack No. 1 and appear at the chosen number in pack No. 2. First, however, to show that by a coincidence the similar card belonging to that pack is not at that number, take the pack, deal six cards downwards and show the seventh, asking if that is the chosen card. Receiving a negative reply, put the seven cards back on the top in their present order thus bringing the extra JD seventh from the top.

Now have the card named and order it to go. Take pack No. 1 and count the cards face up on the table; there are fifty-one only and no JD. Ask the spectator to come forward and take pack No. 2, deal six cards and turn up the seventh. He does so and finds the JD. Tell him to run through the pack and find the regular JD belonging to it, so proving that the identical card chosen has really passed as ordered.

MESMERIZED CARDS

This trick appeared in *The Magic World*, 25th June 1913, contributed by Dr. A. L. Smith.

'Fix a small piece of diachylon to the tip of the forefinger and place a card on the table. Press the finger upon it and it will adhere. Place other cards on the edge of the first and interlock them. By placing the other fingers on the outer cards, they can be raised from the table, and, apparently unsupported, remain attached to the hand. A shake of the fingers and all are instantly released.

DIACHYLON FORCE

The card to be forced is prepared with diachylon and a large tray is required.

Give the tray to a spectator to hold, false shuffle the pack, retaining the card to be forced on the top. Spread the cards with their faces to the audience showing that they are well mixed, then spread them out on the tray face down. A second person is invited to make a free choice of any one card and to push it out of the line of other cards still face down. Gather up the rest of the pack and hold it face down in your left hand. The selected card remains on the tray for the moment. Ask if that is the card that is wanted, then pick it up, put it face down on the pack, i.e. on top of the diachylon card, press it down with the left thumb as you take out a pencil and have a spectator mark the back or initial it.

This force may used as a prediction trick. Write the name of the diachylon card on a slip of paper, fold it, give it to a spectator to hold, then proceed to force the card by the method described.

Card Mysteries Employing Diachylon

THE QUEEN TURNS OVER

Required are a red-backed pack and a double-backed card both sides of which are red. Prepare one side of this card with diachylon, and the face of the QD in the same way.

Hold the QD with the double-backed card squarely behind it, place the AH in front of it and the AS behind it, showing the cards back and front fanned, as being three cards only.

Close the fan and squeeze the cards making the QD adhere to the back of the AH. Holding the cards face downwards remove the middle card, apparently the QD, really the double-backed card and place it red back upwards on the table. Show the two aces back and front as two cards only. Turn them face up, pick up the supposed Q and insert it, still red back upwards, between the two A's.

Close the fan and press the cards making the prepared side of the double-backed card adhere to the back of the QD. Separate the AH from the face of the QD with a slight push and show the three cards are face up, the QD has mysteriously turned over. Backs and faces of the cards can be freely shown.

DIACHYLON BOOK TEST. FORCING A NUMBER

This subtle forcing of cards to represent numbers was originated for use in connection with a book test. It will suffice here to explain the method of forcing only.

Suppose, for instance you desire to force the number 364. From a pack of cards take out any 3 spot, 4 spot and 6 spot and prepare the backs with diachylon. To each of them press any other card so that each pair is back to back. Place the three double cards, the diachylon causing each pair to adhere, on the face of the pack with the faces of the three indifferent cards showing.

When the time comes to force the number introduce the pack, take off the three bottom cards and stand them, faces outwards against a book, a glass or any other object, remarking that they will be used as indicators. Hand the remainder of the pack to be thoroughly shuffled.

Let a spectator cut the pack about one-third down, place one of the indicator cards face up on the lower portion and have the cut replaced. Go to another person and repeat the process, having the cut made about half way in the pack and the last cut about two-thirds down. When putting the double cards face up in the pack be careful no one can get a glimpse of the card below. State that the cards following the face-up indicator cards will be used to represent the number required, pointing out that the method employed ensures that the number is arrived at by pure chance. Run over the backs of the cards and on coming to the first reversed card press the two cards apart, take away the faced card and have a spectator remove the next card himself. Do the same with the next two faced cards. The values of the cards being taken as numerals, the required number is forced.

ANOTHER DIACHYLON FORCE

A special pack is made up of twenty-six ordinary cards and twenty-six all alike. The backs of all the ordinary cards are prepared with diachylon and on each one a card from the other twenty-six is pressed. The pack is then squeezed, making the pairs adhere. So prepared, the pack can be fanned freely, all the faces will appear different. To force any one of the similar cards simply spread the pack face down and have any card pointed to, divide the pack at that card, push forward the top card with the left thumb, separating it from its diachyloned mate, for the spectator to take. Or any number may be called and counted to, the top card of the next pair being pushed off alone.

TWIN ACES   Gravatt

Prepare any indifferent card with diachylon on its face. On this card place an A and press the two cards together. They can be freely handled as one card. Lay this double card upon the table and overlapping it place the other A of the same colour. Have the pack shuffled by a spectator and ask him to take out and retain one card. Take the pack, show the two A's, and retain one card. Take the pack, show the two A's, really three cards, place them on the top, slide off the top card, the indifferent one and, calling it the first A, push it in the middle of the pack. Take the next A and put it on the bottom. Have the selected card put on top of the pack and one complete cut made. The selected card is found between the two A's.

Card Mysteries Employing Diachylon

TURNO

Prepare the face of a card with diachylon and put it at the bottom of the pack. A card is freely selected, then put face down on the face of the pack (i.e. on top of the diachylon card) and is initialled by the spectator on its back. Lift it off with the diachylon card adhering to it and put it face down on the table. Spread the pack with its faces towards you, pick up the double card, the diachylon card now uppermost, insert it in the fan: to the spectators you have simply replaced the initialled card facing the same way as the rest of the pack. In reality when you separate the two cards the initialled card is face up in the face-down pack.

The same trick can be done by wetting the thumb and transferring saliva to the face of the bottom card.

MELROSE

Beforehand smear some diachylon on the tip of your forefinger. Using any pack hand it to a spectator to shuffle thoroughly. Instruct him to put the pack face down on the table and cut about the middle, then take the top card of the lower portion and note what it is. This done tell him to put the card face down on top of the other half which you indicate by touching it with the tip of your forefinger, rubbing some of the diachylon on it, then to complete the cut by placing the other half on top. Pick up the pack giving it a squeeze and hand it to the spectator to again shuffle.

Take the pack back and order the card to vanish. Deal the cards face up asking the spectator to see if his card appears but not to name it. There are fifty-one cards only, the chosen card being dealt with the diachylon card as one card. Announce that you will make the card reappear and instruct him to say nothing but merely think 'Stop' when he sees it. This time hold the pack face up and when you come to the double card push the prepared card off and stop on the next one, the chosen card.

TWO VIEWPOINTS

Any pack of cards may be used but you must have a little pot of diachylon paste in your pocket.

Card Mysteries Employing Diachylon

Hand the pack out to be shuffled and while this is being done get a small daub of the diachylon on the second finger-tip of your right hand. Take the pack and in laying it on the table face down rub some of the diachylon on the face of the bottom card. Invite a spectator to cut, lift up the top card of the lower portion, note what it is, put it face down on the upper part of the cut and complete the cut. The bottom card with the diachylon on its face is thus brought on top of the chosen card. Pick up the pack, giving it a squeeze, and have the spectator shuffle it. In the meantime get a little diachylon on the tip of your left second finger. Take the pack and putting it face down on the table rub the diachylon on the bottom card. A second spectator now cuts, takes a card, notes it and re-assembles the pack in the same way as was done with the first card. Again pick up the pack, give it a surreptitious squeeze and have it shuffled by the second spectator.

Take the pack face down in your left hand, push the cards off one by one into your right hand and drop them haphazardly on the table. You can tell by feel when a double is reached, push the two apart, the top one will be one of the chosen cards, note the exact spot where you drop it. Do the same with the second double card. Borrow a penknife and have your eyes covered with a folded handkerchief. By glancing down the sides of your nose you can locate the positions of the two chosen cards. Move the point of the knife round in circles gradually approaching one of the cards, then suddenly stab the knife down on it. Lift the card on the knife point and have it acknowledged. Do the same with the second card.

DIACHYLON STOP TRICK

Prepare a card with diachylon on its face and place it on the bottom of the pack.

False shuffle, keeping the bottom card in position. Fan the pack and allow a spectator to choose a card freely. Under cut about half the pack and have the card returned on what was the top of the pack. Drop the cut on it thus bringing the diachylon card on top of the selected card. Squeeze the pack as you square it up and tap both sides and ends on the table to prove the card completely lost amongst the others. Have the pack shuffled.

Take the pack back. Instruct the spectator to concentrate on his card and announce that you will deal the cards face down and that although you cannot possibly know either what the card is or where it is in the pack, you will infallibly find it by unconscious cerebration, or any other pseudo-scientific means you care to name. Deal the cards face down. You know by feel when you come to the double card. Push the top one, the prepared card, off and stop dramatically on the next. Have the card named and slowly turn it over.

REVERSED COLOUR SURPRISE

Use a blue-backed pack for this feat and with it one red-backed card, say the QD. Place this card second from the bottom reversed, and the blue-backed QD about sixth from the top. Prepare the back of the top card which may be any card at all, with diachylon.

Force the blue-backed QD. Under cut for its return so that it is put on top of the diachylon card, drop the lower portion on top. Cut the pack, square the cards giving them a secret squeeze, and an overhand shuffle. Order the card to turn over, have it named and instantly spread the pack, backs up, showing the QD face up.

Let the spectator draw the card and hold it face up. Remark, 'I don't know what you are thinking about but the lady is blushing all over.' The card is turned and the red back is revealed. Run over the faces of the pack and show that there is no other QD.

DIACHYLON SUPER COLOUR CHANGE

A red-backed pack of cards, preferably of the bicycle air cushion type, and a blue-backed card with the same back design, are required. Prepare the face of the blue-backed card with diachylon and place it on the face of the pack.

Show the pack, shuffle it, keeping the bottom card in position, and casually make some remark about the shade of red that the backs have. Spread the cards, keeping the blue-backed one covered, and allow a spectator to make a perfectly free selection of a card. Have him note it and show it to several others for a reason that you say will be explained later. Under cut for the return of the card and drop the lower portion on top, bringing the prepared blue-backed card on top of the selected card. Squeeze the pack while squaring the cards, tap the sides and ends on the table showing all fair. Shuffle overhand with the faces of the cards towards the front.

Spread the cards in a wide fan, backs towards you, and ask the spectator and those to whom he showed his card, to set their minds intently on it. Ask if they can see the card in the fan, then say you will pass your forefinger slowly across the top of the fan and when they see it arrive at the card tell them to think, 'Stop.' You have simply to stop with your finger above the blue-backed card. This is acknowledged to be the right card. Draw it up half-way out of the fan and ask the spectator to blow on it. Turn the fan round and show that its back has turned blue. 'Quite natural,' you say, 'you know you blew on it.' The card may be removed and shown on all sides and dropped on the table with perfect safety.

FLYAWAY CARDS

Reverse the two bottom cards of the pack and on the upper of the two put a smear of diachylon.

Allow a spectator to freely select a card; as he looks at it quietly drop your left hand to your side, turning it over, bring the hand up with its back uppermost and the pack will be reversed, but without any alteration in its appearance owing to the two reversed cards. Put the chosen card squarely on the pack face up and have the spectator initial it. The upper of the two reversed cards will adhere to the initialled card as you take it off and insert it face up in the middle of the pack. Again quietly drop your left hand to the side as you say you will make the chosen card vanish and another card reverse itself in its place. Raise the left hand with the pack now right side up. If you can secretly turn the bottom card over to bring it face down with the rest of the cards, do so, if not, turn the top card to show it and replace it, then boldly draw out the bottom card sharply turning it as you do so, show it and put back on the bottom. Spread the pack backs uppermost, the initialled card has gone and another card shows up reversed. Withdraw this card, the initialled card is stuck to its back face downwards, and place it (the two as one) on the table, face up.

Spread the pack and have a search made, the initialled card has disappeared. Insert the double card, still face up in the face-up pack, square the pack and riffle shuffle it thoroughly. Hand the pack to the spectator. Order the chosen card to return to the pack reversed. He spreads the pack face up, one card is reversed, it is the initialled card.

The same trick can be done by simply wetting the thumb and transferring some of the saliva to the back of the uppermost of the two reversed cards.

ACE TRANSPOSITION

Two packs are required, one red-backed, the other blue. From both remove the AH and the AS. Treat the backs of the top cards of each pack with diachylon. In the red pack put the blue-backed AH second from the top and place the red-backed AH in the middle. In the blue-backed pack place the red-backed AS second from the top and in the middle put the blue-backed AS. Fan the red-backed pack face up and remove the AH from the middle, keeping the pack face up, take off about a dozen cards from below, square them up and put them down face up beside the AH. Put remainder aside.

From the blue-backed pack remove the AS from the middle with the pack face up, separate about a dozen cards from the bottom, square the packet and put it face up beside the AS, put rest aside.

Take the red-backed packet, put the red-backed A on top, i.e. on the diachylon card, cut once and squeeze the packet.

Take the blue-backed packet, put the blue-backed AS on top, also on the diachylon card, cut once and squeeze the cards.

Spread the red-backed packet face up, take out the AH (blue-backed) keeping the face to the front and drop it thus into a goblet, place the double card from the packet against the goblet red side face out as an indicator. The remainder of the packet drop behind the AH.

From the blue-backed packet take out the AS (red-backed) keeping its face to the front, drop it into a second goblet on the other side of the table. Take out the double card and place it blue back outwards against the side of the goblet as an indicator. Show the faces of the rest of the cards and drop them behind the AS.

Change the positions of the two indicator cards and order the two A's to pass across to the opposite glasses. Show that the change has taken place and hand the goblets and cards to be examined.

Drop the indicator cards on their respective packs and snap them apart.

REMOTE CONTROL IMPROVED   Orville W. Meyer

This is an improvement on the original trick by Annemann (Chap. 7) in that the use of any special card is eliminated and the trick can be done with any two packs of the same size with contrasting back designs. To prepare, take any card, say 2H and prepare its face with diachylon. Place the red-backed 2H on the bottom of the red-backed pack.

Run through the blue-backed pack and remove the prepared 2H not allowing its face to be seen and have it initialled on the back by a spectator. Announce that you will place the card somewhere in the red pack, put pack and card behind your back and place the card on the bottom of the pack, therefore if anyone has noticed the 2H at the bottom no change is visible, a 2H still shows there.

Bring the pack forward and spread it on the table face up, but keeping the two deuces under the end cards. Have someone indicate any card. Leave that card face up on the table, gather up the pack and put it face down on your left hand. Pick up the chosen card and drop it on the face of the pack for someone to initial on the face. Press the card down so that it adheres to the prepared 2H and they become practically one card. With the left thumb deal the apparently single card face up on the table and hand the pack to a spectator to deal through and find the blue-backed, initialled card. It is not there. Pick up the card on the table, have the initials on the face acknowledged, turn it over and show the blue back, the initials on it are also acknowledged thus proving that from amongst fifty-two cards that very card has been picked out.

CARD IN POCKET

Required a full pack of fifty-two cards and the Joker. Treat the back of the Joker with diachylon and place it on top of the pack.

Riffle shuffle the pack several times, retaining the Joker on the top. Spread the pack face down and invite a spectator to draw out any card and note carefully what it is. Gather up the pack, under cut for the return of the chosen card so that it goes on top of the diachylon back of the Joker, drop the lower portion on top, square the cards, secretly squeezing them, and hand the pack to the spectator to shuffle. Take the pack and put it in your outside right coat pocket. Riffle over the top edges of the cards and locate the double card, that is the Joker and the chosen card stuck together, take them out, face towards you and put them in your upper left waistcoat pocket.

Ask the spectator to remove the pack from your pocket and count them. He finds fifty-one. Tell him to run over the faces and take out his card. In the meantime you have separated the cards in your waistcoat pocket with right thumb and fingers, pushed the Joker right down and drawn the chosen card upwards so that about half its back shows. The spectator announces that his card is not in the pack. He takes the card from your waistcoat pocket after naming it.

It will be noted that the prepared card is subtly got rid of and the pack is ready for any other effects.

THE DIACHYLON DO AS I DO

As usual a red-backed pack and a blue-backed one are used. Prepare by treating the bottom card of the blue-backed pack with diachylon; next above it place any red-backed card from the other pack. Pick out its duplicate with blue back and put it sixth from the top. The red-backed pack is unprepared.

To begin with, force the red pack on a spectator in the usual way. The spectator shuffles his pack while you false shuffle the blue pack. Each puts a card face down on the table, you taking the sixth card, while the spectator puts out any card, neither card being looked at. The packs are squared and placed face down on the table. Place your card on top of the spectator's pack and he puts his card on top of yours. Both packs are given one complete cut. Hand your pack to the spectator, squeezing it as you do so, and he hands you his. Both packs are spread face downwards, the odd coloured cards are pushed out. They are turned over and prove to be the same.

Refer to section 'Do As I Do' for methods with unprepared cards.

A REAL MAGICAL VANISH   Gravatt

From a red-backed pack take out the AH, AS, and QH. Prepare the face of the QH with diachylon. Place a double-backed card, one side red, the other side blue behind the QH well squared together and arrange the two A's in a fan with the QH and the double-backed card between them so that when shown back and front they appear to be three cards only. Prepare the top card of a blue-backed pack with diachylon.

Show the three cards, AH, QH, AS, fanned, back and front. Close the fan and squeeze the cards so that the QH adheres to the back of the AH. Holding the cards face down draw out the middle card, the double-backed card, calling it the QH. The red back shows and as you immediately spread the two aces showing their faces there can be no suspicion that the card is not the Q. Put the two A's, with the Q adhering to the back of the AH in a spectator's pocket.

127

Card Mysteries Employing Diachylon

Take the blue pack, spread it showing backs and faces, square it up and drop it face up on the supposed Q, press down on the pack as you make one complete cut thus causing the red back of the double-backed card to adhere to the back of the prepared blue card.

Order the red-backed Q to pass from the blue-backed pack and rejoin the two A's in the spectator's pocket. Spread the blue-backed pack, every card is blue backed. Take the cards from the spectator's pocket, spreading the Q and the AH apart as you do so and throw the three cards on the table one by one.

Mr. Gravatt describes this effect as a masterpiece, leaving it to the reader to judge for himself upon trying it. We also will leave it at that.

THE ACME SPIRIT TEST

From any pack of cards take five that have a large proportion of white space on the faces, say four 2's and a 3. Prepare the edges of one card by rubbing a little diachylon on them. This card can then be easily picked from amongst the others by the slightly sticky edges.

Place the prepared card in the middle of the five, fan them out and ask a spectator to take one. Usually the middle card is taken, if so ask him to write the name of any deceased person on it. Turn away as this is done, and tell the spectator to put the card in his pocket when he has written the name. In the same way names of living people are written on each of the other four cards. Finally the five cards are mixed up by the spectator and placed face down on your right hand which you immediately put behind your back. If desired you may be genuinely blindfolded. Placing the cards to your forehead one by one you infallibly announce the card with the dead person's name on it—simply by feeling the slightly sticky edge as you place it to your forehead.

If the prepared card is not taken the first time have a name of a living person written on it, hand three other cards for names of living persons and the prepared card last for the dead name.

NUMBER PLEASE

Beforehand place a very small pot containing a little diachylon paste in your waistcoat pocket.

From any pack which has been thoroughly shuffled let a spectator freely select a card, note what it is, replace it and you secretly bring it to the top. Ask spectator to name any number from one to fifty-two. Get a tiny daub of the diachylon on your right thumb and rub it on the back of the top card, the chosen one.

Suppose twenty is the number chosen. Count the cards from your left hand into your right one by one taking each succeeding card under the one before it, so keeping the cards in the same order, the chosen card remaining on top of the cards in the right hand. When you reach the twentieth card put it on top of the packet in the right hand and put the remainder of the pack down. Take the packet of twenty cards in your left hand, square the cards perfectly and press down with the left thumb as you have the spectator name his card. The two cards adhere and you turn them over as one.

THE SYMPATHETIC PAIR—No 1

The top card of the pack is prepared with diachylon.

Invite a spectator to think of any card he pleases and write its name on a slip of paper; you do the same, writing the name of the top card. Spread the pack, face out and ask the spectator to find his card and remove it. Under cut the pack and have the card replaced on top of your diachylon card. Drop the lower portion on top, square and squeeze the pack. Spectator may now shuffle freely by the overhand method. Take the pack, let the spectator open and read the names on the slips, find the double card and push the two apart as you show them.

THE SYMPATHETIC PAIR—No. 2

Two duplicates of cards in the pack are required. Suppose the cards are the 10S and 5D. Cut the duplicates a little shorter and stick the two regular cards together with a little diachylon on the back of one. Put this pair anywhere in the pack, the two short cards on top.

Force the two shorts and have them replaced and the pack shuffled overhand by the spectator. When you take it back and riffle the ends you stop at the double card automatically, separate the two cards and show that they have come together. The duplicate short cards will not appear during the riffle.

THE SYMPATHETIC PAIR—No. 3

Beforehand get a little diachylon under left thumb-nail. From any pack, thoroughly shuffled, allow a card to be freely selected, noted and replaced. Bring it to the top and have another person select a card. As he notes it transfer the diachylon to the back of the top card. Under cut the pack for the return of the second card so that it goes on top of the first one. Drop the lower portion on top, square and squeeze the cards and hand them to be shuffled overhand fashion. Finally the cards are named and you show they have come together; push them apart as you show them.

7

Double-Back Principles in Card Magic

The first double-backed cards put on the market were used in the trick called 'Two Card Monte', and sold by Theodore L. Deland about the year 1910. However, I have reason to believe that the principle was known to and used by Hofzinser many years ago. Deland's trick is more of a joke than a feat of magic but it opened the way for the invention of many fine tricks dependent on the use of the double-back principle.

ALICE IN WONDERLAND

A double-backed card is required. Have this on the top of the pack. False shuffle and cut, leaving it in that position. Allow a spectator to make a free choice of one card and note it. Cut the pack about the middle, at the same time slipping the double-backed card on top of the lower portion, and put the cut face up on the table. The act of turning the cut face up will completely cover the slip sleight. Have the chosen card put face down on top of the face-up cards, then place the other portion of the pack on top also face up. The double-back card is thus just above the chosen card. Take the pack and run over the cards backs uppermost until you come to the reversed chosen card, suppose it is the 6D. Divide the pack at that point and put the cards above it below the rest. The 6D is now on top of the pack and the next card is the double-backed one. Lift the two cards as one and turn them face down. Take off the top card, apparently the 6D, and put it in the middle. Order the 6D to reverse itself and spread the cards, keeping the top card hidden and show a card reversed in the middle; this is the double-backed card but you call it the 6D.

Without allowing time for anyone to ask you to show its face turn the pack face down and run the cards one by one into your right hand, reversing their order. You do this to show that the cards are all backs up, really you spell the chosen card, 6D in this case, and on reaching the last letter throw the packet back on the top of the pack. Seeing that the double lift left the chosen card on the top you have thus put it in position to be spelt out. Order the card to go to that position and proceed to spell it out, turning the card on the last letter.

A false shuffle before the spelling greatly strengthens the effect.

DOUBLE-BACKED CARD ROUTINE   Lane

To present this routine of five effective tricks you require:

> A double-backed card made by gluing two cards face to face.
> AC, JC with one index pip and large pip at the same end changed to S with indian ink.
> One red-backed card, say the 6H.
> Pack of blue-backed cards.

Beforehand arrange the pack with the double-backed card on top, the red-backed card next to it, faked JC anywhere in the pack and the 6H on the bottom.

To present the routine begin by taking the pack from the case, cut and force the lower portion. Take the top, bottom and any card from the middle putting them face down on the table and force the middle one, the 6H.

Assemble the pack with the double-backed card on top. Insert the 6H anywhere in the pack. Cut several times but finally cut at the double-backed card which you always find easily by its thickness.

Make a double lift and show the red-backed 6H. Insert it face up in the pack, allowing part to protrude. Push it home, order it to right itself. Spread pack, it is still face up, take it out, turn it over and show its red back, 'It's blushing for its failure.'

Toss it aside and cut double-back card to top. Cut the pack, take up the lower part and show how, by lifting two cards as one, you can make a card apparently return to the top after being put in the middle. Do this several times till the spectators understand the process (Lane says to do this) but show that it cannot be done with the card on the top. Replace the cut on top so that the double-backed card is the top card.

Have a card freely chosen, under cut for its return and square up. Card is on the double-backed card.

Riffle to double-backed card and then five or six more and cut pack at that point. Chosen card is now about six cards down from the top, with the double-backed card below it.

Feel for this card and turn all the cards above it as one, showing the chosen card. Turn the packet face down, take off the top card and put it in the middle. Again turn all cards above the double-backed card as one, again showing the chosen card. Turn packet face down, put top card in middle and continue showing that the card returns to the top until it alone is above the double-backed card. Leave it face up.

Turn the pack face up and show all the cards face up except the chosen card. Pull it out and show it back and front. Replace it face down, glide it back, draw out the double-backed card and push it into the pack. Turn the pack over and show chosen card back in same position.

Cut double-backed card to bottom. Have a card chosen and noted. Reverse the pack, take the card and insert it in the middle. Reverse the pack, run through the pack and show selected card face up.

Run over the faces of the cards and put the JS on top. On it place any red card and on that the faked JC–JS. Pass to the middle and force the JS. Have it replaced in the same position and pass to the top. Lift three as one and show the JS. Turn the three down, lift the faked card and push it in the middle, leaving the JS end protruding. Turn top red card to show that the JS really has been taken, and as final proof turn pack and show protruding end of faked card. Turn pack down, push card flush, and instantly show JS on top. By spreading the opposite end of the pack you show every card, there is no duplicate.

Cut double-backed card to bottom. Spread the pack for selection of a card. Count the cards as you push them off. Suppose the nineteenth card is taken. As the spectator notes his card, cut the eighteen cards to the bottom thus bringing them under the double-backed card. Under cut for the return of the selected card and throw the lower portion on top. Card is again nineteenth from the top. Let spectator cut several times with complete cuts, then false shuffle and cut at the double-backed card. Announce the position of the card as the nineteenth from the top. Deal and show it.

Cut the double-backed to the top. Have a card freely chosen. Cut for its return, slipping the double-backed card on top of the lower part. Slip the little finger under the card above the chosen card and make the pass. Turn over and show the top card, an indifferent card, then turn over three cards as one, bringing the double-backed card to the top and reversing the chosen card under it. Cut the cards. Have the chosen card named, and instantly spread the pack showing it face up in the middle.

TRANSPOSITION EXTRAORDINARY

Required two packs, one red-backed, the other blue, also a double-backed card, one side red the other side blue, to match the packs. The double-backed card is set, blue side up on the blue-backed pack.

Allow a spectator to take any card from the blue pack, examine it and place it face up on that pack. Suppose it is the 5D.

Hand the red pack to another spectator and have him remove the same card, 5D, from that pack and place it face out on the back.

Pick up the blue pack, make a double lift taking the 5D and the double-backed card as one. Put the pack down, take the red-backed 5D and put it face down below the two cards in the left hand. The two 5D's are now back to back, with the double-backed card between, and its backs face in opposite directions to the backs of the two cards. Turn the three cards over several times to confuse the spectators, then lift the top card off by sliding it towards you, saying, 'I will place this red card on top of this blue pack.' Lay the card, really the blue-backed 5D face up on the face-down blue pack. As the card in your left hand has a blue back showing, the spectators naturally are sure the red-backed 5D has really been put on the blue pack. The double-backed cards and the red 5D are placed face up on the back of the red pack, thus bringing the red back of the double-backed card uppermost.

Put the two 5D's face up into the packs on which they lie, being careful not to expose the backs. Order the cards to return to their respective packs and show that this extraordinary mystery has taken place. You may hand the blue pack to a spectator to verify the return of the blue card, thus both packs will have been freely handled.

INSTO-TRANSPO   Annemann

Effect. Fanning a well-shuffled pack, the performer has a spectator freely select a card on the face of which the spectator's initials are written. The card is openly placed in the spectator's pocket, not quite out of sight and is not touched again until the end of the trick. Now the spectator takes the pack and fans it. The performer selects a face-down card, initials it and places it in his own pocket. Then the miracle happens. The performer takes the card from the spectator's pocket and it is found to be the performer's card with his initials on it. Then the spectator takes the card from the performer's pocket and finds that it is his own initialled card.

Double-Back Principles in Card Magic

Method. On the top of the pack you have a double-backed card to match the pack. On the upper left and lower right corners of each side are light pencil dots, so that no matter how the card is placed in the pack it shows up plainly as soon as the cards are fanned. Under this card is any indifferent card on which you have beforehand written your initials. Riffle shuffle, leaving the two top cards in position.

Fan the pack and have a spectator select any card. Take it and lay it face up on the pack in your left hand, ask the person's initials and openly write them on the face of the card. With the right thumb lift three cards and turn them over as one, that is, you make a triple lift. At once push off the top card with the left thumb, take it and place it back outwards in the spectator's breast pocket without showing its face. You have thus placed the indifferent card with your initials in the spectator's pocket while his card lies below the double-backed card. Hand the pack to the spectator after making one cut. Tell him to spread the cards and you pick out the one below the double-backed card which you recognize by the dot on the corner. Hold the card with its face to yourself and name it as being the card with your own initials on it. Pretend to write your initials on it and put it in your own pocket. The trick is done. Order the change and you each take your cards from the other's pocket.

REMOTE CONTROL   Annemann

Two packs are required; one red-backed, the other blue—also a double-back card, one side red the other side blue. The red side is prepared with diachylon and the card is placed red side down on top of the blue pack. All is then ready.

Hand out both packs to be shuffled. Take them back and from the blue pack take out the double-backed card, first loosening it from the card to which it adheres, and place it, red side downwards on your right hand. Call attention to the fact that no one can possibly have any idea what card it is except yourself. Take the red-backed pack in your left hand and put both hands behind your back, saying that you will put the blue-backed card in amongst the red-backed cards so that nobody can tell just whereabouts it is. What you really do is to put the double-backed card with its red side upwards on top of the pack. Bring the pack forward and spread it face upwards on the table, that is, all except the top two or three cards. Invite a spectator to look over the faces of the row of cards, mentally select one then put his finger on it and push it out of the row, still face up. Gather up the rest of the pack and put it face

135

down in your left hand. Pick up the selected card and lay it face up on the pack, that is, on the prepared back of the double-backed card. Quietly press it firmly and squarely so that the two adhere, then with the left thumb push them, as one card, on to the table.

Hand the pack to the spectator who initialled the blue back and ask him to take out that card. He cannot find it, there is no blue-backed card in the pack. Turn the card on the table, it is blue-backed and bears his initials. By remote control you have caused that one card to be picked from the fifty-two cards of the pack.

INITIALLED CARD TELEPATHY   Annemann

Effect. A card is freely selected and initialled. It is returned and the pack shuffled. The spectator thinks of a number. Performer openly and slowly counts down until the spectator stops him and there is the initialled card. Performer does not know the card or the number until the finish of the trick.

Method. Place a double-backed card on the top of the pack. Put a light pencil dot on the upper left and lower right corners of that card on both sides so that it can be found instantly in a slightly fanned pack. Have a spectator freely select a card and initial its face. Undercut the pack, have the card replaced on the double-backed card and complete the cut. Cut several times and finally by sighting the dot cut to bring the chosen card to the top with the double-backed card below it.

Ask the spectator to think of a number below fifteen so that the effect will not be too prolonged. Now say, 'Your number is odd, isn't it?' If so you continue, 'I thought so, but don't tell me or anyone else just what the number in your thought is.' If the answer is 'No,' say 'Well that's odd. However, don't let me or anyone else know the number you are thinking of.' You know now whether the number is odd or even which is all the information you need.

If even, with your right thumb lift the rear ends of three cards and insert the tip of the little finger. Turn the three cards as one, take off the face-up card and push it into the middle. The double-backed card is now on top, the selected card is face up below it. But if the number is odd simply leave the double-back on the top with the selected card below it.

Riffle shuffle the pack, leaving the two cards in position, and announce that the chosen card is now at the number thought of. Lift and turn three cards as one as you ask 'Are you thinking of One?' On the negative reply take of the top faced card singly. Drop the card on the table.

Double-Back Principles in Card Magic

Again lift three and insert tip of little finger as you ask if he is thinking of Two. If again the answer is 'No' turn the three cards, take off the top faced one and drop it on the table. When finally you get the answer 'Yes,' push off the top face-down card and it will be the initialled card. Try this out with the cards and the details will be clear but the lifting of the three cards as one requires practice.

TURNOVER

Place a double-backed card on the bottom of the pack, first reversing the card above it. Riffle shuffle the pack without disturbing the two bottom cards and being careful not to expose the face card.

Let a spectator select a card freely and note what it is. As he does so quietly turn the pack over, then cut the pack for the return of the card but in doing that slip the double-backed card from the top on to the lower half of the pack. Keep the backs of the cards to the front as you do this.

Have the card returned on top of the double-backed card and drop the right-hand portion on top. You have now only to secretly turn the pack over and the chosen card will be face up in the middle. The double-backed card will be immediately above it and if you slip this to the bottom you have the pack in readiness to repeat the feat.

REPEATING CARD TURNOVER

A pack made up of twenty-six ordinary cards and twenty-six double-backed cards is required. Having the double-backed cards below the others, let a spectator choose any one of the ordinary cards and note it. Have it replaced in the lower half of the pack, i.e. amongst the double-backed cards. Square up the cards and secretly turn the pack over. Order the chosen card to turn over and spread almost half the cards, revealing the chosen card face up amongst apparently face-down cards. Care must be taken not to expose any part of the lower half of the pack. Remove the card and insert it in the lower half face down, i.e. amongst the ordinary cards which are face up. Again turn the pack over secretly and order the card to repeat its somersault. Spread the cards on the table with a wide sweep and once more the selected card appears face up in the face-down pack.

137

A REVERSE LOCATION   Larsen

Required—two double-backed cards. At the start have one of these at the top, the other at the bottom. False shuffle, keeping them in position. The easiest way to do this is to riffle shuffle, keeping the cards well covered with the hands so that in bending the corners for the riffle the lower sides are not exposed. Have a card freely chosen and under cut half the cards for its return. The chosen card thus comes between the two double-backed cards. Order the two cards on each side of the chosen card to turn over. Place the pack face up on the table and spread the cards out in a line. Two cards are revealed backs uppermost with the chosen card between them.

The same effect can be obtained with only one double-backed card. Have this on the top and secretly reverse the bottom card. Undercut as above for the return of the card and finish as before. This is the better method as there is only one prepared card to get rid of, or you may leave the double-backed card in the pack for another effect by proceeding thus: take out the chosen card, slide the lower of the two reversed cards on top of the other, then turn them over together on the face-up pack. The face of the lower card will show and there will be no suspicion attached to the other card. This leaves the double-backed card on the top to be used as you may desire for another effect.

DOUBLE-BACKED CARD FORCE

Two packs are required, one blue-backed, the other red, together with a double-backed card one side of which is red and the other blue. From the red pack take any card and place it face upwards third from the bottom of the blue pack. Under this put the card you wish to force, face downwards, and under this card any indifferent card. You now have the force card second from the bottom with a reversed card above it.

On the red pack put the double-backed card, red side upwards.

To make the force, take the blue pack and riffle shuffle it, being careful not to disturb the three bottom cards. Turn the pack face up and riffle till a spectator calls 'Stop'. Take the double-backed card from the top of the red pack, being careful not to expose its face, and insert it at this point, square the pack and cut it several times. Fan the pack face downwards. The only red back to show will be the card you previously put in the pack reversed. Show all the other cards are blue-backed and allow the spectator to remove the card under the red-backed card. The force is made. Openly remove the red-backed card and return it to the red-backed pack, showing that it is an ordinary card. The double-backed card remains in the blue pack to be used in your next trick or secretly removed, as the case may be.

REVERSI

The effect of finding a chosen card by having it reverse itself in the pack is only suitable for intimate work but the method that follows makes it effective for the stage or platform.

You require a pack made up of fifty-one double-backed cards and one ordinary card which you place on the bottom. One end of all the fifty-one cards is darkened and, in use, you keep this end always towards yourself. From an ordinary pack with the same backs you allow three cards to be freely chosen. In order that the whole audience may follow the trick, turn your back and have the three spectators hold up their cards for all to see. Take the opportunity to slip the ordinary pack in a waistcoat pocket and take out the faked pack. Keep your elbows pressed closely to your sides as you do this so that there is no visible movement of your arms to telegraph that you are doing something.

Have the cards fairly thrust into the pack in different places, letting each spectator push his card flush. Make a false shuffle since it is desirable to keep the three cards well separated. Return to the stage, holding pack in full view, and call attention to an easel on your table which has a board on it with a wide ledge so that a full pack can be stood on it safely. In the meantime you have quietly let the bottom card of the pack fall to your left palm and turned all the other cards over on it. To all appearances the pack is exactly the same but now the three chosen cards will be faced upwards and would show up if the pack were spread.

Stand the pack on the easel with its darkened edge upwards and the face of the bottom indifferent card against the board. The pack now contains fifty-five cards but standing to the rear of the easel you slowly push them off from the left- to the right-hand side of the board counting fifty-two cards only and not exposing the reversed cards. This is possible because owing to the white edges of the chosen cards showing up plainly when you come to the card before one of the chosen cards you push two cards forward as one, thus fifty-two cards are shown all with their backs outwards.

After giving the order for the three chosen cards to reverse themselves, simply push the cards forward one by one on the easel and the three cards show up, and when you come to the fifty-second card pick up the last four as one card. As each card reveals itself take it out and have it acknowledged by the person who drew it. If desired each card can be initialled by the drawer and identified at the finish.

It will be found a help if the ledge on which the cards rest is canted very slightly upwards, the minute projection of the upper ends of the cards being an assistance in removing them neatly.

CHAMELEON BACKS   Vernon

For this clever effect you require two packs, one with red back and one with blue; also a double-backed card one side red, the other side blue. Place the double-backed card on the blue-backed pack with its blue back upwards. Both packs may be shuffled by a spectator if desired. Take the red pack and pick out any black card, put it on the table without showing its face. Fan the blue pack and cut the double-backed card to the top. Then pick out any red card, holding it in the right hand, and the pack face down in the left hand.

Pick up the red-backed card from the table and hold the two cards face down between the fingers and thumb. Show the backs, one red, one blue. Turn them face up, pushing them in opposite directions, and show a black card and a red one. Apparently the blue-backed card has a black face and the red card a red face, just the opposite to the real state of affairs. Repeat the move several times to impress the spectators. Then with the faces upward drop the black card on the floor face up, asking all to remember that it is the blue-backed card.

Drop the red card face up on top of the blue-backed pack, i.e. on top of the double-backed card. Make a double lift and turn over, showing the red back of the double-backed card, thus proving that the red-faced card really has a red back. Turn the two cards again, take off the face-up red card and drop it on the floor. Order an extraordinary change; the cards are turned over, the red card is seen to have a blue back and the black card has a red back.

SATAN BEHIND YOU

Secrete a double-backed card, to match the pack, under your belt at the back.

Have the cards shuffled by a spectator and let him cut the pack into two even packets, handing you one and retaining the other himself. To illustrate what you want him to do, place your packet behind your back, add the double-backed card from under your belt to the top and bring forward the bottom card, look at it and replace it, as you say, on the top of the other cards—really you put it reversed on the bottom of your packet. Spectator puts his packet behind his back, brings a card forward, notes what it is, puts it on top of his packet. You both bring the cards forward, and you put your packet on top of his, thus bringing the card you reversed immediately above the spectator's card. Instruct him to place the pack thus assembled, with his card buried in the middle, behind his back and to take off the top card, turn it face up and push it into the pack.

The spectator does this, brings the pack forward and puts it on the table, face down. Spread the cards, one card is reversed. Push out the card below it, have the chosen card named and turn it up. The spectator has located his card himself. The reversal of the double-backed card has no effect and seeing one card reversed the spectator naturally concludes that it is the card he turned over.

THE DOUBLE CARD PREDICTION

In addition to a double-backed card you require an envelope, a slip of paper and a pencil.

Beforehand take any two cards, say AC and 2S and write their names on the slip of paper. Put this in the envelope and fasten the flap down. Place any indifferent card face up between the face-down AC and 2S and put the three cards on the top of the pack, the indifferent card being the second card and face up. Finally place the double-backed card on the top of the pack.

Begin the feat by handing the envelope to a spectator to hold. Riffle shuffle the cards, keeping the four top cards in position and covering the pack well with your hands in the action to avoid exposure of the faced card. Take off the top card, turn the pack face up, and hand the double-backed card, just removed, to a spectator, inviting him to thrust it into the pack anywhere, face down. Thrust the pack forward and have him do this quickly so that he will have no chance of turning the card over. Have him cut the pack, then turn it face down and spread it on the table. One reversed card is visible and is naturally taken to be the card just inserted by the spectator.

Let him draw out the card above and the card below the faced card, leaving them face down. Invite him to open the envelope and read your prediction. The two cards are turned and prove to be the very ones named.

COMEDY RELIEF

This use of a double-backed card is essentially one for magicians, or to squelch the person who has a smattering of magical knowledge and has been making a nuisance of himself. Casually introduce the old trick of making a chosen card turn face up on the pack by dropping the cards on the table. Then explain the trick and say that owing to its difficulty magicians do not often use it. This is simply to lead the nuisance to say he knows the trick and can do it. Hand him the pack and let him try. Much to his surprise he fails. Try as he will the card obstinately remains back up.

Before handing the pack to the 'wise guy' you bring the double-backed card to the top.

GIANT ACROBATIC CARDS   Grant

For this trick ten unprepared Giant cards and eight Giant double-backed cards are necessary. Set the cards alternately, an unprepared card on top, followed by a double-backed card, then an unprepared card, next a double-backed card and so on.

Begin by fanning the backs towards the spectators. The cards appear to be regular, all facing the same way. Square up the cards and deal nine in the following way: first card face up, next card back up, next card face up, and so on. The ninth card will be face up. Square up the pile, turn it over and put it face down.

Fan the remaining cards backs up, they appear to be facing the same way. Square them and place them in full view. Give the magic command, fan the first stack of nine backs up and all appear to have reversed themselves facing the one way. Pick up pile No. 2 and turning it over faces towards the audience, run them from hand to hand and every second card is face down.

SINGLE CARD FORCE

The double-backed card to be used for this force is made by simply gluing two cards of the pack face to face. If such a card is placed in the pack you can always find it by simply riffling the ends of the cards. When that card is reached there is always a distinct stop. To use it for forcing a single card, place it in the pack with the card to be forced immediately above it. Make a false shuffle, then invite a spectator to insert his forefinger into the pack as you riffle the ends. Time the action so that you push the pack forward to meet his finger just as the break at the double-backed card occurs. Let him look at, or take out, the card above his finger. This makes an easy and certain force.

THE PERFECT FORCE   H. I. Christ

This method may be used for one card or several.

Place a double-backed card on top of the pack and under it, face up, the card or cards to be forced; for example, to force three cards.

Riffle shuffle, leaving the four top cards in place. Put the pack on the outstretched left hand of the spectator and ask him to cut the pack with his right hand. Take the portion he cuts from him, turn it face up and drop it on top of the remainder of the cards on his left hand, saying as you do so, 'We will mark the cut in this manner. Hold the cards tightly for a moment until we are ready to see what cards you have selected,' or any other remark to suit the trick in hand.

Let the spectator remove the face-up cards and take off the three cards from the top of the face-down packet. These are the three cards that were reversed under the double-backed card. The next will be the double-backed card which can be easily disposed of, or ready to use again as your trick may require.

DOUBLE-BACK CARD FORCE

It is a very easy matter to force two cards by the use of a double-backed card.

Beforehand put any indifferent card face up between the two cards to be forced and place the three cards together in the middle. The double-backer you have on the top.

To force the two cards, make a false shuffle, leaving the cards undis-

143

turbed. Take off the top card, the double-backed one, hand it to a spectator and have him push it into the middle of the pack which you turn face up. Push the card quite flush, turn the pack face down and spread it on the table. One card shows up reversed; it is the indifferent card you had secretly reversed beforehand, but the spectator naturally thinks it is the card he just pushed in. He draws out the face-down cards above and below it and you have forced them in an innocent and apparently straightforward manner.

EASY COIN SWITCH

There are several good card tricks which depend on the exchange of the borrowed coin for one of the performer's own. The use of a double-backed card affords an easy, natural way for doing this. Have such a card, with a duplicate coin under it in such a position that you can pick up both with your thumb on top and fingers underneath supporting the coin. Receive the coin on the card and in turning to your table simply turn the card over, securing the borrowed coin with the tip of your thumb. Let the duplicate coin slide off the top of the card into a glass as you call attention to the fact that you do not even touch it.

You can then dispose of the borrowed coin in any way you wish.

THE SYMPATHETIC CARD   Jess Kelly

Two packs of cards are shown. One pack red-backed and the other pack blue-backed.

Performer picks up the red-backed pack and removes one card from the blue-backed pack and explains that generally when a red-back card comes in contact with a blue-back pack it naturally changes colour. The blue-back card is rubbed on the red-back pack and laid face down. When this card is picked up it is now found that the back really has changed colour, from blue to red.

A red and blue double-back card is required for this effect. This card is on the top of the blue-backed pack with the blue side face up. Underneath this card is a red-back card. These two cards are picked up and shown as one and then placed face up upon top of the red-back pack which is held in the left hand. Now the face-up top card is slid off on table (face up) leaving the double-back card on the red-back pack. On picking up the card on the table and turning it over, it is found to be red-backed.

8

Magic Utilizing Double-Faced Cards

DOUBLE-FACED CARDS

This particular principle has not received the attention it deserves from modern card men. Apart from the trick of passing four K's from a hat back to the pack, and vice versa, which was handed down by Hoffmann from prehistoric times of magic, there are but few tricks with double-faced cards ever seen nowadays. Most of the following are due to the ingenuity of Mr. U. F. Grant, the well-known magician and magic dealer. For higher flights of magic to which double-faced cards may be applied the student is strongly advised to study *Hofzinser's Card Conjuring*, translated by S. H. Sharpe.

HAT AND CARD CHANGE   Grant

Required—a double-faced card, say AH–KD. Put this on the bottom of a regular pack showing the AH face, next to it place the unprepared KD and in the middle of the pack, reversed, put the AH.

Begin by taking off the two bottom cards, showing their faces and drop them into the hat. Remove the double-faced card as the KD and vanish by means of a card box, by melting it in a glass of water, or any other way you fancy. Then show that the KD has returned to the hat while the AH has left it and is now reversed in the pack.

THE FUNNY PACK   Grant

In your upper left waistcoat pocket have a blank card, playing-card size, and in right trousers pocket a double-faced card, AH–KD for instance. Borrow a pack and palm the fake card on to it, AH face to show with the other faces. Run through the faces and show there are two AH. Turn the pack over and run over the backs, showing the KD face up, i.e. the faked card. Take this out and in pretending to put it in your waistcoat pocket, palm it and pull up the blank card already in the pocket just enough to show the white edge.

Finally have the pack examined, it is quite regular with one AH and one KD. Take out the card from your waistcoat and show it is simply a blank visiting card.

U CAN'T DO AS I DO
Grant

Fan out five cards face up, a double-faced card being placed second from the right-hand end. Hand a spectator any five cards and tell him to do exactly what you do. Close the cards together faces up. Put the top card on the bottom of the packet face down; top card to bottom face up; top card to bottom face down. Spread your cards and show three cards face up, two cards backs up. Spectator spreads his and they are in the same position. Compliment him. Close up the packets again. Place the top card on the bottom face down; turn the top card face down; turn the cards over and spread them—yours are all face up while the spectator's cards show one card reversed.

Again the spectator does exactly the same as you and again he has one card face down while yours are all face up.

THE SPOTTER CARDS
Grant

Place a double-faced card, say a 7–5, fifth from the bottom of the regular pack, with the 5 side to show amongst the backs of the other cards. Riffle shuffle without altering the bottom packet and not exposing the fake card. Fan the cards face up to show them well mixed and have one freely chosen. The card is noted and then placed on the top of the pack and buried by one complete cut.

Order a card to reverse itself in the pack to indicate the position of the chosen card. Spread the cards and show the reversed card, i.e. the 5-spot side of the fake card. Count down five cards and show the selected card. In the same way you can spell the spectator's name to find his card.

SUNDRY

A double-faced card may be used in the 'Rising Card Trick', with the wrong face showing as it comes up. It is then changed to the right card by pressing the hand over it, that is by turning it round under cover of the hand.

A double-spot card, say a 5–7 may be shown as a 7 first and then changed to the right card by apparently rubbing two spots off, simply by turning the card under cover.

THE FOUR ACES

The plot of the trick is the usual one. Four A's are placed on a table and three indifferent cards put on each. One pile is chosen, the A's vanish from the other three piles and all four are found in the pile selected. The use of double-faced cards makes the trick easy to work and very convincing.

Three special cards are required; double-faced A's of H, C and D, which show indifferent cards on the backs. To prepare the pack; turn it face upwards and put the double cards at intervals near the bottom with the A sides showing. Next place the regular AS between the second and third fake A's. The other three A's of the pack must lie seventh, eighth and ninth from the top.

Begin by turning the pack face up and remove four A's (three faked ones and the regular AS), and lay them face up on the table with the AS as the third card in the row. Be careful not to expose the lower side of the faked cards but you may flash the back of the real AS. From the top of the pack take off three cards, show the faces casually and put them face down on the first A. Take the next three cards, again give a slight flash of their faces and drop them on the second A. The next three cards, the three real A's, you take off and drop on the AS. Without showing the faces, and finally, take three more cards and drop them on the last A.

The third pile must now be forced. You may either use the old method of having the two piles touched, and then one pile—using the old take or leave equivoque—or you may ask for a number between one and four to be named. This leaves two and three the only possible numbers, either of which brings you to the required pile according to which end you begin the count from. In any case pile No. 3 is placed aside.

You order the A's to pass to the chosen heap with whatever hocus

147

pocus you may affect. Pick up the first pile with your right hand, the three top cards face down and the fake A up. Raise the hand, push the top card off and throw it face up on the table with a quick turn of the wrist. Raise the hand again but this time push out the fake A with the fingers and throw it A side down on top of the first card. Continue without hesitation by throwing the next card as you did the first, One card, an indifferent one, remains in your hand; turn it face upwards quickly, snap it with your fingers, showing it freely and drop it on the others. The A has vanished.

Proceed in exactly the same way with the other two piles, but vary the throw of the fake card with each pile. It is advisable to throw the cards all in one heap and drop the pack face up on them after the throw of the last card.

Finally turn the chosen pile face up and show the four A's.

KINGS AND ACES

Four double-faced cards—K's on one side, A's on the other—are required. Place these cards in different parts of the pack but nearer the bottom than the top, with the A's showing with the faces of the other cards. Put the four genuine A's on the top of the pack.

Thus prepared, show the pack face upwards. Remark that you will use the four K's and the four A's and take out the real K's and the prepared A's, laying them down face upwards. As you draw attention to these cards make the half-pass, facing the pack, and bringing the four genuine A's to the lower end of it. Very openly put the four K's on the top of the pack one by one. Put the pack down. Borrow a hat. Take the four A's (the double-faced cards) show them again and put them on the table, covering them with the hat and turning them over in so doing. Pick up the pack, take off the four K's and show them once more, then replace them on the pack.

Order the cards to change places. Holding the pack in your left hand drop the hand to your side as you make a sweeping gesture towards the hat with your right hand. Bring your left hand up with its back upwards, the pack will be turned. Take off the four A's and show them, then lift the hat and display the four K's.

Under cover of this surprise right the pack, bringing the four unprepared K's to the top. Put the double-faced K's on top for a second but immediately palm them off in your right hand. With that hand pick up the A's and offer them and the pack for examination.

Magic Utilizing Double-Faced Cards

THE TRIANGLE TRICK Devant

By way of showing the higher flights to which the use of double cards may be put, a detailed description and explanation of this trick devised by David Devant, the great English magician, follows:

Having invited a gentleman to occupy a chair facing the audience the performer begins by calling attention to a complete pack of cards displayed on a blackboard on an easel and also to a quantity of wide ribbon. He removes the two top rows of cards, half the pack, drops them face downwards on a tray and asks the spectator to take them, cut the pack and put the halves together face to face and then to twist the centre part of the ribbon several times around the cards. He then gives the two ends of the ribbon to two ladies seated at the extreme right and left of the front row, forming as he explains 'The Triangle' of which the spectator is the Apex. He removes the other half of the cards from the easel and puts them face up on the tray.

Each of the ladies is then asked to mentally select one card. This done he gathers up the cards and asks each lady to hold the packet in turn at the end of their ribbon and to wish the card thought of to leave the packet and go to the gentleman's at the Apex. The ladies name their cards, the packet is spread out and the cards are no longer in it. The spectator unwinds the ribbon from his packet and in it he finds the two cards mentally selected.

Method. A prepared pack, several yards of wide ribbon, an easel with a blackboard having four thin strips across it to hold the cards, a tray and a chair are required.

One half of the pack consists of double-faced cards, the cards on the backs being duplicates of the unprepared half of the pack. The cards are placed on the easel so that the two top rows are the ordinary cards, the two bottom rows are the double-faced cards. They overlap a little so that they can be picked up quickly. The performer takes off the two top rows, which the spectator puts into a faced packet and then winds the centre part of the ribbon round it. The two ends of the ribbon are handed to the two ladies. He takes the two remaining rows from the easel and secretly turns them over in getting the tray, thus bringing the duplicates of the cards wrapped in ribbon into view. Each lady in turn is asked to merely think of one of these cards. He gathers up the cards, has each lady hold them to her end of the ribbon and as the cards are named he secretly turns the packet again. Naturally the two cards are no longer to be seen. Since duplicates of these cards have been in the packet wrapped in the ribbon all the time, the spectator on the stage finds them and the trick is brought to a successful end. In the meantime the performer has had ample opportunity to drop the double-faced cards into his pocket and bring out the twenty-six cards necessary to make up a complete pack. This he hands to the spectator for inspection.

DOUBLE REVERSE

Larsen

Required—A double-faced card, one face representing say, a JC, the other the 10H. Place this card second from the bottom of the pack and the J and 10 to match on the top. Force these two cards. Fan the upper portion of the pack and have the two forced cards replaced, faces down, and in different places. Cut the pack somewhere underneath the lower of the two cards so that neither can show up at the bottom. Order one of the two cards to turn over; fan the cards and the double-card is revealed showing say the JC side. Take it out with your right hand, holding it with the J side upwards and being careful not to expose the lower side. Turn the pack face up on it and again cut the pack. If you now turn the cards face down and spread them, the 10H side is revealed and the second card has apparently reversed itself.

NEW CARD MONTE

Grant

Beforehand place in your right trousers pocket a double-faced card, AH–KD.

To begin the trick openly take from an unprepared pack the AH and the KD and place in spectator's side coat pocket. Remove the AH and put it in your right side trousers pocket under the KD side of the double-faced card. Ask the spectator which card is left in his pocket. 'The KD,' he replies. 'Correct,' you say and bring out the double card, the AH side showing. Put this card in his pocket as the AH, turn it and bring it out as the KD, putting it back in your trousers pocket.

Ask him which card is now in his pocket and he naturally says, 'The AH.' Bring the AH from your pocket and throw it on the table. He finds the KD in his pocket. The two cards are perfectly ordinary and the double card remains snugly in your pocket.

Magic Utilizing Double-Faced Cards

A BOOK TEST Grant

In an ordinary pack reverse the AH somewhere near the middle between two spot cards, say a 5 and a 7. On the bottom of the pack you have a double-faced card with the AH side showing. Note beforehand and memorize the seventh word on the fifth page of a magazine or book that you have at hand.

To present the feat turn the pack over and remove the bottom card face up as the AH. Turn the pack face down and have this AH thrust into it face up, being careful that no one gets a glimpse of the other side. Now spread the pack and show the reversed card, the only back that shows, between the 5-spot and the 7-spot, turn the card and show it is the AH. Say that the 5-spot represents the page and the 7-spot the word which is to be read by psychic vision. Hand out the book or magazine to a spectator and proceed to get the memorized word in the usual hesitating fashion.

A CHANGING CARD Grant

A double-faced card, say AH–KD, is placed second from the bottom in an ordinary pack, with the KD side as the back of the card and the real AH on the bottom of the pack.

Thus prepared, execute a riffle shuffle, leaving the two bottom cards as they were. Make the Hindu shuffle, asking anyone to call 'Stop' whenever the spirit moves him. At the word, lift up the packet in your right hand and show the AH. This force is quite convincing to laymen, as it appears that you have stopped at some indifferent card on command. Drop the packet on that in your left hand and order the AH to turn over. Spread the cards and the KD side of the double-faced card shows. Something has evidently gone wrong so you take out this KD, keeping it face up and cut at that point thus secretly bringing the AH to the top of the pack. Take out any two cards and put them face to face with the KD face up between them. Snap a rubber band round the three cards, turning them over in the process.

Order the recalcitrant AH to appear face up between the two cards and the KD to return to the pack. Remove the rubber band, the AH is between them face up. Pick up the pack in your left hand and throw out the two unprepared cards to be examined. Make the bottom change, taking the unprepared AH from the top of the pack and throw it down.

Palm the double card from the bottom in your left hand and spread the pack face up showing the unprepared KD amongst the other cards. Pocket the double card.

THE IMPROVED BURNED CARD   After Annemann

On the bottom of a regular pack you have the AH and next to it a double-faced card, AH–KD, with the KD side showing.

To begin, fan the pack and casually show the faces, keeping the AH at the bottom covered with your hand. Make the Hindu shuffle and force the AH as in the preceding trick. Put the two packets together and order the AH to turn over in the middle.

Spread the cards and show the AH side of the double-faced card. Remove it, keeping it face up and cut the pack at the point, bringing the real AH to the top. Place the double-faced card in an envelope, handling it always AH side up. Burn the envelope and the card and as they burn secretly reverse the AH on the top of the pack and pass it to the middle. Finally spread the pack on the table face up. One card is reversed in the middle. Turn it up and show the AH resurrected Phoenix-like from the flames.

A SPIRIT MESSAGE   Grant

Required is a double-faced card which has both faces representing the same card. On one side write any message which may be appropriate to the occasion. Place this card in an ordinary pack, the unwritten side showing with the faces of the rest of the cards.

Remove this card and two others showing the faces of all three plainly. Snap a rubber band round the three and in the process turn the packet over. Call the spirits into communion and finally reveal the message.

A TRANSPOSITION   Grant

On the bottom of regular pack place the KD, and next to it a double-faced card, AH–KD, with the KD side showing.

Borrow a hat, show the two bottom cards and drop them from the pack into a hat, but awkwardly and visibly let another card fall also. Remove the double-faced card as the KD and place it in a glass, covering it with a handkerchief and give the glass a half turn as you move it away. Order the two cards to change over and take the KD from the hat, uncover the glass and show the AH. When challenged about the third card, bring out an ordinary card, or you may use one with STUNG on it.

9

Card Mysteries Using a One-Way Back Design

This term is applied to cards the backs of which are so patterned that if after they have been arranged exactly the same way of the reversal of a card, end for end, can be detected by the difference in the pattern. The principle is by no means a new one but Charles Jordan was probably the first to apply it extensively. Annemann and others have also devised some very striking effects that can be done by its aid. Probably the best cards for its use are the Bicycle League Back cards No. 808. In the centre of the backs of these cards there are three wings forming a sort of triangle.

one wing up —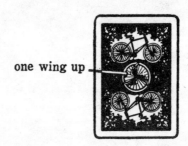

Holding a card one way the centre wing points to the right, but on turning the card around the other way the wing points to the left. The difference is plain to anyone looking for it, indeed a reversed card can be detected at a distance of several yards, yet it will never be noticed by the uninitiated. It will at once be seen that having a pack with this mark pointing the same way on all the cards any card placed in the pack after it has been reversed can be found with ease no matter how much the pack has been shuffled.

154

Card Mysteries Using a One-Way Back Design

Many of the modern bridge cards can be used in the same way as long as the pattern is not too strikingly a one-way design.

It would be impossible to include all the tricks that have been devised upon this principle. From the following selection the reader will no doubt be able to select many that will appeal to him and perhaps devise others himself, which after all is the most fascinating part of card magic.

SUBTLE METHOD OF SETTING THE PACK OPENLY
Annemann

Here is a way to set a pack, which may have been borrowed, right in front of the spectators. Have a card selected, noted, returned and secretly pass it to the top. Bring it to the bottom with an overhand shuffle and sight it, then send it to the middle with a riffle shuffle.

State that you will deal the cards one at a time and instruct the person that when he sees his card he is to think 'STOP,' but if you should pass it by, he is not to say a word. Hold the pack face down and deal the cards on the table one by one, turning them face up and here is where the trickery lies. Suppose that the first card has its indicator at the outer end of the card, turn the card over sideways in placing it face up and turn all the cards that follow with the indicators at the top in the same way, sideways. When you come to a card with the indicator at the inner end, turn it endwise as you lay it face up and treat all other cards pointing inwards in the same fashion. When you turn the chosen card you give no hint that you know it is the card the person selected but you turn the next card in such a way that its indicator will be reversed, and when the whole pack has been dealt it will be the only one reversed.

Confess you have failed and spread the cards out face down, spot the reversed card and running your forefinger along the line thrust it down on the next card above, the chosen card. You have merely to set the one reversed card right and the pack is all set for one-way effects.

DIVINATION SUPREME

This trick depends on a principle that is very little known even by magicians and should be particularly noted.

Hand a one-way pack, properly arranged, of course, to a spectator to shuffle. This done give him the following instructions: 'Fan the cards with their faces towards you, remove any card that you please and put it

155

face down on the table. Close the fanned cards and place them on your left hand. Square the pack and put it on top of your card. Cut the cards and complete the cut. Finally take the pack and shuffle it again, then hand it to me.'

If the reader will follow these instructions with the cards in hand he will find that the action reverses the chosen card. The final discovery of the card can be made in any way you please. You may let the spectator deal all the cards in rows and note the position of the reversed card. Cover the cards with a newspaper, observing a headline or paragraph that comes over the chosen card. Then with your eyes bandaged with a folded handkerchief it is a simple matter to stab the chosen card with a penknife. In this case you do not touch the pack from first to last and the feat is a perfect mystery.

THE PHANTOM STAB

The well-known and popular method of discovering selected cards by stabbing them with the point of a knife, becomes a simple matter by the use of one-way cards.

SHOWING HOW
FAN IS CLOSED.

With the pack set with all the cards pointing in one direction give it a thorough overhand shuffle. Allow a free selection to be made by fanning the pack from left to right. As soon as a card is taken, close the fan by putting your right hand on the left side of it and sweeping it to the right, the action reverses the pack with a perfectly natural action. Have the card replaced and again shuffle the pack. Proceed in the same way for the selection of as many cards as are to be used. Finally have the pack shuffled by a spectator while you borrow a penknife and a pocket-handkerchief. Place the pack on the table, have the folded handkerchief tied over your eyes, let someone hand you the knife with the open blade and have the point directed to the back of the pack. Remember you are supposed to be unable to see anything. Flick the cards off the pack one by one, when you see a reversed card jab the point into it and hold it up for verification.

After taking a stabbed card off the point of the knife remember to feel for the location of the pack with your left hand before resuming the flicking of the cards from the top. Use any artifice to strengthen the impression that you really cannot see anything.

With this method the cards have to be found just as they come, you do not know to which spectator they belong. The next method remedies this defect.

FIVE-CARD STABBING MYSTERY   Annemann

In brief the effect is that five cards are freely chosen from a shuffled pack, the performer, blindfolded, finds them in regular rotation after the shuffled pack has been spread on the table.

The cards Mr. Annemann recommends for this trick are Bicycle Rider Backs. The distinguishing mark is near the upper left corner. There is a loop which ends in a curl at one end of the card and a white dot at the other end.

With the cards all set the one way the pack is first thoroughly shuffled, then five cards are freely selected by as many spectators. Ask each person after noting his card to hold it against his body so that no one can possibly see the face. This tends to prevent any chance of the cards being turned round. Before the cards are returned turn the pack end for end. Have the first card replaced about the middle, and at once square up the cards very openly. For the second card fan the pack, locate the reverse mark and have the card replaced immediately below the first selected card. Again square the pack in such a way that it is plain that the card is really lost (as all think) in the middle. Continue with the others in the same way.

Call attention to the blindfold and state that the cards will be spread on the table and you spread them out in a long row. Then pick them up by scooping them from right to left until the first reversed card is reached. Square this half of the pack and drop the cards on the table, then gather the remainder in the same way, square them and drop them on top of the others. Now the five selected cards are on the top in order of selection. Leaving the pack on the table for the moment have a spectator blindfold you, either with a regular blindfold or a folded handkerchief. In either

157

case you can see down the sides of your nose all that is necessary to be seen.

This done ask a spectator to hand you the pack, do not pick it up yourself, you are supposed not to be able to see anything. Give the pack two genuine riffle shuffles. This is the puzzling feature of the trick even to magicians. The fact is that the first riffle merely distributes the five cards in the upper half of the pack without altering their relative order and the second riffle sends them in the same way throughout the whole pack still in the same order.

Spread the cards and ask spectator to hand you a penknife, which you had borrowed previously and laid with a blade opened on the table. You can now locate each card with ease, stabbing it and lifting it on the point of the knife as you state whether it is the first, third or whichever it may be.

Instead of spreading the cards you may just flick them off the top of the pack stabbing the cards as you come to them. An effective feint to introduce is to stab nothing once and hold up the knife as if it had a card on it. Hold it till told you have nothing there. Most packs of this brand come with the backs in regular order in which case the feat can be done straightaway with a new pack. It is advisable to run over the backs and see that this is so first.

This feat is undoubtedly one of the best card-stabbing effects that can possibly be performed.

A THOUGHT CARD PRODIGY

With the one-way pack set with the patterns in order, have the pack shuffled by a spectator. It is well to indicate that you want an overhand shuffle to be made.

Take the pack and allow the spectator to make a free choice of three cards, then tell him that from the three he is to choose one and concentrate his thoughts on it, foregoing the other two entirely. Let him replace them in the pack, which you have reversed in the meantime, the first somewhere near the top, the second in the middle and the third near the bottom. Square the pack, tapping the sides and ends on the table and make a false shuffle.

Tell the person it is absolutely necessary that he shall have a clear picture of the card in his mind and ask him to take another look at it. Spread the pack before his eyes and when you get several cards past the first reversed card ask him if he has seen it. If not, continue in the same way till you pass the second one and again ask him if he has seen his card. If not you know it must be the third but you continue fanning to the last card.

In this way you know which of the three he has chosen and to reveal it you deal the cards face down until you reach the reversed card you know is his. Make several pretended efforts to lay this card down but it appears to cling to your fingers. Have the spectator name his card and turn it over.

THE FIVE SENSES

From a one-way pack which has been thoroughly shuffled have five cards freely selected and noted. Under plea of having the cards replaced, widely separated, go to the last person with the pack face down on your left hand, having first turned it end for end. Lift off all but about six cards and have him put his card on top, drop six or eight cards from the bottom of the pack on it and have the next card replaced, drop some more on it and continue in the same way up to the last card. Square the pack very openly and give the pack several false shuffles and cuts.

Announce that you will find the cards by using the five senses, seeing, hearing, tasting, smelling and touching. You noted how many cards you dropped before the first person replaced his card, so put the pack behind your back, count to the card and bring it forward, finding the card by sense of touch. The rest of the trick is obvious, do not find the cards in the exact order they were replaced. For instance, you may find the fifth card next, then the second, the fourth and lastly the third. When you pretend to find a card by hearing riffle the pack at your ear, removing small packets till on the last riffle the card is on the top of those left and comes next your ear.

PREMO DETECTION   Jordan

To prepare for this location arrange a pack of one-way cards so that every alternate card is reversed.

By way of satisfying the spectators that the cards will be well mixed deal out any number of heaps of varying numbers of cards but each heap containing an even number. Let anyone assemble the pack by picking up the piles in any order he pleases.

Spread the pack from left hand to right and have a card freely selected.

As the card is taken lift the card that was below it so that it becomes the face card of the packet in the right hand. Keep the packets separated and have the card replaced on top of the left-hand packet. Openly drop the cards in the right hand on it. Lay the pack on the table and have the spectator cut it as often as he pleases with complete cuts.

To locate the card run over the backs until you find two cards facing the same way, following them will be two more cards facing in the reverse direction, the first card of this second pair is the chosen card, waiting for you to reveal it in any striking way you like.

THOUGHT IN PERSON   Annemann

From a one-way pack which has been thoroughly shuffled fan off five cards in the right hand, turn the rest of the cards face down and hold the pack with its outer end pointing to the right.

SHOWING HOW EACH CARD IN
THE FAN IS INSERTED IN A
DIFFERENT PART OF THE PACK.

Hold the fanned five cards with their faces towards a spectator and ask him to mentally select just one card. This done, turn the fan face downwards and insert the cards one by one in different parts of the pack. The action has reversed the five cards. Hand the pack to the spectator for another shuffle.

Take the pack back and holding it in your left hand run cards from the top into the right hand counting them as you do so. Watch for a reversed card and as soon as one appears, run several more cards, lift off the packet, fan the cards, noting the bottom card of the fan, hold them faces towards the spectator and ask him to say whether his card is amongst them. If it is not drop the packet face down on the table and take off another fan repeating exactly the same actions. When the spectator sees his card, square that fan and drop it on the other cards on the table remembering the number the reversed card occupied in the fan.

Finally drop the remainder of the cards from the left hand on top noting the bottom card as you do so.

You know just how many cards the chosen card is below the card just sighted so that by fanning the cards towards yourself you can pick it out at once. If there happen to be two reversed cards in the fan, put one on the top and the other on the bottom. Have the thought card named and show top or bottom card as the case may require.

THINK STOP   Annemann

A pack of one-way cards, Bicycle Rider cards, for preference, in which the mark to be noted is near the upper left-hand corner.

The trick is presented as a purely mental feat and you take pains to apparently eliminate all possibility of trickery. After having the pack shuffled hold it behind your back for the choice of a card. Keeping the pack behind your back and impressing on the spectator the necessity for him to have a clear mental impression of the card, riffle shuffle the cards, turning them round in the process. The card is returned to the pack and the spectator shuffles the cards.

Taking the pack slowly riffle it before the spectator's eyes asking him to make sure his card is still somewhere in the pack and so getting an opportunity of learning its approximate location in the pack as you watch for the reversed card to show up.

Tell the spectator you will pass the cards slowly before his eyes and he is to think 'Stop,' as the card is passed to your right hand. Hold the pack level with the eyes and push the cards off with the left thumb, taking them in the right hand one by one. If the reversed card was well down in the pack turn your head away until you know you are coming near it. Slightly spread three or four of the top cards and glance at them as you take a card, if the card is not amongst them, turn your head away again, if it is there note if it is second, third, or fourth and turn away. So that when the card is taken off you are not even looking at the back. Take the card, hesitate, say that you feel you are compelled to stay right there and ask if it is the selected card.

THE PACK THAT ISN'T

This is a further refinement of the one-way principle but its only practical use is to 'fool' a spectator who knows and is looking for the one-way set-up. To prepare for it first put all the cards in the one-way order. Next separate all the red cards from the black, turn the pile of red cards end for end and riffle the two piles together. All the red cards will have their indicators pointing one way while those of the black cards point in the other direction.

Thus prepared have the pack shuffled and have a card freely selected and noted. Reverse the pack and have the card replaced. Square up and have the pack again shuffled.

Take the pack face down in the left hand and deal the cards face up, telling the spectator to think 'Stop' when his card appears. You watch the designs on the backs and note which way the different coloured cards point. When you reach a card which points in the other direction to the rest of the cards of that colour you know that it is the selected card and accordingly you obey the mental command to stop.

The method can be used for several cards at the same time.

TWENTIETH-CENTURY SORCERY   Jordan

This is a special feat possible only with one make of cards, the Bicycle cards, blue thistle backs, air cushion finish. In packs of this brand there is not only a clearly defined difference in the designs at each end of the backs but two cards are always reversed in packing the cards in their cases. The two cards are the AS and the 2D, the marks to be noted are the vertical lines to the right of the left shin of the capped brownie, there are two at one end but only one at the other.

With such a pack, hand it to a spectator unopened. Write names of the two cards, AS and 2D on a slip of paper, fold it and hand it to some-one to place in his pocket. The pack is taken from its case and shuffled. Deal it face down into a number of irregular heaps but you take care to end one heap with one of the reversed cards and begin another heap with the other. In assembling the packets pick up the cards in such a way that the cards become the top and bottom cards of the pack. If you can, now make a false shuffle and cut. Take the Joker which should have been discarded at the outset, place it on top and have a spectator make one complete cut.

Instruct the spectator to turn the pack face up and take out the card preceding the Joker and the one following it. They are the AS and the 2D. Have your slip produced and read.

(*Editor's Note*.) We cannot say whether the Thistle Back cards used in this trick are still available but we are including the trick because it is one of the earliest descriptions of the reverse principle and shows the ingenuity of Mr. Jordan. The idea of the trick is excellent and with a little thought and pre-arrangement can be worked out with one of the modern packs.

THE FOUR-PILE LOCATION   Annemann

The trick is based on the same principle used in an older feat in which six cards of one suit are placed on the top of the pack and six others on the bottom. Four cards being discarded, including the thirteenth of the selected suit, the remainder are dealt into six piles so that there is one card of the suit at the top and bottom of each pile.

In this case, however, the one-way principle is used to attain the same end in a very subtle manner. The one-way pack is first shuffled. Take it and, to show the spectator what he is to do, deal four cards face down in a row and another four cards on these. Change the pack from one hand to another, reversing it in the process. Scoop up two of the packets and drop them on top of the pack. Put the other two packets together and drop the pack on them.

Hand the pack to the spectator who deals four piles in regular succession one card to each pile, while your back is turned. There will now be four piles of cards having a reversed card on the top and the bottom. He is instructed to take a card from the middle of any packet, note what card it is, place it on top of any other packet and assemble the packets in any order he pleases. The result will be that one pair of reversed cards will have a strange card between them, the selected card. You have only to reveal the card in as striking a manner as you are able.

It will be noted that in nearly all these 'impossible' locations the card is merely picked out and shown. Once the card has been discovered it should be revealed in some magical manner thus enhancing the mystery.

THE CUT PACK LOCATION   Annemann

The one-way pack is thoroughly shuffled and placed face down on your left hand which you hold outwards a little to the left and your head is turned towards the right. Invite a spectator to cut the pack anywhere and note the bottom card of the cut.

As he does this turn farther to the right and your left hand swings around so that you hold the packet behind your back. The cut is then replaced and the pack is taken by the spectator, put on the table and cut several times with complete cuts. (Before the cut was made you noted and committed to memory the bottom card of the pack.)

The halves of the pack now point in different directions, the selected card is thus the last card of one of the halves or the one before the next card that is turned the opposite way.

Remembering the original bottom card that you noted, take the pack and deal the cards into a face-up pile and watch the back of the pack in the left hand. When you see the next card reversed the card dealt will either be the original bottom card or the selected card. If the first, continue dealing until another reversed card appears when the card just dealt will be the selected card.

The conditions in this feat are just about as strict as can be devised for a location.

A CARD IS FOUND ONCE MORE   Annemann

This is one of the subtlest methods yet devised for the use of the one-way pack.

Have the pack shuffled, take the pack back and cut it about the middle. Cut by the ends, holding the cut cards between the right thumb and second finger. Put the left-hand packet face down on the table, turn the right hand over bringing it palm upwards, take the packet in the left hand and put it face down beside the other packet. The action has reversed the cards. One packet has the backs of its cards pointing in one direction, the other in the opposite way.

SHOWING HOW CARDS ARE CUT.

Turn away and instruct a spectator to take one card from either packet, note it and put it in the opposite packet. This done, turn round, pick up the packets with the fingers of each hand at the outer ends and riffle the two packets together. This will bring all the cards pointing in the same direction except the one the spectator changed over from one packet to the other.

You can now reveal the card by having the spectator think 'Stop' as you deal the cards face up, or in any other way you may fancy.

ODD OR EVEN   Annemann

For this feat with a one-way pack the Joker must be discarded and the full fifty-two cards used. Arrange the cards so that the back designs point alternately up and down. By this arrangement you can tell instantly if a number of cards cut off is even or odd. Note the way the design on the back of the top card points, if the top card of those remaining in your hand after the cut points in the same direction an even number of cards has been taken off and vice versa.

Do this twice, allowing a spectator to cut freely. Count the cards without disarranging them and drop them back on top. Put the pack face down on the table and invite a spectator to cut a packet, laying it alongside and from this another few cards so that the three piles lie side by side. Thus you have the bottom part of the pack, the middle portion and the top part, call them 1, 2, 3. Touching each packet you state whether it is odd or even.

By comparing 1 and 3, you know 1: 1 and 2, you know 2: 2 and 3, you know 3. If the points agree the cards are even in number, if they disagree it is odd.

In proving your statements by counting the cards one by one, begin with the left packet, count the second packet on top in the same way and lastly the packet to the right. The cards are then again in the same order.

Follow this with the next feat.

THE ALTERNATE DETECTION   Annemann

With the one-way pack alternated as in the last trick, cut it several times and place it face down on your left hand. Turn your head away, hold out your left hand and have a spectator cut the pack and complete the cut. Tell him to take the top card and note what it is. As he does this invite a second spectator to take the next card and look at it. Have the first card returned face down on the top of the pack and the second one on top of that. Cut the pack once and hand it to a third person.

Instruct him to deal the cards face up into two packets, one card at a time alternately. One of the chosen cards will be found reversed in each packet. The two who took cards having watched the deal know which packet contains their card. Asking the first to hand you the packet with his card in it, shuffle it thoroughly, overhand method, and work the 'Stop' effect. Do the same with the second card.

The preceding trick and this one make two very effective openers for a series of one-way tricks.

A NEW KINK   Annemann

This is an undetectable method for getting a card reversed in a one-way pack.

Let a spectator make a free selection from the pack and immediately hand the pack to a second spectator to hold while the card is returned to it. He then shuffles the cards overhand style and hands the pack to you.

Nothing could appear to be fairer yet you find the card since the mere action of handing the pack to the second spectator has reversed it.

EIGHT IN A ROW   Annemann

This trick can be worked with any one-way pack without having to arrange them all the same way.

Hand the pack to a spectator asking him to thoroughly shuffle it and then deal a row of cards face down. Now you can only turn cards over in two ways, either sideways or endways. The first keeps the cards pointing in the same direction, the other reverses it. Bearing this in mind turn over the eight cards to show their faces and, in turning them, bring them all pointing in the same way.

Invite a spectator to select one card and turn it face down. Note which method he uses in turning the card and turn all the others over with the other method. Slide all the cards together and have the spectator mix them, then deal again in a face-down row. Let your forefinger drift over them back and forth, then suddenly drop it on one card. Turn it up, it is the card.

When doing it with a borrowed pack having a one-way design pattern boldly assert that all cards can be read from their backs and prove it by doing the trick. This will always start an argument especially amongst card players.

GARDENER'S UNIQUE PRINCIPLE   One-Way Locations

This is a new idea which can be applied only to one-way cards, the designs of which extend to the edges of the cards, that is the backs must have no borders. When the cards are fanned it is possible to tell which way each back pattern faces by looking at the exposed left edges. Nearly all the modern bridge-size packs are suitable for the use of this principle. The one-way idea is employed in a very novel and undetectable fashion as will be seen by following explanation of the three tricks following.

I. SECOND CARD LOCATION

A suitable pack being in use it is not prepared or arranged in any way and may be thoroughly shuffled by a spectator to begin with. Take the pack in the left hand and with the thumb fan it slightly so that the left edges of all the cards are exposed. Look at these edges and quickly locate the largest section of cards facing the same way.

Let it be assumed that the cards have either light or dark edges according to the way they are facing. Look for the longest run of either light or dark edges, this group will be referred to throughout as the 'run'. If the desired run does not show up cut the cards and this may bring about the desired result by bringing the top and bottom cards together in the middle.

Usually an obvious run will occur somewhere in the pack but if not you can do several things. You may do some other trick and try for a run after it. Or you can hand the pack to someone else for further shuffling. Again, if there is no run which is obviously the longest there will always be at least two or three runs of about the same size. In this last case use the run that is farthest to the right but until some practice has been had with the system it is safest to wait until one long run makes its appearance.

Let us suppose that you have located a fairly long run. Fan the cards so that the spectator must make a choice near the top or the bottom of the run, or you may force the top card of the run. If, however, the spectator takes a card from another part of the pack, manœuvre so that it is replaced either inside the run or within a card or two of it. All you have to do then is to remember the position of the card in relation to the run. For instance, third card inside the run on the left, or third card outside the run on the right, or as the case may be. Close the pack, square it very openly and have it cut as often as desired, with complete cuts of course.

To locate the card takes an instant only. Simply fan the cards, note the run and you can pull out the card at once or deal with it as you please. In case the spectator insists on pushing his card in at some point remote from the run, you will remember its location by counting, not the single cards, but the groups of cards of the same colour as the long run. A little practice will make the process quite easy.

II. LONG DISTANCE LOCATION

A card having been selected, noted and replaced either just inside the run or just outside, have the pack squared and cut as in No. 1; do not take the pack. Instruct the spectator to stand some distance from you and fan the pack widely, backs to you; he is then to pass his finger slowly over the top of the fanned cards. When his finger is above the card you call 'Stop'. Knowing just where to look for the card it will show up quite plainly.

III. THE SUPER SPREAD

In this case the principle allows of the location of a card under conditions which cannot be duplicated by any other method. Let a spectator shuffle and spread the cards on the table. Look at the edges and locate your run. Invite spectator to touch a card and just lift a corner to note what card it is, as he does this count to the nearest edge of the run by groups of cards as above. Spectator gathers up the cards and cuts as often as he pleases (complete cuts).

Take the pack for the first time and fan it with the faces towards the spectator. Locate the card and then move your finger above the fan until it is over the card, then stop.

You must watch the way the spectator spreads the cards. If he does it the same way that you do all is well, but if he makes his spread the opposite way you must either do the same or turn the cards around before spreading them. Or again you may use the opposite colour in your calculation. If when the spectator spreads the cards the run was of light colour, when they are spread the opposite way it will be a dark colour.

The run may be located by merely pushing the cards a little off square. All you have to see is the edges of the cards so that the colours show up. You can then cut the pack at the selected card.

Card Mysteries Using a One-Way Back Design

SIMPLE TRIPLE LOCATION
Grant

Shuffle the pack overhand and fan the cards, inviting several persons, say three, to choose cards. As each one draws a card tell him to look at it and hold the card close to himself so that no one else may know it. (This prevents them turning the cards round.) In the action of closing the fan, or shuffling, turn the pack end for end and have the chosen cards replaced; thus these few cards will be reversed and easily found no matter how much the pack may now be shuffled. You can disclose them in any number of ways to suit your fancy. For instance, spread the cards face down and stab them with a knife-blade. This is just as easy to do while blindfolded by peeking down along the nose—and much more effective.

NO DICE
Grant

Openly remove from the pack two series of cards, running from 1 to 6, and in doing so set them all one way and shuffle without disturbing this feature. A spectator removes any two cards and if he gets a total of 7 or 11 he wins, as in the regular dice game. If other than these totals he keeps drawing—two cards at a time—trying to make his point. If he draws a total of 7 before making his point, he loses, according to the usual rules. Then he shuffles the cards (overhand) and you draw two cards, say they are a 5 and 4 making 9 for your point, in replacing the cards reverse them. Now, no matter how much the spectator shuffles, you can reach in and remove these two cards at any time, making your point and winning the game.

THE VANISHING MIRROR
Grant

Remove the four A's from the pack remarking that you will expose how gamblers cheat. Show the A's and replace them in the pack reversed and hand the cards to be shuffled. Explain that gamblers have been known to use a small mirror concealed behind something on the table. 'For example,' you say, 'we will hide the mirror behind this book on the table.' Pretend to place a small something behind the book. 'Now, as the gambler deals the cards he is able to tell the identity of each card, and when he comes to an ace he deals it to whichever hands he wishes, like this.' While talking pretend to see the faces of the cards in the mirror behind the book, and when you come to the A's toss them to one side; you know them by the reversed back pattern, of course.

Show these cards to be A's and for the climax, remark—'But if one is a magician he goes the gambler one better . . . will someone remove the book?' And to their surprise there is no mirror there.

THE MARKED PACK
Grant

Wherever card games are played you are likely to find a pack of Bicycle League cards in use. If the game is Bridge most of the modern Bridge packs are one-way designs. Noticing this to be the case you remark that most packs of cards are secretly marked by the manufacturer and, while talking along this line, run through the cards, apparently studying the backs but really sorting them so that all the cards are one way except the A's which you leave reversed. Hand the pack to be shuffled, take it back and as you deal it face down you pick out the A's. There will be plenty of folks to offer you all kinds of money to teach them to read any cards from the backs. This stunt is quite sensational, creates good publicity and provokes a lot of favourable comment.

THE FINGERPRINT DISCOVERY
Grant

Have a card selected, noted, and returned to the pack reversed. Hand the pack to be shuffled and then spread the cards face down on the table. With a remark about the importance of fingerprints in the detection of crime, open your pocket-knife and have the spectator press his thumb on the blade. (A table knife will do.) Now pretend to study the fingerprints on the knife, then look over the backs of the cards, making comparisons. If you have a pocket magnifying-glass use this to build up the deception. Finally pick out the reversed card.

LIVING AND DEAD TEST
Grant

Deal a dozen cards all one way. Ask someone to select one card and write the name of a deceased person on the face. Have it replaced in the group in reversed position and have the packet shuffled. Borrow a hat and put it on the table crown downwards. State that you will endeavour to determine the card with the inscription by the sense of touch. Hold the packet in the left hand, take off the top card and show its face then put it in the hat. Repeat this operation without looking at any of the faces yourself, until you come to the reversed card, which you recognize by the reversed back pattern, and lift two cards as one so that the spectators see the face of the indifferent card. As you put the two in the hat, as one card, flip the upper card face up in the hat so that you can steal a glance at the name written on it. Before placing all the cards in the hat, act as if you had failed and start all over again.

Remove the cards from the hat and put them on the stack again, shuffle and again show one card at a time and drop them into the hat. When you come again to the reversed card, hesitate, concentrate and then say, 'This is the card of death and the spirit from beyond answers to the name of . . . .'

A COUNT DOWN DISCOVERY   Grant

Reverse the top card of the pack. Shuffle, retaining the to pcard, hand the pack to a spectator and turn your back. Instruct him to deal any number of cards he desires face down on the table, look at the top card, remember it and replace the dealt cards. Tell him to square up the pack and give it one complete cut. Face the spectators, pick up the pack and fan it with the backs towards yourself. Tell the person to think intently of his card and you will discover it by psychic force or what you will. Close your eyes and run your first finger over the top edges of the top cards, suddenly stopping upon the very card that was chosen. On trial you will find that you can apparently close your eyes, yet the lids are not completely closed and you can still see enough to spot the location of the reversed card. This is the locator card and the card the spectator looked at will be just below this reversed card.

SIAMESE TWINS   Grant

Have the top card of the pack reversed. Allow a spectator to select any two cards, take one and place it on the top of the pack reversed; the other, also reversed you put somewhere near the bottom. Do this openly, calling attention to the fact that the cards are widely separated. Square up the pack and make one complete cut. Hold the pack face down in the left hand and draw out the cards from the bottom, one by one, placing them face down on the table in a pile. When you deal the first reversed card (the indifferent card that you had reversed on the top at the start), draw back the next card and continue dealing, retaining it at the bottom. When the next reversed card appears, draw out the one you have held back and deal it on top, thus bringing the two selected cards together. Finish the deal, then inquire the names of the two chosen cards. Sweep the pack out face up on the table with a dramatic gesture and show that the two cards have come together in some mysterious fashion.

YOUR CARD, YOUR NUMBER

From a one-way pack, arranged in order, allow a spectator to freely select any card, note what it is and push it back into the pack at any point, you, of course, having first turned the pack around. Shuffle overhand and have the pack cut several times.

Announce that you have such control over the cards that by simply riffling the ends you can find the chosen card. Holding the pack in your left hand face down and close to your eyes, riffle the cards slowly with your right thumb releasing them one at a time. As soon as the reversed card appears, stop, pick up that card and the one below it, remove the two cards, as one, and show with an air of triumph the face of the indifferent card. The spectator denies that the card is his, so you put the two cards, still as one, on the top of the pack.

To retrieve your lost laurels state that you will make the card appear at any number the spectator calls. Suppose he chooses 8. Stand with your left side to the front, hold the pack face down on the left hand with the fingers curled over the right hand side. With the right thumb and fingers lift the two top cards as one as if opening a book—the right hand revolves to the right, showing the face of the card. Count 'One,' and point to the card with the left forefinger (the chosen card is at the back of this card). Bring the right hand down again and take off another card in exactly the same way bringing it against the face of the first, count 'Two.' Continue in the same way up to the seventh card, as you lift this one, the left fingers press against the chosen card at the back of the packet and as the right hand turns, they pull this card on to the top of the pack.

Have the spectator name his card and slowly turn it face up. The moves should be made very slowly and openly. Smoothly done the slip cannot be detected.

ELIMINATION EXTRAORDINARY

Effect. A pack of cards is handed to a spectator who shuffles it thoroughly and retains possession of it (the magician does not touch the pack from first to last). Performer writes a prediction on a slip of paper which is placed in an envelope and held by a spectator. The cards are dealt into a number of piles until after a process of selection and elimination by the person who deals, one card only is left face down on the table. The prediction is read, it is the name of the very card that has been left on the table.

Method. The pack used is a one-way pack in which all the cards have been set the one way with the exception of one which is reversed. It is the name of this card which the performer writes on a slip of paper and seals in an envelope. The pack is shuffled, overhand fashion, and cut as often as the spectator may wish. He is then instructed to deal the cards into a number of face-down piles. The performer has simply to note in which pile the reversed card falls and by playing upon the words 'take' and 'leave' interprets the spectator's choice in such a way that that pile only remains, the others being eliminated. The cards in the pile are again dealt into several heaps and again he notes which contains the reversed card. The process is continued until finally one card only, the reversed card is left on the table.

The trick should be carried through in a breezy style, without giving the spectator too much time to think.

READING THE CARDS   C. O. Williams

This combination of one-way cards with a pre-arrangement is strengthened by the fact that a genuine shuffle is made, and yet the cards can be read while they are face down.

To prepare: first set the cards in one-way order, then separate the D's and C's from the S's and H's. Call the first packet A and the second B. Arrange the A cards by putting the KD face up on the table, on it the 10C, 7D, 4C, AD, and so on, the suits alternating and the values of the cards being three lower with each card.

Turn the cards of packet B so that the indicators point in the opposite direction to those of packet A, then place the KH face up on the table, on it the 10S, and continue the series in the same manner as in packet A. Place packet A on top of packet B and the pack is ready for the trick.

The originator recommends that this prepared pack be substituted for the one in use after several tricks in which the cards have been well shuffled. Then by splitting the pack at the lowest card of packet A, execute a riffle shuffle in a very open fashion, and have the pack cut several times. The arrangement of each series is not interfered with, the cards follow in regular order but the cards of one series are interspersed between cards of the other series. You know which series a card belongs to by the direction in which the indicators point.

In picking up the cards after the last cut sight the bottom card, suppose it is the KD, if the indicator tells you that the top card belongs to the same series, you know at once that the card is the 10C, and that all the other cards facing in that direction follow in regular order. When the first card of series B appears a good plan is to take it off and hand it for examination to prove there are no marks on the cards and sight it. You are then set for the cards of that series as well.

NE PLUS ULTRA LOCATION   Wimborough

To prepare for this effect, first arrange the one-way pack in proper order, that is with the indicators all in the same direction, then reverse thirteen cards on the top and thirteen cards on the bottom.

With the pack in this condition hand it to a spectator, turn your back and instruct him to cut the cards and complete the cut, making it impossible for you to know the position of any card; then to take a card from the middle, remember it, put it on the top and finally cut the pack several times, completing the cut each time. This done you turn, take the pack, and locate the card.

This is made possible by the fact that almost invariably the pack is cut very near the middle so that when the cut is completed the two packets of cards that were reversed at the top and bottom are brought together in the middle, and again at the top and bottom there will be small packets reversed. Therefore if a card is taken from the middle, placed on the top and the pack again cut, it will be amongst a number of cards pointing in the opposite direction.

It has to be admitted that the trick is not infallible but the odds are in favour of success. It is for the reader to decide if he cares to run the risk of a possible failure.

ONE IN TEN DETECTION   Annemann

The one-way pack is first set in proper order. To begin the trick, shuffle the cards thoroughly with an overhand shuffle and then cut at about the middle. Lay the packets side by side with one of them pointing in the opposite direction. To do this use the move described in the trick 'A Card is found Once More' in this chapter.

Ask a spectator to think of a small number and, when you turn your back, to transfer that number of cards from one heap to the other, and square both packets perfectly. This done, turn round, pick up the packets with your fingers at the outer ends and riffle shuffle them together. All the cards with the exception of those transferred will point in the same direction. Shuffle the cards overhand as you tell the spectator that you will deal the cards face up, and that each time he sees a card with the same number of spots as the number he thought of he is to say to himself 'That's my number.' Explain that as this will be repeated four times you are sure to get the right impression by the repetition.

Deal the cards and count the number of cards reversed, then pick out a card having that number of spots and place it face down on the table. When he names his number, let him turn the card himself.

UNI-MENTALITY   Albright

This version depends on the use of a one-way pack. With the pack arranged, the cards being all the same way, let the spectator shuffle it overhand and ask him to think of any card he pleases as he does so. Take the pack and telling him you have an impression of the colour but need a stronger impression of the card, spread the faces of the cards towards him and have him take out five cards, the thought-of card to be one of them. As he looks at these to impress the card on his mind, quietly reverse the pack, and have him place the five cards in different parts of the pack. Give the cards a genuine overhand shuffle. Again have him remove five cards with his card amongst them—the one with the pattern reversed will be his card. Fan these five widely before his eyes with the reversed card in the middle, turn the lower left corner and read the index. Replace the cards in the pack and finish by announcing the colour, suit and value of the card in the usual hesitating manner as if reading his mind.

CHALLENGE OF THE YEAR   Annemann

The Bicycle League Back cards No. 808 should be used for this subtle effect since the reversed card can be detected at a distance of from fifteen to twenty feet.

With the pack in its case you invite two spectators to assist. We will call them No. 1 and No. 2. Take the pack from its case and shuffle overhand. Hand it to No. 1 and walk away. Instruct him to also shuffle overhand, spread the cards in a fan and allow No. 2 to pick out a card and note what it is. He is then to turn his back, hold the pack behind him for No. 2 to push his card back amongst the others. Spectator No. 2 then takes the pack and he shuffles it overhand.

Again you have No. 1 take the pack, stand opposite you, hold the cards face down, lift them one by one and look at each card for a second, then lay it aside.

From a distance of from fifteen to twenty feet the reversed wing can be sighted and this makes the trick a very strong one as any possible suspicion of there being a mark on the cards is thereby erased and the trick is left a complete mystery.

You can finish by calling 'Stop,' or by having No. 2 also watch the faces of the cards and pretend to tell by his expression when the card arrives.

CARD LOCATION SUPREME

This location can only be used satisfactorily with one-way cards that have the distinguishing mark somewhere near the top left-hand corner so that it can be located when the cards are fanned from right to left, the natural way. The advantage is that the cards do not have to be set all the one way.

After having such a pack shuffled by the spectator to his satisfaction spread the cards and allow him to take any card he pleases and note what it is. When he returns his card, by pushing it in the spread, quickly note the way it and five cards above it lie, starting at the fifth card above it and mentally saying to yourself 'Up, down, down, down, up, down,' or whatever the combination may be. Push the card flush, close the spread and square the pack. Put it down and have it cut several times with complete cuts. You can then locate the cards by turning away and running over the cards till you come to the sequence or deal the cards on the table locating it as you do so. There may possibly be a similar sequence by coincidence, in which case you place one of the cards at the top the other at the bottom. Have the card named and show it accordingly.

You can repeat by having the spectator name any number between ten and fifty-two then deal that number of cards face down and note the top card of the pile when the number is reached. In this case mentally subtract five from the number chosen and when that card is dealt memorize its position and the five cards following it. The rest of the pack is dropped on top, the pack squared and cut. In this case as the sequence is reversed, you must either turn your back to find it, or deal the cards with them face up in your left hand, turning them face down as you put them on the table.

When the card is located it is a weak finish to simply hand the card out. Produce it in some magical fashion.

HUMMER DETECTION   Jordan

Any pack with a one-way pattern may be used and it is not necessary for it to be arranged with the backs in order. A borrowed pack will do provided it has the one-way back pattern.

Hand the pack to a spectator to shuffle, remove any card, note and replace it while your back is turned. Two other persons each take a card and retain them. This done turn and take the pack. Deal it into two piles, in one pile place all the cards pointing in one direction, those pointing the other way in the second pile. Remove any card, hold it with face towards yourself, from whichever pile the spectator points to. Ask him to name his card and without showing the card you hold, say 'Correct,' and put it face down on the table. 'Now for the next one.' Put the two piles together so that they all point in the same direction. Have the second person's card replaced, reversed square the cards and shuffle. Run through the faces of the cards, find the first spectator's card and put it on the top. Then turn the pack face down and find the second card by its reversed pattern, put it also on the top, sighting its face as you do so. 'Good.' Name it and ask if you are right, 'Good. Then I'll just place it face down on the........of........,' naming the first spectator's card and suiting the action to the word.

Treat the third person's card in exactly the same way as the second, locating it by the reversed back pattern, naming it and putting it on the other two. Pick up all three, as you say, but really there are four, and put them on the top of the pack. Turn them over one by one, naming them as you do so. The misdirection employed with regard to the first card must be carried through smoothly and without the slightest hesitation. Well done the trick is a very puzzling one.

INSTANT MIND-READING

The trick is nothing more than the location of a card replaced reversed in a one-way pack. To make it effective a great point must be made of having the cards thoroughly shuffled by a spectator before a card is selected and after it has been returned. To do this with the least possible risk of failure hand the pack to someone who habitually shuffles the cards with the overhand method. Have him select a card. Reverse the pack for its return, square up very openly and let him again shuffle to his heart's content. If all has gone well and the cards have not been disarranged, you have merely to hold the pack in your left hand and riffle the ends with your right thumb. When the reversed card appears note what it is and finish the riffle as being a mere flourish.

Take the spectator's hand, put it to your forehead and tell him to concentrate on the name of his card. Finally name the card, colour first, then suit and finally the value.

A COUNTER LOCATION

In a one-way pack with its back patterns all facing the one way, reverse the tenth, twentieth, thirtieth and fortieth cards.

Thus prepared, make several false shuffles and cuts, then spread the cards face down on the table. Invite a spectator to look the cards over making a mental selection of a card, then to merely turn up the index corner and ascertain what it is. This done instruct him to gather up the cards, square the pack and hand it to you. You locate the card at will.

The secret is simple. As the spectator looked at the index corner you had ample time to count the number of cards between his card and the reversed card above it. When the pack is handed to you, a couple of overhand shuffles in which you run off the right number of cards will bring his card to the top to be dealt with as you wish.

A PRINCIPLE IN DISGUISE   Harry Vosburgh

The following clever idea is taken from the *Jinx*, Summer Number for 1935, by the kind permission of Mr. Annemann.

Card Mysteries Using a One-Way Back Design

Arrange your one-way pack so that one half the cards have the patterns pointing one way and the other half pointing in the opposite direction. Have a card freely selected from one half and have it returned to the other. Now cut the pack at the point where the two sections join, and riffle shuffle the halves together bringing the cards all pointing the same way. Then regardless of which half received the card, it will now be the only one reversed in the pack.

Again you may reverse and remember the bottom card, all the other cards pointing in the same direction. Allow a spectator to choose a card freely. As he notes what it is, give the pack an overhand shuffle bringing the bottom card to the top, square the pack and have the selected card pushed in at any point. The direction of the top card of the pack thus jibes with that of the returned card so that if the spectator has any suspicion that the one-way principle is being used he will be thrown right off the track.

THE PERFECT GUESSER   Larsen

For this effect use a one-way pack and arrange all the black cards pointing one way, the reds the other way. Now put the black and red cards alternately. The cards can then be cut as often as may be desired, with complete cuts, of course. By sighting the bottom card, as you put the pack down, you learn the colour of the top card; if the bottom card is red, the top one must be black and vice versa.

Let anyone call for a colour and give him a paper knife to thrust into the pack. Slide the cards above the knife to one side far enough to note which way the card below it lies. Then you allow him to look at that card or the one above the knife as may be necessary.

RED OR BLACK   Annemann

A welcome departure from the eternal 'Please take a card,' type of trick, this depends for its effect mainly on subtle misdirection. A pack of one-way cards properly arranged is required.

Have the pack shuffled by a spectator and then instruct him to turn the cards face up and deal them into two packets—one of red cards, the other of black ones—side by side on to the table. Pick them up one in each hand, fingers at the outer ends and thumbs at the inner, and riffle shuffle. This will set the reds and the blacks with the back indicators pointing in opposite directions. A further overhand shuffle may be made and the pack cut several times with complete cuts. Ask a spectator to cut the pack about the middle and take one of the piles.

You do not know which way either of the colours lie but you say that you will turn up a card from your packet and that from it you will tell the colour of the corresponding card in his packet. Turn your top card and name Red or Black by guess. You have a 50–50 chance, and wrong or right, you now have the key to the remaining cards. You merely pretend to consult your cards, really noting which way the cards of the spectator's point and name them accordingly.

Do not continue the effect for more than ten or twelve cards at the outside.

TRANSCENDENTAL VISION

This feat depends on the use of a one-way pack pre-arranged as to the suits and values of the cards.

With all the cards set one way lay out the following heaps:
1. 8S, 10S, 8H, 9H, JC, QC, KC,   Call this D. value 8.
2. 4S, 6S, QS, KS, 4H, 5H, 7D,   Call this C. value 4.
3. 2S, 7S, JS, 2C, 10C, 3D, 6D,   Call this B. value 2.
4. AC, 7C, 3H, KH, 5D, 9D, JD,   Call this A. value 1.
5. Any seven cards.
6. Any seven cards.
7. Any seven cards.

Reverse the fourth heap, we will call this A: and turn the seven heaps face down. Pick up a card from each heap in rotation, beginning with heap No. 1. Add the three cards left over and the Joker.

Thus prepared, begin by discarding the Joker and the three top cards. Have the pack cut and dealt into seven piles, each pile will then be made up of the pre-arranged cards as above. Let the spectator shuffle each heap separately but have them replaced on the table in the same order. You find heap A since its cards are reversed, heap B will be the next one to the right, C and D following in order. If any one of the heaps happen to be the last in the row, continue the count from the first heap.

Invite the spectator to merely think of any card in an imaginary pack, then show him the heaps in this order: A, B, C, D, asking each time, 'Do you see a card of the same value as the one you are thinking of?' And then, 'Do you see a card of the same suit here?' Ignore the heaps not containing the value of his card but add together the numerical

Card Mysteries Using a One-Way Back Design

equivalents of those that do: eleven signifies a J; twelve a Q; thirteen a K.

If his suit is not in A, it must be Spades; if not in B, Hearts; if not in C, Clubs; if not in D, or if in A, B and C, it is Diamonds. For instance, value is present in A, C, D, but suit is not in B, the card thought of is the KH. The three discards are merely to be used as blinds.

FIND THE LADY   Grant

Remove two K's and a Q, reversing the Q. Hand the three cards to a person to shuffle together so that neither he nor anyone else can know which is the Q, then have them put face down in a row. Borrow three envelopes and hand one of these to a party telling him to take the first card and slide it in so that nobody knows what card it is. You know the Q by the reversed pattern on the back and when you hand out an envelope for the insertion of this card, secretly mark it with your thumbnail. The closed envelopes are then mixed up while your back is turned. Turn and put the envelopes to your forehead one by one. When you get the marked one announce dramatically, 'There is a feminine vibration here.' Toss the envelope to someone to open and remove the Q.

CALL ME UP SOMETIME   Grant

Ask someone to name the four digits comprising their telephone number. Turn the faces of the cards towards yourself and pick out four cards with spot values to correspond with the digits called, but as you do this, secretly bring the four Q's to the top of the pack and reverse them. Toss the four number cards to the table and hand the pack to be shuffled.

Take the pack back, fan it out and apparently place the number cards in the fan haphazardly, really placing them next below each of the reversed Q's. Let the cards protrude a little so that all may see that they go into different parts of the pack. Close the fan and cut. Remark, 'Let's see what kind of a phone number our friend has.' Turn the cards face up and fan them out. Find the number cards one by one and show that each one has located a Q. You say, 'That sure is a good number.'

(Editor's Note): Have the number cards replaced face up in a face-down fan, one above each reversed Q. Let spectator cut the pack, then re-fan the cards backs to the audience so that the number cards stand out. Now have

181

spectator pick out the face-up number cards and at the same time with-draw the face-down card below each, and lay them on the table without looking at the bottom card. Finish as above by dramatically turning up the Q's.

A MIRACLE   Annemann

Hand the pack to a person telling him first of all to shuffle 'like this', indicating an overhand shuffle. Then fan out the pack and allow any other person to freely choose a card. . . . That's right! . . . Now put the pack behind your back and let him replace his card where he likes and push it in flush. This action will have automatically reversed the card.

Now instruct the person who drew the card to take the pack and re-move one card at a time, looking at each one. You watch the backs of the cards as he does this. You can place your hand over your eyes, pretend-ing intense concentration, but you can see through your fingers. When he holds the reversed card to his eyes call 'Stop'. Continue . . . 'I have an impression that you are now looking at the very card you have in mind.' Very effective, from first to last you do not touch the cards.

THOUGHT TRANSFERENCE   Grant

An exceptional mystery for two people. Your assistant leaves the room. Any spectator deals sixteen cards face up in four rows of four cards each. He points out any one card and the entire audience is asked to concentrate on that card. You turn the cards face down. Assistant returns and immediately calls the name of the card.

This is done by means of a code as follows: Starting at the upper left-hand corner of the group the cards are numbered, mentally, 1, 2, 3, 4, from left to right of the first row; 5, 6, 7, 8, in the second row; 9, 10, J, Q, in the third row. The last row signals the suit thus, C, H, S, D. For example, suppose the card was the 5C. You would turn all the cards side-ways in putting them face down except the first card in the second row and the first card in the fourth row, turn these endways. If a K is chosen, reverse a card for the suit only. All the assistant has to do, therefore, is to note the positions of the reversed cards and then announce the name of the chosen card as dramatically as possible.

SAY WHEN

Grant

With the one-way pack in your hand go into the audience and borrow a hat. On the way back secretly drop three cards into it face down. Place the hat crown downwards on the table. Hand the pack to be shuffled and then have fifteen cards counted on your hand. From these have three cards selected and noted, reverse the packet and have them replaced. Have the packet again shuffled.

Step back to the hat, count the cards off into the hat one by one so that they go right on top of the three cards already there. Each time you come to a reversed card drop it to one side of the pile in the hat. Reach in and remove the packet, leaving the three reversed cards, the chosen cards, behind. Recount the cards showing there are fifteen.

Ask anyone to call out any number from one to fifteen. Count to that number slowly and openly and drop that card into the hat beside the three already there. Gather the packet together and again have a number called, count to it and drop that card in, proceed in like manner with a third number. Lay stress on the point that three cards have been selected by numbers freely called by spectators and reach into the hat and bring out the three reversed cards, throwing the remainder of the packets on top of the three in the hat. Have the cards named and show the faces. For club work use an easel to display the cards, putting them face down first then turning them as they are named.

THE DRUNK PLAYS BRIDGE

Albright

Most Bridge packs are natural one-way patterns, which makes possible an excellent impromptu Bridge trick at the conclusion of regular play.

As you gather up the cards to replace them in the host's card case, set all the pack one way except the thirteen cards of the S suit, which you reverse. Now, at the psychological moment say that you will demonstrate how 'some of the boys played Bridge the other night. They were slightly tipsy, but one more so than the others . . . in fact he was practically drunk and everybody thought he didn't know what was going on. So it came to his turn to deal and he shuffled the cards like this.' At this point remove the pack from its case and shuffle, acting the part of the drunk. 'Then he started to deal out four hands, but he got all mixed up and dealt to the wrong hands and everything, something like this.' Still acting drunk, you deal the cards to South, East, North and West, sort of at random instead of in correct rotation. Secretly though you manage to give each man his proper thirteen cards and deal to yourself all the cards with reversed backs. The patter and acting drunk covers this operation perfectly and gets a laugh all the time. 'In the end everybody looked at their hands and would you believe it, the drunk had a grand slam.' Turn over all the hands and show yours to be all S's for the climax.

INCOMPREHENDO   Jordan

The effect depends on the pre-arrangement of a one-way pack. First take out the following cards and make one packet of them in any order, 2, 3, 7, 8, Q of H and S; and the A, 6, 10 of D. Make a second packet of the 4, 5, 9, J, K of H and S and the 2, 3, 7, 8, Q of C. Divide the remainder of the pack into two equal parts and place the first packet at the bottom of the other. Bend the two portions of the pack in opposite directions and place them together. All the cards must have their pointers in one way.

Thus prepared, first cut at the bridge, reverse one packet and then riffle the two together. Shuffle as evenly as possible and the stacked cards will all lie at the bottom, the unprepared cards at the top. Cut about twelve cards from the top to the bottom. Spread the faces to show the cards are well mixed.

Fan the pack for the selection of a card but count twelve cards first and hold a break there, then allow a free selection from the cards in the middle. Note which way the indicator points so that you know whether the card belongs to group No. 1 or group No. 2. If it is from No. 1 the card will spell with thirteen letters and you have only to cut at the break, have the card returned and drop the twelve cards on it. Hand the pack to the spectator and tell him to spell the name of his card, dealing one card for each letter, and turn up the card on the last letter.

If, however, the card is taken from group No. 2 you must drop one card from those separated by the break, so that eleven cards only will be dropped on the selected card. The cards in group No. 1 all spell with thirteen letters, those in group No. 2 with twelve letters. Spell 2, 3, J thus: deuce, three, Jack, not two, trey, knave.

THE ONE-WAY KEY   Sellers

After arranging a pack with their one-way backs all pointing in the same direction, reverse one card.

Shuffle the cards freely, overhand fashion, and allow a spectator to select a card freely. As he notes what it is, spread the cards and locate the one reversed card. Split the pack for the return of the card so that it goes just underneath the key card. A short overhand shuffle will not separate the two cards, so that by locating the key you have the selected card under control.

ONE-WAY PACKS

The following makes of cards are all of the Bicycle Brand, manufactured by the U. S. Playing Card Co. and all have one-way backs.

Rider Backs. There is a small curl in the upper left-hand corner near the top. At one end this curl ends in a white dot, at the other end it has none. This fact is fairly well known to magicians.

Emblem Backs. A reversal of one of these cards is easily detected by the position of the handlebars or the pedals.

Wheel Backs. In the centre of the back there is a circular design in which are three wings. The difference will be noticed at once on reversing a card.

League Backs. This is the best for the purpose. The reversal of a card alters the position of one of the wings in the centre design and the difference can be detected at a distance of fifteen to twenty feet.

Bank Note Back made by the Russell Playing Card Co. The clue lies in the small white dot in the border of small circles surrounding the bank note back.

With a fine pen and blue or red ink it is a very easy matter to make a slight alteration in any design of back that will be perfectly plain to you but unnoticeable to anyone else.

In closing this treatment of the one-way principle I quote from Theodore Annemann who has devoted more time to, and has probably devised more subtle principles with cards, than anyone else. He says, 'I have yet to find a card man using this principle (one-way cards) who doesn't make apparent his scrutiny of the backs in waiting for a card to turn up.'

It follows from this you cannot disguise the fact that you are using one-way cards from anyone who knows the principle even if he doesn't know the particular marking upon which you are relying, and you furthermore run the risk of putting even a layman wise to the method. The best plan would seem to be to 'doctor' your own cards, as suggested above, making the tell-tale mark near the top left-hand and bottom right-hand corners and so plain to you that you can detect it easily with a very slight spreading of the cards. Such a mark will never be noticed by a layman and will enable you to handle the cards without a too-noticeable and fatally suggestive scrutiny of the backs.

10

Mysteries Using Reversed 'Ordinary' Cards

SIMPLIFIED REVERSE   Gibson

With any pack a card having been freely chosen, returned, brought to the top (see Chap. 19), make a riffle shuffle leaving it there. Put the pack on the table, lift off the upper half and spread the cards, keeping the top card behind the others, and ask the spectator if he sees his card. He does not. Square up these cards and take them in the left hand, face down. With the right hand pick up the remainder of the cards and turn them face up just above the cards in the left hand, at the same time push the top card of the left-hand packet (the chosen card) a little to the right with the left thumb.

Spread the right-hand packet on the left-hand cards. The spectator does not see his card there either. Close up these cards carrying away the top card of the left-hand packet. Turn the left-hand packet face up and drop the right-hand packet on top. The chosen card is now face up in the middle of the pack.

UPSIDE DOWN   Wimborough

As with all reversed card effects, cards with white margins on the backs should be used for this trick, otherwise any pack may be utilized and the cards well shuffled before starting. Have a spectator cut off some ten or twelve cards and shuffle them. Tell him that when your back is turned he is to lay out four cards face down in a row, look at one, note what it is, replace it face down and mix the four cards so that he himself will not know which one is his.

187

Mysteries Using Reversed 'Ordinary' Cards

Turn away with the remainder of the pack in your hands; turn these cards face up, reverse the three top face-up cards, put one at the bottom, the next in amongst the others about eight or ten cards down and turn the packet over. The cards will appear to be face up, really the top and bottom cards and one card amongst them are face up, the rest face downwards. The spectator having followed instructions, turn to him. Pick up one of the four cards and insert it face down near the bottom of your packet—to all appearances the card goes in reversed, really it coincides with all your cards but the three. Do the same with two more but put them in together and call attention to it, about the middle, and the last one put about one-third down. These four cards now all face the same way as all the rest of your cards except the three. Turn the pack over, bringing the card that was reversed there to the top, since its back shows the packet seems to be quite regular. With the left thumb riffle the top left corners of the cards until you reach the card you inserted in the packet reversed about eight or ten cards down, cut at that point, leaving it on the top, this brings two of the three reversed cards together and the third is on the top. Call attention to the rest of the cards from which he chose four and tell him to pick them up. As he does so quietly drop your left hand, turn it bringing the knuckles upwards thus turning the pack over. With the right hand draw the pack away and put it on the table.

Have the spectator place the remaining cards on the top and cut the cards. The trick is done. You have already announced that you will cause the chosen card to turn over, but will leave the other three reversed. Have the card named and let the spectator hold the pack. You utter the magic formula, or whatever hocus-pocus you affect, and the result follows. He finds three cards reversed, two of them together, and the chosen card faces with the rest of the pack. If the various steps in the trick are followed with the cards in hand you will have no difficulty, but care must be taken when inserting the cards and cutting, not to expose the fact that the cards are reversed.

U BITE
Grant

Using any pack, secretly reverse the bottom card. Spread the cards and have any one freely selected. After it is noted by the drawer let him return it to the top of the pack. Under cut about half the pack thus bringing the reversed card immediately above the chosen card.

Announce that you will cause the chosen card to reverse itself amongst the others. Riffle the pack and fan it out with the faces to the spectator, a card will be seen turned with its back to them. Cut, bringing it to the top, as all attention is on the spectator as he turns the card over, pull the top card to the bottom with the left fingers turning it over as it goes, a very simple operation. Cut the pack as you put it down on the table. The selected card is now reversed in the middle. The spectator says you have made a mistake, the card is not his. If you act as though you really have made a mistake so much the better; finally try again, this time with the pack in his own hands. He finds his card reversed. Use white margin cards.

It will be noted that this principle can be used simply as an easy method of locating the card, since when it is brought to the top it is ready to be palmed off or disposed of as may be necessary.

THE HALEY REVERSED CARD

The invention of the late Louis Haley, this trick first appeared in print in *The Genii*, Oct. 1936.

First secretly give the inner end of the whole pack a sharp bend by squeezing the inner corners downward between the left second finger and thumb over the first finger which is doubled below the pack. Reverse the lower half facing upwards, with a bridge between the two portions at the rear. Fan the upper face-down cards, being careful not to expose any of the reversed cards, and have a card selected and noted. Take it back in the right hand, face down, and push it into the lower half of the pack. Square the pack with both hands, seize the upper half with the right hand, the thumb finding the break instantly by touch alone, and retain the lower half in the left hand. Separate the hands quickly, and instantly turn the lower half over bringing its cards also face down.

Proceed at once to a riffle shuffle, keeping the cards well covered by the hands as the corners are riffled in so that the reversed card cannot be seen. Give the magical command, have the card named, fan the pack and show it is reversed. This is perhaps the best method yet devised for reversing a single card.

SURE LOCATOR   Grant

Take any spot card, preferably a five-spot, reverse it in the pack fifth from the bottom.

Having done this secretly, have a card chosen, being careful not to spread the cards near the bottom. After the spectator has noted his card, have it put on the top of the pack, under cut about half the cards and drop them on top, burying the card in the middle. Say that you will cause a card to reverse itself in the middle to indicate where the chosen card is. Fan the pack showing the reversed five in the middle. Cut at that card, and throw it face up on the table. Deal off four cards and throw the next one, the chosen card, face down. Have the card named and turn it over.

IN THE DARK

With any pack, a card is freely chosen, noted and pushed into the shuffled pack fairly. A handkerchief is thrown over it, yet you name the card instantly.

After the pack has been thoroughly shuffled, take it and allow free selection of a card. Ask the spectator to show it to a second person. Under cover of this quietly reverse the bottom card and turn the pack over. When the card is now pushed into the pack it really is reversed. Borrow a handkerchief and, as you throw it over the pack, turn the cards over; the pack will now be face down but the chosen card will be face up. Spread the cards as you place them on the table so that the faced card will be exposed and you can read the index through the handkerchief.

UNDER COVER

Effect. Any pack may be used. Performer turns his back. A spectator freely selects a card, replaces it reversed in the middle of the pack, squares the cards and lays a handkerchief over them. Performer lifts the pack and handkerchief and a card is seen to rise from the pack raising the fabric. This is lifted off with the covering and is found to be the chosen card.

Secret. This effective trick depends on the fact that a pack will cut automatically at a reversed card. This can be tested by reversing a card in the middle and holding the pack at the tips of the fingers and thumb of the left hand in position for the Charlier pass. Ease up the pressure of the thumb, and it will be found that the cards below the reversed card will fall. Complete the pass in the usual way and the reversed card will be on the bottom of the pack.

In doing the trick lift the pack in position for the Charlier pass, and make it, as you drape the handkerchief over the cards. You have then simply to hold the pack upright and push up the rear card with the first and second fingers taking the handkerchief with it. Take the card with the fabric from above with the right hand, turn the hand over, letting the handkerchief folds fall down over the wrist and display the card with its face to the spectators.

BEHIND THE BACK

Secretly reverse the bottom card of the pack after you have had the pack shuffled. Allow a card to be freely selected and noted. Under cut about half the pack for the return of the card and drop the cut on top of it. The reversed card will be on top of the chosen card. Square the pack very openly, tapping sides and ends on the table.

Put your left hand with the pack behind your back and make the Charlier pass bringing the chosen card to the top. (See preceding trick.) Bring it forward with the right hand and reverse the bottom card by pushing it off with the left fingers on to the top of the pack, turning it over in the process. This takes but a moment and you bring the pack forward to be examined if anyone wishes to do so.

COINCIDENCE

Two packs are required. Beforehand decide on any two cards you will use. Steam the stamp off a new pack, take out the cards and reverse one of the two cards decided upon at about tenth place from the top, the other about tenth from the bottom. Replace the cards in the case and gum the stamp in position. Have this pack in your pocket. Take the two duplicates from a second pack and put them third and forth from the bottom. You are ready.

Riffle shuffle the pack without disturbing the four bottom cards and have a spectator cut the pack. Count the cards cut while the spectator counts the bottom part—give any plausible reason you please for the counting, it is really only to bring the four bottom cards of the lower part to the top. Show what you want him to do by taking the two top cards of his part, reversing them and pushing them partly into the heaps one in each. Take them out and insert them face down in your heap. Turn your back while the spectator takes the next two cards off his heap (these are the two you fixed beforehand), and inserts them face up, one in each heap. This done, turn around and take the sealed pack from your pocket. Have it opened and the cards removed. Let the spectator cut it about the middle. Pattering about the sympathetic nature of the cards, have him place his hands on top of the packets for a moment, then name the two cards. The cards are spread and the same cards are found reversed. Cards with white margins on the back must be used.

THE REVERSE 'COUNT-DOWN' TRICK

This is one of the easiest as well as one of the most effective presentations of this often seen effect. The magician has a card selected from a group of cards cut from the top of the pack. An elastic band is snapped around the performer's half of the pack and the selected card is returned to the top of the pack by slipping it under the elastic. Next the remainder of the cut is returned on top of the selected card and under the elastic. A spectator calls out any number, the cards are withdrawn one by one from the top of the pack, and on the number called being reached the selected card turns up. This is particularly mystifying because the magician has made no apparent effort to manipulate the pack, in fact the elastic seems to preclude any tampering.

Secret. Before offering the pack to be cut the magician has reversed the bottom four or five cards. The spectator cuts from the top of the pack and holds the cut-off portion in such a way that no one else knows the number of cards he has cut. While he is selecting a card you very deliberately snap an elastic around the pack. Now secretly turn over the pack to bring the reversed cards to the top, and offer the pack for the insertion of the selected card. Assist the spectator by lifting up the elastic. Now, while he shuffles the remainder of his cut-off portion, secretly turn the pack over again so that when he returns these cards they go on top of the original top of the pack, and not on top of his selected card as he supposes. Call for any number and withdraw cards from the original top of the pack to within one of the number decided upon. Fan these to show that the selected card is not among them, and under cover of the fan reverse the pack. The selected card is now on top, and you can let anyone draw it off. While they are looking at the card, withdraw the elastic and reset the pack before offering it for examination.

FRENCH'S EXTRAORDINARY ACES

Here's a different method of doing the 'Four Ace Trick' using the reversed principle and eliminating all palming and intricate sleights.

As in the usual methods, the four A's are removed from the pack and passed for examination as the pack is returned. In turning to the table to get rubber band, the magician makes the Half Pass, i.e. makes one half of the pack face the other half. The rubber band is snapped around the pack and the A's are slid under it on to the top of the pack. Now secretly reverse the pack so that the A's are on bottom. Taking off the three top cards and calling them (Aces), they are laid on the table by the performer. As the third card is laid down, the magician reverses the pack and picks off the top A, glances at it and says; 'and lastly we have the Ace of .... which we will place beside the others.' Under cover of this misdirection the pack is reversed again, and three cards are counted off the top on to each of the first three (Aces). As last card is laid on the third (Ace), reverse the pack again and draw off the three real Aces and stack them on top of the fourth A. Force this pile and finish to suit yourself.

You will find that the spectator's eyes will follow your hand to the table when you lay the cards down, thus securing perfect misdirection for the reversing of the pack.

11

Calculation Tricks With Ordinary Cards

WEIRDO

Effect. Any full pack is freely shuffled. Performer writes the name of a card on a slip of paper, fold it and hands it to a spectator who then calls a number. He counts down to that number and finds the card whose name is on the slip. This is repeated with a second person.

Method. First check the pack to see there are fifty-two cards, if there is a Joker, discard it. Hand pack out to be shuffled and in taking it back note the bottom card. Suppose it is the 8S. Write that on a slip of paper and hand it to a spectator to put in his pocket. Invite him to call any number between thirty and forty. Suppose he says thirty-three. Mentally subtract thirty-three from fifty-two, i.e. nineteen. Acting as though you had not heard you illustrate what he is to do. You say, 'Suppose you choose nineteen, you would deal off cards like this. . . .' Count off nineteen into your right hand and keep your hands separated as you ask the spectator if he understands what he is to do. Then put the two packets together, but place the right packet under the left. Done casually and smoothly this will never be noticed. Hand the pack to the spectator, holding it with the right thumb underneath, fingers on top. Tilt the pack a little and note the bottom card, suppose it is the 3D. Write this on a second slip, fold it, and give it to another person. Now ask first spectator what number he chose. He names it, deals off to it and turns the 8S. Ask him to take out his slip and read it. . . . He finds the correct prediction.

Take the remainder of the pack and drop it on the cards dealt. You have the 3D the nineteenth card from the top. Ask second person to choose a number between eighteen and twenty-five. Put pack on table with the last few cards spread a little so that you can pick up the pack leaving a card or two on the table as if by accident. Suppose he calls twenty-one. You have to add two cards to the top. In taking the pack leave two cards accidentally on the table, put these on top, hand pack to spectator and have your prediction verified by him.

A PREDICTION

A spectator shuffles any pack. Take it and run over the faces of the cards, saying that you will take out two cards to be witness of your ability to foretell events. What you really do is to note the nineteenth card from the top, suppose it is the QH. From farther down in the pack you take any H and any Q, putting them face downwards on the table. Turn the pack face up and let a spectator remove any three-spot cards from the lower portion (the top nineteen cards must not be disturbed). Tell him to lay them in a row face up, the highest card to the left; say they are 9, 6, 2. Hand him duplicates of these values to put in reverse order below, thus: 2, 6, 9. Ask him to subtract and call the figures, handing him cards of the corresponding values (6, 9, 3) as he calls them. Tell him to add these three figures (which total eighteen), then to take the pack and deal off that number of cards (eighteen), and turn up the next card. He does this and finds the QH. You turn your prediction cards, a QH.

In selecting the cards for the subtraction sum, be careful to take the cards from below the nineteenth.

LONG DISTANCE MIND-READING Jordan

Mail to a friend a letter couched in the following terms: 'I am sending you by the next post an ordinary pack of cards. Read these instructions carefully and follow them implicitly. Remove the cards from the case without disturbing their order. Fan them and examine them on both sides. Note that they are neither faked nor arranged in any way. With the cards face down cut as often as you please completing the cut each time. Then make a single ordinary dovetail shuffle. Cut again as much as you like, and finally cut the pack into two heaps as nearly equal as you can. Remove one card from about the middle of either heap, note it, and insert it anywhere in the other heap. Now select either heap, the one you drew the card from or the one now containing it, and shuffle that heap thoroughly. Mail it to me without saying which heap it is and by return mail I'll name the selected card.'

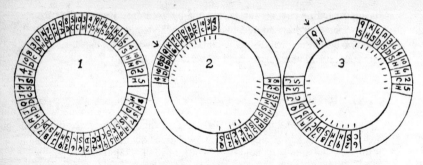

To do this you must shuffle the pack before sending it, but make a note of their order by jotting the names around a circle (Fig. 1). You probably know that complete cuts do not disarrange the sequence of the cards and that is true of a single dovetail shuffle; it merely distributes half the cards through the other half, but each half is still in the same order. The second cutting has no effect on the arrangement. When the pack is finally cut into two packets, the choice of a card from the middle ensures that it will not be an end card of one of the two strings that the original order has been divided into. The insertion of this card into the other packet, and the shuffling of that packet, seems to make its discovery impossible. But all you have to do on receipt of the cards is to mark them off, one by one, on the circle around which you had recorded the original order of the pack. When you have done this you will have either two separate runs of cards, with one card unchecked in one of them (Fig. 2) or, two separate complete runs with one, by itself, checked off somewhere else along the circle (Fig. 3). In the first case he has sent you the heap he drew his card from *and the unchecked one is it*. In the second case, he has sent you the half-pack in which he inserted his card, and the isolated card you have checked off indicates his selection.

TWO CARD LOCATION   Larsen

After a spectator has shuffled a pack of cards, have one freely selected, replace and bring it to the top.

Take about eight cards from the top of the pack, spread them before a second spectator, face down, and ask him to indicate any one card and turn the index just enough to enable him to see what that card is. As he does this count the number of cards from the top card (the first card chosen) to this second selected one; suppose it is five. Close the fan of cards, drop them on the pack and have the spectator cut the pack. Take it and rapidly deal the cards into four heaps, one card at a time. The two chosen cards must thus come together and you may allow the spectator to pick up the piles in any order he pleases. The cards are named, you order them to get together, the spectator goes through the pack and so finds them.

IMPROVED SUPER MEMORY   Gibson

From any pack which has been freely shuffled allow twenty cards to be chosen and retained by different spectators. Collect them face down on top of the pack giving each person numbers from twenty down to one. When Card No. 10 is replaced on the others, secretly bend back the outer left corner with the thumb. When the last card, No. 1 has been taken back lift the top ten cards, the bent corner of the tenth card making this easy, and reverse the cards below. The pack is thus face up with the ten cards numbered from 1 to 10 face down on top of it; the other ten cards, numbers 11 to 20, on the bottom. Put the pack in your trousers pocket and have a blindfold placed over your eyes.

Announce that you will call various numbers, the drawers to name their cards as their numbers are called and you will at once find the cards. You call numbers in the following order:

11, 2, 14; 1, 13, 5; 12, 4, 17; 3, 16, 8; 15, 7; 18, 9; 19, 10; 20, 6;
and you bring out the cards thus:

Bottom card: second from top; third from bottom.
Top card: second from bottom; third from top.
Bottom card: second from top; third from bottom.
Top card: second from bottom; third from top.
Bottom card: second from top.
Bottom card: second from top.
Bottom card: second from top.
Bottom card. Top card.

The patter goes that by intuition you get the thought waves of the persons who are thinking of their numbers and cards.

It's a case of 123; 123; 123; 123; 12; 12; 1; 1.

SPECTATOR'S CHOICE

From any freely shuffled pack deal six heaps of five cards each. A spectator chooses any two cards from the remainder of the pack, writes their names on a slip of paper, folds it and puts it on the table; he then puts his selected cards on top of any two heaps. Gather the heaps so that two of the five-card heaps go on each of the six-card heaps. Remark that you will also select two cards. Run through the packet, note the sixth and twenty-second cards from the top and write their names on a slip, fold it and put it alongside the spectator's slip. Now deal the cards into two heaps beginning at the left and dealing one card at a time. The heap on your left contains the spectator's cards, that on your right has your cards.

Ask the spectator which pair, yours or his, he wishes to have finally left on the table, and which packet is to be 'taken'. If he chooses his cards and the left-hand packet, discard the right-hand packet and say you will discard the right-hand pile throughout. If he chooses his cards and the right-hand packet say you will 'take' that away throughout. Use the same equivocal interpretation if he chooses your pair, to retain the right-hand packet. Supposing he calls for his cards. Pick up the left-hand pile and deal in two heaps as before. Discard the right-hand pile and deal again. Continue until two cards only remain on your left. These two will be the cards whose names he wrote.

If he chooses your cards, deal in exactly the same way but discard the left-hand heap throughout.

MENTALO

A spectator thinks of a number between one and ten. He shuffles the pack, which may be his own, counts down to the number thought of and notes the card, leaving it in the same position. This is done while your back is turned. When he is ready you turn around, take the pack, place it behind your back, rapidly count off nineteen cards, reversing their order, and replacing them on the top. Do this as you say you will put the card at number 20.

Bring the pack forward and ask the spectator the number he thought of, say it was six. Begin your count with that number, dealing the cards one at a time. When you reach twenty let him name his card and you turn it over.

KNOCK OUT COUNTING TRICK

A spectator shuffles his own pack and counts off any number of cards under fifteen. Suppose he chooses six. He looks at the sixth card, remembers it and then replaces the cards in the same order. You turn away while this is being done. Take the pack, put it behind your back and count off fifteen cards from the top and put them on the bottom, but do not reverse their order in counting them. Pretend to be trying to find the card without success; hand the pack to the spectator and tell him to transfer from the top to the bottom the same number of cards that he counted at first, but before doing that, to see that his card is not now anywhere near there.

This done, take the pack and again put it behind your back and transfer fifteen cards from the bottom to the top. The bottom card will now be the card the spectator noted, and you can reveal it as you please. At first the result seems surprising, but a little thought will show that the two transfers of cards you make cancel out, so that when the spectator transfers the cards to the bottom he actually does the trick for you.

A CARD AND A NUMBER

Allow a spectator to shuffle any pack, select any card while the pack is in his own hands, note what it is and finally put it face down on the table. You have your back turned while this is done and keep it turned while he deals two even piles of cards of not more than, say ten cards each. Then he is to put one pile in his pocket, place the other on his card, pick all these cards up and drop them on top of the pack. This done you turn around.

Pick up the pack and put it behind your back and as you expatiate on the impossibility of knowing the position of his card since you ask no questions, count off fifteen cards from the top reversing their order and replace them on the top of the pack. Bring the pack forward and, as you say, to make the problem still harder for you, tell him to take the packet from his pocket and place it on top of the pack. His card will now be the fifteenth card from the top and you can reveal it as you please. You can reverse any number of cards on the top but such number must always be higher than the number contained in each of the heaps he deals.

PROJECTED THOUGHT

Some preparation is necessary. Write on fifty-two small cards 'You will think of the . . . . of . . . . and it will be the thirty-fifth card in the pack.' Fill in the name of a different card on each. Insert these in small envelopes and place the envelopes of each suit, in order from A to K, in four different pockets so that you can readily find the envelope which has the name of any particular card. Thus prepared and with any full pack of cards minus the Joker, you are ready.

Place a small sealed envelope in full view (this an extra one with a blank card in it). Hand the pack to a spectator asking him to shuffle it and merely think of any one card. Then tell him to deal, from the face-down pack, four face-up piles one card at a time. He is to place the pile containing his thought card face up on any two other piles and the remaining heap on those three. Again turning the pack face down he repeats the deal and picks up the piles in the same order as before. He deals a third time. You memorize the ninth card in each pile and watch which pile he puts on two others—the ninth card in that pile is the one for which you must find the corresponding envelope in one of your pockets. To gain time to do this tell the spectator to square the cards carefully, put them face down on the table and put both hands on top. Meantime you have secured the envelope and finger palmed it in the right hand. Pick up the original envelope off the table, fingers covering it with thumb underneath, and apparently transfer it to your left hand; really drawing it back with the right thumb and pulling out the other with the left thumb and fingers. Give this to a spectator on your left. Ask the first person to name the card he thought of, have the envelope opened and the slip read, then have spectator deal thirty-five cards and this gives you your climax.

NE PLUS ULTRA   Donald Holmes

A key card is required, this may be a long card, a double card, any kind of key card that enables you to cut to it by feel. Have this face down on your table. Let a spectator take the pack, shuffle it freely, and take it to the others letting five cards be freely chosen. Take the pack, turn your back and ask the drawers to hold up their cards for all to see. Casually place the pack on the top of the long card. Ask your volunteer assistant to collect the cards face down on his left hand (note the order of the cards) bring them to the table, place them on top of the pack and then cut the pack several times. Finally you cut at the long card thus bringing the selected cards back to the top.

Next by way of giving them a thorough shuffle you lay the cards out a few at a time (really four cards exactly each time), the first four to A, the next four at B, then C and D. Continue dealing by fours in the same way until you have four cards left, deal one on A, the next on B, then on C, and the last card on D. Pick up the

C	B
D	A

packets by placing B on top of A, then C on B, and finally D on C. Take up the pack and deal into four piles, one card at a time as in bridge, and pick up the heaps in the same order as before. The spectators will naturally think the cards are lost in the pack, actually the top card is the second card selected, the third card stands at fourteen, the fourth at twenty-seven, the fifth at forty and the first card at five. These numbers are easy to remember, three of the cards being at intervals of thirteen from the top card. You can then get the number forty for the last card, deal face up and show that is right, mentally noting the fifth, fourteenth and twenty-seventh as you pass them, and then name them by mind-reading. The remaining one, the top card reveal in as striking a manner as possible.

UNI-MENTALITY   Albright

Effect. A spectator merely thinks of a card and the performer finds it and names it. Any pack may be used.

First Method. Spectator shuffles any pack and hands it to you. Tell him to think of any card and concentrate on that card. After a moment or two say that you have an impression of the colour but not the suit, so in order to strengthen the spectator's mental picture of the card ask him to take a good look at it as you run the cards over with the faces towards him. Ask him to say 'Stop' after the card has been passed so as to save time. When he calls 'Stop', bend the inner ends of the cards in your left hand sharply by squeezing them between the thumb base and fingers. Drop the right-hand cards on top and say that you now know the suit. This is a bluff but you have gained knowledge of the approximate position of the card under cover of a pretext.

Cut several times and finally cut at the bend in the inner end of the pack, thus you know that the card thought of is somewhere near the bottom. Again spread the cards before him, fanning them very slowly and tell him to take out five cards, one of which is to be his card. Take your time so that he will have taken out four cards by the time you reach the middle of the pack. Naturally the card he takes from near the bottom must be the thought card. Note where he puts this card amongst the other four, and when you pick up the five cards get it in the middle with two cards above it and two cards below it. Spread the five in a wide fan and hold them up before the spectator asking him to make his mental picture of the card as perfect as possible. With the cards upright it is an easy matter to turn the lower index corner of the middle card with the left thumb and read it. Put the packet down and in your most impressive style read the card in the usual way, hesitatingly—colour—suit—and finally its value.

When showing the faces of the cards to the spectator, insist it is done merely to strengthen his mental picture.

Second Method. The procedure is the same but instead of bending the lower packet when the spectator calls 'Stop', you push the top card of the pack, whose upper right-hand corner you previously bent upwards a little, on the top of the packet in the left hand and close the pack. As before have five cards removed and simply watch the card that is removed just before you reach your key card, the one with the bent corner.

The pulling off of the top, bent-corner card, to the top of the left-hand packet is completely covered by the cards being held upright at the time.

(Note): A better plan than bending the corner of the top card is to put a light pencil dot on the back of the top card near the top left-hand corner and another in the same place near the lower right-hand corner. This can be done at any favourable opportunity before starting the trick. This card is then the one to be pulled over when 'Stop' is called. When the cards are fanned the dot is easily found and the card taken out just before it, is the one to watch.

In all three versions make a great point of the fact that you do not look at the faces of any cards.

For method with one-way cards see Chap. 9.

EASY CARD DIVINATION

A spectator spreads a pack of cards, which he has shuffled, face down on a table. He removes a card from the upper part, notes what it is, and inserts it in the lower half of the pack. When the card is inserted make a mental estimate of about how many cards from the end of the row, i.e. the bottom of the pack, the card lies. Suppose you think it is about four-teenth. Gather the cards and place them behind your back. Count off to within four cards of the estimated position, in the supposed case this would be ten cards and put them on top. Take off four cards from the top and one from the bottom and ask if the card is among the five. If not discard them and repeat the operation. When the card appears you know it is the one drawn from the bottom.

HOUR-GLASS CARDS   Jordan

Anyone shuffles his own pack and removes six cards. From these six he selects one and deals the remainder of the pack into two face-down heaps, a card to each in rotation. He puts his chosen card on top of either half and the remaining five cards on the same heap, or the other, as best suits himself. Instruct spectator to place the half not containing his chosen card on the other half. The pack is laid aside and the time by the performer's watch is noted. Say it reads 3.26. Adding three to twenty-six gives twenty-nine, and the chosen card is found at that number in the pack.

The explanation is simple. The mechanical part ensures the placing of the cards at the twenty-ninth position from the top, and the trick is performed at certain times only, i.e. at 1.28, 2.27, 3.26, 4.25, 6.23, 7.22, 8.21, 9.20, 10.19, 11.18 or 12.17.

EASY CARD DISCOVERY   Lane

Effect. Spectator shuffles his own pack and cuts it about the middle. Spread these two packets face up on the table, one below the other. While your back is turned the spectator takes a card from either row, inserts it in the other row, shuffles that portion, and puts the portion from which he took a card in his pocket. You take the shuffled portion and locate the card.

Method. While you are spreading out the lower portion of the pack, mentally count the spots of the cards in the first row, subtracting ten every time the total amounts to more than that and ignoring the face cards and the tens. If you finish with the number seven, there must be a final three for the second row as the two numbers will always amount to ten. When you turn back again ask which row the card was put into, if it was the top one, count the spots of the packet handed to you in the same way. Suppose you arrive at nine, deduct the previous number seven, and you know the card is a 2. If there are two such cards in the packet you must ask a leading question, such as 'It was a red card, wasn't it?' to get information. If, however, the card was put into the lower heap you have the number three and you work in just the same way.

KEYSTONE CARD DISCOVERY   Larsen & Wright

A borrowed pack having been freely shuffled and returned to you, fan the cards for selection of a card and secretly count ten cards, holding an inconspicuous division at that point. See that the card is taken from farther on. Divide the pack for the return of the card at the division, drop the ten cards on it deliberately and square the pack very openly. Riffle shuffle several times keeping the top eleven cards in top position. Explaining what is to be done, you count off eleven cards into a pile one at a time. Replace these on top of the pack and the selected card is now the top card.

Hand the pack to a spectator telling him to think of a number between five and twelve and 'will the card' to go to that position. He deals face down the number he thought of and looks at the next card, it is wrong. Suppose, for example, he thought of six, replace the packet of six cards on the top of the pack and hand the pack to a second person, telling him to do the same thing but to think of a card between twelve and twenty. Suppose he thinks of fifteen and deals to that number; he looks at the next card and again it is wrong. Replace the packet on the pack and hand the pack to a lady. Let the first two persons tell her their numbers; ask her to subtract the smaller from the larger and deal cards equal to the remainder, which in this case will be nine. She does so and turns up the next card, it is the right one.

Any numbers may be used so long as the second one is larger than the first.

ASSISTANCE CARD TRICK

From any pack take a packet of sixteen cards. Run over the faces and put all the cards of the suit of which there are most together. Rapidly add the values, counting J as eleven; Q as twelve; and ignoring the K. When the total goes above thirteen, or is thirteen, deduct thirteen and start again with the remainder. Subtract the final total from thirteen and remember the result. Ask spectator to take a card but to note the suit only. Spread the cards of the suit you picked so that he must take one of them.

Take the other packet of thirty-six cards and hand it to the spectator. From it he selects any card of the chosen suit he pleases and hands you the remainder. Run over the faces and add the values of the remaining cards of that suit in exactly the same manner as before. Subtract the final figure from the remainder you got from the sixteen pile, the result will denote the value of his chosen card.

THE 52 CARD TRICK

A number is named and a party mentally selects a card. Pack is dealt into four face-up piles, party indicating the pile containing the card. Pack picked up and again dealt in four piles, the pile with card again indicated. This is done twice more and the thought card is found at the number chosen.

The trick depends on the order in which the piles are picked up. All dealing is from the pack held face down, the cards being turned up as dealt. In picking up the piles put them face up on the left hand in the order indicated in the table, turn the pack face down and again deal into four piles.

Table to be memorized:

1. 1. 1. 1.	5. 2. 2. 2.	8. 2. 2. 3.
2. 2. 2. 1.	6. 3. 3. 2.	9. 3. 3. 3.
3. 3. 3. 1.	7. 4. 4. 2.	10. 4. 4. 3.
4. 4. 4. 1.		
11. 2. 2. 4.	12. 3. 3. 4.	13. 4. 4. 4.

This indicates how to pick up the heap containing the chosen card after each of the first three deals when the number given is 1 to 13. After the fourth deal the heap is picked up first if the number is 13 or under. If the number is 14 to 26, subtract 13 from it, deal and pick up the first three times as the table indicates but, after the last deal, pick up the heap second. If from 27 to 39, subtract 26, follow the table, and pick up the pile third after the last deal. If over 39, subtract 39, follow table and pick the heap up fourth.

Examples: Number given is 7. Pick up indicated heap 4. 4. 2. then first. Number is 22; 22 minus 9 equals 13. Pick up 3. 3. 3. then second. Number is 34; 34 minus 26 equals 8. Pick up 2. 2. 3. then third. Number is 49; 49 minues 39 equals 10. Pick up 4. 4. 3. then fourth.

THE MAGI'S DETECTION   Jordan

Effect. A spectator cuts a portion from his own shuffled pack. You run through the cards once, then announce that you have memorized the cards. He secretly removes one card and hands you the remainder. You run through them once and name the missing card.

Method. When you run over the faces of the cards add their values, counting a J as 11, a Q as 12, and ignoring K's. Subtract 13 each time the total goes above that number. At the same time keep tally of the suits by counting S 1, H 2, C 3 and ignoring the D; subtract 6 when the suit total exceeds that number. The two numbers are noted mentally as you pass each card. Suppose the first five cards are QC, 5D, 3H, 9S and JC, you would count 12–3 plus 5–0=17–3; deduct 13 from 17 and go on with 4–3, add 3–2=7–5; add 9–1=16–6; deduct 13–6=3–0; add 11–3= 14–3; deduct 13, and carry on 1–3. A few trials will show that the operation is easy since, there are no large totals, and as you are supposed to be memorizing the cards, a little hesitation is natural, however, the quicker you do it, the more effective the trick.

When the packet is returned to you minus one card, simply repeat the operation and subtract the total from the former one, the remainder denotes the value and suit of the missing card. If the second value tally is greater than the first add 13 and then subtract. If they are the same, the card is a K. If the suit totals are the same it is a D. Suppose the first total is 10–3 and the second 5–3, the remainder is 5–0 and therefore the card must be the 5D.

THE FLUSH TRICK   Jordan

Effect. The A's, K's, Q's, J's and 10's are removed from any pack and mixed. From the twenty cards placed under a handkerchief the performer brings out any Royal Flush called for.

Method. Three simple tables have to be learned. Take the C's face down in the right hand and the S's in the left, mix them by dealing in a single face-down heap as follows:

R.H. 1 card, L.H. 2 cards; R.H. 2 cards; L.H. 2; R.H. 2, L.H. 1; always one card at a time.

Take the H's in the R.H. and D's in L.H. and deal thus: R.H. 1, L.H. 2; R.H. 1, L.H. 1; R.H. 1, L.H. 1; R. H. 2, L.H. 1.

Pick up the ten black cards with the R.H. and the ten red cards with the L.H. Deal again into a face-down heap as follows:

R.H. 1, L.H. 3; R.H. 1, L.H. 1; R.H.1, L.H. 1; R.H. 2, L.H. 3; R.H. 1, L.H. 1; R.H. 1, L.H. 1; R.H. 3.

Hand the packet to the spectator and have him deal them one at a time into three face-down heaps, the nineteenth and twentieth cards going on the first and last heaps. He is to pick them up by putting the third pile on the middle one and these two on the first. Fanning the cards will show the suits to be hopelessly mixed, but have him repeat the same deal exactly and cover the cards with a handkerchief. Impossible as it seems the packet is now arranged thus from the top downwards, five C's, five D's, five H's, five S's.

MODERNISM IN MENTALISM
Hull and Hahne

Any pack may be used and it is a good idea to lead up to the trick by talking of telepathy and the scientific investigations now being carried on regarding it. Have a spectator shuffle the cards, take the pack and run them off one by one before his eyes, you carefully looking away, and ask him to merely think of one. Place the cards one in front of the other in the right hand as you show them so that they remain in the same order. When you have shown nine cards ask if one has been mentally selected, if so replace the nine cards on the top of the pack, but if not, put them on the bottom and continue in the same way with another set of nine cards. If one is chosen mentally from these place them on top, if not, on the bottom, and continue until spectator says he has selected a card, and drop that packet of nine on top and false shuffle the pack.

Say that you will use half the pack only and deal off twenty-six cards in three heaps and, since there is a Joker in the pack, you will take one more card to make the heaps even. Remarking that it is necessary for you to know if the card thought of is in that half of the pack, pick up the first pile of nine and show the cards, if it is there pick up the three heaps with this one on top; if it is in the second put that on top, and if it is neither of the first two you know it must be in the third, so you say you will just take a chance. False shuffle and again deal three piles telling the spectator to watch for his card and try to send you the name mentally. Note the third card in each packet, one of them is the card thought of. With one or two leading questions you can ascertain the card and then name it in the hesitating way the mind-readers affect.

By having the row it is named, you know the card with certainty. In that case gather up the packets with the one containing the chosen card in the middle and it will be the twelfth card down. Deal face up telling the spectator to think 'Stop' when he sees his card. You stop at the twelfth.

FOUR TO ONE DETECTION

Anyone selects from his own shuffled pack any sixteen cards. Take them and deal as follows, face down:

```
        1       2
    3   4   5   6   7
        8       9
   10  11  12  13  14
       15      16
```

Turn your back and tell the spectator to turn up any card, look at it, turn it face down again and leave it in the same place. This done you turn round and pick up all the cards in the same row as his, shuffle them and let the spectator shuffle them. Have the spectator put his cards on top of yours. Shuffle all the other cards and put them on the packet already made. Deal the cards as before face up.

Ask the spectator which row his card is in. It will lie at 7, 8, 9, 10, or 11. There are, therefore, four chances of success to one of failure. The selected card falls at 11 if it is left on the face of his packet after the spectator shuffles; and if you have him shuffle with the cards face up he is not likely to leave it in that position.

A PSYCHIC CARD FEAT

Ask a spectator to take a coin from his pocket and write its date on a piece of paper. Then write the figures reversed and subtract the smaller number from the larger. Suppose the date to be 1935, this reversed would give 5391, and the remainder after the subtraction will be 3456. The spectator is then to take from the pack a card with the same number of spots as the first figure of the answer, and do the same with the other three figures. If there is a 0 he uses a K to represent it. The four cards must be of different suits. This done he is to lay them on the table face down and move them about so that even he cannot tell one card from another, then take any one and put it in his pocket without looking at it.

Pick up three remaining cards and as you add them to the top of the pack, slightly spread them so that you can see the indices. Note first what suit is missing, then mentally add the values and subtract the total from the nearest multiple of nine. In the case given above, suppose the three cards are the 3C, 4H, 6D, the missing suit is S, the total values 13, subtracting this from 18 leaves 5. Therefore the card in the spectator's pocket must be the 5S. The result is surprising since the spectator himself cannot tell what card he picked up.

OUT ON LOCATION   Al Baker

Take any pack, after it has been well shuffled by a spectator, and run over the faces under pretence of taking out the Joker. In so doing note the bottom card, the fifth card farther along, the fifth card from that and finally the fifth card from that one. Do not try to remember the suits of the cards, merely the values. Suppose the bottom card to be the 5D, the other cards at five-card intervals being the 7C, 6H and 3S—simply memorize the figures 5763 as you would a telephone number. This can be done easily as you run over the faces. Then turn the pack face down and under cut seven or eight cards from the bottom to the top and put the pack on the table. Invite a spectator to cut about the middle, complete the cut, look at the top card, bury it in the middle and square the cards carefully. Take the pack, run through the faces and find the original bottom card, the 5D. The figures 5763 will be recalled without effort. Count the cards between the 5 and the 7. If there are five only, count the cards between the 7 and the 6. Somewhere in these groups there will be five cards instead of four. One of these will be the selected card. Cut, bringing these five to the top and glance at them again memorizing the values only. Place the pack behind your back and ask how many spots there were on the card. Bring that card forward and put it face down on the table. The suit is named and you turn the card over, it is the selected card.

In the unlikely event of there being two cards of the same value, put one on the bottom and the other on the top and bring the pack forward. In putting it on the spectator's outstretched hand sight the bottom card. Let him name the card and you turn the top card, or turn the pack over to show the card at the bottom as may be necessary.

COINCIDENCE EXTRAORDINARY

A full pack is required for this trick and it may be shuffled as much as the spectator wishes beforehand. Take the pack and deal the top card face up, then whatever its value deal single cards to make a total of thirteen. Suppose the first card is a 9, deal four cards on it. Deal the next card face up and form another heap in the same way. Suppose it is a 7 spot, deal six cards on it to make thirteen. The J is to be counted as ten, Q eleven and K thirteen. Continue in like manner until you have too few cards left to make another packet. Turn the piles face down and ask a spectator to pick up and hand to you any piles he pleases, but he must leave three heaps on the table. The result of the operation so far is that the number of cards in your hands, less ten, equals the total number of spots on the top cards of the three heaps. That is to say, suppose the top cards to be an 8, a J and a 2, making a total of twenty-one—then the cards in your hands will be 31 in number. Therefore, if you force a 9 spot from amongst your cards and have it added to the three top cards the total will be thirty; while the subtraction of that one card from your packet will leave you with just thirty cards, thus a 'Marvellous Coincidence' is brought about.

To make the trick effective, the dealing should be done haphazardly and great stress laid on the fact that the spectator has a free choice of the packets.

NECROMANTIC CALCULATION   Variation by Hamblen

From a shuffled pack of fifty-two cards a spectator is instructed to deal out, face up, a number of spot cards, say six or seven. Take the pack and deal cards on each of these to bring a total of twelve. Suppose the first card is a 7 spot, deal five cards on it; the next a 3, deal nine cards on it; and so on. This should be done casually without any appearance of having to count. Lay the pack down.

Turn your back and instruct your volunteer helper to turn face down any three heaps he wishes, to take the top cards of these three heaps and place them in his pocket; then to gather the three face-down piles into one packet and put them aside. Finally he is to pick up the remaining face-up packets, add them to the unused portion of the pack and hand them to you. Keeping your back turned tell the spectator to take the three cards from his pocket and add the spots. You seize this opportunity to count off thirteen cards from the top of your packet and palm them in your right hand. When the spectator says he has the total, turn, put your cards on the table and with the right hand pick up the other packet which was made up of the three chosen heaps, thus getting rid of the palmed cards.

Now the number of spots on the three cards the spectator holds is the same as the total number of cards in the packet you have just laid down. Reveal this in the most surprising way you can devise.

12

Mysteries of a Prearranged Ordinary Pack of Cards

PRESENTATION

When a trick depends on a pre-arranged pack it is not enough to merely show the pack and proceed at once with the effect. Either a convincing false shuffle and series of false cuts must be made, or the pack, which has already been used for several tricks and has been handled freely and shuffled by the spectators themselves, must be exchanged, 'switched' to use the accepted term, for the arranged pack.

False shuffling, like all sleights, requires practice but a very easy and convincing method is given in the last section but one of this book which treats of the indispensable sleights for the proper presentation of tricks with cards. A method of false cutting is also included. Once these are mastered, a matter of very slight application, it is hoped that the reader will be sufficiently interested to go more deeply into the subject by studying Erdnase's *Expert at the Card Table*, the *Card Manipulations* series by Jean Hugard and other textbooks.

Several easy methods for switching the pack follow.

SWITCHING THE PACK

1. Place the set-up pack in your inside coat pocket on its side; take any three cards, memorizing them, from the pack to be used for the preliminary tricks (the back must be the same, of course) and put them in the same pocket but on their ends. When you are ready to introduce the arranged pack, have the pack in use thoroughly shuffled by a spectator, take it back and, standing with your right side to the front, pretend to

put it in your inside coat pocket. Really put it in your lower right waist-coat pocket and as you do this with the thumb and first finger, insert the other fingers in the pocket so that the spectators see the pocket bulge out as the pack apparently goes into it. Now give an example of the sensitive nature of your finger-tips by bringing out the three memorized cards from behind the arranged pack, naming each one first. Pretend to re-place them in the pocket, really sliding them into the waistcoat pocket with the same finger subtlety as when the pack was put there. Let a spectator remove the pack from the pocket and you are then ready to begin your pre-arranged tricks.

2. In this case the set-up pack is placed beforehand in the upper left waistcoat pocket and its three top cards are memorized. The same three cards are forced from the pack, replaced, and the pack shuffled by a spectator. The pack is really placed in the inside coat pocket, but the duplicates of the three forced cards are taken from the pack in the waist-coat pocket and this pack is finally removed as if it came from the coat pocket. Three cards are put on top in their proper order and you are ready for the set-up trick.

3. **Al Baker's Method, No. 1.** The duplicate pack is carried in the lower waistcoat pocket. With the pack to be exchanged in the left hand turn towards the table, drop the pack into the outside left coat pocket, at the same time take the pack from the waistcoat pocket with the right hand and put it in the left.

4. **Al Baker's Method, No. 2.** Place the pre-arranged pack in the right-hand outside coat pocket, lying on its side. Sight the two bottom cards of the pack beforehand. Force the duplicates of these two cards from the pack in use and have the pack shuffled by a spectator after the two cards have been replaced in it. Take the pack and put it in the pocket with the pre-arranged pack, but on end. Have the selected cards named and bring out the corresponding cards from the bottom of the set-up pack. Then bring out the rest of that pack and the exchange is made.

A MOVING REVELATION

This is one of the best non-sleight-of-hand tricks extant. The effect is that the performer appears to be able to divine the exact number of cards secretly moved from one end of a row to the other, and is able to continue doing the trick *ad lib*. without re-arranging the cards.

To prepare you place eleven cards in sequence from 10 to A with a J following the A, regardless of suits, on top of the pack. The J is to represent 0. Deal these cards face down on the table from left to right thus:

10. 9. 8. 7. 6. 5. 4. 3. 2. A. J.

Explain that you will turn your back and any spectator may move as many cards as he pleases, one by one, from the right end of the row to the left but not more than ten. To illustrate this you move six cards from right to left. The cards will then lies thus:

5. 4. 3. 2. A. J. 10. 9. 8. 7. 6.

The J has been brought to the sixth position from the right so that 6 will be your key number for the next move. Turn away and the spectator moves, say two cards from right to left making the lay-out:

7. 6. 5. 4. 3. 2. A. J. 10. 9. 8.

Turning around you gaze intently at the spectator, announce that you have read his mind and to prove it you will turn up a card with the same number of spots on it as the number of cards he moved. Turn the sixth card, the two spot. For the next key card simply add two to six which gives eight, the present position of the J, therefore no matter what the number of cards moved, the eighth card will give it by its number of spots. This may be continued indefinitely, whnever the number amounts to more than eleven, subtract eleven and continue with the remainder as the key number. If the J turns up then no cards have been moved.

After divining the number two or three times announce that you will give an illustration of the dominant power of your thought. Pick another spectator and tell him to think of any number between one and ten. Tell him that you have selected a number mentally and that you will force him to choose the same one. To prove your assertion you take a slip of paper and write, 'Turn over the . . . . card,' filling the blank space with the key card calculated for the next move. Put the paper down folded and lay the pencil on it. 'There is my number,' you say, 'Now please move the cards to the number you thought of'. He does so, reads the slip and turns the card showing that number of spots. Gather up the cards, mixing them up, replace them on the pack and shuffle.

The trick is very effective as it is but with the ability to make a false shuffle and false cuts it may be made into a little miracle. With the pack set-up execute several false shuffles and cuts, then deal out five or six of the set cards. Make another false shuffle and several cuts, then deal the rest to complete the row. Any suspicion that you may know the faces of the cards cannot then enter into the minds of your audience and the feat is thereby made very much more effective.

213

DIVINING PACK

Pre-arrange the top ten cards of a pack so that they run from the 10 down to the A. These cards may be of any suits. In offering the cards to a spectator for him to pick one, count the first ten and hold an imperceptible break at that point, making sure that he takes a card from those farther on. Close up the pack and when the spectator has noted his card, cut the cards at the break, lifting the ten cards, and have his card replaced there. Drop the ten cards on top of it and square the pack very openly.

Spread the top ten cards and have the spectator touch any one of them; turn the card face up where it lies, the spots on it will denote how many cards farther on the chosen card lies.

THE TRANSPOSED CARDS   Ziska

Beforehand place thirteen cards of mixed suits running from the K in order of decreasing value down to the A. Begin the trick by false shuffling the pack, leaving these cards on the top. Put the pack down and have a spectator cut it into two parts. Force the selection of the lower heap by the 'your right or my left' equivoque and have him count off any small number of cards, less than ten, while your back is turned, and put them on the other heap. This part is then put on top of the cards remaining in his hands. The fourteenth card from the top will now denote the number of cards counted.

Take the pack, false shuffle if you can, then deal about twenty cards face down, throwing them carelessly but allowing the fourteenth card to be a trifle more exposed than the others. Have a second person choose one of these: if he takes the fourteenth, simply ask how many cards were counted off and have the card turned up. If not have two more cards taken, if these do not include the fourteenth draw it out yourself, put these four in a row and force the right one by having first two cards then one touched by a third spectator, making the eliminations to suit your purpose.

THE CIRCLE OF CARDS   Judah

Beforehand arrange ten cards on the top of the pack, of any suits, but with the values running from 10 down to the A. False shuffle and cut as freely as you can and finally have a spectator cut about the middle. Let him choose a heap: if he selects the top half say that you will have him deal some cards on that heap from the other one: if he chooses the lower one let him take it: in either case he gets the lower heap. Turn your back and instruct him to count off any small number of cards, less than ten, look at the bottom card of the packet, remember it and place the packet on top of the other pile. This done, you turn around, take the remaining cards from him and put them under the other packet.

To discover the noted card and the number the spectator counted off, deal ten cards in a circle, and then four cards in the centre, all face down. After much mental exertion and much uncertain hovering over the cards turn up the lowest card of the packet of four, the eleventh card dealt, the spots on it will denoted the number of cards counted by the spectator and also the position in the circle of the card he noted. You secretly take note of its location, mix the cards up, apparently in a haphazard way, but keeping track of it. Finally draw it aside, have the card named and turn it over.

A TRICK WITHOUT A CLUE   Hamblen

With any pack secretly arrange ten cards of mixed suits, running from 10 to A, the 10 being the top card; false shuffle leaving these ten cards in position. Bend up a corner of the bottom card. Place pack down and have a spectator cut it about the middle; from the lower part instruct him to cut off a few cards after you have turned your back, count them, shuffle them, then note and remember the bottom card of this packet, place it on top of the other part of the pack and finally put the lower half of the pack on the top of both. He is then to cut the pack several times with complete cuts. Turn and take the pack, cut several times, finally cutting to send the bent corner card to the bottom. You now have the pack in the same order as it was before the spectator cut. Deal ten cards rapidly on the table, lift the next one, sight it, then as if you had suddenly changed your mind, drop the card back on the pack, pick up the cards dealt and replace them on the pack. The number of spots on the eleventh card that you secretly looked at, denotes the number of cards taken by the spectator, and the same number subtracted from eleven will give you the position from the top of the pack, for instance if the eleventh card is a 4, then four cards were cut and the card noted will be seven from the top.

Mysteries of a Prearranged Ordinary Pack of Cards

To reveal this knowledge in a striking way, have the spectator cut the pack in half, and each half again, making four packets; keep track of the original top portion. Call the piles A, B, C, D, and suppose D to be the original top portion, to get the seventh and eleventh cards on top of two packets simply have spectator move six cards from D to A, then one card from D to B; next three cards from D to C. This will leave the required cards on B and D. Place one of these on top of each of the other two. Let the spectator take the two top cards and put them face down on the table. He names the number of cards he took and the card he noted. Turn the two cards for the climax.

EYES ALL ROUND

Effect. A spectator thinks of a number between one and ten, counts that number of cards from a pack handed to him, shuffles the packet and puts it in his pocket while the performer's back is turned. Without turning around performer has him remove cards from the top of the pack until he calls 'Stop'. Taking the card stopped at, performer touches the spectator's pocket with it and has the number of cards put there called, suppose it is eight. He turns the card in his hand, it is an 8 spot. The trick is repeated several times with the same result.

Method. To arrange the pack put four sequences of cards regardless of suits, running from A up to 10 on the top, the court cards in any order going below them. When the first person thinks of a number show him what to do. Suppose the number is three, count off three cards, one by one, mix them and put them in your pocket. Take them out, put them on the bottom of the pack which you hand to the spectator. Turn your back. Since the trick works in tens, deduct three from ten and remember 7 as your key card. Turn away.

The spectator counts off the cards to the number thought of, shuffles them and puts them in his pocket. Keeping your back turned tell him to take the packet again and remove a card, then another and another and so on until six cards have been removed. Tell him to place the rest of the pack on top of those counted off. Turn around and have him hand you the next card from the top. Touch the card to the pocket and ask how many cards he has there. He replies 'Eight'. Turn the card, it is an 8 spot.

Put the cards from the spectator's pocket, also the 8 spot on the bottom of the pack. Mentally deduct eight from ten and remember 2 as your next key card. Repeat the experiment only once since after that you might get into the court cards. The spectator's shuffling is merely to destroy the arrangement which might be noticed otherwise.

COUNT YOUR CARDS

A card is taken, noted, replaced and the pack shuffled and cut. The pack is handed to the spectator with the request that he find his own card and save the performer worry and trouble.

Ask him to start dealing the cards face down, to stop at any number he may think of between one and ten so that the trick may not become boresome. He deals and turns up a card. You ask if that is his card and the answer is a negative one. Suppose this card happens to be a six. Tell him to deal another pile and turn up the sixth card. 'Is that your card?' you ask and the answer is 'No'. Suppose this time the card turned up is a 10. Continue, 'Three times and out. You may have one more chance and if you fail this time I'll have to find the card myself. Count one more pile and turn over the tenth card.'

He deals nine cards and you stop him. Ask him to name his card. He does so, turns the next card and it is his.

Method. Beforehand you arranged the first eleven cards, regardless of suits, to run in sequence from 10 to A, followed by another 10. After a false shuffle you have a card selected from below these eleven cards and in so doing secretly count fifteen cards and hold a break at that point. While the spectator is noting his card count another five cards beyond the fifteen and slip the tip of your little finger under the twenty cards. For the return of the chosen card cut off these twenty cards and drop them on top, making the selected card twenty-first from the top. False shuffle and false cut, if you can.

Hand the pack to the spectator and the effect works itself as described above. Regardless of what the first number is the second card must always be a 10 and the chosen card is tenth beyond that.

PYTHAGORAS

Take eleven cards of the following values but any suits and arrange them in this order: A, J, Q, K, 5, 6, 7, 8, 9, 10, Joker, the A being the top card of the packet and the Joker the bottom card. Place the packet face down on the table and invite a spectator to take off any number of cards from the top, not altering their order (not dealing them) and place them on the bottom while your back is turned. Illustrate by taking off three cards and putting them to the bottom. Mentally you subtract three from eleven and remember eight which becomes your key number. Turn away and the spectator does as directed. Turn back and put your left hand on the pack saying that the cards affect your heart beats so that you can tell the number transferred; also that you will not only discover the number but that you will turn up a card denoting the number by its value. Explain that a J counts 2, Q counts 3, K counts 4 and the Joker—0, the other cards according to their spots.

You have merely to turn up the eighth card which will give you the number of cards transferred. To repeat, glimpse the bottom card of the packet and subtract from eleven, this will give you the key card for the next transfer. If no cards are moved you turn up the Joker, value 0. The trick can be repeated indefinitely.

KNOCK 'EM DEAD
Buckley

Take out the H's from A to 10, place an indifferent card between each and an indifferent card on the top. Prepare a small wooden plug with ten holes bored in it, in each of these holes place a slip of paper rolled into a pellet, each slip bearing the name of one of the ten H cards. Put this plug in your right-hand outside coat pocket, the slips arranged in order so that you can instantly find any one required.

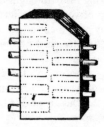

Provided with the prepared pack, the plug with the pellets, a slip of paper and pencil and having a hat on the table, begin by writing something on a slip of paper, pretending to drop it into the hat and have a spectator call any number between one and twenty. If the number called is even, hand him the pack and tell him to count down to that number and note the card, if the number called is odd he is to count down to that number and look at the next card. In the meantime you have simply to halve the number to obtain the value of the card, remove the corresponding pellet from the plug and drop it into the hat secretly as you bring it forward to have your prophecy verified.

SELF-WORKING MYSTERY   Larsen

With a pack of strippers arrange the first ten cards to run from a 10 down to an A using mixed suits, and reverse them. Begin by shuffling the cards thus—strip off the top ten cards and make a riffle shuffle. Apparently cut the pack, really strip the ten cards out and drop them on top. Invite a spectator to freely choose a card from anywhere but the ten top cards. For its replacement cut off the ten cards, their reversal making this easy, have the card put back, drop the ten cards on it and square the pack. The chosen card is now the eleventh card and you false shuffle, keeping it in that position.

Again cut the top ten cards and put the remainder of the pack on the table. Fan the ten with both hands and let spectator remove one card. Separate the cards at the point from which this card is taken, with the left hand drop all the cards that were below it on top of the pack, then pick up the pack and put it on top of the cards remaining in the right hand. The spots on the card taken from the ten will indicate the position of the chosen card from the top of the pack. The counting must, of course, be done faces down.

STOP AND THINK   Jordan

Separate the cards of any full pack into their suits, then separate each suit into odd and even cards, J and K being odd and Q even. You thus have eight packets. Put the two red odd with the two black even cards and shuffle them thoroughly; do the same with the two red even and the two black odd cards. From these two packets take one card alternately in one pile until the cards have all been taken. The cards will appear to be well mixed.

With the pack so arranged begin by having it cut several times with complete cuts. Deal the cards into four heaps, one card at a time. Suppose the letters A, B, C, D, represent the heaps it will be seen that if A and C are put together and also B and D we have the two original packets, red odd and black even, and red even and black odd. Ask the spectator which he will have, the odd packets or the even. Whichever he takes let him put them together and shuffle the cards. You do the same with the remaining packets.

219

The spectator takes any card from his and pushes it into yours which you give to him to shuffle. Taking it back you have only to find the one card that does not match up with the odd and even cards that you hold. It may be an odd black, all the rest of the blacks being even and so on.

NOVEL CARD DISCOVERY   Jordan

To set up the pack first separate the odd cards from the even, the J and K being taken as odd cards and the Q as even. Put thirteen odd cards face up on the table, on them put thirteen even cards, then the rest of the odd cards and finally the remainder of the even cards. Turn the pack face down. Now if it is cut at the middle the odd cards will be on the top of each portion and the even cards at the bottom, therefore if the two packets are riffled together the top part will consist of odd cards and the bottom of the pack will have the even cards when the riffle shuffle is completed. There will be a few mixed cards in the centre but that will not interfere with the effect.

After the arranged pack has been riffle shuffled, have it cut into two packets as near equal as possible. Invite a spectator to take a card from the middle of either heap and push it into the middle of the other packet. The cards being dealt, the one even card amongst the odd cards or vice versa, must be the chosen card.

IMPROVED MARVELLOUS PREDICTION   Jordan

In this trick you actually set up a borrowed pack into the odd-even arrangement. Deal the cards into four heaps by putting in the first two only odd S's, and H's, and even C's and D's. Into the second two heaps deal only even S's and H's and odd C's and D's. Put first two heaps together and have a spectator shuffle them while you shuffle the other two. Cut the spectator's packet into two portions putting them side by side. Cut your packet placing the halves on top of the other two packets. Top of each now contains even S's, H's; odd C's, D's, bottom portions of each are S's, H's; even C's, D's.

Have a spectator riffle these two packets together. There will be only a few cards of both kinds mixed in the centre, the cards at the top and bottom of the pack remain as set up. Have the pack cut into three nearly even piles, discard the centre one and have two spectators each take one of the others. Each selects a card from the other's packet and shuffles it into his own. Have the packets put together, the original top heap going on top.

The cards are now called one by one from the top of the pack. The first odd S or H, even C or D is one of the chosen cards. After a card or two more has been called, have the packet turned over and have the cards called from the face of the pack. This time listen for an even S or H, odd C or D. This will be the other card. Reveal the cards as you please.

READY RECKONER   Jordan

To prepare for this trick sort out the odd and even cards of each suit and reassemble the pack by putting the odd S's and H's with the even C's and D's in one packet, and the even S's and H's with the odd C's and D's in another. Put the packets together making a bridge between.

Thus prepared, take the pack and hold a break at the bridge with the pack face down in the left hand. Let half the cards below the break drop on the table, then drop the rest of the cards below the break besides the first lot. On each packet drop half the remaining, now dovetail the two packets together and as the lower half of each packet consists of one kind of cards and the upper half of another when the shuffle is completed the pack will be in two kinds of cards, with a few mixed in the middle.

Instruct a spectator to cut the pack into three heaps, pocketing the top packet and handing you the middle one. By merely glancing at the cards you tell him how many cards he cut. The only kind of cards he can have in his pocket are odd S's and H's and even C's and D's. A glance at the cards handed you will show how many of such cards are in it, subtract the number from twenty-eight and you get the number of cards cut.

Follow this with 'The Pair Detection'.

THE PAIR DETECTION   Jordan

This trick is designed to follow the 'Ready Reckoner'.

While the spectator verifies your total, secretly add the spots of the only odd S's and even C's in the packet which you still hold, subtracting thirteen each time your number exceeds that, and you know the number of points in his packet when all the thirteens in it have been cancelled. Tell him to shuffle his packet and to remove any pair from it, pocketing it.

The only pairs in his packet must consist of a card of each colour, either a S and a H, or a C and a D. Place the packet you hold face down on the table and put the other packet, which has not been touched, on top of it. Taking his packet, you merely add the spots of the black cards in it, subtracting thirteens. Subtract this total from what the total should be and you have the denomination of the pair. If it is odd they are S and H, if even, C and D.

Follow with 'Dead Easy Location'.

DEAD EASY LOCATION   Jordan

Continuing after 'The Pair Detection', have the spectator replace the pair and put his packet on top of the pack after he has thoroughly shuffled it. Tell him to cut the pack at about the middle, note the card on top of the lower portion, put it on top, reassembling the pack and make several complete cuts.

Then tell him to deal the pack into several rows, turning the cards face up. You can now locate the card. Owing to the way in which the two lower portions were placed, cutting the pack at the middle forced the spectator to choose a card from among the even S's and H's, odd C's and D's, and this is placed on the original top of the pack, his whole packet of cards being of the other variety. In glancing over the cards dealt, locate the long string that must have been his packet and the card dealt next before the first of this string must be the selected one.

ODD OR EVEN   Jordan

The trick requires a special arrangement. First sort out the suits and arrange each to read from back to face,

6, 4, 10, A, Q, 2, J, 7, 8, 5, 3, K, 9

cut each of these packets so that a card of different value is at the bottom of each. Riffle shuffle the S's and H's together once only and do the same with the C's and D's. Put the two packets together with a bridge at the division.

To present, cut at the bridge and riffle shuffle once only, then cut the pack. Fan the pack from left to right, the faces outwards and have a spectator choose a heap. Pass the cards from left hand to right and as spectator tells you that a card is of a suit chosen, place it face down on the table. When complete the cards are in the set-up order except for being cut. On a small card, which you can palm on to the back of the rest of the pack, you have the following table.

OOOO–8	EOEE–6	OEOO–2	EEOO–3	OEEO–10
EEOE–4	OOEO–J	EEEO–K	OOEE–A	
OOOE–7	OEEE–9	EOOE–Q	EOOO–5	

A spectator cuts the packet with complete cuts and you turn your back. He puts the top card in his pocket without looking at it or letting anyone else see it. He deals the twelve remaining cards into four face-down heaps, a card to a heap in rotation. He then turns the top card of each heap face up and calls Odd or Even for each, J is odd, K Q even. Consulting your table you at once name the card in the spectator's pocket the face of which no one else has seen.

If desired you can repeat with any one of the other suits.

THE WONDER FORCE   Jordan

A. This can be used as a prediction trick or as a method of forcing a card for any other trick.

Suppose you wish to force the QH. Firs. divide the pack into its red and black cards. Place six red cards face down, on them twelve black cards, then six more reds and on them the QH, and on it any black card. Arrange the rest of the pack in another pile, first a black card, on it seven reds, then twelve blacks, and lastly the rest of the reds. Put the second packet on top of the first making a bridge between them.

If you are simply making a prediction write 'Queen of Hearts' on a slip of paper, fold it and give it to a spectator to hold. Cut the pack at the bridge and riffle shuffle them together. The centre portion of the pack will consist of black cards. Ask a spectator to give the pack another riffle shuffle and as he must cut amongst the black cards no red card can fall above the force card, the QH. Tell him to take out the first red card he comes to. Your prediction is read and the card shown.

Two or more cards of the same colour can be forced in the same way.

B. Second Method. Place a duplicate of the force card next above the bottom card of the original upper half of the pack. When shuffling let these two cards fall first. This time there is a force card the first red card from either end. Spectator riffle shuffles and then cuts the pack into two portions. He chooses one, if the top half, he takes the first red card from the top, if the lower heap, the first red card from the face. Again you may use two different red cards and have from twenty to thirty cards dealt into a heap, reversing their order so that the first red cards taken from each heap will be the force cards.

PSYCHIC PREDICTION   Jordan

Here is an arrangement which will force the number twenty-seven. It may be used simply as a prediction effect, the number being written beforehand on a slip which is placed in an envelope, sealed and held by a spectator, or in any effect requiring the forcing of a number. Other numbers can be arranged for on the same lines. For twenty-seven arrange cards as follows:

2S, 3H, AS, KH, 9S, 10H, 5S, JH, QS, 4H, 8S, 6H, KS, 3H, AS, 2H, 9S, 10H, 5S, QH, JS, 4H, 8S, 6H, 7C, KD, 2C, 10D, 4C, AD, 3C, 8D, 9C, QD, QC, 4D, 7C, 2D, JC, 10D, 4C, AD, 3C, 8D, 9C, JD, KC, 4D.

Bridge the cards so that you can cut at the 6H.

With cards thus arranged, first write the prediction, then cut at the bridge, riffle shuffle once only and call attention to the genuineness of the shuffle. Show the faces of the cards rapidly, the duplicates will not be noticed and the cards appear to be perfectly ordinary. Hand the cards to a spectator telling him to think of a suit. Cutting the pack wherever he pleases he picks off a card at a time from the top, noting each. Those not of his suit he places face up. No matter where the pack is cut or what suit he selects the total for six cards thus taken will be twenty-seven.

PROPHESIED SPOT TOTAL   Jordan

Remove the 3's, 9's, K's, 6's, A's, 4's, 7's, 10's, J's, and 5's, and paying no attention to suits, arrange them in four sequences, so that all four sets of ten are in the same order. Place these sets together and on top of them put the remaining twelve cards of the pack.

With the pack thus prepared, begin by writing a prediction, sixty-nine, on a slip of paper, fold it and give it to someone to hold.

Take the pack, deal off ten cards and openly add their spots, spectator checking. Replace them on top, then put half a dozen to the bottom and again deal off ten cards, the values of these are added and checked, giving a different total. Invite a spectator to cut the pack, deal off ten cards and add up their values. He does so and gets a total of sixty-nine. Your prediction is opened and read aloud. It is the same.

The arrangement does it all, any ten cards of the forty taken in sequence add up to sixty-nine. It is advisable to have the spectator cut about the middle.

CAGLIOSTRO'S VISION   Jordan

The pack used for this trick must be a complete one of fifty-two cards. Arrange the following cards in this order at the bottom of the pack: 2H, AC, 2C, 3C, 4C, 5C, 6C, 7C, the 2H being the bottom card.

To begin, make a riffle shuffle, leaving these cards in position at the bottom. Put the pack on the table and turn away. Instruct the spectator to remove two cards from the middle of the pack, putting one at the top and one at the bottom so that you cannot possibly know the cards occupying these positions. Tell him to fix on any number between one and ten, deal a face-down row of cards from left to right to that number, look at and remember the last card of the row. Next he is to go back to the first card of the row and deal one card on each one in the row, continuing as long as there are enough cards to complete a deal on the whole row. When there are not enough to do that he is to lay them aside. Tell him to assemble the heaps by placing the last heap on top of the next one to the left, these two on the next and so on, finally cutting the complete pile several times completing the cut each time.

Turn around, note the number of cards left over; if there are none his card will be the next behind the 2H, the pack being face up. If there are two cards left over, his card will be next behind the 2C, if three over, next behind 3C and so on.

QUADRUPLE PACK MYSTERY   Jordan

Take the AC from each of three red-backed packs and discard one of them entirely. Place two of the A's at the rear edge of your table, the ends projecting over it slightly and conceal them by laying a blue pack in its case over them. Have the three red packs thoroughly shuffled, placing them together as one huge pack. Pick up the blue pack with the two hidden A's below it and taking back the triple stack rest the blue case on it for a moment leaving the A's on top. Lay the triple pack down and hand the blue pack, taking it out of its case, to a spectator. Turn your back or leave the room.

Instruct the spectator to take any card from the blue pack and put the rest of the pack in his pocket. Ask a second person to deal a row of cards face down from the triple pack on the table, the second person to stop him at any time and put his blue-backed card face down at the right-hand end of the row as the last card. A small identical number of cards is then dealt in turn on the back of each card in the row and the heaps are to be assembled by picking up the one first dealt at the left end, putting it on top of the second, these two on the third and so on. A third person now takes the pack so assembled, cuts some and, holding it face up, deals the cards one by one, calling their names as he does so. When he calls the first AC you start counting the cards to and including the next AC, the number will be the number originally in each heap and the chosen blue-backed card will lie exactly that number of cards from the second AC.

You call 'Stop' and turn around. The second spectator names his card, it is the one the third spectator has in his hand. He turns it over, it has a blue back.

MEPHISTOPHELES' TOUCH   Jordan

Take out all the 2's, 3's, 4's, 5's and 6's from a complete pack and arrange the remaining cards in four sequences of 8 cards, thus:

> 9S, 7H, KC, 8D, QS, JH, AC, 10D.
> 9H, 7C, KD, 8S, QH, JC, AD, 10S.
> 9C, 7D, KS, 8H, QC, JD, AS, 10H.
> 9D, 7S, KH, 8C, QD, JS, AH, 10C.

It follows from this arrangement that no matter what card is taken the eighth card down from it will be of the same value and the next suit in the order of S, H, C, D. Place the twenty low cards on the top of the arranged packet bridging them.

Begin by showing the pack, cut at the bridge and riffle shuffle the low cards into the others. Have a spectator cut. Take the pack face up and throw out all the low cards as you come to them. The arrangement of the remainder is unaltered though no spectator would believe this even if you told him.

Turn away, ask a spectator to make a complete cut and note the top card, putting it face down on the table. Tell him to deal eight cards on top of it, lay the pack aside and shuffle the nine cards. Turn and spread the packet face up. There will be one pair of cards amongst them and his card is the one that comes first in the suit order. For instance KH-KC being the pair, the spectator's card will be the KH.

FAIR AND SQUARE
Annemann

With any pack arrange the cards according to suits only. Rotate the suits throughout the pack, paying no attention to the values. For instance, you may have the suits, C, H, S, D, C, H, S, D, and so on all through the pack.

Cut the pack several times with complete cuts. Fan the pack for the free selection of any card. While the spectator is looking at his card run off four cards from the point at which he removed his card and have it returned there. Square up the cards and have the spectator make several complete cuts.

To find the chosen card you have simply to run through the faces of the cards and note when you come to the two cards of the same suit together. The selected card will always be the one of these two which is nearest the face of the pack.

YOUR CARD
Orville W. Meyer

In doing this feat lay great stress on the fact that you never see the face of any card. You hold the pack behind your back and allow a spectator to freely remove one card. Still holding the pack behind your back, bring forward two cards and lay them face down on the table. State that these two will reveal the chosen card, one telling the suit, the other the value. And they do.

You have the pack stacked by the Si Stebbins system in which the suits and values rotate regularly. When the spectator cuts the pack behind your back for the selection of a card, have him take the top card of the lower portion, take the cut from him and place it below the lower packet. In short the pack is cut at the point from which the card was taken.

Now because of the system the fourth card from the top of the pack will be of the same suit as the selected card and the thirteenth card down will be of the same value. So that all you have to do is to bring out these two cards to reveal the suit and value of the chosen card.

(*Note.*) When removing the thirteenth card behind your back slip the tip of your left little finger in marking the spot. You can later on easily put it back in its proper place. The card taken from the fourth place can be replaced in position and you have your set-up ready again.

ONE IN FOURTEEN

Annemann

The pack is arranged in the 'Eight Kings', the Si Stebbins, or any other system in which the sequence runs in four cycles of thirteen values; such system as Nikola's is not suitable for this feat.

False shuffle the pack and allow a spectator to make several complete cuts. When he is satisfied that the cards are well mixed invite him to take the top card, look at it; put it face down on the table and deal thirteen cards on top of it. The remainder of the pack is put aside. Tell him to pick up the fourteen cards, shuffle them thoroughly and then hand the packet to you.

To find his card you have simply to look over the faces and find a pair of cards of the same value. There will be one pair only in the fourteen cards and one of the pair will be his card. Suppose the pair to be the KC and KH, and the arrangement of the suits in the stacked pack to be C, H, S, D—the spectator's card will be the one that occurs first in the suit order, thus in this case it will be the KC.

Having found the card so simply, reveal it in as magical a manner as you can devise.

(*Note.*) In running through the packet to find the selected card re-arrange the cards in the same order. Take out the selected card and drop the cards on top of the pack. Replace the chosen card on top and you have the pack in order for any other trick depending on the arrangement.

THE FIFTEENTH CARD

(After Jordan)

From any pack take out all the black cards and arrange them in the order following:

A, K, 2, Q, 3, J, 4, 10, 5, 9, 6, 8, 7, 7, 8, 6, 9, 5, 10, 4, J, 3, Q, 2, K.

There will be one A left over, place it on the top of the pack. It will be noted that the arranged cards make two sequences, one ascending value, the other descending, and that any two adjacent cards will total fourteen or fifteen in value, the J, Q, K, being reckoned as eleven, twelve, thirteen. Put the black cards, thus arranged, on top of the red, note the red card that is fifteenth from the bottom and put the pack in its case.

To show the feat, begin by writing the name of the fifteenth card on a slip of paper, fold it and give it to a spectator to put in his pocket. Take the pack from its case, split it at the lowest black card and mix the cards, calling attention to the genuineness of the procedure. Hand the pack to the spectator and have him deal the cards one by one into two piles, the red cards in one heap, the black in the other. The cards will be in the same order but reversed, the noted card being now fifteenth from the top of its packet.

Ask the spectator to choose one of the packets. If he takes the blacks go right ahead with the effect. If he chooses the reds tell him to put those cards in his pocket and to remember he chose the packet freely. Have him thrust the blade of a knife into the black cards and let him take the two cards below, the two cards above, or the single card above and the single card below the blade. Any of these pairs will total fourteen or fifteen. If fourteen tell him to deal fourteen cards and lay the next face down on the table, if fifteen, to put out the fifteenth card, then to take the slip from his pocket, read your prediction and turn the card he arrived at.

The procedure is so apparently genuine that it will puzzle anyone not acquainted with the secret.

SENSATIONAL CARD MYSTERY

The secret is that cards are generally arranged in a certain order when they come from the makers, usually H, C, D, S with values from the A to the K.

Introduce a new pack and hand it to a spectator to open. He takes the pack out of its case and puts the cards face down on your left hand. Invite five or six spectators each to cut a small packet of cards from the top, look at the face card of the cut and then hold the packets against their chests so that neither you nor anybody else can get a glimpse of the face cards. Retain a few cards on your left hand and in returning to your table sight the top card of this packet. This will indicate the face card of the last spectator's cut. Suppose your sighted card is a 9S, you know the spectator cut an 8S. Take his packet, drop it on top of the cards in your left hand, sight its top card and so get knowledge of the next cut card.

Proceed in exactly the same way for the rest of the spectator's cards.

(*Note.*) The reader is advised to test the various makes and brands of cards before relying on this 'secret'.

NEW X-RAY TRICK

Use the 'Eight Kings, etc.' arrangement and introduce the trick after switching the arranged pack for one that has been freely handled and shuffled by the audience.

Have a spectator freely select a card and pass all the cards below it to the top. Sight the bottom card and so memorize the chosen card. Go to a second spectator, have him cut off a packet, shuffle it, retaining one card and passing the rest to a third person to do the same. This person hands the cards to a fourth who also picks out a card. Have these cards replaced in different places in the arranged pack retained by you.

Drop the cards into a goblet and throw a handkerchief over them. Talk about the progress being made in telepathy, now a proven scientific fact and so on. Ask each person to concentrate on his card and after much stress name the first card. Take the cards out of the goblet, run through them to remove the card just named and note another card out of the regular order. Put the cards back in the goblet, cover them and proceed to get the name of the card you just noted. Continue with the rest in the same way. Shuffle the cards after you note the last card and you can let anyone remove the cards from the goblet after you name it. There will be nothing for anyone to find as a clue to the trick.

SHARK FOOD

Pack is in any arrangement you prefer to use. If you cannot make a satisfactory false shuffle, the pack in use which has been freely handled and shuffled by the spectators should be secretly exchanged for the arranged pack. Hand this to a spectator and have him make several complete cuts. Turn your back and tell him to deal cards face down on the table, stopping whenever he pleases, then he is to take the next card, look at it, insert it in the cards he holds and shuffle them. This done, turn around, take the cards from him, open the packet for the return of the cards dealt on the table. Slip the tip of your left little finger under the top card of this packet, lift off all the cards below it and shuffle them on the top. This leaves the last card dealt by the spectator at the bottom of the pack. Sight it and you know by the set-up what his card is and you can reveal it as you wish.

THOUGHT FORETOLD   Jordan

Effect. Performer writes a prediction, seals it in an envelope and hands it to a spectator. This person chooses a colour, red or black, and from a shuffled pack draws one card. This he puts in an envelope and burns it. He segregates the cards of the colour he chose. One card is missing and its name is found to have been predicted by the performer as proved by the slip in the sealed envelope.

Method. Separate the red and black cards of any pack and take out one red and one black card, remembering their names. Cut the two piles in half and put the black halves on the red halves. Bridge the two packets and put them together.

Thus prepared ask a spectator to choose between red and black. Whichever he names, write the name of the card of that colour on a slip of paper, seal it in an envelope and give it out to be held. Divide the pack at the bridge and give it a careful riffle shuffle, calling attention to its genuineness. The shuffle will put all the black cards together at the top and all the reds at the bottom of the pack, with perhaps a few mixed in the middle. Whichever colour was named, fan the half of the pack of the opposite colour for the selection of a card. This card is not looked at but placed in an envelope and burned. This ensures that when the spectator picks out the cards of the colour he chose there will be one card only missing. Naturally this is taken to be the one burned since the card named in your prediction is missing.

MYSTERIOUS DETECTIVE   Jordan

Effect. Spectator cuts a pack and takes the top card of the lower heap, and two other people do the same. The performer takes a card from the pack, touches each man's pocketed card and names them correctly.

Method. Arrange the red cards from face to back—AH, 2D, 3H, 4D, etc., to QD, KH, AD, 2H, etc., the suits alternating and the values in sequence. Do the same with the two black suits. Cut the reds bringing 8H to the face, and the blacks with the 2C in same position. Put the two packets together, bridging them.

To present, cut at the bridge and riffle shuffle. Show the faces rather rapidly, pack looks well mixed. Allow first spectator to lift off a packet, laying it aside, then take the top card and pocket it. A second spectator lifts off another packet in the same way and pockets card, third spectator follows suit. Assemble the pack by replacing the packets to bring pack to its original order except for the three cards removed. Note the bottom card and name a card a few points lower in value which will be near the top of the pack, saying that card is your detective card. Run through the pack face up and note first two cards of the same suit near together without a card of the same colour but different suit between them.

Suppose you see the 8C and 10C and no S between them, you know that a 9S has been removed. There will be two other similar combinations giving you the names of the other two cards. Memorize the cards and after taking out the so-called detective card, touch each man's pocket, put the card to you ear, and name the card.

SUPER COUNT DOWN   Vernon

Arrange the pack red, black, red, black, etc., the colours alternating throughout the pack.

After a false shuffle hand the pack to a spectator, asking which he prefers odd or even. If he says odd ask him to think of any odd number from one to fifty. Turn your back instructing the spectator to first cut the pack several times, then count off on the table singly cards to the number thought of and to note the next card. Put this card on those dealt and drop the pack on top of all. Finally he is to cut again.

Take the pack and fan the faces towards yourself, note where two cards of the same colour come together. Openly cut at this point so that one goes to the top, the other to the bottom. Run through the cards again and count as you do so until you reach two of the same colour together. The first of these will be the noted card and the number that this card is from the bottom indicates the number thought of.

If the spectator has thought of an even number he is to note the top card of the heap on the table instead of the top card of the pack. In this case when you receive the cards instead of cutting when you reach the two cards of the same colour, simply jog the second card slightly inwards with the left thumb and continue running over the faces until the second two of the same colour is reached, cut at this point, between the two cards, turn the pack face downwards and make a break below the jogged card. Lift the cards above the break, they correspond to the number mentally selected.

FATE AND THE JOKER   Jordan

Effect. A spectator selects a card by thrusting the Joker into a shuffled pack. Performer names the card by merely looking at the Joker.

Method. Separate the red cards from the black. Put all the H's and D's together in pairs whose value is fourteen, thus 7D, 7H, KH, AD and so on; J, Q, K, values being eleven, twelve, thirteen. In the same way arrange the S's and C's in pairs of value fourteen. Put the two packets together making a bridge.

To begin, show the pack, cut at the bridge and riffle shuffle the halves slowly and openly calling attention to the genuineness of the shuffle. Remove the Joker, hand it to a spectator and invite him to thrust it into the pack wherever he pleases. This done let him take the card above or the card below the Joker.

Take the pack, turn it face up to remove the Joker and note the card near it which hasn't a mate near it of the same colour but opposite suit to make up a total value of fourteen, then subtract its value from fourteen and name the other suit of the same colour. For instance you find a 2H alone, the card drawn was the QD.

PSYCHOLIA
Jordan

From two packs of cards take out all the low cards from 6 to 2 and discard one set of these entirely. Shuffle one of the thirty-two-card packs thoroughly and then arrange the cards of the second pack in exactly the same order. Place this pack in your pocket. Put the low cards of the other pack on top, bridging the packets.

To begin, show the pack, cut at the bridge and riffle the two packets together slowly, calling attention to the thoroughness of the shuffle. Turn the pack face up and discard the low cards from 6 to 2 so that the cards will be in the same order as those of the pack in your pocket. Let a spectator cut the pack in about two equal piles and you hand the heaps to two persons, noting the bottom card of each as you do so. Now leave the room.

Take out the duplicate pack, cut it to make the face cards the same as those you noted in the spectator's packets. Spread the two packets face up some distance apart. Note which packet contains the AS. Now call to the spectators: 'Have five cards chosen from whichever packet contains the AS and one card from the other packet, note the selected cards and shuffle them into the opposite heaps from which they were drawn. Now put the two heaps together with the AS heap on top. Kindly read aloud the names of the cards as they lie from the top.' As each card is read discard its duplicate from your AS heap. One card will be read which is not in your AS heap. This is the one the spectator removed from his AS heap. Pick it out of your as yet unused heap and keep it separate. Let the reading continue until your AS is reduced to but five cards—these, and the one you have laid aside, are the selected cards.

Announce their names with dramatic effect.

THE WIZARD'S DREAM   Jordan

Arrange the cards of each suit from A to K in sequence of value, A, 2, 3, 4, 5, 6, etc. The order of the suits being S, H, C, D. Cut a small card to the face.

Show the pack and put it on the table. Turn away and have a person cut the pack as often as he likes with complete cuts then give it a riffle shuffle and finally tell him to cut the pack about the middle. Invite him to take any card from one heap and put it in the other.

You turn around, take whichever packet he wishes and find the card. The principle is simple, a single dovetail shuffle does not destroy the arrangement, it merely divides the sequence into two strings and by following each of them without regard to the interlying cards any strange card or any missing card can be detected at once.

DIABOLICAL TRANSPOSITION   Jordan

Effect. Two packs of cards are used and four spectators join in the trick. The first two spectators are each given a pack of cards which they cut several times and then each deals off a packet of twenty-six cards. The first man pockets the lower half of the pack and hands the counted off twenty-six-card packet to one of his neighbours; and the second man does the same. The two assisting neighbours both stand and each fans his packet of twenty-six cards, and proceeds to mentally select any one card. The magician causes these two mentally selected cards to leave the assistants' packets and fly back to the original halves of the packs still in the first two spectators' packets. Upon examination this amazing transposition is found to have taken place, and the packs may be examined without discovering the secret.

Method. Using two complete packs of the same back patterns, you thoroughly shuffle one pack and remove twenty-six cards just as they come from the top. Take the duplicate twenty-six cards from the other pack, arrange them in the same order, and place these two duplicate half packs together. Do the same with the other two half packs. Each pack is therefore the complement of the other, i.e.; the twenty-six cards missing from the first arranged pack are in the second arranged pack, and vice versa, and the dealing of twenty-six cards will always leave their duplicates in the hands of the party originally holding them. It is now obvious that, when the procedure described in the first paragraph is followed, no matter what cards the assistants note their duplicates are already in the half packs held by the first two spectators. Before the audience realizes what is about to happen, however, the magician takes back the two (counted off) twenty-six-card packets and boldly switches them, either by the pass or in laying them on the table—and the trick is done. Due to this little swindle the selected cards appear to vanish—on command of the magician—from their respective packets and are found to have returned to the original halves of the pack still pocketed by the first two spectators. Further examination of both complete packs will give no clue to the mystery.

CARD MEMORY Annemann

Effect. Pack is shuffled, divided in half, one half is chosen by a spectator and read through once to the performer, who then leaves the room but remains within hearing distance. Spectator spreads the cards in a row face up and the performer names the cards in order both ways and names the cards at any numbers or the number of any card.

Method. The cards are arranged but the arrangement can vary every time. Separate the black cards from the red, shuffle the reds and spread them face up from left to right. Take the black cards and arrange the values in the same order exactly, but where you have a H in the reds use a C in the blacks and for D's use S's. Therefore supposing the sixth card in the red packet is the JH, you know that the sixth card in the black packet will be the JC and so on. Put the two packets together making a bridge between them.

To begin, show the pack, cut at the bridge and riffle the two packets together, calling attention to the fairness of the shuffle. Say that a full packet makes the effect too lengthy and that you will use half the cards only. Turn pack face up and deal one by one, the reds in one pile, the blacks in the other Turn them face down and have a spectator choose one packet. Carelessly drop the other into your pocket. Have him cut the chosen pile several times and then call the names of the cards to you just once. Listen, pretending intense concentration, but remember the last card only. Leave the room, take the packet from your pocket, cut so that the card corresponding with the last card called by the spectator is at the face thus putting it in exactly the same order as the other packet.

Hold the packet face down and deal them face up and overlapping in a row from left to right, naming each card aloud as you turn it. After every fifth card jog the next five up and down alternately about an inch. After you have called all the cards you can locate any number instantly and call the card at any number named and vice versa.

SENSITIVE THOUGHTS   Annemann

This is worked on the same principle as 'Card Memory'.

Arrange a pack exactly in the same way with a bridge between the two sets of reds and blacks.

Show the pack, divide it at the bridge, execute a riffle shuffle and then deal the packets, reds and blacks, just as in the preceding trick. Both packets are in the same order as set up.

Ask a spectator to choose a packet, to think of any number from one to twenty-six and name it. Address a second spectator and tell him he is to take the other packet, run over the faces of the cards and think of any card he may see. As you say this you have picked up the packet and run over the faces as if showing the second man what he is to do, really you locate the card at the number called by the first person. To do this quickly, subtract the number from twenty-six, count as you fan from the face card, and when you reach the number note the next card, which tells you the card in the first packet at the number called. If it is the 7S for instance, you remember the 7D.

The second spectator names his card. Have the first person hold his packet to your forehead as he repeats his number. You name the card, and as he deals face up counting to that card note where the second person's card lies and remember the number. He, in his turn puts the pack to your forehead and you call the number at which his card lies in his packet. If the mate of the card does not appear you must pick up the first packet and quickly continue the count as you show that all the cards are different.

RED AND BLUE BACK MIX-UP   Annemann

Effect. The performer announces that a very peculiar affinity exists between cards of the same suit and value. To illustrate this he brings out two packs, one with a blue back, the other a red.

Mysteries of a Prearranged Ordinary Pack of Cards

Each pack is snuffled by a member of the audience, then the performer puts the packs together and shuffles the double pack. He drops the cards into a borrowed hat and, holding it above his head, he has each of three people call any number up to ten. He brings out cards one by one, dropping them aside until he comes to the number given by the first person, this card is seen to have a red back and he stands it back outwards against a glass or displays it on an easel. He repeats the process with the second number called, that card proves to have a blue back, and lastly at the third number the card is a blue-backed one.

The three persons are asked to call numbers again and bringing out cards accordingly the first card arrived at is blue. Continuing with the next two numbers the cards come out red and blue. Finally the six cards are turned faces outwards and they are seen to consist of three matched pairs.

Method. The whole thing depends upon a mere arrangement of six cards, three taken from each pack. They are arranged 1, 2, 3; 1, 2, 3; red, blue, red, blue, red, blue. This packet is loaded into the hat secretly, ample opportunity for this is afforded while the two packs are being examined and shuffled by the audience.

TWO PERSON LOCATION   Annemann

The pack used for this effect of pretended telepathy must be pre-arranged according to any system with which you and your assistant are familiar. Send your assistant out of the room. Give the pack a false shuffle and series of cuts and allow a spectator to make a free selection of the card. Casually cut the pack at the point from which the card was taken. Instructing him to concentrate his thoughts on his card, go to a second person and have him select any card. As you turn back to the first person secretly slip the card that was above the second chosen card to the bottom.

Have the first card pushed back into the pack at any point by the first spectator and square the pack perfectly. Do the same with the second person's card. The pack is taken to the assistant. All he has to do is to note the two bottom cards and take from the pack the two cards that follow these in the system and bring them into the room one in each hand.

Note.—You can put the pack in an envelope and fasten the flap before sending the pack to your assistant. He has a duplicate envelope in his pocket. He simply tears the envelope open, takes out the pack, notes the names of the two cards, writes them on the face of his duplicate envelope and puts the pack into it. He fastens the flap and returns to the room. The denouement follows.

DUAL SYMPATHY   Annemann

Two packs are required, one of which is set up according to any system for the whole pack that you may be familiar with.

By means of the usual equivoque force the unprepared pack on the spectator to shuffle while you false shuffle the set-up pack. Change packs and instruct the spectator to do exactly as you do. Cut your pack several times. He does the same. Take off the top card, look at it, push it into the middle and square the pack. The spectator follows suit. Lift your pack and place it against his forehead, he puts his pack against your 'aching brow' and in doing so gives you a flash of the bottom card. From this you know the card he looked at.

The packs are replaced on the table, cut, and the packs exchanged. The spectator takes his card out and puts it face down. You pretend to take out the card you looked at but really find the card that follows the one you sighted, according to the system. The cards are alike.

See also the chapter 'You'll Do As I Do Card Mysteries . . .'.

ANOTHER SYMPATHETIC MYSTERY   Annemann

The effect is that the performer never approaches the spectator, yet he is able to pick out from his pack the duplicate of the card picked by the party himself.

You ask a spectator to hold a pack face down, cut it at any spot and note the card, then to replace the cut and square the pack. While he concentrates on his card, you run over the faces of your pack and finally take out one card. Spectator removes his card. The two cards are the same.

Two stacked packs, same system, are required. When the spectator cuts his pack, note the approximate position at which it is made. When the spectator replaces his cut, start running through your pack at a point as near as you can estimate that his cut was made, so you must come fairly close to the card selected. Because of the system of arrangement the suits rotate and the colours alternate, making the next part easier. You will have to ask a few leading questions as the person thinks of his card. You may say, for instance, 'It's a red card, isn't it?' or, 'You are thinking of a Heart, aren't you?' If the answer is 'Yes,' take the H nearest on either side, which includes a range of nine cards, and it is next to impossible that you would be that far wrong in making the location. With one query such as 'High or low?', 'Odd or even', 'Spot or picture card?' you have the identity of the card fixed and take it out. Only one or two leads are necessary.

A QUAINT HAPPENING
Annemann

Two packs of cards are provided. A spectator takes one and you take the other. Spectator shuffles his pack, cuts and notes the card cut at. You simply ask the value of the noted card and count off that many cards. The card at that number in your pack proves to be a duplicate of the one noted by the spectator in his pack which you have not even touched.

Both packs have to be arranged. In pack No. 1 take out all the C's and H's and assemble the pack thus: six indifferent cards, thirteen H's and C's, in any order, thirteen indifferent cards, thirteen H's and C's, seven indifferent cards. Put the pack back in its case.

Pack No. 2: Take the H's and the C's and arrange them from the A to the K in sequence. Face the remainder of the cards and put the H's one one side, the C's on the other, replace this pack in its case also and remember on which side the suits are.

Show the two packs and have the spectator hand you one. If he gives you No. 2, let him take No. 1. If he selects No. 1, remove it from its case and give it to him. Tell him to cut the pack and riffle the halves together which will bring all the H's and C's to the middle of the pack. When he cuts about the middle he must get a H or a C. One question, 'You are thinking of a red card,' and the answer gives you all the information you need. You know how to remove your pack from its case so that the proper side is uppermost. Ask the spectator to tell you the value of his card. Suppose he says 'Five'. Count off the cards from the top of your pack and hold the fifth card face down. He names the card he looked at in his pack and you turn over the card you hold.

£1,000 TEST CARD LOCATION

You hand a pack of cards to a spectator and ask him to mix them well. He is then to square them up, make one complete cut, look at the top card of the pack and push this card into the pack so that it is lost. The pack is put on your outstretched hand and you name the selected card.

The method is not absolutely sure-fire but if it fails you repeat and it has never failed on the second trial so far. The pack is pre-arranged in the system you prefer. When you hand it to be shuffled and as soon as the spectator begins to shuffle say, 'When you have them mixed, square the cards up on your left hand. Ready?' This is an innocent way of hurrying him and cutting the shuffle short. He cuts, completes the cut, looks at the top card and thrusts it into the pack.

What has happened is this, the complete chain of the stacked sequence has been broken but there are now a number of packets of cards that are still stacked and the shorter the shuffle the more cards there will be in each bunch. After the cut, which the chances are will be made in one of these bunches, you have simply to sight the bottom card and name the card that follows it in the sequence of the system.

You will be correct at least 80 per cent of the time but if it fails hand the pack back and try again. The odds are very big against a second failure.

SEEING WITH THE FINGERTIPS   Albright

No. 1. Lip-Reading Test

The pack in use must be a pre-arranged one, a switch being made with the ordinary pack of similar backs.

Allow a spectator to make a free selection of one card from the set-up pack. Cut the pack and sight the bottom card. Proceed to name the chosen card from it by pretended lip-reading with the tips of the fingers. Patter about the facility with which deaf people, by simply placing their fingertips to a person's lips, can understand what is being said and continue with: 'Please whisper softly under your breath the name of your card and I will attempt to tell what you are saying by feeling your lips.' Place your fingertips to his lips and name the card.

No. 2. Here's Your Card

Continue with the same pack after making a false shuffle or at least several cuts. Invite someone to call the name of any card. Point out that no one can possibly know just where it lies in the pack. Glimpse the top and bottom cards and calculate its exact position by the system. Have someone blindfold you. Take the cards off the pack one by one pretending to read the index of each with your fingertips. When you reach the card announce it dramatically.

No. 3. The Master's Touch

In gathering up the cards after the last trick, reset the pack and continue as follows:

After false shuffling the pack and having it cut several times with complete cuts, borrow an envelope and hand it with a pencil and a pad to a spectator. Approach another person, fan the pack behind your back and ask him to take out a group of cards, half a dozen or so in a bunch. Say, 'Don't look at them yet, just have them put in the envelope without even counting them and seal the envelope.' While this is being done, cut the cards so that the card just above the packet removed becomes the bottom card of the pack. This bottom card indicates where you are to start when naming the cards in the envelope, while the top card gives the clue for the card to stop it.

Have someone genuinely blindfold you this time since all the information necessary has already been acquired. Touch the envelope with your fingertips and ask the spectator holding the pad and pencil to be ready to jot down the names of the cards as you call them. When you call the last card ask how many you have named, say it is six. Pretend to weigh the envelope carefully and then declare the number is right.

Have the cards taken out, their names called and verified.

PERFECT CARD DIVINATION   Albright

The effect is that a spectator simply thinks of a card. He does not touch a card or write anything. The performer gets the very card thought of.

The pack is pre-arranged thus in groups of six and seven cards:

AH	7C	5S	JD	9D	3D	
JH	10C	2S	6S	7D	3C	
6C	4C	7H	5D	6D	QD	
9H	8S	10S	JC	10D	QS	
6H	2H	8D	5C	5H	AD	KD
9C	2D	8C	JS	KS	AC	4S
QC	9S	QH	KC	3H	2C	3S
8H	KH	4H	7S	4D	AS	10H

In order to assist the spectator in making a mental picture of his card, take off the first group of six, show them and ask spectator to say 'Yes' or 'No', if he sees a card of the same value as his card. Do the same with the following three sets of six cards. Each of these groups has a value, 1, 2, 4 and 8. Add the value every time he says 'Yes'. J is eleven, Q twelve and if he says 'No' four times his card must be a K.

The next four groups of seven cards are to determine the suit. They represent S's, H's, D's and C's. When he says 'No' to a group then the suit that group represents is the suit of his card.

You don't look at the faces of any cards, just drop them aside after being looked at by the spectator. By switching the pack you can introduce the feat at any time.

UNIQUE TELEPHONE TEST   Albright

A spectator just thinks of a friend and mentally recalls his telephone number and name. In order to have several persons concentrate have him write it down and show it to them. From a shuffled pack placed in his pocket, the performer removes cards one at a time, placing certain cards aside face down. Spectator calls the phone number and the cards are turned one by one revealing it. Performer then announces the name.

The shuffled pack is switched for a pre-arranged pack by means of the pocket switch or by any other method you prefer while the phone number and name are obtained by using Baker's notebook, or Anneman's Mental Masterpiece, or any other means at your disposal.

Knowing the number, you have simply to take the cards off the set-up pack in your pocket and each time a card of the required number is reached lay it aside face down. By starting a new heap each time a card is reached the pack can be kept in order for other tricks with the arranged pack.

The name you simply pretend to get by telepathy.

PSYCHOLOGICAL DISCERNMENT   Albright

Effect. Any card thought of revealed. A shuffled pack placed in performer's pocket, the cards brought out one by one, stopping on the card thought of.

Method. Having divined the name of a thought of card by the method explained in 'Perfect Card Divination', or in any other way at your disposal, switch the pack for a pre-arranged pack in putting it in your coat

242

pocket. Then bring the cards out one by one and stop dramatically when you have the right card in your hand.

ANOTHER IMPOSSIBILITY

Two packs are required. In one, which we will call A, the top ten cards are arranged in the Si Stebbins order as follows:

AD, 4C, 7H, 10S, KD, 3C, 6H, 9S, QD, 2C.

From pack B remove the corresponding ten cards and place them at intervals of five cards throughout the pack. Thus the AD's will be the fifth card, 4C's the tenth card and so on. Put this pack on your table, hidden by a handkerchief.

Thus prepared, show pack A and spread the faces showing them all different, then execute the overhand jog shuffle, followed by a riffle shuffle and several false cuts, keeping the top ten cards intact. Fan out the top ten cards widely and ask a spectator to mentally select a card. This done hand him the pack and let him shuffle it thoroughly. Take pack and apparently put it on table as you pick up the handkerchief, really dropping it into a well and bringing the prepared pack to light, or use any other switch you may prefer.

Have the handkerchief folded and tied over your eyes. Take the cards off the pack in batches of five and show the faces to the spectator, repeating to yourself the name of the special card in each set of five. When finally the spectator sees his card and removes it you know its name and you can name it in the usual hesitating way, as if the mental impressions were coming through by degrees.

COUNT THE CUT   Jordan

The pack is arranged in the Si Stebbins order. In the right-hand upper waistcoat pocket place eight cards of any suits from a pack with backs of the same pattern as the stacked pack, as follows: A, 2, 4, 8, K, 3, 10, K.

To begin, execute a false shuffle and have the pack cut several times with complete cuts. Finally ask a spectator to cut off a packet and put the cards in his pocket, doing it in such a way that no one can even make a rough estimate of the number of cards taken. Pick up the lower part of the cut and, in putting it in your inside coat pocket you easily sight the bottom and top cards from which you calculate just how many cards were cut.

Announce that you will draw out cards haphazardly whose total spot values will indicate the number of cards cut. The cards you produce come from your waistcoat pocket and with these you can make any total that is necessary. It is only necessary to remember the order in which they stand in your pocket.

A DISCARD TRICK   Jordan

This trick is designed to follow the 'Count the Cut' trick just explained.

Have the extra cards used for showing the total, in your left hand and with that hand remove the cards from your breast pocket leaving the extra ones behind. Put the pack together in its arranged order. Cut the pack, then have a spectator cut about one-third of the pack, note the next card, place it on the cut-off portion and bury there by placing on it about half the remainder of the pack. He notes the next card also, putting it on top and the rest of pack on top of all.

Instruct him to deal seven heaps, face down, a card at a time. Next to reassemble the pack but putting the last heap on the next to the left, these two on the next and so on. There will be three cards left over, glimpse the bottom one, it is the card that originally lay over the first card the spectator noted. That gives you the first card. To find the second card have him deal the pack into six heaps in the same way as before. There will be one card left over, sight it and since it is the card that originally lay below the second selected card, you are now able to reveal the cards as you please.

CREMO CARD RESTORATION   Jordan

The trick depends on a subtle method of forcing a card. A duplicate card is required, suppose it is a 9D. Arrange the bottom eighteen cards in the manner following, X representing an indifferent card, and D any indifferent D.

   D, X, X, X, D, X, X, X, D, X, X, 9D, X, 9C, X, 9H, X, X.

Place the duplicate 9D near the top of the pack.

Begin by making a false shuffle, not disturbing the stacked cards. Hand the pack to a spectator, telling him to think of a number from ten to fifty-two and then cut the pack into two piles. Force the selection of the packet that formed the bottom of the pack and have him count it, thereby reversing the order of the cards. On the pretence that his packet may not have a sufficient number of cards have him transfer four cards at random from the other packet to the top of the packet he has chosen. The choice of the packet, the counting and this transfer of cards makes it seem impossible there could be any prearrangement. Ask him now to name the number he has mentally selected. When he names it calculate the number of letters in its spelling.

If it is an odd number instruct him to deal a card for each letter, look at the card at the last letter and remember its value, then repeat the spelling and note the last letter card as the suit. If it spells with an even number of letters tell him to turn the next card. This process it will be seen, from the formula above, infallibly forces the 9D. Instruct him then to shuffle the whole pack and deal face up until he comes to the card, the 9D, then to put the pack in his pocket, tear the card into small pieces and hand them to you. Wrap them in a piece of tissue paper, vanish them by palming or switching for a packet of flash paper which you touch off with a lighted cigarette. He takes the pack from his pocket and in it he finds the 9D restored.

STRANGE COINCIDENCE   Jordan

Arrange an ordinary pack thus: any four court cards, four 5's, four 9's, four 8's, four 7's, four 6's, four A's, four 2's, four 3's, four 4's, 4 court cards, four 10's, four court cards.

Ask two spectators to call two numbers, the first to name a number between ten and twenty-five. If it is divisible by four tell the second person to name a number between twelve and seventeen; if, however, there is a remainder of one after such division give him thirteen and eighteen; if a remainder of 2, give him fourteen and nineteen; if one of three give him fifteen and twenty. By this ruse no matter what number the first party chooses, the spots on the card there plus those on the card at the second person's number invariably total ten. Deal down to the numbers called and put the cards aside face down. Replace the dealt cards on the top and ask a third person to call any number over four. If his number is five, six, seven or eight you have ten at each of them by dealing from the bottom. If he gives a larger number than eight, simply draw back one of the tens until the number is reached. Place the ten face up alongside the other two cards. Turn them over and show that the combined spots also total ten.

When drawing the cards from the bottom, deal them face down if you have to go beyond the first ten.

PREMIER BOOK TEST   Annemann

Some preparation is necessary. First remove two A's, then set up all the other cards, regardless of suits, so that any two cards taken together from anywhere in the pack will have values totalling fourteen or fifteen. For example—7, 8, 6, 9, 5, 10, 4, J, 3, Q, 2, K, A, K, and so on. The pack us course, can be cut indefinitely without upsetting the arrangement. Put the pack in its case with the two A's on the top. Open the book to be used in the experiment at pages fourteen–fifteen. On the inside front cover of a small, end-opening notebook write in two columns the first thirteen words from pages fourteen and fifteen, and put the book in your pocket.

To present the feat, remove the cards from the case and leave the two A's inside. Place the pack down beside the book and ask a spectator to step up. Ask him to cut the pack several times, then cut again, take the two cards cut at, and take them and the book to a far corner. Tell him to add the values of the two cards and open the book at the corresponding page.

Invite a second person to take the pack, thoroughly shuffle it, spread the cards face down on the table and turn up any one he wishes. He calls out the value of the card to the man with the book who is told to count to the word at that number on the selected page and memorize the word. You know the page as soon as he begins counting, the even numbered page being always on the left, odd on the right. Take out your notebook and a glance at the inside cover as you open it gives you the word. Write it on the first page, tear this out, fold it and give it to the second spectator to hold. The first man calls the word and the second man reads your writing.

BETWEEN THE LINES   Annemann

This is considered to be one of the cleverest book tests with a pack of cards ever devised. It is simple yet effective.

An ordinary book novel is used, plus a pack of cards stacked in the Si Stebbins order of A, 4, 7, 10, K, 3, 6, 9, Q, 2, 5, 8, J, A, 4, 7, etc.; with suits rotating.

Start by giving the pack a false shuffle or several straight cuts. Put the pack on the table with the book and walk away. While your back is turned you direct a spectator. Tell him to give the pack a complete cut. Then say, 'Better give it another.' Continue, 'Now hold the pack in your hand and deal three cards in a face-up row from left to right from the top of the pack. These cards are going to indicate a page and word in the book. By the way, are there any picture cards among the three?'

If the spectator says 'YES,' you say, 'They're too confusing. Push those three cards away and deal three more the same way. Are there any picture cards there now?' Suppose he says 'No'.

You go on, 'Look at the first two cards. If they are a six and a seven, open the book to page 67. If they are a five and a two, open the book to page 52.'

'You have it? Now look at that last or third card. I want you to start at the top of the page you have and count across on the top line to the word at that number. If it is a three, count to the third word. If an eight, count to the eighth word.

'Now turn the cards on the table face down so I can't see them, and keep your finger on the word you have located.' At this point you turn around, and proceed to reveal the word.

This effect can be got only through the use of a Si Stebbins' stack and no other. There are only four possible combinations of three cards without pictures, A-4-7, 4-7-10, 2-5-8, 3-6-9.

Therefore you previously have looked up and memorized four words, the seventh word on page 14, the eighth word on page 25, the ninth word on page 36, the tenth word on page 47. A good method is to write the words on the left thumbnail. Two of these page numbers are even and two are odd. When you turn around and note spectator holding book with his finger on a word, you know it is an odd or even page because all even numbered pages of all books are on the left and all odd numbered pages of all books are on the right when book is opened before you. Therefore you are immediately down to two words. Start by giving the first letter of one of the two words. If right, continue. If wrong, say, 'Well, the last letter is . . . . .' And you name the last letter of the OTHER word, and spell out the word backwards. Whenever a spectator deals three times on table and has a picture card each time, the fourth or next deal of three will always be A-4-7. In such a case you don't even have to turn around, but can name the word immediately. If you get used to a book you can also judge which of the two words it is as the odd numbers are twenty-two pages apart and the evens twenty-two pages apart too. A book of sixty to eighty pages will be found perfect for this effect.

FATHOMED THOUGHT Annemann

Effect. A spectator cuts off a portion of the pack and takes the next three cards for himself. He adds the values of these cards and opens a book at the page of the same number as the total arrived at. He notes the value of the highest card of the three and counts to the word at that number from the top of the page. The performer announces that very word.

Method. Stack the pack in the Si Stebbins order. There are only thirteen possible combinations of the values of three consecutive cards as shown by the following table. The card represents the card above the three removed by the spectator after he cuts, and you sight this as you assemble the pack following the cut.

Card	Page	Word	Card	Page	Word
Ace	21	10	Eight	16	11
Two	24	11	Nine	18	12
Three	27	12	Ten	22	13
Four	30	13	Jack	12	7
Five	20	11	Queen	15	8
Six	23	12	King	18	9
Seven	26	13			

Use a small pad about three inches by five. Along the top edge write as small as possible the thirteen values and the words which you have taken from the book to be used. When the spectator cuts the pack and removes three cards, reassemble the pack and sight the bottom card. Take out the pad and pencil and note the word in the list. As soon as the page and the word have been found, write it on the lower half of the top sheet of pad, tear off the half-sheet, fold it and give it to be held by a second spectator. Have the word read aloud by the first spectator, then the second man opens your slip and reads the same word.

WINNING THE CUT

Arrange a pack in two packets each containing two A's, two 2's, two 3's, two 4's, and so on, up to two K's.

To begin, false shuffle and false cut, then cut the pack at the two K's which you can easily spot since you pretend to be anxious to cut the pack as near as possible into two equal portions. Have a spectator choose one heap, you take the other. Tell him to shuffle his packet while you shuffle yours, falsely of course.

The packets are placed on the table and you invite the spectator to cut and show the card cut at. Seeing this card, and knowing the arrangement of your cards, you can with a little judgment always cut a higher card than his. Contrive if you can to beat him by one spot, or if he cuts an A, you also cut an A.

Finish by exchanging packs, each shuffling again. In shuffling locate an A and hold a break, or jog a card. You both cut once more and again you win. Cards can now be examined and nothing suspicious can be found.

WIZARD'S WILL   Jordan

Prearrange a pack of cards in any order that you are thoroughly familiar with. False shuffle if you can, if not have a spectator cut as often as he pleases, each time completing the cut. In taking the pack sight the bottom card, from which you know the top card. Deal the cards face down in rows of irregular length, remembering the first card and, by going through the formula as you deal, memorize also the first card of each row.

Now name any card you please and tell the spectator that you will make him select that very card. Invite him to touch a card. Whatever card he touches you know what it is by its position in the arrangement. Pick up the card and lay it aside, not looking at it nor letting anyone else see what it is. Have him touch another card as you name the one just put aside. Continue for three or four cards in just the same way, but if by chance the spectator happens to touch the card you called first, stop right there, turn the cards over and show that he has picked out the very cards you called for.

If, however, he does not touch that card, you do so yourself, calling it whatever the last card may have been. With this card scoop up the packet of cards laid aside, turn the cards face up and they will be in the exact order called.

CARD DIVINATION   Vernon

Arrange the top twenty-six cards of any pack thus: KC, 9C, 5H, 4D,

3S, 2C, 6C, 2S, 4H, JS, AS, 9H, QH, 6S, 7C, 10C, AH, AC, 10H, 4S, 7S, JD, QD, 8S, 5D, 8D.

False shuffle keeping top stack intact. Hand pack to spectator and instruct him to lift off about half the cards and return whichever portion he wishes. If top half is returned, fan the cards for him to make a mental choice of one card. If the lower half is returned use it to show spectator how he must fan his packet in order to mentally choose a card. Selection is always from top packet.

Replace arranged packet on top and shuffle thus; undercut about one-third of cards, injog first card and shuffle on top. Under cut to injog, run seven cards, injog eighth and throw balance on top. Square up making break below jogged card. Cut the pack at break and put the packets on the palms of spectator's outstretched hands. For description of injog see chapter on 'Indispensable Sleights'.

Ask spectator to name his card. The instant the card is named you are able to give instructions for him to find it in the most convincing way. There are twenty-six possible selections and each one is located in a different manner. A careful study of the table below and a few trials will show the simplicity of the proceedings.

Always place the top half on the spectator's left hand. The bottom card of this packet is 2S, top card 4H. Top card of the other heap 6C, and bottom card an indifferent one not used. These three cards are indicators to locate card spectator selects, except in case of a few which are spelt out. If either of these happens to be taken you force the heap and reveal it. For the twenty-three other cards proceed thus:

Seventeen cards are on spectator's left hand, they will be referred to as the right-hand heap since they are on your right hand, the other six are on top of the other cards, call it the left-hand pile.

Right-hand heap. To locate card:

JS.	Show the 2 spot on bottom of R. heap, count down two.
KS.	do as above, but turn the next card.
9H.	Show 4 spot on R. heap, count down four.
QH.	same, but show the next card.
6S.	Show 6 spot on top L. heap, count down six.
7C.	do the same, but show next card.
10C.	Spell out TEN CLUBS.
AH.	Spell out ACE HEARTS.

The remaining cards of this heap spell out either on the final 'S', or by turning the next card. For the last three spell THE.

Left-hand heap. To locate card:

2C.	Show 2 spot at bottom of R. heap, count down two.
3C.	do the same, but show next card.
4D.	Show 4 spot of R. heap, count down four.
5H.	do the same, but show the next card.
9C.	Show 6 spot top of L. heap, count down six.
KC.	do the same, but turn next card.

The list is simple in practice. Do not attempt to memorize it, simply use it as a guide until various combinations have become familiar. It is very effective to have two cards thought of by different persons and locate both at the same time, very often the spots on one card will locate the other.

DOUBLE DIVINO   Jordan

Use two packs which have similar back patterns. From each you discard the same two cards of the same value, suit and colour, as for instance, the 2S and the 2C. Shuffle one pack and then place the cards of the second pack in exactly the same order. Put the two together making one large pack of 100 cards. If you can false shuffle and false cut this enlarged pack it will strengthen the effect, but in any case a series of straight cuts should be made. Next deal the cards into four face-down piles, one card at a time with the fifth card falling on No. 1; the sixth on No. 2; and so on until there are four piles of twenty-five cards each. Let the spectator choose a heap; if he takes No. 1, you pick up No. 3 and vice versa.

The same rules will then apply as in the preceding version but in this case you can actually produce the same card. After working one of the effects with two packets, put them aside and let the spectator take one of the remaining two, while you take the other. Place your packet behind your back and cut it to bring the cards in the exact order of the spectator's packet. Instruct him to lay his cards out in a face-down row and then to push forward any two or three cards he pleases. From your packet, behind your back, you bring forward the same two cards placing them opposite the spectator's cards. Each pair is then turned up and prove to be the same cards.

THE MISSING PAIR   Jordan

For this a new unopened pack of Bicycle cards must be used. These come packed with the Joker at the face, followed by the court cards, then C's, H's, D's and S's. Open the case, take out the cards, discard the Joker and false shuffle. If you cannot do that, then make a series of quick cuts. Hand the pack to spectator who also cuts (complete cuts) as often as he pleases. Instruct him then to deal the cards into four face-down piles, to choose one and shuffle it. Tell him to examine it and if it happens to contain any 2-spot cards of the same value, to pocket them, if not to take any one of the other packets until he finds a pair. This last is a bit of misdirection, there are pairs in every pile.

Pick up the pile from which he has removed a pair and note the C's left, from these you at once know the value of the C taken and therefore the card taken with it. After the cards are dealt into piles, the A, 5, and 9 of C and D, will always be in one heap, the 2, 6, 10, in another, the 3, 7, in a third and the 4, 8, in the fourth. The C and D are the only spot cards that can be paired by the deal.

Note.—Better run through the cards and see that the cards are stacked in the order given.

PREMIER CARD DISCOVERY   Jordan

Arrange the pack beforehand thus, counting from the top: fourteen odd cards, twelve even, fourteen odd and the last twelve even cards. Count the Q's as even cards and the J's and K's odd, discard the Joker, and mix the suits in any order. Spread the cards and no set order will be noticeable. Invite a spectator to cut about the middle and riffle shuffle. Tell him to shuffle so that everyone can see it is thorough (the more evenly the cards fall the better). The central part of the upper half of the pack will consist of odd cards only and the central portion of the lower half will be made up of even cards.

Invite the spectator to divide the pack into two heaps about even, take one card from the centre of either heap, note what it is and place it in the middle of the other heap. The cards are dealt face up and you simply have to watch for an odd card in a series of even cards, or an even card in a run of odd ones. Having spotted the card you can reveal it as you please.

LOCATION   Lane

During the course of other tricks an opportunity can easily be found to get four cards of the same value to the top. Say, for instance, you have got the four J's to that position. Riffle shuffle, leaving them there and have the pack cut. Complete the cut but keep the tip of your little finger between the two portions. Spread the pack, keeping the four J's in the most prominent position, and force one of them. Let it be replaced in another part of the pack, square it up and have the spectator shuffle. On running through the pack you find the J that is by itself and reveal the card in any way you please.

With the same set-up you can allow any card to be drawn, then dividing the pack between the four J's have the card replaced at that point. Shuffle the cards yourself so that you do not disturb the middle cards and let the spectator cut as often as he wishes. You can locate the card at will.

A SIMPLE LOCATION

The necessary pre-arrangement in this case is very simple. Have all thirteen cards of one suit together in the middle. Have a card selected from either the upper or the lower portion of the pack, and see that it is replaced amongst the centre thirteen cards of the one suit. The pack may be cut with complete cuts as often as desired, and you have only to run through the pack to find the odd card amongst the thirteen.

This can just as easily be worked by having a card drawn from amongst the arranged thirteen, and replaced amongst the other cards either above or below. After the cutting you have only to look for the single card of the set suit, or run through the remaining twelve to see which is missing.

OUT OF SIGHT   Larsen

The pack used must be prearranged according to a system with which you are familiar. False shuffle and false cut, or if unable to do that, simply have the pack cut as often as desired, completing the cut each time. Turn your back and, holding the cards behind you, allow a spectator to remove one as you push the cards from the left hand to the right. Split the pack at the point at which the card is taken and, turning slightly towards the spectator say, 'Please look at the card but give me no chance of seeing it.' This action will take the cards behind your back momentarily out of range of the spectator's vision and you push off into

253

the right hand the card that was above the chosen card, that is, the lowest of the cards now in your right hand.

As you again turn your back squarely to the spectator, bring your right hand in front of your body. A glance at the palmed card will tell you the name of the selected card, it being the next in the order. You may drop the palmed card into a waistcoat pocket or add it to the top of the pack in taking the cards from your left hand. Take back the chosen card and slip it under the top card, the pack will again be in the set order ready for further tricks depending upon it.

PROPHESIED DISCOVERY   Larsen

Beforehand separate the red and black suits of a pack. Sort fifteen red cards in the following groups from the face towards the back:

$$10; 9, A; 3, A, 6; 4, K, 2, 4; J, 2, 5, Q, 3.$$

Ignoring the court cards, the spot cards in each group add to ten. Note the tenth card from the face of the packet of black cards, say it is the AC, and write that on a slip of paper. Place the two packets together and you are ready.

Show the slip with the prediction and put it face down on the table. Cut the pack at the colour division and riffle shuffle very openly. Hand the pack to a spectator asking him to sort out the black cards from the red. He will naturally do this holding the pack face up and dealing the cards also face up, thus when the sorting is completed and the packets are turned face down, the AC will be the tenth card of the black pile; and the first fifteen cards of the red pile will consist of the arranged cards. Let the spectator choose either heap. If he chooses the black, hand it to him to hold; if he takes the red, pick it up and deal one card by itself, then separate piles of two, three, four and five cards. Now have him choose any heap and add the values of the spot cards. Due to the prearrangement, he must arrive at ten. On dealing to that number from the top of the black pile he turns up the AC, which conforms with the prediction previously written on the slip you put on the table.

FROM ANOTHER PACK   Larsen

Two packs are necessary. Prearrange one pack in four series of thirteen cards running from the A to the K from the bottom upwards, without regard to suits. From the second pack take the four K's, arrange them in order C, H, S, D, and put them in your right-hand outside pocket. Thus prepared hand the ordinary pack to a spectator to shuffle while you false shuffle the arranged pack. Both packs are then placed on the table side by side and the spectator selects one. Interpret his choice so that he gets the arranged pack. The other is laid aside. Instruct the spectator that while your back is turned he is to cut the pack and complete the cut; then cut off a packet and turn it face up on the table, note the card on its face, take the remainder of the pack and deal cards face down on the table to the number denoted by its value and note that card. He is to count a J as eleven, a Q as twelve and a K as thirteen. Thus if he cuts a 3, he must deal three cards, if a Q, twelve cards and so on. This done his count will always end on a K. You will have to get the colour and suit by leading questions, having these, you name the card in full. Have the other pack shuffled and then drop it into your pocket joining the four K's. Knowing the order in which these are you can produce the right one instantly.

DIVINO   Jordan

From any full pack of cards throw out two of the same colour and value but of differing suits, say for instance the 6D and 6H. Put these aside, fifty cards only being used in the trick. Sort these into their suits in any order, and then place the C's and the H's together in one packet and shuffle them thoroughly. Spread the cards face up on the table and sort the S's and the D's into exactly the same order as the C–H packet and put the packets together.

To present the trick, let the spectators cut the pack as often as they please but see that each cut is completed. Then have a spectator deal the cards into two face-down piles, a card at a time in each packet, and select either heap. If he takes the heap on the first card dealt, cut the other heap which you pick up at the thirteenth card and place these at the bottom. The cards of the same value and the same colour will now lie in exactly the same order in each packet, that is, if the 6D is the top card of your packet, then the 6H is the top card of the spectator's pile. If, however, he takes the No. 2 packet you must cut off twelve cards and put them at the bottom of your pile to attain the same result. When the spectator names any number between one and twenty-five and looks at that card in his packet you have merely to look at the card occupying the same number in your packet and you instantly know the card he's looking at. (His card will be the same value and colour but the other suit.) You can now reveal it in various ways, such as:

1. The spectator having called a number and noted his card, find the matching card and note it secretly. Have both packets shuffled, put together and the pack placed in your pocket. Draw the cards out one at a time until you reach the selected card, throw it face down on the table, have card named and turn it over.

2. After the number is called turn away and find the card in your packet. You may then reveal it simply as a mental feat.

3. A number having been called by the spectator and your packet cut to bring both in sequence, both deal cards face down in unison and stop at the chosen number . . . the cards are the same value and colour.

4. The packet may also be left in the same order as dealt. In that case a very simple calculation will determine at what number the card he calls will lie in your packet, since you know that the fourteenth card of your packet will be of the same colour and suit; if he chose the other packet your thirteenth card will match the top card of his packet. When he has found the card at the number he called, deal cards face up from your packet to show they are well mixed, until you have passed several cards beyond the matching card. Gather them up and name his card in any dramatic way you please.

5. Having sighted the matching card, have the two packets put together and the whole pack shuffled by the spectator. Afterwards run over the faces towards him to prove that the card is still in the pack, and so regain control of it, producing it as you desire.

If the spectator keeps his cards in the same order when counting to the number he chooses the trick can be repeated.

The value of this trick and all others depending on a set-up is greatly enhanced if the pack which has been in use for several tricks, and which has been freely handled and shuffled by the spectators, is switched for the arranged pack.

WILLIAMS'S CARD TRICK

Beforehand arrange a pack of cards so that every second card from the top is a H, thus; the second card, the fourth card, the sixth card and so on are all H's, running from the A up to the 10. In your right-hand coat pocket have a set of duplicate H cards in the same order. Ask a spectator to call a number between one and twenty-one. If it is an even number ask him to count down and look at the card at that number, but if an odd number is called, tell him to deal to that number and look at the next card, and then shuffle the pack. In the meantime, standing at ease with both hands in your trousers pockets, you have ample time to count to the duplicate of the chosen card and palm it in your right hand.

Throw your handkerchief over your right hand, take the pack back in your left hand and lay it on the handkerchief just over the palmed card. Turn your hand so that the pack is upright and facing the front. Fold the back of the handkerchief over to the front, then fold it back on both sides of the pack so that the card at the back is securely held. Grasp the fabric by the four corners and the folds, letting the pack hang down in the improvised bag. With a little shaking the card will be freed from the folds and gradually appear, seeming to come through the fabric.

RED OR BLACK

For this trick it is best to use a new pack of Bicycle cards, preferably of the air-cushion finish, with white border. Sort out the black and the red cards. Place a red card and a black card back to back and continue this arrangement with all of the cards, so that all the black cards are face upwards and the red cards face downwards. Show the pack fanned, it will appear to consist of all black cards, the backs of the red cards will not show, partly owing to the white borders and partly because the backs tend to stick together and do not slip as perfectly as the face surfaces.

Square the pack, covering the cards with the right hand and holding the face card only with it. Now drop the left hand about an inch carrying with it the rest of the cards, and slip the tip of the left thumb under the outer side of the pack and rapidly turn it over sideways. Take off the face card with the right hand, blow on it and put it on the bottom. Again spread the pack, this time the red cards only will show.

EXCELLO CARD DISCOVERY

Sort out the pack into its four suits, the cards in haphazard order, making one pile for each suit. Assemble the pack by picking one card from each packet in rotation. When you present the trick make a false shuffle and cuts if possible, if not, make a series of straight cuts. Have a card freely selected but keep the two parts of the pack separated at that point. Push four cards from the top of the bottom portion over to the right and hold the division at that point. Divide the pack here for the return of the chosen card. It will be, therefore, four cards lower in the pack than it was originally.

Let the spectator make as many complete cuts as he likes. To find the card, run over the faces and when you come to two cards of the same suit together, the one nearest the face of the pack will be the card. You can bring it to the top or bottom by cutting and then deal with it as you please.

NAMING CHOSEN CARD

Beforehand place all the even cards at the bottom of the pack, counting the Q's as even cards, J's and K's as odd. Memorize the bottom card. You give a spectator the following instructions—he is to cut about one-third of the pack, note the card at the bottom of the cards so cut, riffle shuffle the cut cards into the remainder of the pack and then cut the pack with complete cuts several times.

When you return you have merely to run through the pack face up and find the card which is the first odd card above you key card, that is the original bottom card of the pack.

PSYCHIC CARD TEST   Annemann

Two slates, two pieces of chalk and a stacked pack is required for this trick.

False shuffle and cut the pack if you can, if not simply make a series of quick cuts with the pack in your hands in position for shuffling. Spread the pack on the table in as long a row as you can manage. Have a spectator draw a card from the line and note the spot it is taken from. Tell him to take one of the slates and piece of chalk, go to a distant part of the room and draw a rough picture of his card. In the meantime you have casually picked up the cards, first the part of the row above the spot from which he took a card and then gathered up the rest using these as a scoop. A glimpse of the bottom card allows you to calculate what card the spectator took. Place the pack aside, pick up the other slate and also draw a rough picture of that card. The whole effect depends upon the presentation.

A CARD AND A NUMBER   Baker

Two packs are required and both must be arranged in the same order such as the Si Stebbins or the 'Eight Kings, etc.'. Have both packs in their cases and allow a free choice of either. Hand the chosen pack to a spectator to place in his pocket. Ask another person to call any number from one to fifty-two. Suppose twenty-three is called. Break the pack as near to that number as you can estimate, a glance at the bottom card at the break will at once give you the position of the twenty-third card. You will rarely be more than two or three cards away from it. Proceed to force this twenty-third card on a second spectator.

You announce that you will show a strange effect of sympathy between the two packs, by making the same card as that chosen to locate itself at the very number called in the pack which was placed in a spectator's pocket before the number was called. The spectator takes the pack from his pocket, counts down to the number called and finds there the duplicate of the chosen card.

The trick is very effective and the ideal system to use for it is Nikola's for two reasons: the cards are known by their numbers in the pack and the pack can be shown and handled freely since the cards are not in any recognizable order, that is to the layman.

MEDIUMISTIC STUNT NO. 1   Si Stebbins

Pack is handed to a spectator with a request to turn his back and cut wherever he pleases. He is then to deal as many cards as he pleases, stopping at any card whatsoever; he is to look at this card and note what it is, then put it face down on the table and deal four cards on it. These five cards he mixes together and then hands them to you.

To find the card you look for two cards of the same suit amongst the five and name the higher one. The pack has been set up in the Si Stebbins order, each card being three points higher than the preceding one and the suits being in rotation. The result given must follow.

MEDIUMISTIC STUNT NO. 2   Si Stebbins

The pack is set up in the Si Stebbins order. Make a false shuffle and execute several false cuts. Invite a spectator to take out a bunch of cards, all at once, from any part of the pack. He is now to take one and lay the

259

rest aside. This card is sealed in the innermost of a nest of three envelopes which you hand to him. While this is being done you reassemble the pack by placing the remainder of the spectator's bunch of cards on the pack, which you had cut at the point at which he removed them. A glance at these will tell you which card is missing from the sequence.

Go to a second spectator and have him draw a card. By cutting at the point from which it was drawn and sighting the bottom card of the upper packet you know the card he holds and so proceed to read his mind. Replace his card on the top of the bottom packet and return to the first person. Let him place the nest of envelopes on your left hand and with the usual hesitation get the colour, suit and value of his card.

Open the envelope, show the card and replace this card in its proper position—the pack will again be in order.

SYSTEM

Beforehand the pack is arranged in the 'Eight Kings, etc.' order, but each of the four suits is arranged separately. Put the pack in its case and hand it thus to a spectator when you are about to present the trick. Instruct him that he is to remove the pack from the case, cut it into two portions and riffle shuffle them carefully, once only, select one card from each heap and have their names noted. He is then to riffle shuffle the two packets together, square the pack and replace the two cards in it anywhere he pleases, either together or separately, and place the pack on the table. While this is being done you turn your back or leave the room. Be sure that the spectator thoroughly understands what he is to do.

When you turn around or re-enter the room, you take the pack, run over the faces of the cards and pick out the two chosen ones. You are enabled to do this infallibly because when the four suits are segregated the first riffle shuffle distributes the cards of each suit throughout half the pack in the same order and the second shuffle sends them throughout the pack still in the same order. Therefore if the intervening cards are removed each suit will be found in the original 'Eight Kings, etc.' order. To find the selected cards follow each suit through the pack; the two cards out of place will be the selected cards.

THE KNOCKOUT   By Clayton Brown

Effect. Two ordinary packs of cards are introduced and shuffled. One is temporarily placed upon the table, while the performer takes the other and has three cards freely selected by as many spectators, who immediately place the cards in their pockets without even looking at them. The performer's assistant is then introduced as the medium and is handed the other pack from the table. Without a word from anybody, she immediately locates the selected cards. The first pack is left in the hands of some disinterested party after the cards have been selected.

Secret. Two packs of cards with backs alike are essential. One pack is arranged in the well-known Si Stebbins style, or 8, K, 3, 10, 2, etc.— whichever is preferred. Come forward with the two packs and offer one to a spectator to shuffle, while you false shuffle the other (the prepared one) Place the pack that the spectator has shuffled on the table, in plain sight of all. Now for the under-handed business: Offer a card to be selected from your pack (the prepared one) in the same manner that you would in any other trick, but in closing the fan, slip out the card that was over the selected one, into the palm of the right hand. Then calmly place it on the top of the pack. This is the tell-tale card that furnishes the clue as to what the selected card is. The spectator places his card in his pocket without even looking at it, and particularly without letting those around him see it. Repeat these operations until you have three cards selected. Then you will have key cards on the pack. Step over to your table and pick up the other pack, placing the three key cards on it. You have previously palmed these off and given the pack to someone to hold. Hand the other pack to the medium and step into the audience without a word. The medium looks at the three top cards in running through the pack and figures back three cards according to the system, picking out the duplicates of those originally selected.

This effect should be played up strong, and the cards drawn out one by one with great 'concentration'. The wise ones will be fooled the most, for they are all looking for codes.

A PREARRANGED PACK OF CARDS THAT CAN BE SHUFFLED

Arrange your pack in the Si Stebbins order, then with the pack face up deal the first card face down and on top of this card place the next card and continue until you lay out twenty-six pairs. Now take each top card and trim it short and narrow. You now have the cards in pairs, assemble and you can now riffle shuffle pack with freedom. Each pair will fall separate. A card is removed while performer riffles the pack by looking at the card below (long card); performer knows the value of the selected card, by adding three points and suit. Should the card be the 10C, the selected card must be the KH.

AMAZING MEMORY   Annemann

To arrange a pack for this feat first sort out the cards of each suit, then take the C's and the H's and shuffle them thoroughly. Spread the cards and then sort the S's and the D's in exactly the same order with the S's corresponding with C's set-up and D's with the H set up. Deal the S's and D's face down on the table, thus reversing their order, and then put the C–H packet on top. Thus the top and bottom cards will be of the same colour and value and, knowing one, you can at once name the other.

With a pack so arranged, execute a false shuffle and cut, and show the faces to prove the cards are well mixed. Next turn the faces towards you and run over the cards rather slowly pretending to memorize them. Offer the pack to a spectator asking him to make a free choice. Run the cards one by one counting them and note the number of the card chosen. Turn the pack and run over the cards from the bottom. To find the key to the card selected. For example: suppose the card drawn was the sixteenth from the top. You have merely to note the sixteenth card from the bottom to find the card of the same value as the other suit of the same colour. Note the next card and continue running the cards until you reach the corresponding card of the same colour, stop, call the name of the chosen card and have it returned at this location. The pack will then be in order for a repetition of the trick.

SIX PILES

For this trick you must make an impromptu set-up with twelve cards of any one suit, six at the top and six at the bottom. To do this run through the pack to take out the Joker and seize this opportunity to get several cards of one suit, say H's to the top and bottom of the pack. Remarking that you have also to eliminate four other cards, take out one card of the suit decided on, H, and any three cards of other suits. The pretence of searching for special cards covers the placing of the remainder of the H's in the required positions. Lay the four discards and the Joker aside. Riffle shuffle without disturbing the six top and the six bottom cards. Hand the pack to a spectator telling him to deal six cards in a row and continue dealing one card at a time on these in rotation. The result is that each pile has a H at top and bottom.

Instruct the spectator that, while your back is turned he is to take a card from the middle of any heap, note it, place it on top of any other heap and assemble the piles in any order he pleases. Finally he is to write the name of the card on a slip, fold it and put it on the table. Turn around and spread the pack face up on the table, run your hand over the line telling him to think 'Stop' when you reach his card. Take a mental note of the card between two H's but do not stop. Gather the pack and lay it aside, then pretend to get the name of the card by putting your hand to his forehead. Name it in the usual piecemeal manner. The slip is opened and your mind-reading is verified.

MEPHISTO'S MESSAGE

Beforehand arrange sixteen cards of mixed suits on the top of the pack as follows: 3, 2, court card, 5; 2, court card, 5, 3; court card, 5, 3, 2; 5, 3, 2, court card. Note that these cards make up four groups of four cards, the spots on which, counting court cards as two, amount to twelve. Count to the twelfth card from the bottom and write its name on a slip of paper and seal it in an envelope.

Thus prepared, have a spectator cut the pack in half. Tell him to deal the cards in the lower packet face down and count them, and then snap a rubber band around them and put the packet in his pocket. Next instruct him to deal from the upper packet four hands of four cards each. It makes no difference whether he deals four cards at a time or, separately, but whichever method he adopts, remark that you meant him to deal the other way but let it go. Let him select any pile, and place his hand on it, while you pick up the other three and shuffle them back into the pack. The spectator counts the spots on the four chosen cards and gets the total twelve. He then takes the packet from his pocket and counts down to the twelfth card and finds we will suppose, the AC. On opening the envelope he finds this card named in your prediction.

NAME OF CARD   R. W. Hull

Prearrange the cards of a full pack with the Joker as follows—JC, 4S, AH, 4H, 3C, 8H, 10C, 5C, 9C, 9S, 9H, QC, QS, 6H, 5S, 5H, 7H, 6S, 3D,

6D, 5D, 9D, 8D, 3H, Joker, 2D, AS, 2S reversed, AD, 2H with an X on its face, 7D, 4D, 10D, 3S, QD, KD, JD, QH, KS, 10H, 7S, 7C, KC, JH, 10S, 2C, 6C, 8S, 8C, 4C, AC, JS with an X on its back, KH.

With a pack in this order in hand, false shuffle and false cut, then ask someone to think of a card and then name it. Proceed to discover it either by spelling its name, and this applies to forty-two cards, or in different ways applied to ten special cards, these are:

JC, KH, 2S, AS, 2H, JS, JS, 2D, 2D, 3H and the Joker.

If one of them is called proceed as under:

JACK OF CLUBS. Snap the back of the pack ordering it to rise to the top. Show it.

KING OF HEARTS. Same procedure sending card to bottom.

TWO OF SPADES. Reversed in the pack. Simply order it to do so.

ACE OF SPADES. This is the card above the reversed 2S. Order the card below it to reverse itself.

ACE OF DIAMONDS. Order card above it to reverse itself.

TWO OF HEARTS. Show that you have foretold the choice of this card by marking an X on it.

JACK OF SPADES. Same as for 2H but mark is on the back.

TWO OF DIAMONDS. Order the Joker to locate the card.

THREE OF HEARTS. Same as for 2D.

THE JOKER. Take a card for each letter of the sentence, 'You have called for the Joker' and turn next card.

Detailed spelling table for the other cards

Where an X appears turn the card after the last letter

HEARTS

ACE. Spell 'HEART' and hold the five cards face down and ask if 'ACE' shall be spelt from top or bottom. Either fits.

TWO. THREE. See above.

FOUR. Spell 'FOUR' remove the cards, snap on the back saying, 'You want a Heart?' Show the 4H.

FIVE. Spell 'THE FIVE OF HEARTS.' X.

SIX. Spell 'THE SIX OF HEARTS.'

SEVEN. Spell 'THE SEVEN OF HEARTS.'

EIGHT. Spell 'EIGHT' take next card and say 'HEART'. Show it.

NINE. Spell 'NINE HEARTS.' X.

TEN. Spell 'THE TEN OF HEARTS' from the bottom of pack.

JACK. Spell 'JACK HEARTS' from the bottom.

QUEEN. Spell 'THE QUEEN OF HEARTS' from the bottom.

KING. See above.

DIAMONDS

ACE. See above.

TWO. See above.

THREE. Spell 'THE THREE OF DIAMONDS.' X.

FOUR. Spell 'THE FOUR SPOT OF DIAMONDS' from bottom.

FIVE. Spell 'THE FIVE SPOT OF DIAMONDS.'

SIX. Spell 'THE SIX SPOT OF DIAMONDS.'

SEVEN. Spell 'THE SEVEN SPOT OF DIAMONDS' from bottom.

EIGHT. Spell 'THE EIGHT SPOT OF DIAMONDS.' X.

NINE. Spell 'THE NINE SPOT OF DIAMONDS.' X.

TEN. Spell 'THE TEN SPOT OF DIAMONDS' from bottom.

JACK. Spell 'THE JACK OF DIAMONDS.'

QUEEN. Spell 'THE QUEEN OF DIAMONDS' from bottom.

KING. Spell 'THE KING OF DIAMONDS' from bottom.

CLUBS

ACE. Spell 'CLUBS' from bottom, then 'ACE' from top or bottom of these five cards.

TWO. Spell 'TWO CLUBS.'

THREE. Spell 'THREE' then 'CLUBS' with the same cards and show.

FOUR. Spell 'FOUR' from bottom, then 'CLUB' with same cards and show.

FIVE. Spell 'FIVE CLUB.'

SIX. Spell 'SIX CLUB' from bottom.

SEVEN. Spell 'SEVEN OF CLUBS' from bottom.

EIGHT. Spell 'EIGHT' from bottom, then 'CLUBS' with same cards.

NINE. Spell 'NINE CLUBS.'

TEN. Spell 'TEN CLUB.'

JACK. See above.

QUEEN. Spell 'QUEEN OF CLUBS.'

KING. Spell 'KING OF CLUBS.'

SPADES

ACE. See above.

TWO. See above.

THREE. Spell 'THE THREE SPOT OF SPADES.'

FOUR. Order to top. Turn top card to show it is not there first then make a double lift.

FIVE. Spell 'THE FIVE OF SPADES.'

SIX. Spell 'THE SIX SPOT OF SPADES.'

SEVEN. Spell 'SEVEN OF SPADES.'

EIGHT. Spell 'EIGHT' from bottom take off two cards on last letter and spell 'SPADES' show card.

NINE. Spell 'NINE SPADES.'

TEN. Spell 'TEN SPADES' from bottom.

JACK. See above.

QUEEN. Spell 'QUEEN OF SPADES.'

KING. Spell 'THE KING OF SPADES' from bottom.

NEW PACK DETECTION   Jordan

For this trick arrange to have a new unopened pack of Bicycle cards. Hand this to a spectator and ask him to break the seal, take out the cards, cut them several times and then deal two face-down heaps, a card to each. Two persons each take one heap and each shuffles thoroughly. Then each draws a card from the other's packet and shuffles it into his own. You find both cards at will.

The trick depends on the fact that Bicycle cards are packed in one of two ways:

1. A to 10, S: 10 to A, D: 10 to A, H: 10 to A, C: J to K, C: J to K, S: J to K, D: J to K, H: Joker.

2. A to 10, C: A to 10, H: A to 10, D: 10 to A, S: K to J, S: K to J, C: K to J, H: K to J, D: Joker.

Fan the pack and discard Joker. When the spectator cuts and deals into two packets each will consist of a certain easily learned set of twenty-six cards, so that when a strange card is introduced into either set it is readily recognizable.

FOUR-FOLD SYMPATHY

Two packs are used, one with blue backs, the other with red backs, and both having white borders around the back patterns. Remove from the blue pack the KS, AH, 10D, 3S, and put them on the top in that order followed by an indifferent card as the top card. Also take out the 7C, and put it on the bottom. From the red pack take out the same cards making a packet of them in the same order, with an indifferent card on the top and the 7C as the bottom card, and place this packet of red cards at the bottom of the blue pack.

To perform the trick, place the two packs on the table and force the red pack on a spectator using the usual equivoque. Ask him to shuffle his pack while you shuffle the blue pack. You can do this by a riffle shuffle without disturbing the top and bottom cards, but the cards must be well covered by the hands to avoid exposing the red-backed cards on the bottom. Secretly make a break with your right thumb at the inner end of your pack separating the six red cards from the blue cards. Take the red pack from the spectator with your left hand and put the two packs together for a moment pretending to judge the thickness of the pile to decide how many packets you should make. Really you let the six red cards join the red pack at the top. Separate the two packs again and place them on the table. Cut the blue pack into two packets and invite the spectator to do the same with the red pack. Again cut each of your piles in half, the spectator follows suit. We will call the piles A, B, C, D. In making the cuts see that the spectator does exactly the same as you do so that the resulting packets are opposite one another. In each case the arranged cards are on top of pile D. Turn the top cards of your four piles face up, spectator does the same. Call attention to the fact that they are just any cards at all and have them all turned down again. Now move the top cards of your four piles from one heap to another apparently in a haphazard fashion, but in such a way that ultimately you have one of the four cards, KS, AH, 10D, 3S, on top of each heap. The spectator makes each move as you do, so that the four duplicates in his pack are brought to the same locations. The top cards are turned and shown to match, and are put aside.

The 7C, will be the bottom card of your packet A, while the red 7C is on the top of the spectator's heap D. Assemble the pack by placing D on C, DC on B and DCB on A, the spectator doing the same. Turn your pack face up showing the 7C, and tell the spectator to turn over the top card of his pack, and it also proves to be the 7C.

TELEPATHIC CONTROL

Under the pretence of taking the Joker out of a well-shuffled pack, rapidly memorize the five bottom cards. The quickest and easiest way is to first take the values only, as for instance 7, 5, Q, 9, 4, then memorize the suits in the same fashion. Riffle shuffle several times, but do not disturb these five bottom cards.

Hand the pack to a spectator and have him make several complete cuts. He then fans the pack and hands you four cards as you call for them. The first three cards called are just indifferent ones, but are not among the four cards, name the bottom card of the five memorized and have the pack cut at this point, thus bringing the other four cards to the bottom of the pack. Tell the spectator to deal the cards into four face-down heaps with the result that you have the four memorized cards one at the top of each heap. Spectator chooses a heap and looks at the top card. You tell him to cut the packet, look at the card, cut and tell you if it is odd or even, then you name the top card. This odd or even business is for misdirection only.

The other three cards can be read in the same way. *Note.*—It is easier to have five cards set up in a formula you know by heart and add them to the bottom of the pack just before you do the trick.

CARDS AND POCKETS   Buckley

Effect. After shuffling and cutting the cards the performer instantly calls the number of cards in a packet cut off. After repeating this effect several times he divides the packet into four portions and puts each packet in a different pocket. Any card called for is then instantly produced.

Method. The cards are arranged in four sections thus:

No. 1. AH, 2H, 3S, 4S, 5S, 6D, 7D, 8D, 9C, 10C, JC, QH, KH.
No. 2. AC, 2C, 3H, 4H, 5H, 6S, 7S, 8S, 9D, 10D, JD, QC, KC.
No. 3. AD, 2D, 3C, 4C, 5C, 6H, 7H, 8H, 9S, 10S, JS, QD, KD.
No. 4. AS, 2S, 3D, 4D, 5D, 6C, 7C, 8C, 9H, 10H, JH, QS, KS.

Refer always to the first packet as the H packet; the second as the C packet; the third the D packet and the fourth the S packet. Having the packets so arranged face down, put No. 1 on No. 2, these two on No. 3, and these on No. 4. Thus assembled the top card will be the AH and the bottom card the KS. The packets being in numerical order (J counting eleven, Q, twelve and K, thirteen), the value of the face card of the packet cut off will denote the number of cards in the packet, for instance, if the face card is a 7 and the packet contains a few cards only their number is seven; if, however, there are obviously more than seven cards, simply add thirteen and call twenty as the number of cards. Finally, if you cut more than half the pack you must add twenty-six to the value of the face card of the cut.

For the second effect riffle the ends of the cards, locate the KH (thirteenth card), lift off packet No. 1 and put it in your left side coat pocket; riffle next to the KC and put packet No. 2 in your right side coat pocket; divide the remainder at the KD and put No. 3 in right trousers pocket and No. 4 in left trousers pocket. A very simple formula will enable you to find any card called for. Divide the numerical value of the card by three and the answer, ignoring the remainder if any, will designate the pocket containing the card. For example the 7H is called for. Three goes into seven twice, so two therefore is the key number. The suit being H refer to the H pocket (left side coat pocket) and count two, counting the right coat pocket one and the right trousers pocket 2; the required card must therefore be in the right trousers pocket and as the packet is in numerical order it must be the seventh card.

Again, suppose the JC is called for; three into eleven gives three for the answer. The suit being C, refer to the C packet in the right coat pocket and count three from it in the same direction as given in the first example, bringing you to the left coat pocket in which the card lies. Since the A and the 2 cannot be divided by three, they will be found in the pocket of the suit called for.

Place the packets in the pockets with the faces outwards. When a card is brought out do not remove it singly, count to the card, square the others behind it and bring them all out as one card, then replace them in the pocket so that the order of each packet is not disturbed.

COUNT DOWN DETECTION   Larsen

Arrange thirteen cards (seven red and six black) in some well-known order such as the 'Eight Kings, etc.'. In presenting the trick make a false riffle leaving the packet on the top undisturbed. Hand the pack to a spectator telling him that, when you turn your back, he is to count off any small number of cards, look at the card counted to, remember it, replace it anywhere in the pack and shuffle the cards thoroughly. This done you turn around and take the pack. Ignore the first two cards of the arrangement, the count will always be more than two. Of the eleven cards remaining there are six black and five red. Ask whether the card was red or black as you run over the faces of the cards. If the answer is red, bring the five red to the top in their arranged order. Boldly announce that you have put the card on the top of the pack. The card is named and you show it as being the top one by turning two or more as one card. If the card is a black one do the same thing with the six black cards.

It has been suggested that after the colour of the chosen card has been ascertained, one of the five or six cards be reversed in the middle, one or two brought to the bottom, one or two to the top and one palmed off and put in a pocket. When the card is named it can at once be shown in one of these positions and the necessity for the lifting of perhaps five or six cards is eliminated.

THE ADVENTURES OF DIAMOND JACK By Namreh

A little story based on the pack of cards. First, let me introduce our hero, Diamond Jack (JD). No relation to Diamond Joe. Jack was just twenty-six (2S, 6S), handsome, a regular King of Hearts (KH). He had been an Ace (AD) in the war, but now he was poor. In fact, he had not been flush (flush in S's, K-Q-J-10-9) for a long time. He often felt blue (show blue back of card) because he belonged to only one club (AC) while his friends belonged to two or three (2C and 3C). But Jack was proud; his hands (two fans of cards) had never turned a spade (AS).

One day at seven (7S) he had a date with a swell queen (QD). She was a 'pip' (snap spot of Q), but when he arrived she was not on *deck* (look for Q on top of pack). 'That is a nasty cut' (cut the cards, said Jack. So he picked up another blonde queen (pick up QH from table) and ate (8S) with her. The head-waiter said he had a full-house (8H, 8D, 8C, 3H and 3D), but he seated them anyway, as head-waiters will. And say, she ate (8H) and ate (8D) and ate (8C). She ordered several club steaks (throw down 8C) and everything on the card (hold up 3H, back to them). The waiter brought tray (3H) after tray (3D) of food.

But finally, as she was finishing off with a fancy, cherry-coloured pear (7H and 7D), Jack realized he had only a ten and a five (10D and 5D). Luckily the bill was only thirteen spots (10C and 3S), but when the waiter added two more (deal last two cards on table), Jack asked, 'What for?' (4S).

'My tip,' said the dirty knave (JC).

'The deuce (2D) you say,' said Jack. 'I don't mind forking (4C, KC) over 10 per cent (10H), but this is outrageous.'

Here is where the queen dropped out of sight (drop QH on floor).

Then the waiter spotted the diamonds (6D) on Jack's cravat and snatched for them. Jack pasted a grand slam in his fifth rib near the heart (5H). 'Nein, Nein, Nein,' (9D, 9C, 9H) cry the German waiters excitedly. But the manager sicks (6H) the police on them. In fact, he called out half of the force (4H, 4D). In the shuffle (shuffle cards on table) that followed, Jack fanned a few (fan), but he had the whole pack after him, and finally six or seven clubs (6C, 7C) descended at once. His mind went blank (blank card).

When he awoke he was facing Judge King (KD). A lawyer was appointed to handle the case (pick up card case from table). 'Your name,' said the Judge.

'Diamond Jack,' (JD) shouted our hero.

'Not so much snap,' (snap the cards) said the Judge.

Just then Jack saw his old sweetheart, Mary McClub (QC) from Oireland, who was acting as court stenographer.

'Your Honour, I was almost robbed by a knave (JH), a *highjacker* (hold JH above your head), but this little girl will testify to my character.'

'Let me get this *straight*' (K-Q-J-10-9 of S, same as used before), said Judge King.

'I love her with an aching heart,' (AD, KD, AH) said Jack.

'So hearts (AH) are trumps?' asked the Judge.

'I'm no joker,' (Joker) said Jack.

'So you want to marry her?'

'I do,' said Jack, handing over a *solitaire* (AD).

'Accept my stamp of approval,' (snap revenue stamp on card-case) finished the Judge.

And so they became two of a kind (5S and 5C), two minds with but a single thought, two hearts (2H) that beat as one (AH). Finis.

SEQUENCE

In the following prearrangement please note that the italic cards (QH, JD, AD, KD, QC, AH and the straight flush in S's) are used two and three times. These are to be laid aside, so that they may be obtained later without hesitation:

QH on table, *JD*, 6S-2S, KH, *AD*, *K-Q-J-10-9 of S*, blue, AC, 2C, 3C, 2 fans, AS, 7S, QD, pip, pack, cut, pick up *QH*, 8S, full-house (three 8's, two 3's), 8H-8D-8C, 8C, card, 3H-3D, 7H-7D, 10D-5D, 10C-3S, deal 2, 4S, JC, 2D, 4C-KC, 10H, *QH*, 6D, 5H, 9D-9C-9H, 6H, 4H-4D, shuffle, fan three, 6C 7C, blank, *KD*, case, *JD*, snap, *QC*, JH high, *QC*, *K-Q-J-10-9 of S* as used above, *AD-KD-AH*, *AH*, Joker, *AD*, stamp, 5S-5C, 2H, *AH*.

13

Magic With a Svengali Pack of Cards

THE SVENGALI PACK

This special pack consists of twenty-six ordinary cards, all different, and twenty-six short cards all of the same suit and value. The latter may be narrower as well as shorter, but short duplicates only are generally used. The pack is set up by arranging the two sets alternately, thus every other card from the top of the pack is a card of the same suit and value. Burling Hull in his *Sealed Mysteries* claims its invention and that he copyrighted it in 1909. The Svengali pack soon leaped into wide popularity and into the hands of street pedlars. Many thousands of packs must have been sold, and are still selling, and yet its use must not be despised by magicians on that account. Like many other weapons in the magicians' armoury it can be used even amongst people who know the principle without their suspicions being aroused.

VARIOUS METHODS OF HANDLING THE PACK

Briefly the pack is used thus: After giving the cards a riffle shuffle, which does not disturb the arrangement, square the pack and hold it face down with the outer end slightly raised towards the spectators. Slowly ruffle the cards by placing the tip of the right forefinger on the outer edges of the cards, bend the pack slightly upwards and release the cards rather slowly, every card will be seen to be different. The short cards do not appear since the cards fall in pairs. Lowering the pack, again ruffle the cards and invite a spectator to insert his finger-tip (or the blade of a knife), at any point he desires. No matter where he does this his finger will rest on the back of one of the short cards. Divide the

272

pack at this point, let the spectator take out that card and the force is made.

It will be noted that the bottom card of the portion lifted off with the right hand is an indifferent card as is also the top card of the left-hand portion after the card has been withdrawn; by showing these cards the apparent fairness of the choice is established.

From this simple principle many astonishing effects have been developed and it is safe to say that there are possibilities of further card miracles waiting to be evolved by ingenious minds.

The greatest effect is obtained by switching a pack that has been used for several tricks, in the course of which the spectators have freely handled and shuffled the cards, for a Svengali pack. Results can then be obtained which to the layman appear miraculous. In the following pages a method will be found for secretly exchanging the duplicate cards for twenty-six indifferent cards which, with the other twenty-six cards of the Svengali pack make up a complete pack that can be freely handled and examined by the spectators, thus leaving no clue to the feats performed.

Besides the ruffling method of showing all the cards different you may cut small packets from the top laying them down face up. Every face card will be different since you can only cut at a long card. Assemble the pack again and have it cut several times. This is a very convincing method.

In addition to the thrusting of a finger or knife blade into the pack for the choice of a card, you may cut the pack by the ends into several piles and have any one of them chosen. The top card of the heap chosen is lifted off by the spectator.

A second method of showing all the cards different is to hold the pack upright in the right hand, thumb at the top, fingers at the bottom, release the cards slowly from the thumb and they will fall forward in pairs, every card showing a different face. This is more convincing than the ruffle.

Magic With a Svengali Pack of Cards

SIMPLE EFFECTS

Before explaining some of the special tricks that have been devised for the use of this pack and to enable the reader to become used to the proper handling of the pack, some of the simpler feats will be described first.

1. Show the cards all different by ruffling them, riffle shuffle and make a series of cuts each time showing a different card on the face of the right-hand portion. Invite a spectator to insert his forefinger-tip at any point he desires. Let him remove the card, note it and you read his mind by naming the card. Casually show the bottom card of those in your right hand, that is the cards above the one he removed and also the top card of the portion in your left hand.

2. Have the card replaced in the same position and drop the right-hand portion on top. Square the pack and cut several times to make the impression that the card is lost in the pack. Announce that you will place the cards, one by one, face down on the table and invite the spectator to call 'Stop' at any time he wishes. Seeing that cutting the cards has left one of the shorts on the top, it follows that you have only to stop on any odd number to have a duplicate of the selected card in your hand. If, however, the spectator calls on an even card simply place it on top of the cards already on the table and say, 'And the very next card will be your card.' Turn the next card and show it, then place it on top of the pile on the table, pick up the pile, being careful not to expose the bottom card, and place it on top of the remainder in your left hand.

3. Hand the top card, the one already chosen and ask the spectator to place the tip of his forefinger on its back and hold it there for a few seconds, then placing your left hand with the pack behind your back, you take the card in your right hand and say you will push it into the pack behind your back so that no one can possibly know just what position it will occupy. Pretend to do this but simply put the card on the top of the pack. Bring the pack forward and again show that every card is different by making a series of cuts. Then ruffle the cards inviting the spectator to insert his finger-tip anywhere he likes. He does this and you lift off the portion above his finger, while he names the card (you have forgotten what it was?). Ask him to draw out the card and turn it over—and he finds it's his card. Again show that the card preceding it and the card following it are quite different cards.

4. The above effects may very well follow one another but, of course, you cannot keep on using the same forced card indefinitely.

Magic With a Svengali Pack of Cards

A pretended prediction trick can be easily worked with the Svengali pack. After showing the cards all different and riffle shuffling the pack, you write the name of the force card on a slip of paper, fold it, and hand it to a spectator to hold. Have a spectator select a card as above with his finger-tip, or a knife blade, as you ruffle the cards, or by his making a simple cut. Lay the card face down on the table, have the spectator read your prediction then let him turn the card over.

5. Naturally, the use of this pack makes a sure-fire force. It can be used to force two cards by having two sets of thirteen similar cards instead of the usual twenty-six. However, you should be prepared to make a switch to an unprepared pack after the force. Various methods for effecting this will be explained here since they are indispensable if you wish to do a series of tricks with Svengali packs. It is hardly necessary to point out that the back patterns of all the packs must be the same.

SWITCHING PACKS

1. Pack in right hip pocket. Give some reason for putting the pack behind your back. Have it in your left hand, as the right hand goes to the back, pull out the pack from the hip pocket, change the packs and slip that just taken from the left hand into the right hip pocket. A slight turn to the right should be made to cover the right hand going to the pocket. The belt may be used in the same way.

2. Place duplicate pack in upper left waistcoat pocket. When you turn away on some pretext, drop the pack in use from the left hand into your inside breast pocket while the right hand takes the duplicate pack from the waistcoat pocket and put it into your left hand. Be careful to keep the elbows pressed to your sides as the change is made.

3. Duplicate pack is on your table covered with a handkerchief. Pretend to put down the pack in use as you pick up the handkerchief; in reality keep the pack in your hand, covered with the handkerchief, and the pack on the table appears to be the one put down. Use the handkerchief and put it and the pack in your pocket.

4. A bold method suitable for the smaller-sized bridge packs is to have the duplicate pack in your right-hand trousers pocket. Apparently put the pack in your left hand, palming it in the right. Toss the cards from the left hand to the spectators, thrust right hand into the trousers pocket, leave the palmed pack and bring out the duplicate.

5. On a chair seat have several sheets of paper and under them the duplicate pack. With the pack in your right hand lift up the sheets, drop

the pack and take up the duplicate. This is a useful method in any trick such as the card stabbing in which the pack is wrapped in paper.

6. With the duplicate pack in its case in your right-hand outside coat pocket, replace the pack in use in its case as if you had finished. Put it in your coat pocket, then decide to do one more trick and bring out the other case.

7. A standard method for a set performance is the use of a card servante on the back of a chair. The switch is simply done by dropping one pack into the bag of the servante and gripping the duplicate from its clip as you place a chair for a spectator to sit on facing the audience.

Other methods will be given in the special section devoted to sleights.

THE THREE HEAPS

To avoid repetition it will be taken for granted that you have shuffled and cut the pack and show all the cards to be different by one or other of the methods given above. This will be taken for granted in the description of each trick.

Cut the pack by the ends into four heaps and place one aside to be used later as an extra. Have a spectator choose one of the three remaining heaps after you have lifted the ends of the top cards to show them all different. You simply lift two as one, the lower long card making this an easy matter. Whichever packet the spectator chooses order the top card to change to whatever your force card may be, suppose it is the 8S. Lift the top card and show it. Drop the extra packet on top and at once show the faces of all the cards. The 8S has vanished. Turn the top card of one of the other two heaps, it is the 8S. Drop the extras on top of this pile and show the faces. Again the 8S has gone. Lift the top card of the third pile, it is the 8S. Drop all the rest of the cards on top and again the card has disappeared only to show up finally on the top of the pack.

CUTTING THE PACK WITH A KNIFE

When a knife blade is thrust into the ruffled pack it will, as has already been seen, rest on the back of the force card. If, however, you want to have the card appear as the bottom card of the upper portion, thrust the point of the knife in a downward direction which will bring it below the short card. If you wish to bring the knife above the short card without ruffling the pack, thrust the knife point into the pack in an upward direction. In both cases show the card preceding the force card and the one following it.

THE WRAPPED PACK

The card is selected, returned, and the pack wrapped in paper. A knife is thrust through the paper into the pack and the card will rest on the knife either above or below it.

ANY HEAP

After the return of a card cut the pack into six or seven heaps. Have one heap freely selected. Place a coin on top of that heap. Gather up the others, then show the chosen card under the coin.

REVERSED CARD

Surely this is the simplest of all reversed card effects. Reverse one of the force cards beforehand. Have the card returned, ruffle the pack and the card has vanished. Turn the pack over and let the card fall from the right thumb as already explained, and show all the backs. Then hold the pack upright, fan it with the backs to the onlookers, and the card shows up reversed.

THE UNSEEN CARD

A spectator takes a card (force card) and without looking at it, puts it in his pocket. Another person is invited to take a card, replace it and then names it. His card is ordered to leave the pack, fly to the first spectator's pocket and his card to return to the pack. Show the faces, the card has vanished and the first spectator finds that very card in his pocket.

THINK OF A CARD

Again a spectator takes a card (force card). It is returned and the pack shuffled and cut. Drop the faces of the cards before a second spectator asking him to merely think of one card that he sees. Square the pack and riffle to the card he names, draw it slightly out of the pack and ask the first person if he wants his card above or below the mentally selected card. Cut the pack and show his card accordingly.

CARD STABBING

Card chosen as usual and returned. Deal the pack into two heaps on the floor. One heap chosen, forcing the heap of duplicate cards by the usual method. Blindfolded you take a knife and stab any one of them. It will be the chosen card.

SVENGALI PREDICTION

In addition to the Svengali pack you must have twenty-five cards which added to the indifferent cards of the pack will make up, with one of the force cards, a complete and unprepared pack. Put these twenty-five cards in your left outside coat pocket.

Begin by writing a prediction, i.e. the name of the force card on a slip of paper, fold it and have it placed in a spectator's pocket. Shuffle the pack and have a spectator cut and look at the top card. He thus gets a force card. Replace the cut, again shuffle the pack, then deal the cards in two packets, a card to each alternately. Force the unprepared pile on the spectator and have him look through it to see if his card is there. It is not, so you have him pick any five cards from the other pile, without looking at them and put them face down on the table. Invite him to put his finger on the back of one of the five. Gather up the other four, add them to the rest of the force cards and hold the packet in your left hand. Now have your prediction read, the spectator turns his card, it is the card originally cut and the one named in your prediction.

Under cover of this surprise drop the force cards into your left coat pocket and bring out the unprepared cards there. You will now have a full pack of regular cards with the exception of the one force card which you can then use as a short.

Any small variation in the working, such as having the prediction already written and sealed in an envelope and having the card chosen by first shuffling and then spreading the force cards on the table, may be left to the reader's own fancy.

This trick and Jordan's 'Mystery Problem' are two of the best that can be done with the Svengali principle.

THE MYSTERY PROBLEM   Jordan

Some special preparation is necessary for this effective trick. The twenty-six long cards of the pack are ivory-finish Bicycle cards while the twenty-six force cards are air cushion finish. The remaining cards of the ivory-finish cards are placed in your right outside coat pocket with a rubber band around them. Suppose that the force cards are 4H, prepare a message reading 'The Four of Hearts——17th card,' seal it in an envelope and you are ready.

Hand the envelope to one spectator to put in his pocket. After the usual preliminaries force a 4H on a second spectator and leave the card with him for the time being. Return to your table, say that you need only half the pack for the experiment and deal cards rapidly into two heaps. When the card was drawn you cut the pack at that point so that after the deal all ivory-finish cards are in one heap and all the other force cares are in the other.

Snap a rubber band around the force cards and drop the packet into your right coat pocket, putting it behind the packet already there. Pick up the twenty-six ordinary cards, have the force card returned to it and let the spectator shuffle the cards thoroughly.

Take the packet back and to further mix the cards deal them into three piles. Detecting the chosen card by touch, it is the only air cushion card present, and note the packet into which it falls. Pick up the packets with this one in the middle and deal three piles again. This time pick the piles up with the chosen-card packet on top, and at the end of the third and last deal place this packet second. The chosen card now stands seventeenth from the top. Have the prediction read and deal sixteen cards turning up the seventeenth. Carelessly take out the packet of ivory-finish cards from your pocket and put it on the table. The pack is then complete and no clue is left to the mystery.

THE CARDS AND THE DICE

The card having been forced, returned and the pack cut freely, deal out six cards in a face-down row, with each card slightly overlapping the preceding one. Continue in the same way until you have dealt six rows. It follows that the first, third and fifth cards in each row will be force cards, that is if you start the count from the left end of a row, but if the count is begun from the right-hand end they will lie second, fourth and sixth. Hand the spectator a die, or borrow one if you can. Have it tested by trial throws and when all are satisfied that it is unprepared, ask the spectator to make a throw to determine which row shall be chosen. Whatever the result gather up the other five rows and replace the cards with the rest of the pack. Have a second throw made to indicate the position of the card in the row. If it is an odd number count from the left, if an even number from the right. Push the card out of the row and pick up the five remaining cards in such a way that the alternate set-up will be completed when the last card is put on top.

Have the chosen card named and turn it over.

SVENGALI CLAIRVOYANCE

Effect. The performer's assistant is genuinely blindfolded and seated with his back to the audience.

The performer shuffles a pack of cards and shows them to be well mixed. One of the spectators freely chooses a card, replaces it and the pack is again shuffled and cut. They are then dealt face down on the table. Suddenly the assistant calls 'Stop'. The spectator names the card he selected, the card stopped at is turned, it is the very card.

Method. The trick is self explanatory once it is known that a Svengali pack is in use. After the usual preliminaries the assistant has merely to call 'Stop' on an odd card. Well presented the trick will baffle any audience.

THE PRIZE WINNER

Two packs are required, one unprepared and one Svengali. Suppose the forcing cards of the latter pack are 10S's. Remove the 10S from the ordinary pack and put it in your right-hand trousers pocket.

To begin, show the two packs and put them on the table. Borrow a hat and while getting it palm the 10S from your pocket and secretly drop it into the hat as you lay it crown downwards on the table. Have a spectator choose one of the packs, interpreting the choice to suit yourself, i.e. if he points to the Svengali pack, then that is the pack to be used and you hand the other to him. If he chooses the ordinary pack just hand it to him to hold. Write 'Ten of Spades' on a slip, fold it and give it to a second spectator to be held.

After the usual preliminaries with the prepared pack force a 10S and put the pack away. Instruct the spectator now to take from the other pack the card of the same value and suit as the one just freely selected. He searches for it and the card is not there. Tell him to count the cards, there are only fifty-one, the card is missing. Invite the second spectator to take out your slip and read it aloud. You have predicted the card. Finally the borrowed hat is turned over and out falls the missing card.

THE MIRAGE PRINCIPLE   R. W. Hull

In addition to the Svengali principle of twenty-six force cards cut short, these cards are also cut a trifle narrower. The faces of all the indifferent cards and the backs of the force cards are prepared as for the slick card principle, while the faces of the force cards and the backs of the indifferent cards are slightly roughened. The result is that the cards tend to stick together in pairs and the pack can be handled almost in any fashion and the force cards will not show. They may be fanned, thumbed through, shuffled both by the riffle and the overhand method, sprung from hand to hand or spread with a sweep on the table and all with perfect safety. There would even be little risk in handing them to a spectator for a casual overhand shuffle. There are several ways of forcing a card with this pack.

1. Ruffle and let spectator insert his finger.
2. Have knife blade inserted in the ruffle.
3. Have a number named and count down to it.
4. Deal the cards slowly and have a spectator call 'Stop'.
5. Spread the cards face downwards on the table and have a spectator point to any card.
7. Put the pack face downward on the table and have a spectator cut by the sides or ends anywhere he pleases.

The following tricks are good examples of what can be done with this improved Svengali pack.

MIRAGE PACK   R. W. Hull

After the usual shuffling and cutting have a card selected and have it placed on the face of the pack which you hold up towards the spectators. Suppose the card is the QH. Fan the pack, show that there is no other QH in it. Hold the pack vertically, the sides parallel with the floor, ball of right thumb at the centre of the upper side, the QH facing the audience. Patter about optical illusions and allow the cards to fall forward showing all the faces alike, i.e. all QH's. This results from the sides of the force cards being narrower. Square the pack and spread it face upwards on your right hand and every card shows a different face, thanks to the rough and smooth alternations keeping the cards in pairs.

THE EYE POPPER   R. W. Hull

Have the force card selected by one of the methods given, looked at and returned to the same position. Square up the pack, push off the two top cards as one and show the face of the indifferent card, turn the pack over and show the bottom card. Put the pack face down on your left hand, snap the pack and draw the top card off alone and the chosen card has apparently jumped to the top. Turn the card face down, push off two as one and bury them in the middle of the pack. This may be repeated several times quite safely. Owing to the preparation of the cards the moves are quite easy.

By riffling along the side edges the principle of narrow cards comes into play and you can cut a force card to the bottom at will.

SVENGALI MIND-READING

The pack is riffle shuffled, cut, shown all different, and then cut by the spectator.

Any number is then called by a spectator and you cut the pack into that number of piles. Turn up the index rear corners of the top cards and pretend to memorize them, then after much mental exertion write the name of the force card on a slip of paper (the top cards of the piles are all alike, of course). Fold the paper and put it on the table. Instruct the spectator that when you say 'Ready,' he is to seize the top card of any pile he feels impelled to take, and without looking at it, to put it face down under his hand. Stare intently at him, then suddenly call 'Ready'. The spectator does his part. You now gather up the piles, with the chosen packet on top.

Have the slip opened and the name of the card read aloud. The spectator turns up his card, it is the card you predicted.

THE SIAMESE SVENGALI PACK   Lu Brent

Make up a pack which is the exact reverse of a Svengali pack in this fashion: Cut short twenty-six different cards and paste these to the face of twenty-six ordinary force cards—gluing the junction about half an inch at the bottom.

With such a pack you cannot only riffle the cards to show them all different but you can fan them fairly and freely and shuffle either overhand or by the riffle method. Any card riffled to, can be shown instantly on the top of the pack and many fine combinations can be worked out.

SVENGALI FORCE

An easy but effective force for stage or platform work can be made with the Svengali pack. An unprepared easel is required which has a ledge on which you can stand seven or eight packets of cards.

Having shuffled and cut the prepared pack, show the faces all different. Next, while exhibiting and setting up the easel, invite a spectator to call a number between five and ten. Cut that number of piles from the pack, placing them face out on the easel. Call attention to the fact that all the cards are different and then turn all the packets with their backs outwards. The top card of each packet is a force card so it makes no difference to you which of the heaps is selected.

14

Magic With a Mene-Tekel Pack of Cards

THE MENE-TEKEL PACK

It is not certainly known who devised this variation of the combination of long and short cards, but the title, 'Mene-Tekel', was first applied to it by the late W. D. Leroy, the well-known magical dealer of Boston. Like the Svengali pack it consists of twenty-six ordinary cards and twenty-six short cards but instead of the short cards being all of the same suit and value, they also are all different, each short card being of the same suit and value as its neighbouring ordinary card so that the pack consists of twenty-six pairs of cards, one short and one ordinary card of the same suit and value in each pair.

To construct such a pack obtain two packs of cards, with the same back patterns, the cards preferably being thin and pliable and not too slippery. Thoroughly shuffle one pack and count off twenty-six cards. Then from the second pack take twenty-six cards of the same denomination as in the first and arrange them in the same order. You will then have two packets of cards exactly similar. From the ends of one set shave off about one-sixteenth of an inch. This may be done with a photo-print trimmer, or, better still, a bookbinder's guillotine if you have access to one. Having thus shortened one set of cards, arrange the whole fifty-two in pairs, the short card being the top card of each pair, and the Mene-Tekel pack is set-up.

To show the cards apparently all different riffle the ends slowly before the audience, the faces of the ordinary cards only will show up. Or, you may hold the pack upright, thumb at the top end, and let the cards fall forward on to the left hand, again showing only the faces of the ordinary cards. The pack may be riffle shuffled without disarranging the cards.

284

Magic With a Mene-Tekel Pack of Cards

To do this, square up the pack by tapping one end on the table to settle the short cards, then while the pack is on end, divide it about in half so that a short card is on the top of the lower portion. Riffle the two halves one into the other in the usual way, the cards will fall in pairs and the sequence of the prepared pack is not destroyed. The pairs will occupy different positions, but each pair will be intact. In similar fashion the pack can be cut indefinitely with complete cuts without separating the pairs, since the cut will always be made at one of the ordinary cards.

To illustrate the use of the pack for controlling a freely chosen card slowly riffle it and request a spectator to insert his forefinger, or a paper knife, anywhere he pleases and take the card next below his finger or the knife. In every case that card will be a short card and the next card (ordinary card) will be the duplicate of the one chosen. As the spectator takes the card raise the portion in the right hand and separate the hands a little, then casually place the two portions of the pack together but put the cards in the left hand on top of those in the right hand. This departure from the regular way of assembling the pack will never be noticed, however, if it is preferred you may openly cut at the point from which the card was removed. The result is that you now have on the top of the pack the duplicate of the card chosen. The card may then be dealt with in any of the following ways.

1. The spectator, having noted his card, replaces it in any part of the pack which you at once square up very openly. Request him to blow on the top card, name the card he drew, and turn the top card, it is his card. If it is desired to repeat the trick you will have to find the odd one and again bring it on top of its duplicate.

2. The duplicate may be revealed by holding the pack a short distance above the table, secretly push the card a little off the pack sideways, and the action of dropping the pack will cause the card to turn over and appear face up.

3. The card may be forced right out of the pack and passed through the table. To do this, secretly wet the back of your right hand. Show the spectator how you wish him to apply pressure. Put the back of your right hand right on top of the pack and your left hand palm downwards on that. Press down firmly and the top card will adhere to the back of your right hand, which you pass under the table top. The spectator places his hands on the pack in the same way and presses firmly. Have the card named and produce it from under the table.

4. As the spectator notes his card, secretly glimpse the top card. Tell him to concentrate his thoughts on the name of his card and you read his mind in the usual fashion, first getting the colour of his card, then

the suit and finally the value. By having the card returned to the top the pack will be in order for another demonstration.

5. After the card has been selected and the shift made bringing the duplicate to the top, put the pack in your left outside coat pocket for a moment, thumbing off the top card and leaving it in the pocket. Bring the pack out again under pretence of having forgotten to have the chosen card replaced. Have it pushed into the pack and at once place the pack in your right-hand pocket. Have the card named and order it to pass across into the left pocket, from which you produce it.

6. After the return of the card to the middle, square up the cards very openly, then hold the pack upright in your right hand, face of the bottom card towards the spectators. Order the card to rise and push up the top duplicate card with tips of the first and second fingers. It will appear to rise from the middle of the pack.

CONTROLLING SEVERAL CARDS

Bring the duplicate of the first card to the top as already explained, leave the chosen card in the first spectator's hands and go to a second person. When he draws a card do not pass the upper portion to the bottom as before, simply lower the top packet to the side of the lower one and with the thumb of the left hand push the top card of the lower on top of the right-hand packet and replace this packet on top. Thus the duplicate of the second spectator's card is now on top of the pack, and the first person's duplicate card is the second card. You follow exactly the same process for as many cards as you wish to have chosen so that finally you have duplicates of all the cards on the top of the pack, but you must remember that these are in the reverse order to that in which the short cards were drawn.

CARD INTO POCKET. A SECOND METHOD

A card having been drawn and the duplicate brought to the top, you very thoughtfully turn your back to enable the spectator to show the selected card to everyone else. Seize the opportunity to note what the top card is and slip it into a pocket. Turn around, have the chosen card replaced, ruffle the pack sharply and name the card. Order it to leave the pack and fly to your pocket, from which you instantly produce it.

Magic With a Mene-Tekel Pack of Cards

FROM A HAT   J. F. Orrin

Have three cards selected and pass the duplicates to the top in the manner explained above. Each spectator then pushes his card into the pack which you square up each time in the fairest possible way. Drop the pack into a borrowed hat and proceed to mix the cards, apparently, by shaking the hat vigorously with a lateral motion which does not alter the relative position of the cards at all. Ask the third person to name his card, reach quickly into the hat and produce it. You simply bring out the top card. In like manner you find the second person's card and finally the third. Or you bring out the three cards in any order the spectators may require, and do it just as easily.

CARD AND NUMBER   J. F. Orrin

A card having been chosen, its duplicate brought to the top, the card itself replaced in the pack and the pack squared up, have a number called, suppose it is fifteen, and announce that you will make the card pass magically to that number. First, however, show that it is not already at that number by dealing off fourteen cards on to the table, reversing their order and bringing the duplicate to the bottom of the fourteen cards. Show the fifteenth card and replace it on the cards in the left hand but so placed that about an inch of the right-hand side overlaps the rest of the cards. Pick up the fourteen cards from the table and apparently place them on the top of the left-hand portion, really slip them under the overlapping card, thus bringing the duplicate card to the fifteenth position as required.

ONE IN FOUR   J. F. Orrin

A card chosen, duplicate brought to the top as usual, turn your back while the card is shown to all. Take two cards from the bottom of the pack, the bottom card and the third from the bottom and put them on the top. The four cards on the top of the pack will then be all different and the third from the top will be the duplicate of the chosen card.

Have the spectator's card returned to the centre of the pack, square the pack and at once deal the four top cards on to a card stand commencing on your right-hand side. Now you must have one of these selected and it must be the third from the right-hand side. Ask someone to call a number between one and four and, of course, the answer will be two or three. If three is chosen, count from the right-hand side, if two is the number called, count from the left. In each case the chosen card is arrived at. The impression left on the minds of the spectators is that, although you did not express yourself any too clearly, still you intended to give a free choice of all four cards.

THE POCKET RISING CARD
J. F. Orrin

A fake is required consisting of two pieces of cardboard, a little larger than a card, fastened together around two sides and one end by adhesive tape or pasted paper. There should be space enough between the pieces of cardboard to take three cards. Half an inch from the top of each piece and midway between the sides is a hole, large enough for a thread to pass freely. Put a thread between both pieces and make a knot at one end to prevent it slipping right through. Thread the other end in a needle and put the fake in your upper left waistcoat pocket. Pass the needle through the bottom of the pocket and thence inside the waistcoat and trousers and finally through the lining at the top of the left trousers pocket. Withdraw the thread from the needle and tie a small wire ring to the end. If a card is pushed into the fake the thread will be carried down to the bottom of it, and a pull on the thread will cause the card to rise apparently from the pocket.

With a fake thus prepared have a card selected and bring the duplicate to the top. Turn away so that the card may be shown, take the duplicate and slip it into the fake. The real chosen card is then replaced in the pack, the pack squared and you order the card to leave pack, go to your waistcoat pocket and then rise from it. The necessary motive power is given by your thumb which you slip into the ring in your left trousers pocket and pull gently downwards.

CARDS AND SLATES
Gravatt

You require two slates one of which is prepared with a dab of wax. Have these on your table, waxed slate on top of the other. A card having been selected and the duplicate brought to the top, hold the pack in your left hand, pick up the top slate with the right hand and show both sides. Pass the slate to your left hand so that the wax is pressed on the back of the top card. Hold slate and cards in the left hand and pick up the second slate with the right hand. Show both sides of this one. Take both slates in right hand and lay the pack on the table. Put the top slate under the other, which has the card adhering to its lower side, thus bringing the card between the slates. Have the selected card returned to the pack or put in a card box. Order the card to vanish and appear between the slates. Take the slates apart and show the card.

COINCIDENCE MENE-TEKEL

Gravatt

For this effect, which Mr. Gravatt considers one of the best of the tricks of its type extant, you require a Mene-Tekel pack having red backs, and an ordinary pack with blue backs.

Show the red-backed cards all different, have a card selected, and bring the duplicate to the top. Take the chosen card and place it casually on the top of the pack, then lift the top two as one, showing the face of the lower one, and place the two, as one card, in a glass tumbler with the backs to the audience. Both cards being the same no suspicion can be attached to this move.

Have the unprepared blue pack shuffled, any card selected but not looked at, and place it in the glass behind the other two cards so that its back is nearest the audience. In your patter lay great stress on the fact that the two cards were freely selected from different packs. Turn the glass around, remove the front card, leaving the duplicate facing the audience. The two cards are the same. Show the red back of the card in your hand, then turn the glass and show the blue back of the other.

15

Magic With a Stripper Pack of Cards

THE STRIPPER PACK

Probably there are extremely few people who handle cards in any way, either as card players or magicians, who do not know what a stripper pack is, and probably every magician living has at some time or other made use of the stripper principle. The principle is simple in the extreme, the cards taper at the ends, that is one end of each card is slightly narrower than the other. It follows that if a card is turned end for end it can be instantly found because of the projection of its broad end amongst the narrow ends of the other cards.

The use of this expedient is too often condemned by unthinking magicians as being a of childish nature and of use only to those to whom the difficulties of the more pretentious and elaborate methods of sleight of hand are insurmountable. But any road that leads to the desired result, that of deceiving your audience, is as good as any other, and where simplicity is achieved, it may be much better. After all the deception of your audience is your ultimate goal. Complication for the sake of being complicated is a fool's trick and is not the same thing as being clever. In ordinary life, in which conjuring has no part, it is called by the less attractive name of self conceit.

The reason generally given for not using the stripper pack is that it is so widely known, even to the average schoolboy, which may be true but that does not in itself render the principle useless. One might almost as well say that since practically everyone knows there is such a thing as palming, therefore the magician should not use his hands. The value of an accessory depends largely upon the skill and subtlety, with which it is used. A simple device in one person's hands may become a stroke of genius in those of another. The ordinary straightforward use of the stripper cards, with the cards coarsely cut does certainly reduce the pack almost to the level of schoolboy conjuring. But a well-cut pack, such as a professional would insist on, should not betray the secret even under a free handling by the spectator.

The first thing to be mastered is to be able to turn the pack imperceptibly for the return of the chosen card. To begin with, have the narrow ends nearest your body so that when the chosen card is returned to the reversed pack the projecting sides will be at the inner end. To effect this reverse, spread the pack in a wide fan in the left hand from left to right. As soon as a card is withdrawn close the fan by placing your right hand on the left side of the fan and closing the pack towards the right, thus bringing the narrow end pointing to the left and the wide end to the right. Retain hold of the cards with the thumb and fingers of each hand at the ends.

If the spectator has taken a card by its wide end and has not changed his hold, you offer the pack to him in your **right hand**, slightly spreading it with the thumb and fingers. Square the pack and the wide end of the chosen card is at the inner end. It may happen that the spectator will turn the card round himself in showing it to another spectator, in that case you offer the pack for its return with your **left hand** again slightly spreading it fanwise, this time with the left thumb and fingers. By holding the pack in the position named, the necessary turn is half made and can be imperceptibly completed by taking the cards in the right hand for the return of a card, or nullified by taking them with the left hand.

Another very good method is to square the pack and hold it by the ends in the right hand, fingers on the outer wide end, thumb on the inner narrow end, square the sides of the pack with the left thumb and fingers, the left forefinger curled up under the pack, and the right forefinger curled in on the top. Now it is an easy matter to riffle either end of the pack for the return of the card. If the spectator has not turned his card, remove your left hand from the pack and with it pull the right sleeve a little, at the same time turning the right palm upwards bringing the pack upright, right thumb on the narrow ends. Bring the left hand against the face of the pack and riffle with the thumb for the return of the selected card. If, however, the spectator has turned his card, simply riffle the wide ends with the tip of the right second finger.

These two methods obviate the necessity for any palpably awkward reversing of the pack and will pass without notice even by those who know something about the stripper principle.

The latest and best method for the return of a card to a stripper pack is of comparatively recent introduction and is calculated to deceive even an expert if he is unacquainted with the procedure. Before offering the pack for the choice of a card, secretly turn half the pack so that the upper half of the cards have their narrow ends pointing outwards, the lower half has its wide ends pointing inwards. Allow a card to be selected freely from either half of the pack, but have it returned to the other half. Or if the card itself is turned by accident or design see that it is pushed back amongst the cards it was taken from. Square up the cards, cut at the projecting end of the lower wide cards and lift off the upper portion with the right hand, thumb on the inner end, fingers at the outer end, grip the lower portion in the same way, thumb on the inner end, fingers on the outer end, turn the hands in the opposite directions bringing the thumbs together and riffle shuffle the cards by the ends. The result is that all the narrow ends and all the wide ends are brought together, leaving the chosen card the only one reversed.

Some practice should be given to stripping the cards apart after some have been reversed. This should be done so neatly that the move should pass for an ordinary cut. It is only necessary to hold the pack rather loosely and quite flat when it will be found comparatively easy to separate them with one quick movement. An illustration of the subtle use of a stripper pack in presenting a series of tricks depending on prearranged cards follows. The main thing in such effects is to convince your audience that the cards are honestly shuffled and therefore thoroughly well mixed: this can be done by using strippers. Simply cut the arranged pack for a riffle shuffle, turning one packet endways. The result will be a thorough mixing of the cards and this will be recognized by the on-lookers; but by simply stripping the two sections apart under cover of a pretended cut, as explained and dropping one portion on the other, you have the cards in the same order as before. This subtle process is calculated to allay all suspicion as to the pack being arranged in any way and is therefore, invaluable in all such tricks.

Another practically unknown method of reversing the pack for the return of a card is to spread the cards on the table for the selection of a card. As soon as one has been withdrawn pick up the pack with the right hand between the fingers at the outer end and the thumb at the inner end. In the course of some remark, such as asking the spectator to remember the card, turn the right hand palm upwards bringing the pack upright, then take it by the sides in the left hand turning it face down and execute an overhand shuffle. The pack is reversed. Spread it on the table again and have the card pushed in the spread. Gather the cards once more and again shuffle overhand. Nothing could appear to be fairer.

TRICKS WITH THE STRIPPER PACK

The following tricks are arranged beginning with the simplest possible feats and proceeding to the more subtle effects which are worthy of the attention of the most expert card handler.

TO SEPARATE THE RED CARDS FROM THE BLACK

Beforehand separate the red suits and the black into two packets. Reverse one packet, put the two together and shuffle the pack thoroughly. Show the faces of the cards proving they are well mixed, then separate the reversed packets with an apparent cut as already explained. Until you can do this deftly the separation had better be done behind your back. Show all the reds in one hand and the blacks in the other. Turn the outer end of the left-hand packet towards the right and put the right-hand packet on top, thus bringing all the narrow ends together, and the pack is ready for further feats.

THE FOUR ACE TRICK

Pick out the four A's and put them on the table face downwards. To show them, take them by their outer ends and turn them over lengthwise. They must be in a packet one on top of the other. Now turn them face down sideways and they will have been reversed. Replace them thus in different parts of the pack which you hand out to be shuffled by the overhand method. Take the pack back, put it behind your back, strip out the A's and put them in your hip pocket. Hand the pack to a spectator asking him to take out the A's. He cannot find them and you take them from your pocket.

FINDING A CARD IN ANY POSITION

A card having been freely chosen, returned to the reversed pack and the card well shuffled, take the pack and put it behind your back. Ask what number the spectator would like it to appear at. Strip the card out and put it second from the bottom. Bring the pack forward, show the bottom card, turn the pack face downwards, draw out the bottom card and deal it face up, pull back the next card about half an inch and deal the next card face up, keeping the chosen card at the bottom. Proceed in the same way until the chosen number is reached, draw the bottom card out and put it on the table face down. Have the card named and turn it over.

SELECTED CARDS PASS THROUGH A HANDKERCHIEF

With the selected card reversed in the pack as usual, hold the pack by the two ends between your hands, face downwards. Ask the spectator to throw a handkerchief over the pack. Then saying, 'Perhaps it will be better to have the pack in sight all the time,' draw the pack away with one hand, the other hand retaining the reversed card and letting it drop on the table under the handkerchief. Immediately drop the pack on the handkerchief just above the card under it. Give the pack a sharp blow ordering the chosen card to pass through it on to the table. Lift the pack and the handkerchief and show the card face down. Have it named and turn it over.

THE TURNED CARD

A chosen card being in the reversed pack as usual, make an overhand shuffle holding the pack on end with the narrow ends upwards. The protruding sides of the reversed card will be detected easily by the sense of touch alone and it becomes a simple matter to finish the shuffle by leaving it on the top. There is no need to look at the cards. Place the pack on the left hand, face downwards and cover it with the right hand, fingers at the outer end, thumb at the inner. Secretly push the top card a little way over the side of the pack with the left thumb, the right hand hiding the action. Have the card named. Now drop the pack from a little height on to the table and owing to the resistance of the air the top card will be turned over face up on the top of the pack.

FINDING ANY NUMBER OF SELECTED CARDS AT
ONCE OR SEPARATELY

It is just as easy to deal with a number of cards as with one only, but each card should be returned to the reversed pack before the next is chosen. Suppose four or five have been drawn and returned, you can then put the pack behind your back and produce them all at once or singly, giving the spectators the choice. Or you may do the same thing with the pack covered by a handkerchief, or a hat, or by holding the cards under the table.

FINDING ALL BUT A CHOSEN CARD

Holding the pack upright with its back towards the audience, narrow ends upwards, it is very easy to retain the selected card between the thumb on one side and the fingers on the other, as the rest of the cards fall. This done, have the card named and turn it around.

COMPANIONABLE KINGS

Remove the four K's from the pack and throw them out face up on the table, turning them lengthwise as you do so. Show the faces of all the cards to prove the pack has no duplicates. Pick up the K's one by one, turning them sideways so that they go into the pack reversed in different places. Hand the pack out for an overhand shuffle. Strip the K's out in apparently making a strip cut, or put the pack behind your back, pull the K's out and put them on the top. Place the pack on the table. Let someone make one complete cut and take the pack. Order the K's to get together in the middle. The pack is spread face up on the table, the four K's are together.

PASSING A CARD THROUGH A TABLE

This trick is only suitable for performance when seated at a table. A selected card being reversed in the pack as usual. Say that you will try to make it pass through the table and, with an indicatory gesture, put the pack under the table holding it with both hands. Strip the card out and let it fall in your lap. Put the pack on the table and strike it sharply. Then bring the card out, it having apparently passed through the table into your left hand. Have it named and turn it up.

THE ANIMATED CARD

To one end of a long hair fasten a small black pin. Bend the pin and fix it in the bottom of your waistcoat underneath. To the other end attach a small pellet of good adhesive wax. Stick the pellet on one of your waistcoat buttons. After the usual preliminaries when the pack with the reversed card is returned to you, cut at the protruding edges bringing the chosen card to the bottom. Take the pack in your right hand, faces of the cards towards you and tap the edges of the pack on the table, looking at the cards as you do so. With the left hand secure the pellet of wax. Put the pack back in the left hand and press the wax on the face of the bottom cards, near the inner end. Cut half the pack and drop on the table and put the left-hand packet on top bringing the chosen card attached to the hair to the middle. Spread the card, command the card to walk out and gently move your body backwards. Hold your hand at the edge of the table and receive the card with the fingers under it, thumb on top. Scrape the wax pellet off with the tip of your second finger, have the card named and throw it down face up.

By the same method you can, after spreading the cards out in a row, suddenly lift your side of the table causing all the cards but the chosen one to fall to the floor.

CUTTING AT A CHOSEN CARD

This item is self explanatory. It is only a matter of having the pack with the chosen card reversed in it, shuffled and put face down on the table. Make a quick and apparently casual cut, really cutting at the projecting edges of the chosen card. Hold the cut face down, have the card named and turn the packet face up showing the card. In spite of its simplicity, or perhaps because of it, the little feat has a fine effect.

THE BLOWN CARD

A card having been chosen, returned in the usual fashion and the pack shuffled, take the pack back and hold it face downwards in your left hand with the narrow ends outwards. Put the right hand over the pack, thumb on one side of the narrow end, fingers on the other. Raise the pack to your mouth and blow hard at the same time thrusting your right hand quickly forward taking the card with it and throwing it out into the air.

CARD FROM SPECTATOR'S POCKET

With the card, or cards, returned to the pack as usual, the pack is shuffled and then placed into a spectator's pocket. It is best to put the pack in the pocket with its narrow end upwards, you can then produce the cards with ease, either all at once or singly. If you are dealing with one card only and wish to name it before producing it, simply cut at the card first and sight it as you put the pack in the pocket.

THE 'CUT' COUNT

Simply reverse the twentieth card beforehand. By cutting at this card you can announce that you hold twenty cards, while there are thirty-two on the table.

OUT OF THE ROOM DISCOVERY

If you have a friend who understands the method, you go out of the room. A card is selected and your friend attends to the usual pre-liminaries. The pack is placed on the table and you proceed to discover the reversed card in as striking a manner as possible.

THE COURT CARDS

Under pretext of showing there are no duplicates throw out all the court cards face up in a packet on the table. Pick them up by drawing them off the table with the right hand, turning them over lengthwise as you put them on top of the remainder of the pack. Have the cards thoroughly shuffled and show that the court cards are distributed through the pack. With a strip cut or after placing your pack behind your back, produce the court cards only and throw them on the table.

NAMING THE CARDS

Beforehand reverse any three cards in different parts of the pack, remembering their names and their order. Have the pack cut several times and finally make one cut yourself, cutting at one of the reversed cards and sighting it. This card gives you the clue to the other two which you produce naming them before you do so. Cut the pack once before producing the third one and then bring it out of the middle.

MAGNETIZED CARD

Have the card in this case chosen by a lady. After it has been replaced in the usual way and the pack shuffled, hold the cards upright in your left hand, narrow ends upwards, and the backs outwards. Ask the lady to rub the top of the pack with her fingers and then to allow you to touch her fingers with the tips of your right first and second fingers. Put these two fingers on the top edge of the pack, the thumb resting on one side of the pack and the third finger on the other. Press slightly inwards with the thumb and third finger and raise the right hand. The reversed card will be lifted out as if clinging to the fingers by magnetic attraction. Have the card named and turn it around.

AT ANY NUMBER FROM POCKET

When the shuffled pack with the reversed chosen card is returned to you, cut the pack once at the chosen card bringing it to the bottom. Place the pack in a spectator's pocket, sighting the card but not allowing anyone else to see it. Have a number called. Bring the cards out one by one taking them from the top until you reach the number chosen, then bring out the card pretending to read it first.

CARD THROUGH HANDKERCHIEF

The effect is that a card is selected, replaced in the pack and the pack wrapped in a handkerchief. This is then gently shaken and the card penetrates it.

After the pack with the reversed chosen card is returned to you, lay it face up on your right palm with the narrow ends inwards. Throw the handkerchief over the pack with the left hand and at the same time draw the pack forward towards the right finger-tips, stripping the reversed card nearly all the way out of the pack and gripping its wide edge between the root of the thumb and the tip of the little finger. Reach under the handkerchief from the front and bring out the pack, leaving the handkerchief face up and just over the card under the handkerchief. Fold the front part over towards the right wrist, then fold the sides down and under the right hand so that the card below is overlapped and held securely in place. With the right hand then take the folded ends of the handkerchief and hold it so that the pack hangs down, front to the spectators. Have the card named and a gentle shaking up and down will cause the card to work its way out of the folds with all the appearance of coming through the fabric.

JUST THE REVERSE   Jordan

Effect. A pack of cards is shuffled and any card is freely chosen and noted by the spectator. The card is returned to the pack. The performer then shows the card case is empty and places the pack inside. He removes the cards and asks the drawer to run through the cards to make sure they are all facing one way and there really are fifty-two cards in the pack. The pack is returned and replaced in the case which is held on the performer's outstretched hand. Performer reads the spectator's mind and slowly the chosen card. The pack is removed from the case and the card is found reversed in the middle.

Working. One side of the card case is thinned for about half an inch near the bottom until it is only as thick as a piece of paper. This is done by dampening the side and then removing the surplus cardboard with a nail file. This is much easier than merely scraping the card with a knife. The case is then reassembled and is to all appearance normal. But when the stripper pack, with the selected card reversed is placed in the case, by grasping the thinned part between the thumb and first finger that card is retained in the case.

When this has been done there are still fifty-two cards in the pack since the Joker is in it. Have the spectator run through the cards and count them face down each time. Glimpse the chosen card in putting the pack back in the case and also get the retained, chosen card in the middle and face up by inserting the pack cornerwise. Push the flap in and put the pack on your left hand. Proceed to read the spectator's mind in the usual hesitating way, suit and value. Finally the chosen card is found in the middle of the pack and it is reversed. The effect will be found to be well worth the slight trouble of preparing the card case.

THE FOUR KINGS

Secretly reverse three cards at the bottom of the pack and hold the pack so that the wide ends of all the other cards point outwards. Have the four K's removed from the pack which is examined to prove there are no duplicates. In returning to your table momentarily put the K's, which you hold in your right hand, under the pack and strip off the three reversed cards on to the back, so that you then have seven cards in that hand instead of the four K's only as the spectators think. Keep the packet facing the front so that they see the face of the outer K, then drop the packet on top of the pack. State that you will deal the four K's in a row and deal the four top cards—three are indifferent cards and the last one only is a K. Take three cards from the bottom of the pack and put them face down on the first indifferent card. Then take three cards from different parts of the pack and put them on the second card, cut the pack and place three cards from the lower portion on the third card; replace the cut and put the three top cards (K's) on top of the last card (a K).

Force the choice of this packet, the K's, in any way you wish, and place the other three packets in the pack in different positions. Hand the pack to a spectator, order the three K's to leave his hand and join their confrère. He searches the pack and finds no K's, while you turn the chosen packet and show all four.

'STRIPPER' STABBING

After the usual preliminaries, the pack with the chosen card reversed in it is returned to you. Shuffle it overhand by the ends and bring the chosen card to the top. Put the pack on the table, and cut it into two heaps. Borrow a handkerchief and a penknife, open one blade and lay the knife down. Fold the handkerchief and have it tied over your eyes. You still can see all that is necessary down the sides of your nose. Ask a spectator to stand alongside of you, to guide your hands on to the two packets of cards, then to place his hands on top of yours. Now move your hands and the spectator's around and around, thoroughly spreading and mixing the cards but carefully keeping the selected card, which was the top card, under your left thumb. Thus at the end of the spreading you can see exactly where the card lies. Ask for the penknife, don't pick it up yourself. Move the point around in circles, then suddenly and dramatically plunge it down, stabbing the card. Have the card named, lift off the blindfold, and show the card on the point of the knife.

CARD IN THE HAT

A card is selected, replaced, the pack shuffled and the card stripped to the top in the usual way. Take a hat and show it, holding the brim at one side with the right hand, the left hand with the pack at the other side. Tip the hat forward so that the audience can see it is empty. In turning the hat back towards yourself and putting it down, push off the top card with the left thumb so that it falls into the hat. Leave the hat on the table and hand the pack to the spectator. Order the chosen card to leave the pack and appear in the hat. The pack is searched, the card has gone. Turn the hat over and the card falls out.

REUNION

A spectator makes a choice of any two cards that are together in the pack. The cards are noted and replaced in different positions and the pack shuffled as usual. Shuffle overhand and strip the two cards out to the top. Put the pack on the table and cut once, bringing the two cards to the middle. Hand the pack to the spectator and order the two cards to fly together again. He runs through the pack and finds them together in the middle.

SATAN'S MAIL

Card selected, returned, pack shuffled and the card brought to the top by the usual methods. On a waistcoat button you have beforehand placed a pellet of wax, and on your table you have an empty envelope. Hand the envelope out to be examined and gummed down. As this is being done, get the wax pellet and fix it on the back of the top (chosen) card. Hold the pack in your left hand, face down, and take back the envelope in your right hand. Pass it to your left hand, secretly pressing it down on the pack with the left thumb, while you show an empty hat with the right hand. Put the hat on the table, take the envelope with your right hand and drop it into the hat, being careful not to expose the card which is now stuck on the back by the wax pellet. Hand the pack to the spectator and command the card to pass into the envelope. The pack is examined, the card has gone. Take the envelope from the hat with the attached card to the rear. Hold it up to the light and the shadow of the card is seen. Tear off one end, insert your fingers and apparently draw the card from the inside, really from the back.

CARD AND PLATE

Use a pellet of wax as in the preceding trick. After the usual preliminaries, strip the card to the top. Hand a plate for examination and seize the opportunity to fix the wax pellet to the back of the top card. Take the plate back, put the pack face up on it and press hard while you pull up your sleeves. Take up the plate and toss the cards into the air, turning the plate slightly towards yourself. Suddenly thrust the plate into the shower of falling cards and quickly jerk it back. Show the card on the plate and have it identified as the chosen card.

ANOTHER RISING CARD

Chosen card brought to the top in the usual way. Shuffle freely leaving the card in that position. Hold the pack in your left hand, upright, facing the audience and the back of the left hand in front of the cards near the bottom. Stand with your left side to the front. Clench your right hand, fist fashion, but leaving the forefinger extended. Rub this finger on the top edge of the pack and lift it. Nothing happens. Rub it vigorously on your coat and replace it on the pack. Under cover of the pack extend the little finger of the right hand and press it against the back of the top card. Push the card upwards as you slowly raise the right hand. The card will appear to be attracted by the forefinger and rise clinging to it.

THE STARTLER

The selected card being in the pack reversed and the pack having been shuffled, take it back and give it a shuffle yourself. Ask a spectator to step forward to assist you. Use the diversion to get the top card to the bottom, reversing it in so doing. Simply press the fingers of the left hand firmly on the top card and raise the remainder of the pack with the right fingers letting the top card slip to the bottom, turning face up in transit.

Ask the spectator to hold out his hand and take the pack with his thumb on top and fingers below. The chosen card is named and you give the pack a quick and rather sharp downward blow, knocking all the cards from his hand except the chosen one which is left in his hand and stares him in the face.

CARDS FROM THE AIR

Two cards are selected and treated as usual being reversed in different parts of the pack. After being shuffled the pack is returned to you. Strip the two cards to the top under cover of an overhand shuffle, then by means of the move explained in the preceding trick, pass the top card to the bottom of the pack face upwards. Hold the pack firmly between the fingers and thumb of the right hand. Swing the hand upwards sharply, let the cards slip out from between the top and bottom cards. As soon as these two are alone in the hand press them tightly together and dash them against the falling pack, scattering the rest of the cards in all directions. The effect is that you have caught two cards from the shower. Have the cards named and show them.

ACROBATIC JACKS

Turn the pack face up, run through and throw out the J's face down, turning them end for end as you do this. Show the faces of the cards to prove there are no duplicates. Turn the four J's over face up, sideways this time so that they remain reversed. Push them into the pack in different places and hand the pack to be shuffled. When it is returned give it another shuffle and strip the four J's to the top. A story such as 'The Four Burglars' should accompany the trick. The pack being the house which they enter in various ways, finally being disturbed they escape by the roof, thus providing the finale by showing all four together on the top.

THE CAPTAIN CARD

Selected card stripped to the top in the usual way. Borrow a hat, show it empty and place it on the table. Take the pack in the right hand face down, thumb at one end and fingers at the other. Place your hand over the hat and spring the cards into it, retaining the top card in the right palm. With the same hand take the hat by the brim with the fingers inside and thumb outside, thus concealing the card. Shake up the pack in the hat while pattering that the hat is a ship, while the pack represents the passengers and crew. A storm comes up (shake hat violently) and the passengers and crew take to the boats (empty out the cards on to the table). Let the palmed card slip into the hat and put it down. Gather the cards and hand the pack to the spectator, he finds his card (the Captain) is missing. It is found in the hat . . . the captain stayed with his ship.

FLYING CARD

In the usual way a card is selected, replaced, pack shuffled and returned to you. Shuffle and strip the selected card to the top. Take out any five cards and show their faces to the spectators asking whether the chosen card is amongst them. Of course it isn't. As your hand comes down it passes over the top of the pack held in the left hand and carries away the top card underneath the five. Drop these on the table. Hand the pack to the spectator. Cut the five cards to bring the chosen card to the middle and false count them as five. Hand the pack to a second person and order the card to pass from the pack to the five cards. This is then verified.

POSITIONS UNKNOWN   Jordan

A pack of cards is examined and shuffled by the audience and returned to the performer who is then blindfolded. The pack is handed to him behind his back and he asks for the name of any card to be called. Almost immediately he brings forward a portion of the pack with that card at the face. This is repeated, then at request he brings forward the A, K, Q, J, 10, of any required suit. A colour is called and immediately the whole twenty-six cards of that colour are shown. Laying down the red suits the performer requests anyone to name one of the black suits, which he at once produces. Finally he also separates the two red suits. The whole pack is shuffled and handed for inspection.

Working. The pack first shown and given for inspection is an ordinary one and must later be exchanged for a stripper pack. This pack is prearranged as follows: 2, 3, 4, 5, H; 2, 3, 4, 5, S; 6, 7, 8, 9, H; 6, 7, 8, 9, S; 10, J, Q, K, A, H; 10. J, Q, K, A, S; 2, 3, 4, 5, D; 2, 3, 4, 5, C; 6, 7, 8, 9, D; 6, 7, 8, 9, C; 10, J, Q, K, A, D; 10, J, Q, K, A, C,

All the black cards are reversed. Thus when the pack is held behind your back a half-stripping movement will separate the colours, leaving six banks of each colour. It is not desirable to pull the cards more than half-way out. By cutting to the nearest set, squaring up, then rapidly thumbing the necessary one, two, or three cards from the other half of the pack, the card called for can be produced quickly. Getting out a set of A, K, Q, J, 10, is easier still, though to the audience the difficulty would seem to be greater. The production of all cards of one colour is merely the separation of the hands. When showing the twenty-six cards they are kept on the move and not fanned widely so that the fact that the suits are separated will not be perceptible. At the end, the two packets are riffled together putting the cards in order for the tricks that follow.

EDUCATED DIE

After the usual selection, replacement and shuffling, take the pack and strip the selected card to the top. Remove four cards from various parts of the pack, one of them being the selected card. Place the cards in a row, the chosen one being the third from your left. Show a die (borrow one if you can) and have it thrown. If one or four turns up tell the spectator to throw again to prove the die is not loaded. If three is uppermost count from your left; if two, count from your right; if five count from your left to four, then back to the selected card as five. If six is thrown count from the right and back again to selected card.

STOP ME AT ANY TIME

For this effect the reversed card must be stripped to the bottom in the course of an overhand shuffle which will be found just as easy as bringing it to the top. Take the pack face downwards in the left hand as for dealing. Bring the right hand over the pack, slip the thumb below the pack so that it touches the bottom card, while the tips of the fingers rest on the front edges of the cards. Draw the cards back a little starting with the top card inviting the spectator to call 'Stop' whenever he wishes. When he calls draw all the 'pulled back' cards to the rear and free from the pack at the same time pulling off the bottom card with the thumb. This card automatically becomes the face card of the packet drawn off the pack, so that it makes no difference when the spectator stops you, his card will always be at the bottom of the packet.

THE FOUR ACES

With the pack in proper order run through it face up and take out the four A's, putting them on the table face downwards thus reversing. Show that there are no more in the pack. Turn the packet over face up sideways. Fan the pack and insert the A's in different places, leaving them protruding so that their separation is plainly visible. Close the fan and push them flush. Overhand shuffle by the ends stripping the four to the top. Deal sixteen cards face downwards, the aces will be the bottom cards. Put the remainder aside. Pick up the sixteen cards and deal four heaps of four cards. Complete No. 1 heap first, then dealing four cards into a second heap and so on. The A's will be in the fourth heap.

Force the fourth heap in the orthodox manner, placing the other piles back in the pack. Order the A's to pass, show there are none in the pack and turn the A's face up.

RISING CARD

'A stripper pack is good to use with a rising card windlass because you can palm strip the card with the left-hand movement while facing the audience and while the right hand remains stationary until the palmed card is added to the top of the pack by the left-hand movement.'

REVERSIBLE CARDS

With the stripper pack in order, take the pack face downwards in the left hand with the wide ends pointing outwards. Deal the first card face down, the next face up turning it over lengthwise and laying it down so that it overlaps the first card. Continue in the same way making a line of face-down, face-up cards, which overlap one another, so that everyone can see the condition of the cards. Gather them up as they lie. Show the faces by fanning the cards. Square the pack but hold the cards loosely, do not squeeze them. Put right hand at the outer end above the pack, thumb at one side, little finger on the other, three fingers over the end of the pack. Left hand holds the rear end of the pack between the thumb and first and second fingers. Gently pull back the left hand to start the separation of the two packets, and strip the left-hand packet out, covering the action with the right hand, and then turn the faced cards over and put the packets together again. Ruffle and show all the faces the one way.

THE SHUFFLED SPELLER

A card having been freely selected, returned and the pack shuffled, take the pack back and hold it in the left hand, narrow ends outwards, in about the position for dealing, but about an inch farther forward. Note the position of the reversed card by its projecting sides. Bring the right hand to the pack with thumb above the cards and fingers below, so that the first and little fingers are against the sides of the pack near the ends and can feel the reversed card. Have the card named. Deal off a card for each letter by drawing it off the pack with the thumb and turning it face upwards. When you reach the last letter do not exert any pressure with the thumb but grip the sides of the reversed card between the sides of the first and little fingers, draw it clear, drop the thumb on it and deal it face up just as the other cards were dealt. The position of the right hand gives excellent cover for the sleight which is not difficult but requires a little practice.

LIKE THOUGHTS

Two packs are required. One the regular stripper pack, the other a 'reader' pack, that is, one by which you can read the cards by the backs. In the usual way have a card selected freely from the stripper pack and control it. After the pack has been shuffled, take it back and hold it in the left hand, faces towards you, thumb at the upper left corner and forefinger curled against the back. Feel the projecting edge of the reversed card and as you raise the pack to your forehead make a break with the left thumb and quickly note the index of the reversed card. Lay the pack aside.

Hand the reader pack to be thoroughly shuffled, then deal it in rows

307

face downwards. Pass your hand slowly over the cards, hesitate, let it be drawn to one card, which is, of course, the duplicate of the card you sighted. Hold it face down, have the chosen card named, then turn it over.

THREE CARD REVERSE

Three cards are selected and treated one by one in the usual fashion, so that when you receive the pack after the final shuffle the three cards are in various parts of the pack. Strip them to the bottom in executing an end overhand shuffle. Hold the pack face down on the left hand as for dealing. Bring the right hand over the pack, with thumb at the rear end. Bend the ends up slightly, let the three bottom cards slip away and insert the tip of the left little finger between them and the rest of the pack. Now push all the cards above these three about an inch forward in the left hand. Take off several of the top cards and spread them to show that none of the chosen cards is amongst them. Replace these, and taking hold of the protruding packet with thumb on the back and fingers below, quickly turn them lengthwise, bringing them face up on top of the three cards, separated at the bottom. Spread a few and show that none of the chosen cards is amongst them either. Cut the pack while it is still face up bringing the three chosen cards, now reversed, to the middle. Execute several riffle shuffles covering the cards well with your hands to avoid any exposure of the reversed cards. Order all three to turn over and fan the pack outwards showing the three face-up cards.

FINDING THREE CARDS

Have three cards selected and deal with them singly in the approved method so that they are reversed in different parts of the pack. Strip them to the top in shuffling end fashion. Sight the two top cards and put the pack behind your back. Have a card named. If it is not one of the two you know, bring out the third card. A second card is called for. Ask at what number you shall produce it. Bring forward cards from the bottom to a number one less than that chosen then produce the top card, or the second, as the case may be. Slip the remaining card second from the bottom and bring the pack forward. Ask the drawer of that card at what number he would like it to appear from the bottom. Show the bottom card, turn the pack face down and deal it face up. Pull the next card back a little with the left finger and deal the one above it. Continue in the same way till the number is reached, draw out the chosen card and put it face down on the table. Have the card named and turn it over.

CARD DIVINATION

As usual a card is selected, returned and pack shuffled. Strip it to the top and square the pack with your right hand, thumb at bottom, fingers at the top. Lift the pack to your forehead, at the same time turning up the lower index corner with your right thumb and sighting it. Now announce the name of the card in the mind-reading fashion. Colour first, then suit, finally the value.

LIFTING ANY NUMBER OF CARDS CALLED FOR—No. 1

Beforehand reverse-end every tenth card. With very little practice you can divide the pack at the round numbers and run off backwards or forwards to make up the number called for. In counting the cards do not reverse them, but replace them on the pack in the same order.

LIFTING ANY NUMBER OF CARDS CALLED FOR—No. 2

In this method the cards are reverse-ended in alternate packets of four. The cards may now be counted rapidly with the left thumb in packets of four or eight; the odd cards being arrived at by adding a card or two, or discarding them as may be required to make the exact number. You can also pretend to judge the number of cards, apparently cut at random, by their weight. The counting by the left thumb at the rear of the pack is hidden by the right hand which is lifting the cards for the cut. After the demonstration make a strip cut pulling the reversed packets apart, turn one packet and riffle shuffle thus putting it in order for the regular stripper effects.

A DIVINATION EFFECT

An effective use may be made of the stripper pack in conjunction with the Si Stebbins system or any other full pack prearrangement.

For instance, the performer invites someone to take a batch of cards, put their names down on a piece of paper, then cut the pack and place it in his pocket after returning the chosen packet to the middle. The performer, by simply gazing into the person's eyes, reads the names of the cards and actually removes them from the pocket as he names them.

The effect is mysterious but the means of accomplishment are very simple. You have merely to reverse the top card and the bottom of the pack, so that when the cards are returned to the middle by cutting the pack one reversed card is brought above the packet and one below. You already know the first card of the batch by having sighted the card above it when the packet was removed. When the pack has been put in the pocket you find the card to begin at by feeling the first reversed card. Continue in the same way until you come to the second reversed card.

SYMPATHETIC NUMBERS   Jordan

Method. A pack is shuffled and cut by the performer who then takes off a small packet and seals it in an envelope which is placed on an easel. A sealed envelope containing a prediction is also put on the easel. The remainder of the pack is cut into four equal portions and the top cards of each are placed on the easel without their faces being seen. A choice is then given of the four remaining top cards or the four bottom cards. Whichever may be chosen the cards are taken, their values are added together giving a total of ten. In the envelope is found a slip bearing the written number TEN; the packet of cards in the envelope is counted— ten again; and finally the cards on the easel are turned, they are all tens.

Working. Arrange a stripper pack as follows— Any nine cards, any one reversed, a 10, a 4, any seven cards, a 4 reversed, a 10, an A, any eight cards, an A reversed, a 10, a 3, any seven cards, a 3 reversed, a 10, a 2, any eight cards and a 2 reversed. This last must be a long card.

To perform the trick, cut the pack several times and finally at the long card, bringing it back to its original order. Cut at the first reversed card which gives you ten cards, put these in the envelope and close it. Divide the pack into four packets by cutting at the reversed cards. The four top cards all tens, are removed and put on the easel faces inwards. Either the four top cards or the four bottom cards of the packets will now add ten. Whichever is chosen remove the cards add the spots and conclude the trick as given above.

THE ADVANTAGES OF THE STRIPPER PACK

In his book Mr. Gravatt writes as follows:

'It is sometimes desirable to get rid of certain selected cards entirely so that at the conclusion of the effect the reproduced cards may be shown to have actually left the pack. This can only be achieved with an ordinary pack by dint of considerable skill and manœuvring and keeping track of the cards by means of the pass, slip, false shuffling, etc., all of which call for no common degree of skill in card manipulation. With the aid of a stripper pack the thing becomes a simple job, it being perfectly easy to extract say half a dozen cards with one swift movement and either dispose of them entirely, or else bring them all together at the top or bottom of the pack for future manipulation. Since this can be accomplished even after a genuine shuffle, it serves the purpose better than the elaborate methods. Especially until the performer's skill will permit him to be clever for the somewhat dubious satisfaction of being clever.

'When it is a case of forcing a card, or several cards, it is a matter of anxiety to many to be able to handle the pack naturally and yet not lose sight of their force cards whilst casually shuffling the pack. More than one ambitious but nervous amateur have accidentally shuffled in the very cards they intended to force, and must restore matters as best they can. The stripper pack always allows you to do a perfectly genuine overhand shuffle, or, for that matter any other kind, yet you have your forcing cards ready at any time.

'To the performer to whom neat handling of cards is not second nature, it is not so easy to raise two or more cards together and handle as one card, a thing which is often necessary in certain kinds of tricks. There are innumerable performers who can silently and quickly count with accuracy any desired number of cards by merely running the thumb over the end of the pack. There are, on the other hand, any number to whom such a feat would present insuperable difficulties and who, faced with such a proposition before an actual audience, would end up by balling up the entire trick from sheer nervousness. If the required cards are counted off and reversed in one clump to start with, they may be found and brought to the top at any time and the projecting edge allows the performer to lift the desired number whether it be 2, or 20, without a glance at the cards.

'One reversed card in the pack will form a key at which, after a series of cuts, the pack may be given a final cut to restore it to the original condition before it was cut at all. A reversed card serves also to mark off

311

any desired number of cards to be palmed off the pack and added to others, such as the cards to the pocket, etc. The performer is able to secure the exact number quite automatically.'

It has been my experience gained through a long period of intimate connection with magic and magicians, professional, amateur and would-be, that without a certain degree of mastery of the fundamental sleights no one can present even the simplest of the so-called self-working feats with any degree of satisfaction to himself or his audience. Tricks do not work themselves and there is practically not a trick in the whole range of magic that does not depend upon the performer to be really effective. This is especially the case with card tricks. There are, of course, numerous tricks which are really only puzzles, such as those depending on numerical calculations. The interminable counting and dealing in such tricks make them utterly useless for these days. Any performer attempting the presentation of such feats would find his audience bored to tears before he was through with the first one and if he attempted to continue with others would find himself playing to empty benches.

On the other hand with a fair degree of skill the most banal effect can be transformed into a striking feat. With regard to the use of strippers it is easy to say that 'with one swift movement' any number of cards can be extracted from the pack and disposed of, but that does not help the would-be magician towards his one end, the deception of his audience, since that 'swift movement' and the disposal of the cards would be perfectly palpable to onlookers. My conclusion is this, to anyone with the few indispensable sleights at command the stripper pack is a very valuable accessory but to attempt to depend upon it solely will lead to disaster.

To acquire the necessary degree of skill does not require any great amount of application. In the older textbooks great stress was laid upon the Pass. One hour a day for a period of three months was said to be necessary to get a working acquaintance with it. Modern ingenuity has devised other methods of attaining the result in far easier ways and the same thing applies to the other necessary sleights. I will undertake to teach any person who can handle cards sufficiently well to shuffle a pack overhand fashion neatly, the half-dozen indispensable sleights in five lessons of an hour's duration each.

I do not mean that in that time anyone could become a skilled sleight-of-hand performer, but I do maintain that sufficient skill would be acquired to enable one to present card tricks capably and with the necessary confidence.

END STRIPPERS

While the principle of stripping the ends of cards has been known and used by gamblers for generations and was certainly originated for the purpose of cheating at cards it has remained practically unknown to magicians generally speaking. This is rather a curious fact since there are many fine effects possible only with end strippers while everything that can be done with the side strippers can also be done with the end variety. Again the cards can be so finely cut that detection is practically impossible and such cards can be freely used even with those that know all about side strippers without arousing suspicion.

With the cards all set the one way the various methods for getting a chosen card reversed in the pack which have already been explained for the side strippers, can be brought into play. When the card has been reversed, or the pack reversed, which comes to the same thing, the projecting edge can be detected instantly in the mere act of squaring the pack with the thumb on one end and the fingers on the other. It is an easy matter then to make a break under the card and make the pass bringing it to the bottom, or to break the pack at that point and execute a riffle shuffle bringing the card to the bottom; or again to secure the card in the right hand by means of the side palm; or simplest of all to make a regular overhand shuffle, the projecting edge making the reversed card cling to the fingers so that it can be put at the top or bottom as the last movement in the shuffle.

All the tricks for which side strippers are generally used can be done with the end strippers. As for the special effects which can only be done with the end strippers space will permit of the explanation of but a few of them. The reader will no doubt find out novel applications of the principle for himself.

A 'STOP' DISCOVERY

After the pack has been shuffled by a spectator, secretly reverse one card and have it near the middle. Allow the free selection of a card. After the spectator has noted it cut the pack by the ends at the reversed card and have the chosen card replaced at that point, replace the cut and square up very openly. Make a partial shuffle bringing the reversed card and the card below it, the chosen card, to a position about one-third of the pack from the top. Hold the pack by the ends and drop small packets of cards from the bottom in different places on the table telling the spectator to call 'Stop' whenever he pleases. When he does call drop all the cards below the reversed card. Have him name his card and turn the top card of the last packet.

The trick may be repeated with added effect. When 'Stop' has been called palm the top card of the last packet and turn over the next, showing it but not looking at the card yourself. Turn it down and replace the palmed card on top. When the spectator says you have shown the wrong card, affect incredulity and work the argument up. Finally invite him to turn the card up himself. Before the shock of the surprise has passed it is well to assemble the pack, losing the first card shown amongst the others.

RED OR BLACK

I am indebted to Mr. E. L. Whitford for the following very effective arrangements. Separate the black suits from the red, turn one packet round and then put the two packets together. Hold the pack as for an overhand shuffle. Press on top and bottom cards with the left thumb and fingers, then pull out all the cards but these two, letting them fall well into the crotch of the thumb. Repeat the action with the new top and bottom cards, letting this pair fall on the first pair. Continue the action until all the cards are exhausted. The result is that you have the black and red cards alternately throughout the pack all the cards of one colour being reversed. This is the simplest way of making such an arrangement, the whole action taking a few seconds only.

Now, with a red card on the bottom if you riffle the top ends of the cards at one corner red cards only will show, then by slipping the top black card to the bottom and riffling by the corner, black cards only will be visible. The principle is exactly the same as with the Svengali or Mene-Tekel packs, the short cards do not appear.

Again, by taking two packs, one with a red back, the other with a blue back and using the red cards with red backs and the blue cards with blue backs, and arranging them as above, you can show all red faces and turning the pack over show all red backs. Then by slipping the top card to the bottom and riffling on the opposite corner show all black faces and follow that by showing all blue backs.

By applying the principle of roughening the backs (see Svengali section) and then arranging the cards in pairs one red, one black, with the backs together, and also carrying out the reverse stripper arrange-

314

ment as above for each colour you cannot only show all red and all black by riffling but also by fanning cards.

Properly introduced, that is by exchanging the pack that has been freely handled by the spectators, these results will be incomprehensible, even startling, to the layman and indeed to the average magician.

THE AMBITIOUS CARD

The use of the end strippers makes this trick as near perfection in handling as is possible. I am indebted to Mr. Annemann for permission to detail some of the moves he uses. In his hands the trick is perfect. Begin by having a card chosen, replaced, then bring it to the top by whatever means you prefer, making no reversal of the pack or the card. Order the card to the top and show it has arrived. Take it off by putting your finger-tips under it, thumb on top and turn it endwise to show the face. Replace the card face down by turning it over sideways. This is a perfectly natural way of showing the card and by using it you have reversed the card without any possibility of arousing suspicion.

Show the chosen card again and push it under the next card. Order it to the top, lift the two cards as one, thumb at one end and fingers at the other. The projecting edges makes this the easiest thing in the world. Replace the two cards, take off the top card and push it under the next. This time, of course, the trick works itself, the chosen card is on the top. Lift it by the ends to show it in the same manner as when handling two cards.

Again push the reversed card under the top one, make the double lift and show its face, push off the top card over the side of the pack a little and slide the two cards under it. This time lift three cards, just as easily as two, show the face of the reversed card and replace on top. Slide off the top card, not showing its face and push it into the middle, show the face of the next card, also an indifferent one, to prove the chosen card really has gone to the middle, riffle, make the double lift, and show reversed card back on top.

Have the spectator hold out his hand palm upwards, slide off the top card on to his hand and drop the pack on top. He finds his card has returned to the top.

The moves can be varied *ad lib.*, and for close work it is one of the most effective that can be performed.

16

Magical Mysteries With Special Packs, etc.

IMPOSSIBLE CARD DISCOVERY
Baker

Two packs are required, one a forcing pack with all the cards alike, the other being a regular pack minus the card of which the forcing pack is made up. Place the forcing pack in your left outside coat pocket on its side.

Thus prepared, fan the regular pack with the faces to the audience and then have it shuffled. Take it back and illustrate to a spectator what you want him to do, saying, 'I want you to put the pack in your left coat pocket so' (put it in your left pocket upright) 'then draw a card from the middle of the pack thus and, without looking at it, hold it close to your body and place it in your right-hand pocket so,' do this with a card from the upright pack. Take the forcing pack from the left pocket and the card from the right-hand pocket, which you put on the bottom of the forcing pack. Hand this pack to the spectator and he puts it in his pocket. While you turn your back he takes out one card as directed and places it in his right-hand pocket.

This done, you turn and take back the pack. You ask him, 'Did you do as I directed? Now put the shuffled pack in your pocket in this manner—(put the forcing pack in your left pocket on its side) you withdrew one card only and put it in the other pocket—(take a card from the regular pack and put it in the other pocket). Is that right?' Take the regular pack from the left pocket and the card from the other pocket and put the pack down. You slowly name the card and the spectator takes it out and shows it. This card added to the pack on the table makes it complete and no clue is left to the mystery.

ONE AHEAD   Jordan

Effect. Performer shows two packs, red- and a blue-backed respectively. From the blue pack he throws a card face down on the table. A card is freely chosen from the red pack and is retained by a spectator. The blue card is turned, it is the same as the card freely chosen from the red pack.

Method. The blue-backed pack is unprepared but has at the top a double-backed card, one side red the other blue, with blue side uppermost. The red-backed pack consists of twenty-six pairs of duplicate cards. The backs have a one-way pattern and the cards of each pair point in opposite directions. All the first cards of each pair point one way, the second cards the reverse way. The pack can be riffled to show all the cards are different. Place the double-backed card from the top of the blue pack on the table, carefully avoiding any exposure of the lower red side. Riffle the red pack showing the faces to the spectators and they will appear to be ordinary cards. Spread the pack and allow a spectator to make a free choice. As he takes it you note the way the pattern lies so that you will know whether the duplicate is above it or below. Cut the pack to bring the duplicate to the top. Take it and with it execute the Mexican turn-over, thus leaving the duplicate card face up on the table and carrying away the double-faced card which you turn over in your fingers so that the red back shows to the spectators.

THE MENTALIST'S CARD STAGGERER   Annemann

A little preparation is required. You need five cards of the same suit and value, say 8H, with backs to match the pack in use. From the pack take the 8H, put four indifferent cards on it and put the packet in your inside coat pocket with the backs outwards. Take from the pack the KD, put it amongst the five 8's of H, between the third and fourth and put the six cards on top of the pack. In the coat pocket have some letters or papers.

Take the pack from its case and slowly fan it, from left to right, faces to the spectators, remarking that it would be a wonderful thing if you were to have one of the cards merely thought of and then find it. You say you cannot do that but you have had some success with a small number of cards. By this time you have spread all the cards but the special cards at the top and you close the fan. Riffle shuffle several times keeping the six cards intact on the top. Hand the cards to a spectator asking him to deal five cards face down in a row. This done take the pack back. Tell him you will turn your back and he is to turn and look at any card he wishes, being careful in picking it up not to bend it and after putting it face down again to move all the cards slightly so that no possible clue will be left. Illustrate by picking up the fourth card, the KD carefully, then as you are about to replace it, as if struck by an afterthought push that card back in the pack and deal the top card, the fifth 8H, all five cards are then 8H's.

Turn away; spectator looks at one card and replaces it; turn to the table again and pick up the five cards keeping the faces towards yourself. Hold the packet in your right hand, with the left remove the letters, etc., from your breast pocket, then turn your right side to the front, take the five cards in your left hand and hold the edge of your coat with the right. Apparently place the cards in the breast pocket, really thrust them into your upper waistcoat pocket but insert the free fingers of the left hand into the pocket making a slight bulge which is visible to the audience. Open the coat and let them see your hand coming away from the pocket. With the left hand reach into the pocket and take out the top card of the packet there and repeat the action three more times. For the last card let the spectator put his hand in the pocket and certify that just one card remains. Have him name the card he looked at originally, then bring out and show the card he now holds. It is the same card.

The pack is now complete and can be freely examined as no clues remain.

COINCIDENTALLY   Jordan

Any two packs may be used after being shuffled by the spectators. One pack is put on each of your palms and you deal the top card from each pack face down on the table about a foot apart. Ask a spectator to choose one of them and as your hands swing back after the deal change the two packs from hand to hand behind your back. Pick up the card not chosen and put it on top of the pack it apparently came from, actually due to the switch it goes on to the pack which has a duplicate of it. Run over the faces, find the duplicate, put it on the bottom and put the pack down. Look at the other chosen card, note what it is but call it as being the card returned to the pack, keeping its face away from the spectators, and replace it face down on the table.

Take the second pack, take out three cards, naming them, one being the duplicate of the card on the table, and put them face down, the duplicates being No. 1 and 2 in the row. Riffle the other pack, asking spectator to call 'Stop' whenever he pleases. At the word separate your hands, right hand holding the original lower half, left hand the upper half, and put them side by side. Top card of one, or bottom card of the other, is chosen and put aside, and the packets put together so that the duplicate card remaining becomes the top or bottom card as the case may be. Let spectator throw a die. No matter what number shows, you count to one of the duplicates, pick it up and put it on top of the pack in right hand. Left hand takes other pack. Ask spectator to turn up the three remaining cards and as he does so swing packs behind your back and push the duplicates on the top or bottom to the opposite pack to which they belong. As the missing card is named, deal it with the right hand from pack to which it was just transferred. The card from the other pack is turned up and proves to be the same.

The two packs must have the same back pattern.

MAGNETIC MENTAL CONTROL

Two packs are required. One with blue backs, unprepared, and one with red backs, prepared as follows: Take twenty-six red-backed cards and twenty-six blue-backed ones, and set them up alternately to make a regular fifty-two-card pack. Roughen the faces of all the red cards and the backs of the blue cards so that when the cards are spread the red backs only will show. Thus prepared the pack can be fanned, spread on a table and even shuffled by the overhand method without revealing the blue-backed cards. Take the bottom card of the pack, it will be a rough-backed blue card, and put it on top of the unprepared blue pack.

To show the trick. Take the blue pack from its case, fan it to show the faces and the blue backs, and throw out the Joker. Take out the red pack, and exhibit it in the same fashion. Put the red pack down and take up the blue-faced cards. Shuffle the top card to the middle, then take it out, not allowing anyone to see its face, and place it on the top of the red pack and make one cut. This returns the card with the rough blue back to its mate the red card with roughened face. So far as the audience is concerned you have simply taken a blue card from the blue pack and placed it in the red pack, burying it with a cut and you next shuffle the reds with their faces to the front. Spread these cards face up and invite a spectator to touch any one of them; cut at the card, slide it out of the fan and hand it to the spectator face up. Ask him if he had a free choice.

Then have him turn the card over, it is a blue-backed card. Turn the rest of the cards and fan them, they all have red backs. He has found the very card you just before transferred from the blue pack.

MOVIE COLOUR CARDS

Two packs are required, one with blue backs, the other with red backs, and card cases to match. Also two double-backed cards, one side red, the other side blue. Place one of these, red side upward on top of the blue-backed pack and the other blue side upward on the red-backed pack. Place the red pack with blue top card in the blue case and the blue pack with the red top card in the red case.

The effect of the trick is to apparently make the packs change places. Take the cards from the blue case and to make them appear all blue backs, first hold the pack so that the blue-back card on top is seen by the spectators. Turn the pack with its face to the front in the left hand as if about to overhand shuffle face upwards. Lift the rear half of the pack with the right hand and turn it so that the blue-back card on top can be seen; drop some cards from the face of this packet on to the packet in the left hand and again turn the right and show the blue back. Repeat this several times, remarking 'a blue-backed pack of cards'. In squaring the pack, keep its face to the audience and secretly reverse the top card, bringing its red side uppermost. Replace this pack in the blue case.

Perform the same operations with the other pack to prove it is a red-backed pack and, after reversing its double-backed top card, place it in the red case. It only remains to work up the effect as strongly as possible: order the change to take place and show that the red cards are in the blue case and vice versa.

TRANSPO COLOUR CHANGE

Two packs are required, one with blue backs and one with red. They are placed in your trousers pockets, one pack in each. The packs change places.

First show your pockets are empty, and then place the red pack in the right pocket, the blue in the left. Openly take the packs from the pockets and show what will take place by changing the packs from one hand to the other, the left hand taking the red pack, the right hand the blue. Put the packs in the pockets again, order the invisible transfer, take them out and show that the red pack has passed back to the left pocket and the blue to the right. When you took the packs out of the pockets to demonstrate the change, one card was left in each pocket, so that at the finish the audience see only these single cards of the opposite colours.

INVISIBLE FLIGHT   Hamblen

Two packs are necessary, one with blue backs, the other red, and a duplicate of one blue-backed card, 5S, for instance. Steam off stamp on the red pack's case, insert the duplicate 5S in the middle of the pack and reseal it. Put this on your table with the blue-backed pack on top of which you have placed the 5S, together with five slips of paper, an envelope and a glass.

To begin, hand the sealed red pack to the spectator for safe keeping. False shuffle the blue pack keeping the 5S on top, then have five cards drawn, amongst them must be the 5S, with five chances you can hardly fail to force the 5S, but remember which person drew it. Hand slips of paper and pencils to the five persons, asking them to initial the faces of their cards and to write the names of the cards on the slips. This done, gather up the five cards getting the 5S to the bottom of the packet. Tell the five spectators to wad their slips into small balls, and as you turn to your table to pick up the envelope let the 5S drop on top of the pack. Turn to audience and slowly place the four cards (supposed to be five) in the envelope and give it to be held. Collect the wadded slips in a glass, take particular note of the 5S slip so that you will be able to pick it out. Shake the pellets around and toss them on to the table.

Pick out the 5S pellet, hand it to the spectator who has the red pack. He reads the name on the slip, opens the pack and finds the duplicate blue-backed 5S. Take this card from him to show it to everyone and ask the person holding the envelope to open it and see that the 5S has gone. As he does this you change the card in your hand for the initialled 5S previously dropped on the top of the pack. Hand this to the person who drew it to identify his initials.

BLIND MAN'S BUFF   Hamblen

Two duplicate packs are required, one unopened and other prepared as follows. Suppose you use Bicycle Rider cards which have a small white dot in the circle on the backs. With red or blue ink according to the colour of the backs cover up this white dot. Put about forty of the cards thus prepared in your left outside coat pocket so that they lie, well squared, on their sides. Thus prepared hand out the unopened pack to a spectator to break open, after which he is to shuffle the cards thoroughly and have ten cards selected by other spectators. This done you take back the remainder from him and tell the choosers of the cards to mark their cards inconspicuously on the faces. Your volunteer assistant is then to collect them. While this is being done you have all the time in the world to put the remainder of the pack in your left coat pocket and bring out the forty marked cards. Casually place these on the table. Let your volunteer assistant put the collected cards in the pack and then shuffle as thoroughly as he pleases.

Have a folded handkerchief tied over your eyes as you stand behind the table, and have the pack placed down in front of you. You can see down the sides of your nose and as you flick the cards off the top one by one spot the white-centre cards, which are the selected ones, show them and have them acknowledged. Place them aside face up. A good blind is to let your hand stray from the pack after you have found half a dozen or so and hover over one of the cards already turned up. Pick it up, turning it and ask 'Someone's card?' You will be told you have already found that one. Ask your helper to put the cards aside as you find them. This clinches the impression that you cannot see anything.

You may easily get the very last card on top of the rest as you pretend to search for it. Gather the pack, take off the blindfold and palm the card. Have it named, plunge your hand into your pocket and produce it. 'No wonder I couldn't find it,' you say.

SPEAKING OF PINK ELEPHANTS

A blue-backed pack of cards is shown to contain no duplicates. A mentally selected card is removed by a spectator and is found to have become red-backed in his own hands. Knockout number two comes when he discovers that the whole pack has turned red-backed. He replaces his card without your seeing it and as soon as he names it you spell out its name, removing a card for each letter and turning it up on the last one. The pack is now cut in two portions and a card selected from one of them vanishes and reappears in the other.

Bicycle cards, whose backs have white margins, are most suitable. From a red-backed pack remove these cards: 2, 3, 7, 8, Q, of C's; 4, 5,

9, J, K, of H's and S's. Cut a narrow strip from the ends of these and glue each to the back of a card taken from a blue-backed pack being sure that none of these red-backed cards are duplicated by the blues. Lay the double cards out face up, glued ends all one way. Now from a second red pack remove the duplicates of the fifteen named above. Cut them short and smooth their cut corners with sandpaper. Lay them out face up in the same order as the rear ones of the glued pairs already laid out.

To assemble: On the first single card place the eighth double one, then the second single, ninth double, third single, tenth double, etc., to the ninth single on which goes the first double, tenth single, second double, etc., until all are picked up. The duplicate of any rear card of a glued pair is thus about half the pack removed from it, the pack having been assembled face up, and all glued ends the one way. Turn the pack face down and place on it an indifferent blue-backed card.

Hold the pack face down, glued ends inwards and with the other hand riffle the free ends, from back towards face of pack. Do not call attention to it but everyone will notice that all backs show blue. Raise the pack vertically, so that it faces the company and freely show the blue-backed card at the back, transfer it to the face of the pack. Riffle the free ends from the back towards the face, or fan the cards, the faces now showing, owing to the upright position of the pack. Demonstrating that the cards are all different, have someone mentally select a card as you riffle them. As he can only see the faces of the short rear cards of the glued cards, his choice is limited to them.

Fan the pack requesting the man to remove his card. Naturally he removes its single duplicate and his free handling of it is what makes this so convincing. Square the pack and turn it face down, concealing its back for the present. Tell him to return his card. He turns it face down to do so and discovers it is red-backed. Before he recovers you begin fanning the pack from the left hand to the right, counting as you do so. The whole pack is now red-backed.

When you have counted eleven cards of the fan into the right hand, have him insert his card there, and continue spreading the cards, being careful not to expose the single blue-backer at the pack's face. Close the pack and have him name his card. Then deal a card at a time on the table for each letter of its name, as 'DEUCE OF CLUBS', and turn up the last card. It is his card. This is because each of the fifteen cards he could choose all spell with twelve letters.

As your right hand turns the card up your left hand slips the blue-back card at pack's face into left side coat pocket. Fan the pack until you feel two adjacent double cards and insert his between them, where it originally came from. Replace the spelt off cards on the pack one at a time to restore the original order.

Fan the pack to show there are no duplicates, then cut it into two heaps. Riffle the end of the smaller heap so that only the rear cards of the glued pairs can be seen. The spectator mentally selects any one save the heap's face card. Riffle the other heap similarly to show his card isn't there. Now fan the first heap showing each card separately. His card has gone. Fan the other heap and its short single duplicate is found and may be removed and examined as it is unprepared.

CARD TELEPATHY

The performer's assistant, acting as the medium, is escorted to another room. From a pack of cards a spectator freely selects a card which is shown to everyone and then put in the spectator's pocket. A blank slip of paper is placed in a plain envelope and together with a pencil is sent to the medium. The envelope is returned and being opened by one of the audience is found to have a message written on the slip of paper giving the name of the card.

The information is conveyed by the envelope and the pencil. If the card is a C gum down the right side of the flap only; if a H gum the left side, if a S the tip only and if it is a D simply push the flap inside. The value of the card is marked on the pencil with the finger-nail on the wood beside the letters denoting the trade name, etc. For instance, if the card is an A make a mark opposite the first letter, if a 2 mark the second letter and so on.

CARD X

The pack is thoroughly shuffled by a spectator and the performer takes the pack. He introduces his assistant who is to act as the medium. She is seated on a stool and a blindfold placed over her eyes. In adjusting this some eight or ten cards, previously memorized by the lady, are added to the pack by the operator taking them from her sash at the back. Cards are then held up with the faces to the spectators, backs to the medium. With the customary hesitation, slight mistakes and corrections she calls their names.

SIGHT UNSEEN

This trick is arranged for two people, performer and medium, preferably a lady, and is only suitable for private performances or small clubs.

You arrange that you and your assistant shall be introduced to members of your audience and you take care to both note the first three people. Classify them in the order of the first letters of their surnames, for instance Mr. Bell, Miss Jones and Mrs. Smith. It is understood between you that the first person will represent the AC; the second person the AH; the third the AS and any fourth person in the audience will stand for the AD. When the feat is to be presented the medium is escorted into another room. From any pack lay out the four A's, face up and invite one of the three people first introduced to step forward and touch a card. Supose you call Mr. Bell and it happens luckily that he selects the card he represents, you tell him to simply concentrate on the card he touched, go into the next room and the medium will tell him the name of that card. The medium, of course, knows the card she is to name the moment he enters the room and does so with the proper acting. If, however, he touches another card you ask him to sit down again telling him to keep his mind fixed on the card. Suppose it was the AH he selected, then to get a double concentration, you would ask Miss Jones to go to the medium. If the AD is the card touched send any member of the audience outside of the three special persons.

As with all similar feats the presentation is practically the whole thing.

MIRACLE CODE

A simple code is used covering the cards of a pack. The order of the suits is C, H, S, D, and the cards of each suit run from the A to the K. Thus one is AC, thirteen the KC; fourteen the AH and so on up to fifty-two which would be KD. Therefore any card having been selected if you convey the corresponding number to the medium he can name the card.

Your assistant is taken to another room by a committee. From any pack a card is freely chosen, you take and fold it in half, noting what it is. Hand it to a spectator telling him to continue folding it in the same way into the smallest possible compass. As he does so tear a corner about six inches square from the top of a page in a magazine you have lying handy, the page number corresponding with the number of the card in the code. Take the folded card and wrap it in the paper so that the proper page number is on the outside. The package is carried to your assistant, he places it to his forehead, reading the page number as he does so, and after due concentration he names the card.

TELEPATHIC CARDS

A pack is shuffled and spread on a table face up. Members of the audience touch any cards and remember them. Cards are gathered up and again shuffled and a spectator takes the pack out of the room to an assistant who acts as the medium. In a few moments she makes her appearance and hands to the spectator a sealed envelope containing the chosen cards.

A blank playing card and a short pencil repose in your right-hand trousers pocket. As the spectators touch the cards, one at a time, write an abbreviated name for each, thus, JD, 10H, 3S, and so on. Palm the card and add it to the pack when you gather up the cards. Cut or shuffle the cards after adding the palmed card. The spectator himself is thus the innocent bearer of the necessary information. For impromptu work with a borrowed pack palm one of the two's and use it for writing the names of the cards.

TOY TELEPHONE READING

Assistant is seated on the stage, performer carries a pack of cards and a toy telephone amongst the audience. A spectator selects any card then whispers softly into the telephone a request for the medium to name the card. She does this correctly. This may be repeated as often as desired.

The information is given by a silent code as follows:

SUITS. Hearts: Phone in right hand, receiver on hook.

Diamonds: Phone in left hand, receiver on hook.

Clubs: Phone in right hand, receiver off hook.

Spades: Phone in left hand, receiver off hook.

VALUES. Divide into four sections, omitting the K:

(1) A, 2, 3.   (2) 4, 5, 6.   (3) 7, 8, 9.   (4) 10, J, Q.

1. Hand spectator the phone and ask him to stand up.
2. Ask him to stand, then hand him the phone.
3. Have him stand up, hand him the phone, then sit down.
4. Merely hand him the phone.

Signal position in each of the sections thus:

    1st number, if performer does not remove telephone from spectator.
    2nd number, if he takes telephone with right hand.
    3rd number, if he takes telephone with left hand.

DUO-MENTALITY   Albright

This is a trick for two people, the name of a card being apparently transmitted to one of them without any apparent means of communication.

The secret lies in the use of an Eversharp pencil, known as a propelling pencil and which has a transparent barrel. In this barrel there is a series of spirals, one of which is red. By holding the nickel tip and turning the barrel the lead is forced out and the red signal moves down one spiral towards the tip. It follows that any number from one to thirteen can be signalled by bringing the red point to the required spiral, so covering the value of any card. The cap band can be replaced in four different positions in relation to the barrel of the pencil; let these indicate C, H, S, D.

With the pencil in hand let any card be named and while the spectator finds the card, removes it and puts it in his pocket, set the pencil; it is best to have this at the tenth spiral and move the red signal back or forward as may be necessary. Send the pencil to the medium (who previously had left the room) together with a pad, an old envelope or a piece of paper. She reads the signals, writes the name of the card and this is proved to be correct by the card in the spectator's pocket.

THREE IN ONE CARD TRICK   R. W. Hull

You require a pack, one extra card with the same back pattern and two visiting cards. Discard the Joker and any one of the other cards, inserting in its place the extra card, say the 7D. Find the 7D belonging to the pack and put it on top, the duplicate on the bottom. On one of the two visiting cards write 'Seven of Diamonds'. Turn the written side downwards and put the blank card on top, now put them in a waistcoat pocket, blank card outside.

Show the pack by spreading the faces without exposing the top 7D and riffle shuffle leaving top and bottom cards in place. Divide the pack into two packets of twenty-six cards, by counting off twenty-six from the top without reversing the order of the cards; then count the remainder reversing them in the count. You have thus two packets of twenty-six with a 7D on the top of each. Ask a spectator to call a number between one and twenty-six. Count to that number reversing the cards, bringing a 7D to that position. Put the packet down, take out the visiting cards. Let the top side be seen to be blank, turn over the two and on the blank side of the lower one write the number just called. Put this card on top of the packet, 7D side downwards. Take the other packet and have someone else call a number, count down to it again reversing the cards. Write the number on the second visiting card letting both sides be seen. Force the choice of the first packet, hand it to the spectator to deal to the number he called where he finds the 7D. Hand the visiting card to him and he finds the name of that card written on it. In the meantime you have wet your thumb with saliva. Pick up the packet, transferring the moisture to the back of the top card. Place the 7D on it, cut the cards burying it, unobtrusively squeeze the packet and order the 7D to pass to the other packet at the number chosen freely and recorded on the other visiting card. Let a spectator pick up that packet and hold it. Deal your cards face up, the 7D sticks to the back of the wet card; it has vanished. The other 7D is found at the chosen number.

THE MIDNIGHT MARVEL   V. F. Grant

Effect. A spectator takes the four 2's from his own pack, replaces them in different parts of the pack and shuffles. The pack is handed on again. The four 2's are reversed in the pack. They are taken out. The spectator holds the rest of the pack. The lights are put out and on again, the 2's are again reversed in the pack, and the performer holds four indifferent cards.

Secret. In your waistcoat pocket you have four 2's from a strange pack, the back pattern doesn't matter since it is never seen. When the spectator takes the four 2's and replaces them, tell him to be careful not to put any of them within six cards of the top or bottom. When the lights are put out you simply take out your own four 2's, put them in different parts of the pack reversed, take off four cards from the top of the pack and put them in your pocket.

When the lights are on again, spread the pack backs up and the four 2's (your strange cards) are seen to be face up. Draw them out towards yourself and put them in a face-up packet, being careful not to allow a glimpse of their backs. Run through the pack, saying you will reverse the four cards in different places, any four, you say, but you really reverse the four 2's, this time being careful not to allow a glimpse of their faces. Lights out—put the four 2's (our stranger cards) in your pocket and take out the four indifferent cards you took from the pack in the first phase of the trick.

Lights up—you hold four indifferent cards and the four 2's are again found to be reversed in the pack. The pack is again complete, the stranger cards are safely out of the way and no clue is left.

It is advisable to carry two sets of 2's, one bridge size and one poker size, you are then prepared for whatever cards may be used.

THE LIMIT FOUR ACE TRICK   Billy O'Connor

The four A's are shown and laid singly on the table in a row, or on a card stand. On top of each A three other cards are placed. One pile is now selected and is shown to contain but one A and three indifferent cards, and is placed in a glass facing the audience. The other three piles are picked up, shown to be as represented and are placed back into various parts of the pack. On command the A's are caused to leave the pack and enter the pile on the table; the pack is riffled through and no A's are to be seen, while on fanning the packet which has been standing in the glass they are found to be the four A's.

Preparation. Seven A's are required—One AS and duplicates of AD, AC and AH. These latter six A's are all cut short, and one of each suit is prepared as follows: Paste each one on to the face of an indifferent card, gluing them together at the bottom only, so that you have three double cards with an A showing on the face of each. These three double cards are the ones that will be later dealt on to the AS pile, so it is obvious that when this pile is picked up and ruffled at the top (loose end) by the thumb, only the AS and the three indifferent cards will show, yet when the packets is fanned it shows four A's. Place the prepared duplicate A's third, seventh and eleventh from the top of the pack, and the other three short A's and the AS among the lower cards of the pack.

Routine. Fan the pack and pick out the four single A's and set them in a row on the card stand with the AS in third position. Deal three cards on to each A, one at a time, bringing the prepared duplicate A cards on to the AS. Force this pile, riffle it as explained above to show only the A on the face and three indiferent cards and, set it up in a glass facing the audience. Take up each of the other piles, riffle them in the same fashion and put them back in the pack. Tap narrow edge of pack on the table to settle the 'short' A's and riffle the top edge of pack slowly to show that the A's have disappeared. Fan the packet which has been standing in the glass and show the four A's.

ZEN'S CARD MIRACLE

You will require two packs of readers, that is with marked backs, and a small easel made to hold twenty-five cards in five rows of five cards each. To prepare for the trick sort out the two packs, separate into odd and even cards, counting J's and K's odd, Q's even. From each of the odd packets discard three cards, the 3's of C, S, and D, for instance. You have now two packets of odd cards, twenty-five cards in each. Shuffle one set, then sort out the other into exactly the same order and stack one set on top of the other. Put this pack on the table face down.

Take one of the piles of twenty-four even cards and discard any four, say the four 2's, leaving twenty cards and put these in your upper left waistcoat pocket. Take the other pile of even cards, add one set of the discarded 3's to them making twenty-seven cards and put them in your right-hand coat pocket with a handkerchief over them. Discard entirely the other set of 3's and 2's.

To present the trick, have a spectator cut the pack and count off twenty-five cards. Let him have four cards taken and retained by any four persons. Casually pick up the remaining twenty-five cards and put them in your right coat pocket under the handkerchief with the twenty-seven cards already there making a complete pack. When the helper returns to you take the cards from him and let him choose a card. When you turn your back so that all the five chosen cards can be held up for all to see, quietly take out the twenty even cards from your waistcoat pocket and drop into it the twenty odd cards. Do this without moving your elbows. Have the helper replace his card in the packet and shuffle the cards, then go down and collect the rest, having the cards shuffled as much as is wanted. Taking the packet you lay the cards out on the easel, note the five odd cards and later pick them out as dramatically as you can. Finally switch for the pack in your right coat pocket.

A NOVEL CARD PROBLEM

Two packs are necessary, one ordinary the other with all the cards cut a trifle shorter. Put the short pack in your right-hand coat pocket on its side and you are ready.

Let five or six persons each pick out a card and hand the pack along. This done, go to the first person, have the card returned, bring it to the top and false shuffle, leaving it there. Put the pack in your coat pocket upright. Say that you will bring the card out at any number that may be called. Suppose 7 is the number chosen. Draw out six cards from the short pack and on the seventh bring out the top card of the ordinary pack which is the first card chosen. Bring out the short pack and add the six cards previously drawn from it but leaving the chosen card on the table.

The remaining chosen cards are now returned to the short pack which is given a vigorous shuffle, and you find them with ease and reveal them in various ways. Deal with one card at a time and throw each card as you discover it on the table.

GET IT IN THE DARK   Annemann

Three forcing packs are required. Suppose for the sake of illustration that one pack is made up of A's, the second of 2's and the third of 3's. Remove these three cards from a regular pack and place a forcing pack in each of your outside coat pockets and the third in the right hip pocket. To show the trick:

Have the regular pack shuffled and examined. Take it back and have the lights turned off. At once take forcing pack No. 1 from right coat pocket and drop regular pack into left hip pocket. Let a spectator take the forcing pack, take out one card and return it to your hand. Meantime with your left hand take out pack No. 2. Take back pack No. 1 in right hand and at once give No. 2 to a second spectator with your left hand. Your right hand meanwhile drops No. 1 pack into your right coat pocket. Take No. 3 pack from your right hip pocket, receive pack No. 2 in your left hand and hand out No. 3 with the right. Take out the regular pack from the left hip pocket and when the No. 3 pack is returned slip it into your hip pocket and have the lights turned up. Name the three cards, varying the method of pretended divination each time. These cards being returned complete the pack, and no clue is left to the *modus operandi*.

ZENS' MIRACLE POCKET TO POCKET TRICK

Three packs are required, all with the same backs. Take any fifteen cards from one pack and mix them. Take the same cards from each of the other two packs and put them in exactly the same order as the first fifteen. Stack the three piles together. This pack can now be cut, with complete cuts, any number of times and the first fifteen cards and the next fifteen cards will always be duplicates. Three small envelopes are necessary. In one place any twelve cards from one of the original packs, seal it and put it in your inside or outside breast pocket. Take three more indifferent cards from the same pack, put them under the two remaining envelopes and put the envelopes and cards near the edge of your table, but slightly overlapping it, so that you can pick up cards and envelopes together and keeping the cards concealed below it.

With these preparations complete invite a spectator to cut your prepared pack, complete the cut and deal off fifteen cards. Pick up the two envelopes and the cards, drop them on top of the fifteen, thus imperceptibly adding the three cards to the packet. Have the helper choose one of the envelopes, put the cards into it, seal it and put it in his pocket. Again have him cut the remainder of the pack and deal off fifteen more cards. Taking these down to the audience, he has three cards selected by different people and replaced. He then brings the cards back, shuffles them and puts them in the remaining envelope which is sealed. Take it from him, pointing out that you have not touched a card, and push the envelope into your coat pocket but instantly bring out the one already there which contains twelve cards only. Give it to someone to hold. (If you use the outside breast pocket the envelope can remain there in full view.) The trick is now done and you have simply to work up the dramatic part. Order the three chosen cards to pass from one envelope to the other. One is found to have twelve cards and the other eighteen, with the duplicates of the three chosen cards amongst them.

NEAT CARD DETECTION

The cards of a Bicycle Air Cushion finish pack can be divided into two classifications. The parallel ridges and depressions which run the length of the backs of the cards do so in different directions. The few on which they run straight up and down should be discarded beforehand. Sort the cards accordingly into two packets, making a bridge between them. To locate a card simply cut at the bridge, hand one packet to a spectator and keep the other. He takes any one of his cards, notes it, and pushes it face down into your packet. Let him take the packet immediately and shuffle it. You can readily find his card by the backs alone. Reveal it in as striking a way as possible.

NEW CARD LOCATOR

Take any court card face downward and place a sixpence on the centre of its back. Hold the coin firmly with the thumbs and press firmly and evenly with the fingers from underneath all around the card. The shape of the coin will be clearly impressed on the card, a rim, imperceptible to the eye, being left on the face of the card. The cards may be freely shuffled by a spectator and the prepared card will pass unnoticed, yet you can find it instantly by squaring the pack and cutting. After a card has been chosen simply cut at the prepared card, have the selected card returned on top of the lower half and drop the cut fairly and openly on top. You have simply to square the pack, cut at the locator card and riffle shuffle, leaving the chosen card at the top to be dealt with as you please.

Or you may hold the pack as for the Charlier Pass, relax the pressure of the thumb and the pack will always break at the prepared card.

THE FOURTEEN PACK   R. W. Hull

This pack is so arranged that after a spectator has shuffled it and then, while still retaining it, has thrust the Joker into it anywhere, the cards above and below it, or the two cards above or below, will always give a total of fourteen if their values are added together.

The cards must first be set up, then their backs and faces prepared. For the set-up make four piles of cards in order from A to K with the suits well mixed in each pile. From the first draw out the top and bottom cards, A and K, putting them together; then the Q and 2, Jack, 3, 10 and 4 and so on. Each packet will give six pairs totalling fourteen, and the four 7's making two more pairs you will have twenty-six pairs with the Joker being the odd card. Place the pack so arranged face down on a table. The back of the top card must be polished and its face roughened: the second card must have its back roughened and its face polished; the third, back polished, face roughened, and so on throughout the pack.

Finally, roughen both sides of the Joker. For the process of polishing see p. 95, for roughening p. 104.

A pack so arranged and prepared may be handed out to be shuffled overhand without fear since the pairs cling together. If a spectator prepares to dovetail shuffle, stop him under pretence of not wishing to have the cards bent. Now if the Joker goes in between two rough surfaces it will push the cards above and below it out a little on the opposite side, in this case the card above it and the card below will always total fourteen; but if it goes in between two smooth cards, the two cards above or below will total fourteen.

Whether all this trouble merely to force one number is worth while is for the reader to decide for himself.

TELEPATHY?

Effect. The performer fans a borrowed pack of cards with the faces towards himself. He borrows a pencil and puts any mark or initial a spectator may call on one of the cards. He shuffles the pack and asks the spectator to call the name of any card that comes into his mind. He fans the pack, locates the card named and hands it out. It bears the mark or initial that was called. No other card in the pack bears any mark.

Working. This depends on the use of a 'thumb writer'. The borrowing of the pencil, the pretended writing and the return of the pencil, merely built up the effect psychologically. Nothing is written at that time. The card is marked at the moment when it is found in the fan and withdrawn from the other cards.

Thumb writers of various kinds from the thumb-tip to the tiny flesh-coloured metal bands fitting over the ball of the thumb, can be had from the magic dealers. Ingenious performers will find many uses for this gimmick.

THE WHISPERING ENVELOPE   Jordan

Take an envelope of thin paper, insert a red card and show that it is quite opaque. Return the card to the pack and have someone shuffle it. Take the pack and count the cards to see that there are fifty-two, but as you do so run all the red cards to the bottom. Turn your back and holding the cards behind you spread the black cards and have one freely chosen. Put the pack aside. Pick up the envelope, hold it open, address side downwards and parallel with the floor. Have the card inserted face down, press it well into the lower left corner of the envelope, moisten the flap and fasten it. Fold the right-hand end of the envelope over as far as it will go and also the top. Let the spectator hold the envelope by the top right-hand corner. Strike a match and set the lower left corner alight, holding the match for an instant close to the corner when the index of the card will clearly show to you.

When the envelope and the card are destroyed proceed to read the person's mind with the usual hesitation, getting first the colour, then the suit and finally the value.

GREAT PSYCHIC CARD FEAT

This trick is purely bluff but with proper presentation can be made very effective.

You require a red lead pencil and an exact imitation of it, made of wood with the point painted red. Explain to a spectator that you are going to have him mark a card under such conditions that he, himself, will not know what card he marks. Take the red lead pencil from your pocket and mark several small red crosses on a piece of paper to show him what he is to do. Put the pencil back in your pocket, and hand him a pack of cards in which you have already marked a card with a small red cross. Have him shuffle the cards and then hold them behind his back face up. Tell him to cut the pack anywhere he pleases and, if he likes, to cut the pack again. Point out that neither he, nor anybody else can possibly know the card now on top of the face-up pack. Take out the fake pencil, hand it to him and tell him to put a small red cross on the top card. Take back the pencil and put it in your pocket. Have him cut the cards, turn them face down and shuffle them, then bring the pack forward. You can pretend to look right through the cards by par-optic vision and name the card with the red cross on it. Having marked the card yourself you have no difficulty in naming it. He searches the pack and finds that very card marked with a red cross. Casually bring out the red lead pencil and leave it on the table.

CARD STABBING

A card having been chosen, returned to the pack and the cards shuffled, it is discovered by a stab with a dagger although the cards after being scattered are covered with a newspaper.

The newspaper is prepared by having a duplicate of the card concealed in a pocket made by pasting a duplicate piece of newspaper over it. After the cards are spread on the table or floor, lay the newspaper over them in such a way that the card pocket is not directly over any of the cards. A blindfold is tied over your eyes and the dagger is handed to you. Look down the sides of your nose, locate the pocket and after moving the point over the paper in gradually smaller and smaller circles, suddenly plunge it through the paper and the concealed card. Take off the blindfold and tear away the paper, destroying all evidence of the paper pocket.

MIRACLE CARD LOCATION   Vernon

Put a small quantity of gambler's daub, red or blue, on the flap of your own card case in such a position that the case cannot be opened naturally without some of the daub being smeared on the thumb. Ordinary lipstick may be used for red cards, and eye-shadow, the grease variety, for blue.

Hand the prepared case to a spectator to remove the cards. When he pulls out the flap, a small quantity of daub will have been left on the ball of his thumb, so stop him and suggest that he use his own cards. Have him spread them in a row on the table, pick up any card, note what it is, return it to the pack and shuffle the cards as thoroughly as he likes. You leave the room as he does this. On returning you locate the card easily by the daub mark on the back. Use a small quantity of the daub, a few experiments will quickly indicate the right amount.

MIRACLE LOCATION CLUB VERSION   Vernon

A prearranged pack and a small dab of gambler's daub on or under a waistcoat button are required. To present the trick the pack should be false shuffled and cut, or at least a series of straight cuts made. Several spectators are allowed free selection of cards but each time a card is drawn you make a light smear with the daub taken on your second finger-tip from the waistcoat button on the card above. Four or five cards may be taken and the pack handed out for their return and shuffled as much as the spectators wish.

To locate the cards you have merely to find the cards marked with the daub and pick out, in each case, the card following it in the system used. Place these cards face down on the table. When you have them all, pick up the packet and hold it with the backs of the cards to the spectators. The drawers are asked to call their cards in turn and you pull each card slowly from the packet and show it.

The same system can be used effectively as a mediumistic stunt.

TELEPATHIC SELECTION

James Maxwell
Magic Wand, March 1920

This is the first description of a carbon card and since the invention has been claimed and sold by so many since the date it appeared, this belated credit should be given.

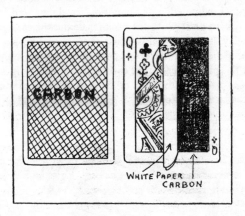

WHITE PAPER
CARBON

To prepare, take a spare card, either the Joker or the plain card usually supplied with a pack. Soak this for some time in water and carefully peel off the back, then dry it with blotting paper placed between the leaves of a book to keep it flat. Cut a piece of carbon paper slightly smaller than the card and gum this to the prepared back, the tracing side outwards. Next take a court card from any spare pack and with a razor blade cut on the line that encloses the picture along the top and bottom and one side, so that the centre of the card will open like a book, the uncut left side acting as a hinge.

Paste the prepared back on top of this card, leaving the central flap quite free. Fit a small piece of thin white paper between the flap and the carbon sheet, adding a dot of gum at each corner. This paper can be used for two cards but must be renewed for each performance. This card is on the top of the pack which is used as a rest when the name of the card thought of is written. When you take the pack and run through the faces it is necessary only to lift the flap and read the impression. The prepared card can then be palmed and disposed of. Methods for using the card are left to the reader.

MENTAL MASTERPIECE

Annemann

Buy a pack of Bicycle Cards, the case of which contains a replica of the back design of the cards. Cut this out of the case. Split one of the cards and to its back paste a piece of good black pencil carbon paper cut to size, the prepared side of the carbon paper downwards. Paste around the quarter-inch white edge of the cut-out card case and lay the prepared carbon card on it. With the pack inside put the case under heavy pressure to dry. To use this faked case put a card with but few spots, such as one of the 2's, on the face of the pack and put the pack in the case so that this card is next to the carbon paper. Anything written on a piece of paper placed on the back of the case will be reproduced by the carbon on the face of the top card. The pencil used should be a hard one

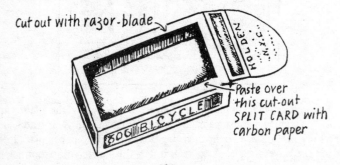

Cut out with razor-blade

Paste over this cut-out SPLIT CARD with carbon paper

and not more than three inches long so that the writer is induced to bear down heavily.

To present the trick, or rather a trick, since the fake can be used in many ways, invite a spectator to step forward. Tell him to merely **think** of any card in the pack, he can change his mind as often as he likes till he fixes definitely on one card. Merely as a matter of precaution and as a means of helping him to concentrate on the card, hand him a piece of paper and a pencil and ask him to write the name of the card. Casually take the pack and place it under the paper as a support. Turn away while the writing is done, telling him to fold the paper and put it in his pocket. Take back the case and the pencil and impress on the subject that he must concentrate his thoughts on the card while you run through the pack. Take this out with the cards facing you, read the impression on the top card and after the proper amount of hesitation and searching, take out the card and lay it face down on his outstretched hand. Have him take out the paper and read the name of the card then hold it up for all to see.

AUTOMATIC SECOND DEAL   Vernon

To achieve a perfect second deal, make a small hole in the corner of a card at the point at which the ball of the thumb lies when the pack is held in position for dealing, in the left hand. This hole must be just large enough to allow part of the ball of the thumb to touch the card below when the prepared card is placed on the top of the pack. With the card thus placed the left thumb can push off two cards evenly. The lower card is then pulled out by the tip of the right second finger (the first finger acts as a shield) and is seized between the thumb and second finger and dealt on to the table, the left thumb simultaneously pulling back the prepared card to the top. It is this pulling back of the top card that makes the deal so deceptive.

To give a demonstration, have the faked card sixth from the top. Turn up the inner index corner of the top card and miscall it as the prepared card. Deal five cards very rapidly, then take off and show the prepared card, covering the hole with the finger and thumb. Replace it on top and say you will deal seconds again but more deliberately, then deal as described above, throwing the cards face down or face up as your fancy dictates and every now and then showing the top card still in position. With a minimum of practice a very convincing demonstration of second dealing can be made.

MAGICARDO

This trick is performed with a pack that has a hole cut lengthwise through the centre of the cards. The slit is about two and a half inches

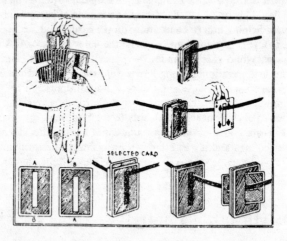

SELECTED CARD

long and about half an inch wide, so that a card can be pushed through it if turned endwise. It is cut slightly nearer to one end than the other. If the pack is set with all the slits coinciding and one card is reversed the end of that card must protrude slightly when the pack hangs on a ribbon passed through all the slits. That is the secret.

When any card has been freely chosen, simply turn the pack round before the card is replaced. Thread a ribbon through the slits, throw a handkerchief over the pack and then give the two ends of the ribbon to be held. The end of the chosen card will protrude above the others. Reach beneath the covering and find the protruding card, separate the pack at that point and push the card right through the holes in the cards on one side of it or the other. Push the pack together and bring the card out upright like the others. Remove it from the ribbon and show that it is the chosen card. The card may be marked and several may be used at once.

STEREOTYPED—Reading the Cards

A spectator shuffles the cards and takes one. You feel it with your hands behind your back to get the vibration? With a piece of chalk you draw a correct picture of the card on a slate or blackboard.

The cards are prepared beforehand by tracing the indices with Carter's red ink for the red cards and any good black ink for the black suits. You moisten the tip of right forefinger and when pretending to feel the card simply press the finger-tip on the index and so get an imprint of it. This can be read under cover of handling the chalk if you finish the trick using a slate or a blackboard.

Editor's Note.—Dr. Bates of Freemont, Ohio, was the first to show this trick. He used indelible blue and red pencils to trace the indices.

THOUGHT CARD DISCOVERED   Devant

Invite a spectator to think of any card and then remove it from the pack, put it face down on the table and spread a handkerchief over it. While this is being done take a small black pin, which you had placed beforehand in the lower edge of your waistcoat, and hold it, point down, between the second and third fingers of your right hand. Put this hand on the handkerchief just over the card, place your left hand on top of your right and have the spectator put his hands on top of yours. Telling him to concentrate his thoughts on his cards. Push the pin into the top right-hand corner of the card, which will raise a tiny lump on its face. Then let the spectator replace the card in the pack and shuffle freely. Quietly drop the pin on the carpet. Take the pack and deal the cards face up, and when you reach the marked card, the tiny protuberance can be felt by forefinger. Note what it is but go right on. Accuse the spectator of not concentrating. Spread the cards face up, grasp his hand and sweep the other hand over the line of cards. Drop it dramatically on the chosen one.

IMPROMPTU DETECTION

This trick had better be done with a pack of well-used cards. After such a pack has been thoroughly shuffled take it and secretly draw your thumb-nail obliquely across one side, leaving a scratched line. Hand the pack to a spectator to cut the cards while he decides on any number under twenty. He then deals cards face down to that number, note the next card and replace the dealt cards on top of it. Finally he is to cut the cards again so that all possible trace of his operations is lost. This is all done while your back is turned.

You locate the card by the scratch. When the spectator first cut the pack, the line is divided into two parts. When he counts off a number of cards their order is reversed and the scratch on their edges will slant the opposite way. All you have to do is to see that all the cards with the reversed slant are in the same group, cut at lowest of these cards and the next card will be the one noted by the spectator. You can learn its identity by cutting so that it is the bottom card of the top half and sighting it as you riffle shuffle. Reveal the card in any way you wish.

NINE IN TEN DETECTION

Mark any card with a pencil dot on the top left corner and the lower right corner. If you are working with a borrowed pack you can do this during some previous trick in which you have had occasion to turn your back.

Hand the pack to be thoroughly shuffled. Take it back and fan it, faces of the cards to the front to show it well mixed, spot the dotted card and cut to bring to the top. Divide pack and riffle shuffle, sighting the bottom card of the left-hand portion and letting it drop first, and retaining the marked card on top of the pack. With the pack face down on your left hand, seize about half the cards near their inner ends between the right thumb and second finger, the forefinger pressing down on the middle, lift the cards, giving the end of the packet a rather sharp squeeze and put it on the table. Take the remainder in the same way and drop them on top. Apparently you have made a simple cut, really you have made a bridge at the inner end of the pack while the outer ends of the cards lie flat.

Put the pack face down on your left hand and invite a spectator to cut and note the card at the face of those taken off. He can only cut at the ends and in all probability will cut at the bridge. If the dotted card is at the top of those remaining in your left hand you know he has cut at the card you sighted, so you hand these cards to him and let him shuffle as much as he likes. You can reveal the card as you wish. If, however, he cut at another point, let him put his packet face down, yours going alongside it. Cut both packets, yours at the crimp, and in putting them together, see that the bottom part of his packet goes on top of the crimp, then cut at the crimp for a riffle shuffle and sight his card in the action. You will not often have to do this, however,

Magical Mysteries With Special Packs, etc.

IT'S UP TO YOU

This trick can be done with any pack. Have the cards shuffled by a spectator, take them and under pretence of finding out if the pack is complete, count the cards face down on the table. As you deal the second, third and fourth cards press the nail of your second finger on the face of each card near the top right-hand corner. A slight lump will thus be made on the backs of these three cards in just the position to be felt with the ball of the left thumb in dealing the cards. After the count the three marked cards will be second, third and fourth from the bottom.

Allow a card to be freely selected and noted. Put the pack on the table, the chosen card is placed on top and the pack cut by the spectator, burying it. Tell him to deal the cards one by one into two, three, or four heaps as he pleases. Infallibly this will bring his card above one of the marked cards. Let him look through the packets and hand you the one containing his card, face down. Pretending you have to know just how many cards are in the packet, deal the cards face down. When you feel the lump you know that the card just dealt is the chosen one. Count the number of cards you deal on top of it and you know its exact position enabling you to reveal it in any way you please. Present the trick as being dependent on an intricate mathematical formula.

17

The Use of Short Cards in Magical Effects

Probably the earliest device in the way of preparing cards for secret use in performing tricks was the wide or long card. As the name implies, one card is a trifle wider or longer than its fellows and therefore projects slightly either at the end or the side. To prepare such a pack have all the cards but one slightly shortened or narrowed by means of a printer's guillotine. Later came the thick card, two cards glued together and dried under pressure, which can be easily found by the fingers in riffling the edges. Variations of this idea such as cutting the picture of a court card from its frame and gluing it to the face of a duplicate court card, cutting out the spots and gluing them over the spots of a duplicate card, etc., but all of these devices are liable to detection when the pack is handled by a spectator. The most satisfactory method is that of cutting one card a trifle shorter than the rest. Such a card forms an invaluable key card, it can be found immediately by riffling the pack and is practically indetectable to anyone who does not already know of it.

As with strippers, to handle the short card intelligently requires some practice and the card should be lightly cut that the difference in length would only be revealed by minute inspection. The use of a card cut so short that the pack divides at it, when riffled, with a loud click, simply ruins an artifice that is invaluable when intelligently used. To anyone having a working knowledge of the few indispensable sleights the short card is a very valuable accessory. The danger is that it renders some operations so easy that the beginner especially comes to depend on it entirely.

The drawback to the short card is that it has to be prepared and therefore can only be used with your own pack. On occasion this can be overcome by carrying a small pair of scissors and working an effect that entails your leaving the room. By carrying off one of the cards in use you can cut off a shaving and secretly return the card to the pack. There is, however, a plan for getting the same effect easily and quickly with any pack at a moment's notice. This was, I believe, devised by Louis Nikola, the English magician, at any rate he was the first to record it in print in his book *The Nikola Card System* which was published in 1927. The plan he recommends there is to bend up the bottom left-hand corner of a card and work it between the thumb and finger until it is soft. Only a small corner is necessary, say to within an eighth of an inch or so of the edge. When the cards are riffled with the thumb across this corner, the cards will break at that point, so that such a card may be put practically to all the uses of a short card.

The following tricks with a short card have been selected from *Tricks with a Short Card*, by U. F. Grant, the well-known magician and magic dealer. They will serve to illustrate the uses to which the principle can be put. It would be impossible to give more since there is hardly a card trick in which a short card could not be employed. I reiterate that the short card should not be used constantly but only on occasion, when it becomes an invaluable weapon for throwing the spectators off the track.

CARD FROM NOWHERE

You may have a duplicate of the short card planted in one of your pockets or in any other place you please. Having forced the short card by the riffle force simply order it to leave the pack and go . . . to wherever you have the duplicate hidden. Riffle again and show that the card has vanished, then produce the duplicate.

ON THE TOP

Force the short card by the riffle, or any other way you have at your disposal, have it replaced and the pack shuffled by a spectator. Take the pack and bring the short to the top secretly, if you can, if not then by simply cutting at the short.

Lift the two top cards as one, the top card being short makes this an easy matter. Replace the two cards as one, order the chosen card to mount to the top and show it.

The Use of Short Cards in Magical Effects

X-RAY EYES

Place the short card ninth from the bottom. Have a spectator select a card from anywhere above these nine. Lay the pack on the table and instruct the spectator to put his card, after noting it, on top of the pack and cut the cards burying his card in the middle.

Pick up the pack, quietly riffle to the short card and cut at that point bringing it to the top. State that you have X-ray eyes that can pierce through the thickness of the cards and detect at what number the chosen card lies. Put the pack on the table and have the card named. Gaze intently at the back of the pack and finally announce that the card is the tenth card from the top. Let the spectator deal nine cards and turn up the tenth, his card.

It must be remembered that the chosen card is always one card farther down than the number at which you place the short card from the bottom.

A COLOUR CHANGE

Use a blue-backed pack and on the bottom place a red-backed short card. Fan the pack for the free selection of a card being careful not to expose the red-backed card at the bottom. Have the chosen card noted, put on the top of the pack and bury it in the middle with a complete cut. Square the cards very openly, tapping the ends and sides on the table to obviate any suspicion that you mght keep the location.

Put the pack behind your back saying that you will try to pick out the selected cards under impossible conditions. Riffle to the short, take off that card and the next, the selected card, as one card and bring them forward showing the face. The spectator admits that the card is his and you ask him if he knows how you could possibly know it was his card. He says 'No'. 'Because it has a red back' you say, turning the card and showing the back. Drop the two on the pack and take off one only. Snap it to show it is a single card but don't show the face again.

CUT CARD FORCE

Have two or three cards cut short and put them in the middle of the pack. Square the cards and place the pack on the table.

Invite a spectator to cut about the middle and the cut will always be made right above the topmost of the short cards, the card that is to be forced. In using this force always place, or better still hold, the pack so that the cut is made naturally at the ends.

ANOTHER FORCE

With the short card on the top of the pack, shuffle several times leaving the card in position on the top. Ask a spectator to call any number from one to twenty. Suppose ten is chosen. Count off nine cards keeping them in the same order and put them on the bottom of the pack. Have the spectator look at the top card, note what it is and replace it. Let him then cut the cards burying his card in the middle.

As you go to a second person, find the short by riffling and make the pass at that point, or openly cut the cards. Tell him you will count down ten cards and have him look at and remember whatever card is at that position now. Go through the same routine and he naturally gets the same card as the first man.

Go through exactly the same procedure with a third spectator and you have forced the same card on all three. Finish the effect in any way you wish.

TO ANY NUMBER

To begin have the short card on the bottom, have a card selected, noted, placed on the top of the pack and make a complete cut. Secretly find the short card and cut, or make the pass, including the short card, bringing it again to the bottom and the chosen card to the top. Ask the spectator to call a number, suppose he says 'Five'. Count off five cards at one time on to the table and drop the pack on top of them. Lift off the top card, then stop and say, 'Oh, my mistake, this is the sixth card and you said five. We will start all over again.' Riffle to the short and cut bringing that card to the bottom. The chosen card is now fifth from the top.

HOROSCOPE CARD FORCE

Have the short card on the bottom and the card you want to force on the top of the pack.

Ask a spectator what month he was born in, suppose he says 'May'.

Illustrate then just what you want him to do. Deal the first card on the table calling it January and continue the deal calling the next card February, and so on until you reach May. Leave that card on the top telling him that would be the card he would look at if he were dealing the cards. Drop the pack on the cards dealt and give the cards a complete cut. Find the short card and make the pass, or make a cut openly, bringing the short card to the top.

Hand the pack to the spectator. He counts down to his month, May, and he will get the card that was originally on the top of the pack, thus making a very novel force. You may write 'Happy Birthday' on the card beforehand and then force it.

A SPELLING TRICK

Prepare by placing on the top of the pack four cards whose names will spell with twelve, thirteen, fourteen and fifteen letters in that order. You may use any cards that fill the requirements such as the 8C, 7H, KD and 8D. The short card you place eleventh from the bottom and you are ready.

Give the pack a quick riffle shuffle not disturbing the set-up at the top and bottom. Fan out the four top cards to a spectator and have him mentally select any one of them. Close the fan, drop the four cards on the top of the pack and make a complete cut. Cut again at the short card and hand the pack to the spectator telling him to spell his card by removing a card from each letter and on the last letter to turn the card over. He does so and turns up the card he thought of.

THE LOCATOR   Maxwell

With a short card on the top of the pack have any card selected and returned to the top of the pack. Hand the pack to be shuffled. Performer takes back the pack and riffles for the short card and cuts the pack bringing the short card to the top and the selected card will invariably be on the bottom to be produced as desired. The chances of the short card and the selected card staying together during the shuffle are about 90 per cent.

BEHIND THE PACK   U. F. Grant

Have the short card on top of the pack which you hand to a spectator.

Instruct him to fix on any number in his mind and, while your back is turned, deal cards one by one face down to that number, then look at the next card, remember it, replace it face down on the pack and put the dealt cards on top. Finally, tell him, he is to make a complete cut. You turn away and the spectator carries out your instructions.

Turn and take the pack. When the spectator dealt cards from the top the short card naturally became the bottom card of the pile, and when he replaced the pile on the card he looked at, the short card was brought immediately above it. All you have to do, therefore, is to cut the short card and all the cards above it to the bottom and you have the chosen card on the top of the pack. To simply lift the card and say, 'Here is your card,' would be too crude a finish. Having the card so easily at your command every effort should be made to devise some striking method of revealing it.

DOUBLE LOCATION

Shuffle the pack freely, locate the short card and cut it to the bottom. Invite a spectator to cut the pack into two piles, call the top half A, the bottom half B, take the top card of B, note it and put it on top of A, then place pile B on top of pile A. The short card has thus been brought immediately above the spectator's card. Take the pack, riffle to the short card and cut, complete the cut and you have the short card on the top of the pack.

Ask a second spectator to do exactly as the first spectator did, that is, make a free cut, look at the card on the top of the lower heap, put it on the upper heap and complete the cut. This time the chosen card has gone on top of the short card and it therefore lies between the two selected cards. Take the pack, riffle to the short card and draw it out, but as you do so retain the location by slipping the tip of the left little finger in at that spot. Show the card as being taken at random, turn it face up and thrust it into the pack again apparently at random but really being careful that it goes in at the break.

After giving some plausible reason for the two chosen cards being attracted to the reversed card, fan the pack with the backs outwards, the reversed card showing about the centre. Draw the short card upwards about half-way out of the pack and do the same with the card on each side of it. Ask the spectators to call the names of their cards. Turn the two cards and show their faces.

The Use of Short Cards in Magical Effects

A REVERSED LOCATION

Place the short card on the bottom of the pack, shuffle overhand retaining it in that position, then fan the pack and have a card freely selected. Place the pack down, have the spectator put his card on the top and make a complete cut, then carefully square up the cards. Take the pack and riffle it showing the faces to the audience to prove that there are no reversed cards in it. The short card will not be exposed since it will fall with the card immediately in front of it as one card.

In accordance with whatever plot you have arranged for the effect, fan the pack and show that a card has mysteriously reversed itself, take out the card next below it, have the spectator name the card he chose, turn the card and show it.

VANISHING CARD

Have the pack freely shuffled, take it back and locate the short card by riffling the ends. You require it to be in a position a little above the middle of the pack and if it is not just right make a cut to bring it where you want it. Go to a spectator and explain to him that you will riffle the ends of the cards so (riffle them), and that you want him to call 'Stop', whenever he pleases. Start the riffle rather slowly and at the call of 'Stop' let the cards break at the short card. Separate the cards at this point and have the spectator remove the short card, look at it and replace it in any part of the pack he pleases. Square the card and hand them out to be shuffled.

Take the pack and order the chosen card to vanish, ruffle the cards slowly before the spectator's eyes and apparently his card has left the pack, the short card cannot possibly show since it falls simultaneously with the card preceding it. Quietly riffle to the short card and bring it to the top secretly, or by simply making a cut. Order the card to return, have it named and turn the top card showing it has obeyed orders.

After having shown that the card has apparently left the pack you may go to a second spectator, have him shuffle the pack then force the short card on him also. Let him take it out holding it face down. Ask the first spectator to name the card he chose and have the second person turn over that very card.

18

More Miscellaneous Tricks

EVERYWHERE AND NOWHERE

This brilliant trick was the invention of the late Dr. Hofzinser of Vienna, who was regarded as the greatest card conjuror in the world. In his hands this experiment must have been a veritable masterpiece of artistic card conjuring and the modern magician will find this latest adaptation* a decided addition to his repertoire.

This is one of the most effective card tricks ever devised. The reason that it is so seldom seen is probably because the explanation given in the textbooks are unnecessarily complicated and give the trick the appearance of being difficult. The moves in the routine that follows have been arranged to simplify the procedure as much as possible.

The only requirements are—a small stand or card easel, or failing that, three glasses, against which to stand cards for display, an ordinary pack of cards with two extra duplicate cards, two 10S's for example. Any card can be used but the black suits are preferable if the feat is to be performed before a large audience since the spots stand out so much more plainly under artificial light. Let us suppose that 10S's are used, place all three on top of the pack. Begin by shuffling the pack overhand in this manner—under cut about three-quarters of the pack, injog the first card and shuffle off. Ask a spectator to draw a card, insert the tip of the left little finger below the jogged card and, spreading the pack, force

---

* Reprinted from *Card Manipulations* by Jean Hugard (p. 112–15). The five sections of this book are now published by Max Holden, N. Y. C. as one volume, and comprise the very latest tricks and all the sleights known to modern card conjuring. Four versions of 'Everywhere and Nowhere' are given. Other presentations of this trick will be found in T. Nelson Downs' *The Art of Magic*; and in *Modern Card Effects and How to Perform Them*. Hofzinser's original version will be found in his book *Card Conjuring* by Ottokar Fischer and edited by S. H. Sharpe.

one of the three 10's. This is much easier and more natural than making the pass to bring the 10's to the middle. The shuffle, being quite genuine as far as the cards actually shuffled are concerned, tends to throw the spectator off guard and renders the force easier. In any case there should be no difficulty in forcing one of the three 10's.

As the spectator notes his card, close up the pack and insert the tip of the left little finger above the two remaining 10's. Hold the pack in right hand, fingers at the outer end, the thumb at the inner end, holding the break. As you ask the spectator to replace his card allow a few cards to drop from the bottom of pack on to your left palm, then a few more, finally let drop all the cards below the break and hold the left hand out to receive the chosen card which is thus returned on top of the other two 10's. Make the pass, bringing the 10's to the top.

It is necessary now to place the 10's so that one shall be next to the bottom card, one on top of the pack and the third one third from the the top. To do this the simplest way, grasp the pack with the right hand as for an overhand shuffle, press firmly on the top and bottom card with the fingers and thumb on the left hand and lift all the cards but these two with the right hand. The top card, the first 10, will fall on the bottom card and you drop the cards from the right hand on top of them, thus placing the first 10 next to the bottom. Do this casually, while talking, then as if having changed your mind as to the manner of shuffling split the pack in half and riffle shuffle. Let the two lowest cards in the left-hand packet fall first, then execute a genuine riffle until the packets are reached. Hold back the top card of the left-hand packet and let it fall between the two top cards of the right-hand packet, i.e. between the other two 10's. The three cards are now in the position required—one on the top, one third from the top and the last next to the bottom card.

The usual patter runs to the effect that by means of a scientific system a card can be found in a shuffled pack in not more than three trials. 'The most likely position,' you say, 'is the top of the pack.' Make a double lift and show the second card.

'Is this..........of..........your card?'

'No.'

'Then I'll put it here on the table out of the way.' Turn the two cards down, as one, take off the top card, the first 10S, and put it face down on the table or easel, or stand it upright against one of the glasses.

'The next likely position is on the bottom. Here is your card, the ....of...........' Say this confidently as if sure of its being right and hold the pack upright in the left hand, the bottom card facing the audience.

'What? Wrong again? Then I must put this card with the other one.' Drop the left hand and by means of the Glide draw out the second 10S and put it beside the first. Now shuffle overhand by first running one card, then drop about half the pack on it, injog one card and shuffle off. The last 10 being the next card below the jogged card, make a break at that point with the right thumb at the inner end of the pack, separate the next two cards, 10S and an indifferent card, from the rest and push them forward, as one card, till they protrude from the outer end of the pack for about an inch. Turn the pack upright and with the right hand, thumb at rear and fingers in front, pull the two cards up for about three-quarters of their length above the pack. Assert now with the utmost confidence that you have succeeded.

'I have only this one more chance and as my system has never failed yet this..........of..........simply must be your card. No again? You are sure? Pardon me, but did anyone else see the chosen card? Oh, excuse me. I don't doubt you for a moment, but it is such an extra-ordinary thing for the trick to fail I thought you might have made a mistake. This is not your card.' The more bewildered and anxious you can appear to be, the better the final effect. Drop the left hand, push the lower of the two cards flush with the pack, draw out the upper card, a 10S, and put it with the other two on the table.

'I must finish the trick somehow. You all say that not one of these cards (point to the easel or the glasses) is your card? Very well. May I ask you what was the card you chose? The 10S? Do you think it would be possible for me to make you see any one of these cards as the 10S? No? Let us try. Which one shall I take? The middle card?'

Take that card and hold it with its back to the audience.

'Of course it isn't really a 10S, but it will appear so to you.'

Wave your hands in pretended hypnotic passes, then turn the card face out.

You all see it as the 10S? Very well, I will replace it here.'

Make the bottom change in the swing towards the table and put the indifferent card down face inwards.

'You are still sceptical? Let me prove that you are all under hyp-notic influence. Of these two which would you like to see as the 10S? This one? Very well.'

Repeat the same business and again change the card for an indifferent one by the bottom change, placing this card down with the first.

'One card only is left. You will see this also as a 10S.'

Show the card as before, but this time it must be changed by the top change. Show the card upright, holding it with fingers on top end, thumb on the lower. The left hand holds the pack close to the body about waist high, as you say:

'Of course the card is not a 10S. The real 10 is here in the pack'

Drop the right hand bringing the card on top of the pack and at the same moment push the top card of the lower pack over to the right. Release the 10S from the right hand and grip this top card in exactly the same way. A moment later the left thumb pulls the 10 squarely on to the pack and moves away, the right remaining stationary. Finally place the indifferent card with the other two.

'Let me give you further proof. You see this top card?'

Make the double lift and show an indifferent card. Name it and turn the two cards, as one, face down. Take off the top card, a 10S, and after more hypnotic passes turn its face to the spectators.

'Now you see it as the 10S.' Replace it on top. Wave your hands again.

'Now look at the bottom card. It also is the 10S.'

Hold the pack upright and show the 10 on the bottom. Under cover of this surprise make the pass and hold a break with the right thumb between the two packets. Show the pack upright in the right hand, bottom card facing the audience, an indifferent card is now seen to be there.

'It is all an optical illusion. The cards are not really 10S's. They only appear so.'

Place the pack in the left hand and slip the tip of the left little finger into the break. Lift off the top card and show it is an indifferent card now.

'But when I put you under the influence you can see the 10S only, look.'

Cut the pack at the break and hold the top portion upright, a 10S again faces the audience. Insert the tip of the left little finger under the top card of the lower packet, i.e. the third 10. Replace the top packet and make the pass, bringing the three 10's to the bottom, riffle off the inner ends of these three cards and insert the tip of the left little finger between them and the rest of the cards, and hold the pack in position to execute the bottom palm. (Erdnase, p. 86.)

'I know exactly what you all suspect, that I have been trying to mislead you and that all the cards are 10S's. I wouldn't do anything as barefaced as that for worlds. Look! This card is not a 10.'

Palm the three 10's in the left hand and at once turn the first card on the table face out. 'Nor this,' turn the next, 'and this last one is not a 10 either.' Turn it also.

'You see there is not a single 10S in the pack.'

Spread the cards face up on the table with a flourish turning your right side to the audience as you do so and slipping the three palmed cards into your left trousers pocket at the same moment.

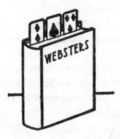

'In fact knowing that card is an unlucky one for my trick, I put it in my pocket before I began. Here it is.'

Thrust your left hand into your pocket, bring out one of the three 10's and throw it on the table.

Smoothly executed and well acted the feat has an extraordinary effect. It is one of the few card tricks suitable for performance before the largest or the smallest audiences. Paul Rosini, the Philadelphia *presti-digitateur*, makes a feature of the trick and in his hands it is a master-piece.

A very good plan for displaying the three cards when performing the trick in the parlour, is to take a large thick book, stand it upright and insert the cards as shown in the illustration. This is another idea of Dr. Jack Daley's who also makes a speciality of the trick. In his hands it leaves nothing to be desired.

THE ORIGINAL 'STOP' TRICK

It would seem almost as if the old-time magicians had used all the plots possible for the presentation of card tricks and that all that is left for the successors is to improve the method by which the old effects were done. This fact is one of the reasons why the public generally com-plains that magic is always the same. While to a magician a modern method of doing an old trick will convert it into a new trick, to the layman it remains simply the same old effect. Not knowing, nor caring to know, the vastly improved methods used to bring the effect about, he simply asks, 'Why do magicians always do the same things?' The best audiences to a skilled magician are those composed of people who know something of the technical part of magic and can therefore appreciate his skill. There would seem to be a good argument here in favour of a widespread promulgation of our so-called secrets, exposures if you will, but that is apart from our subject.

The first of the 'Stop' tricks was used and described by Robert Houdin almost a century ago. Briefly the effect was this—three cards were selected from a pack, replaced and the pack shuffled. Standing beside a table the magician removed cards from the top one by one and laid them down, at the same time inviting the first of the spectators who had taken a card to call 'Now' whenever he chose, and stating that no matter when the call was made the card then in his hand would be the spectator's. Such proved to be the case and the same effect was repeated with the remaining cards.

The Effect as Worked by Ralph W. Read

Props and Preparation. A regular pack and a three-bank forcing pack to match; also the well-known 'Card Servante'.

The forcing pack consists of 'short' cards, say sixteen each of 9D, JS and 2H, with a 'long' card between each bank and one 'long' card on the bottom. These three 'long' cards are all alike, say QH. Now add two indifferent 'long' cards to the pack, say a 7S on bottom and a 4D on the top. This pack now has fifty-three cards which go in clip of the card servante on back of table or chair.

In the regular pack locate the 9D, JS and 2H placing them on top of pack, and all is ready.

Performance. False shuffle regular pack and force the 9D, JS and 2H in order. Let spectators shuffle their cards back in, then you take pack, return to the platform and state what has been done, stressing the fact that each spectator shuffled. While talking you cut the pack a few times, but don't expose any cards.

You now reach for the table (bearing servante) with hand holding the regular pack ready for the switch, bring the table forward, and with forcing pack now in your hand, casually expose the bottom card (7S) . . . 'I shall now remove the cards' (you glance at 7S) . . . 'I hope no one took this bottom one' (remove 7S and lay face down on the table) . . . 'I shall take them one at a time' (remove top card—4D—and give the audience a flash of it) . . . and place this on the table (lay down 4D) . . . 'Will the party who selected the first card please say "Now" when he feels the impulse?' You are slowly removing cards (9D) one by one, placing them on the table as you speak and of course you hold his card when he calls 'Now'.

If they delay saying 'Now,' you remove cards at snail's pace—you can be as slow as they, and need never run beyond the sixteen bank. You can by play as to 'this one, or the next?'—'Do you want to change your mind?' etc., before you expose the card, and always have them name it before you turn it over.

You make the pass at the first 'long' card before starting on the second selection, and likewise for the last card. If the bottom card is accidentally exposed, the same QH gives mute evidence that there has been no manipulation.

A later addition to Robert Houdin's trick provided for the spectator striking a bell of the push button variety instead of calling 'Now'. For stage purposes the trick as described is still one of the most effective possible with cards but it is not suitable for close work or small audiences. The method that follows is specially adapted for such cases.

'SAY WHEN'   Al Baker

A forcing pack is still used but it is made up of two different cards instead of three. On top are placed about seven indifferent cards and another indifferent card is on the bottom. Near the centre of the pack the top card of the lower set of force cards is cut short and right above this is another indifferent card. Thus when later the pack is cut at the short card this indifferent card becomes the bottom card of the pack.

A hat rests on your table a little to your right. First, two of the force cards are taken by spectators. They are replaced amongst their own kind and you explain that the spectators will practically find them themselves without knowing where they are. In explaining how the cards are to be passed illustrate by passing one at a time the seven top cards of the pack over to the hat and putting them inside. In doing this stand the cards on their side with the backs outwards.

Now apparently remove these cards, really taking only a couple, and place them on the bottom of the pack. Begin taking the duplicates of the first card, moving each card slowly across the intervening space and dropping it into the hat, until the spectator calls 'Stop'. He names his card, turn the one in hand around, it is the right card.

Reach into the hat to retake the cards dropped in, tip over several of the indifferent cards that stand on their sides so that they fall face up on the force cards. Bring the bunch out openly with the face of the packet to the audience and remark, 'I'm glad you called out at that spot, if you'd called out sooner you'd have missed it.' Place these cards at the bottom of the pack and openly cut it, or secretly make the pass, at the short card.

The third spectator next calls 'Stop' at any card he pleases. As soon as you show that again the stop has been made on the right card, tip over the remaining indifferent cards face up on the force cards in the hat and show the faces of these as you bring out the packet. The subtle use of the indifferent cards completely camouflages the forcing pack and the use of such an expedient will not be suspected.

A MEANS TO AN END   Douglas Dexter

The modern magician specially prides himself on being able to produce with a borrowed pack effects which originally called for the use of specially prepared cards or forcing packs. This is a brilliant example of the solution of one of these problems. The 'Stop' effect is here produced with a borrowed pack. Two hats and a length of wide ribbon are the only accessories required. Place the hats, crown downwards, on the seats of two chairs about four feet apart and stretch the ribbon between them, one end in each hat. A small weight should be attached to each end of the ribbon to hold it in position.

In placing the hats and adjusting the ribbon you have taken the opportunity to introduce into the right-hand hat some ten or twelve cards, previously palmed from the pack. Next have two or three cards freely selected, noted, replaced and brought to the top in whatever way you prefer. Thoroughly shuffle the cards and drop them into the left-hand hat.

Take a card from the bottom of the pack, slide it along the ribbon explaining what you intend to do, just before dropping it into the second hat, turn it around and show that it is an indifferent card, Next take the top card, slide it along the ribbon, back outwards of course, put it quietly into the second hat and instantly back palm it. Dip your hand into hat No. 1 and bring out the same card at your finger-tips. Pass this along the ribbon fairly slowly and repeat the movements until the spectator calls 'Stop'. The card is named and turned and shown to be the one. Repeat the same process with the second and third cards, finally the spare cards are taken out of the second hat and returned to the pack as being those actually passed.

If soft hats are used, have a small tie clip sewn to the ends of the ribbons in lieu of the weights which have a tendency to drag the hats over sideways. These should be sewn so that the ribbon will be vertical and not flat between the hats. The use of a bell or a small whistle instead of the spectator calling 'Stop', makes the trick even more effective. This brilliant method is particularly interesting as being one of the few in which the back palm is put to its legitimate use as a secret sleight and as an example of what might have been done with it had its use not been practically limited to juggling flourishes.

THINK 'STOP'   Al Baker

Effect. Any pack of cards is shuffled by a spectator and handed to the performer, who lays it face down on the table and asks a person to cut the pack at about the centre; to look at and remember the card on the top of the lower part, replace the card and put the portion cut off on top. The spectator squares the cards carefully, cuts it several times and hands it to the performer, who then deals the cards face up, instructing the spectator to merely think 'Stop' when his card makes its appearance. He stops at a certain card which is acknowledged to be the correct card.

Working. All that you require is a tiny pellet of wax, about the size of a pin-head in such a position that you can secure it when you want it, a good place to carry it is on one of your waistcoat buttons. Proceed exactly as described above. When you place the pack on the table request a spectator to cut it about the middle and as you say, 'and put the top half here,' touch the table just to the right of the pack and deposit the pellet of wax. When the pack is cut, and the cut put at the spot you indicated, the wax pellet adheres to the face of the lowest card and therefore is carried to the back of the selected card when the cut is replaced. The two cards stick together, the squaring of the cards bringing their edges together, and the pressure exerted in the further cutting cements them still more securely.

When you deal the double card it is apparent to the touch and you have only to push off the top card of the two and stop on the next. With proper presentation the trick becomes a little miracle.

Editor's Note.—An effective presentation of the above trick can be worked by using a pack with a one-way back, and having the chosen card reversed in the pack. (See Chap. 9.)

THE PSYCHOLOGICAL STOP TRICK

Performer has any card freely selected and returned to the pack. Pack is shuffled and handed to the spectator who is instructed to deal the cards one at a time on to performer's hand and any time he feels like it to stop and the selected card is found there.

This effect is about 97 per cent perfect and when it works is a real miracle in card magic. Paul Noffke, a very clever card man, works this effect and in his hands it is 100 per cent perfect. Max Holden worked it for Tommy Downs and Eddie McLaughlin and had them completely stumped. As the title implies it is a psychological trick and depends on the manner in which the performer instructs the spectator to deal the cards on to his hand.

Working. Any card is selected and while the spectator is looking at his card, performer thumb counts nine cards from the bottom of the pack. These nine cards are removed and taken in the right hand in the action of cutting the pack and the selected card being replaced on the top of the pack the cards in the right hand are placed on top and a false shuffle is made keeping the top ten cards intact.

The pack is handed to a spectator and he is instructed to deal the cards one at a time face down on to performer's hand. When the spectator has reached the third card performer says FASTER. At the fifth card performer says STOP ANYWHERE and times himself in the manner in which he says this. As a rule it will be found that the spectator will stop on the ninth or tenth card. All that remains is to work it up and show the tenth card as the selected card that the spectator found himself. If the spectator stops at the ninth card, performer says, 'Now turn over the next card.' He does so and it is his card. If he stops when the tenth card is on the performer's hand, he just turns it over. In case the spectator goes beyond that card, performer notes the position of the tenth card on his hand and side steals it out bringing it to the top and then revealing it.

The thumb count is very useful in many card effects. Pack is held in the left hand, thumb on one side and fingers on the other. Right hand is on top of the pack, fingers at one end, first finger bent on top and the thumb at the left corner nearest himself. This corner is riffled with the thumb and it is an easy matter to count nine cards as they are riffled. A break is now held here with the left little finger which holds the break until the cut is made.

NUMBER PLEASE   Al Baker and Audley Walsh

Some years ago a trick in which a card was revealed over the telephone by an assistant was very popular with magicians; unfortunately it fell into the hands of the folks who exploited for sales promotion purposes and has become too widely known to be any longer of use to a magician. It is to be hoped this fine trick will not share the same fate.

This is a novel card effect in which the performer tells the selected card by telephone.

AUDLEY WALSH METHOD

Mr. Walsh calls a friend on the telephone and offers to do a trick with cards. The person called is to shuffle a pack of cards and then look at the bottom of the pack and note what card is on the bottom and remember it. He is then to count from the top of the pack, on the table the same number of cards. Say there was a 5C on the bottom of the pack; the person would count five cards from the top of the pack on to the table and then place the balance of the pack in hand, on top of the cards on the table. He is then asked to turn the pack face up and call the cards from the bottom one at a time, slowly. After a number of cards have been called Mr. Walsh names the card that was on the bottom of the pack at the start and remembered by person on other end of the telephone. The means used are very simple, yet the person doing the naming of the cards is thrown right off the track.

You have a pad from one to thirteen written on it.

1	2	3	4	5	6	7	8	9	10	11	12	13

After the person has noted the bottom card and counted the same number of cards to correspond with it and then placed the pack on top of the counted cards he is to turn the pack face up and call the cards slowly one at a time.

As he calls the first card, performer does not count this, but as he calls the second card, JH for instance. Performer notes this on pad under number 1, third card under number 2, etc. For example:

1	2	3	4	5	6	7	8	9	10	11	12	13
JH	4D	6S	2H	5C	8H	9S	3C	9D	6D	QS	4C	2D

All performer does is look over list and see what card corresponds with the number over it. In this case the 5C is under five so that should be his selected card, but very often there will be another card under a corresponding number, say, a 9D appeared under the number nine.

Then it could be one of the two, so you boldly say, 'It was a diamond.' If he says 'No', you know it was the 5C. If he says 'Yes', go right on and finish the trick.

It is necessary that you perform or go through this routine before going to the next method as the second method will not be confusing after this one is learned.

The part that throws the person off the track is—He is calling names of the cards and does not know that you are counting and his attention being on the names of the cards, he does not count.

AL BAKER METHOD

In my method I have a person shuffle the cards and then divide them into two portions. He selects one heap and lays the other heap aside.

Again after shuffling the heap he has, he is asked to note the card on the bottom of the pack, remember it, and then count on to the table the same number of cards as the value of the card on the bottom of the pack. If, say, the 7S was on the bottom of the pack, he must count from the top of the pack on to the table seven cards. He is then asked to place the balance of cards in hand, on top of the cards on table and square the pack.

If he were now to cut the cards it would be impossible to find the selected card and yet, this is what you lead him to believe actually takes place.

You ask him to pick up the cards and call the cards from the top of the pack, slowly. As he calls the first one, say for instance, the AC, you say, 'Just wait a minute, put that card back on top, I forgot something.' He places the A back on top and you continue, 'I wanted you to cut the cards and complete the cut. Will you please do so?' He cuts the cards, BUT, the AC is now your key card. Just remember 'AC'.

Have a pencil and pad handy and now ask him to call the cards by name from the top of the pack. Suppose he called the following cards— you would jot them down in this fashion:

3C AD 5H 2S KH JS QD 7S 3H 8C 5S 6D 2H 4S 9D AC
      7   6   5   4   3   2   1   0   0

When you hear AC you jot this down but let him go on naming cards, but you need not note any after the A is called as this is our key.

To find the selected card you start at the AC and count to your left or back in this manner. You don't count the A nor the next card but at the next or third card you start, 1, 2, 3, 4, 5, 6, 7, 8, and as you come to seven, if there is a 7 card marked down that is his card.

If you count back as you count nine, if there is a 9 corresponding with your count, his card was a 9.

Sometimes there will be, say, a 5 at the five count and a 10 at the ten count. Boldly say, 'Was it a ten?' If he replies in the affirmative, name the 10. If he says 'No', name the 5.

Of course, it is understood, should there be a picture card on the bottom of the pack, at the beginning of his count, say a J, he should count eleven cards on to the table—A Q twelve and a K thirteen.

THE CASE OF THE FOUR KINGS   John J. Crimmins, Jr.

Any pack may be used and there is no preparation required for this effective impromptu experiment.

Remove the four A's and the four K's from the pack and show plainly by running over the cards with their faces to the spectators that there are no duplicates of either. Pick up the K's with the right hand, spread them fanwise and place them on top of the pack held in your left hand. As you close the fan slip the tip of your left finger between the third and fourth K's.

Take the A's, squared together, by the top and bottom outer corners between the right thumb and forefinger and show the face of the outer A. Turn a little to the left in the action of placing the A's on the top of the pack. At the moment that the right hand covers the pack, straighten out your left fingers and carry the three K's upward making an opening between them and the rest of the pack, bookwise. Drop the four A's into this opening and at once close the left fingers bringing the three K's on top of the A's. The pack must be held with its back to the front and almost vertical, the action of raising the K's being completely covered by the back of the right hand.

Deal the four A's, as you say, really three K's and one A, turning the A face up on the other three cards. Deal four K's, really three A's and one K, turning the K face up. Smoothly carried through there can be no doubt about the piles being really the K's and the A's as they appear to be. With your patter running on the lines of 'birds of a feather flocking together' or any other plausible plot, transpose the visible A and K, and then for your climax turn the two piles faec upwards, the other three A's and K's have apparently followed the leaders.

THE J. M. RISING CARD

(Reprinted from *Genii*, Vol. I, No. 1. Sept. 1936)

We are pleased to be able to offer through the courtesy of Jack McMillen, the inventor, a new method of working the rising card experiment that is certain to take its place among the thousand and one ways of working it already in existence. For impromptu work this has many distinctive features. Nothing is required save the cards, which may be borrowed. The card rises actually from the centre of the pack, yet it is held squared up, neither thumb nor fingers being inserted in the pack to push the card up. And the principle employed to attain this effect is absolutely new.

At the request of the performer anyone shuffles the pack and then deals off three cards. The magician picks up these three and requests a spectator to look at one of them. Nine times out of ten it will be the centre card that is selected, but if not, the performer simply asks that a card be taken, and then has it replaced between the other two, so that it becomes the central one of the three.

The three cards are laid momentarily face down on the table, while the pack is placed in the left hand, fingers on one side and thumb along the other. The top card of the three on the table is picked up and shoved into the centre of the pack, but only half-way, being left projecting half its length from the end of the pack. The left thumb holds a break beneath it. The right hand takes up the next card from the table—the noted card—and shoves it half-way into the pack from the end, apparently directly below the card already pushed in. Actually the left thumb releases the card below the first of the three, so that there is a card between the two extending half-way from the pack. The last of three cards is picked up and pushed in below the others, but again the left thumb releases one of the cards of the pack so that the third card is inserted below. Thus we have the pack with three cards extending half their length from its end; unknown to the audience they are separated from each other by indifferent cards.

The pack with the cards still projecting is turned over in the left hand so that the faces of the cards are to the audience. The pack is held with the first finger projecting out beyond the end, other fingers at one side and thumb at the other. The right hand is brought up so that it conceals the inner end of the pack. Now the left first finger pushed the three projecting cards into the pack, flush with the rest. This action causes the indifferent cards between the three to be pushed out the other end by friction. These two projecting cards are concealed by the right hand. Now the right hand held in such a manner that it keeps the projecting cards hidden, bevels the end of the pack spreading the cards downwards slightly at the end from back to front. The performer calls attention to what he is doing and explains that he is about to make the chosen card rise and is spreading the cards so that the spectators will be able to see that the card actually rises from the place where it was inserted. This feature does, incidentally, serve to make the feat more effective, but the real reason for spreading the cards downwards from the end is so that the face cards of the pack are brought down enough to conceal the projecting cards behind them when the right hand is taken away.

The pack is held in the left hand with the fingers on one side and the thumb at the other, near the lower end, the cards being held upright. When working for just one or two spectators, there is no need to worry about angles. When working for more, the pack is held with the left side slightly towards the spectators. From this angle, the left fingers, holding the pack completely screen the cards projecting from the centre, downwards, behind the front cards.

The left little finger is placed under these two projecting cards and they are pushed up flush with the rest of the centre cards. This causes the card between them, the selected card, to rise from the upper end of the pack. Due to the way the cards are spread it can be seen that the card is rising from the centre of the pack. During the rising, the upper end of the pack is tipped slightly towards the spectators, to conceal the movement of the little finger. As soon as the projecting cards have been pushed up flush with the rest, the little finger resumes its place at the side of the pack as the performer offers it to the spectator that he himself remove his card from the position in which it has risen. All the cards are now in the position to which they were openly adjusted and examination of the chosen card, and the remainder of the pack as well will give no clue to the method employed.

MIRASKILL by Stewart James
(Reprinted by permission from *The Jinx*)

I don't know where Mr. James got his title for this mystery, but any time anyone can produce such a problem I'll be the last to argue over what it is to be called. Certainly no concocted effect has in years been so original in effect upon the watchers.

I have used the problem any number of times since learning it, and I have yet to find people who aren't amazed at the outcome. I won't go into any reason why it works because of limits in space, but it does work, and that's about the most important.

The performer has a pack of cards and two pieces of paper with a pencil. The pack may be a borrowed one which has been in constant use. A spectator mixes the cards, and the performer asks if he prefers black or red. Without touching the pack or seeing any of the cards, performer now writes a prophecy on one of the papers and puts it with the writing side down on the table. The spectator is now asked to remove the cards from the shuffled pack two at a time and turn them face up. If two reds are together he is to keep them in a pile before him (we are pretending he wanted red—if black he'd keep black pairs). If two blacks are together he is to put them in a pile before the performer, and if the two are of opposite colour, they are to go into a third or discard pile.

The spectator does as directed, taking the cards off in pairs, and putting them in their correct pile. As soon as all of the cards are separated in pairs, the performer asks the spectator to count the number of cards in his pile and then the number of cards in the performer's pile. Then the spectator is asked to look at and read aloud the written prophecy which has not been touched. It reads, 'Your pile will have four more cards than mine.' AND IT'S RIGHT, **despite the fact that the performer did not touch the cards after the genuine shuffle by spectator.**

Immediately the performer tells another spectator to gather together the cards and shuffle them thoroughly. He writes a prophecy on the second piece of paper AND THEN ASKS spectator which colour he wants for himself, telling him to place pairs of that colour in front of himself, pairs of the other colour in front of the performer, and pairs of mixed colours to the side. Again, the cards are separated and again the two piles are counted. The prophecy, this time, reads, 'We will both have the same number of cards this time.' **And everything may be examined as there is no trickery to find.**

This trick practically works itself. It is based on the actuality that, if a full pack of fifty-two cards be so separated after a genuine mixing, the red and black piles will always contain an equal number of cards. There is no way of telling EXACTLY HOW MANY will be in each pile, but they positively will be the same. Before starting, or during another effect, steal four cards of one colour from the pack. We shall say red. By stealing four cards of a colour you unbalance the pack so that the red pile will be four cards less than the black when finished. If you steal four black cards, the black pile will be four less than the red. You can also steal two or six cards of a colour and the pile of that colour will be two or six less, but four is about right. Don't ask me why it works. It does. Put these four stolen cards facing the body in right trousers pocket.

Now have the pack shuffled. Ask first spectator which colour he prefers. Then write the prophecy to fit. If he wants the 'short' colour, write that his pile will have four less than yours. Now explain how he is to separate the cards and let him go ahead. The outcome will be as you prophesied. About half-way through the cards you drop your hand to pocket and palm the four stolen cards. All eyes and attention being on the two piles, you carelessly pick up those in the discard, square them, and put back, you have added the stolen cards which set you for the second time. No one ever pays any attention to the discard.

The first prophecy having been found correct, the performer, without touching the cards, asks that they be picked up and mixed again. This time you write the prophecy BEFORE asking the spectator which colour he wants. As the pack is now complete, the piles will be the same and it doesn't matter. Now try out this masterpiece and you'll find it to be one of the best card mysteries in years.

MASTER CARD LOCATION   Gibson

With any pack that has been freely shuffled by a spectator, fan it out from left to right for the spectator to select a card, having first secretly noted the card on the bottom. Count the cards as you run them off and when you have reached twelve say, 'Put your finger on any card as it goes by,' and continue to count. When he touches a card, remember its number, turn your head away as he lifts the index corner and notes the card. This done, square the cards very openly and let the spectator cut several times with complete cuts.

To find the card, run them over face up, cut at the original bottom card and count to the number memorized.

MIRACLE CARD LOCATION
Ben Erens

A card having been selected from a shuffled pack you fan the cards in your left hand and allow the spectator to push it in anywhere he pleases. Hold the inner ends of the cards firmly preventing the card from going right home. Close the fan and push the card flush with your right forefinger at the same time giving it a slight nick on the edge with your finger-nail. Take the pack in your right hand and offer it to the spectator to shuffle. The action turns the pack bringing the nicked end of the card towards you. No matter how the pack is shuffled you can detect the card instantly. When you take the pack back simply divide it for a riffle shuffle with the nicked card at the bottom of the right-hand packet. You can then control it as you please.

CARD DETECTED BY PULSE BEAT
Conrad Rheiner

After a spectator has shuffled any pack, take it back, sighting the bottom card as you do so. Turn away and hold the pack in your left hand behind your back. Ask the spectator to cut off a packet freely. Turn to face him and ask if he is satisfied and seize the opportunity to slip the bottom card to the top of those remaining in your left hand. Turn away again and have him look at this card, assemble the pack, put the card in it and shuffle thoroughly.

Now take hold of the spectator's left wrist and press the fingers against the pulse. Instruct him to deal the cards face up and whenever he comes to his card you will detect it by his pulse beat. Knowing the card you have merely to act your part.

IMITATION SECONDS

Secretly get the four J's to the top of the pack with one indifferent card between the third and fourth J's.

False shuffle and cut, retaining these five cards in position. Offer to give an exhibition of second dealing, and rapidly deal out two hands, one to a spectator the second to yourself. When you take off the sixth card to deal it to yourself, don't throw it down, use it as a scoop to pick up the other two cards dealt to your hand and place the three cards on the pack. The three cards dealt to the spectator are turned over, they are three J's. Drop then on top and again deal two hands. Again the spectator gets three J's; one will be of a different suit but you do not allow any time for a close scrutiny. Pick the cards up quickly and repeat the trick two or three times, each time, of course, scooping up your cards as described. It is this action that makes the trick possible, since by it the sixth card dealt, an indifferent one, is brought below the other two cards of your hand, one indifferent card and one J. Thus the set-up is the same every time, three J's, indifferent card, followed by the fourth J.

The trick will be found effective if worked quickly and will pass for an exhibition of super second dealing.

PSYCHOLOGICAL FORCE

This is a method of forcing one card out of four placed face down on a table. Assuming that the spectator is right handed, place the four cards face down in an even row in front of him with the card to be forced in the second place from the right end of the row according to his point of view, the left from yours. When a spectator is induced to take one of four cards quickly this succeeds in about nine out of ten trials.

Another plan is to deal five cards face down in front of the spectator so that they stretch out in a line diagonally away from him. In this case again the choice is almost certain to fall on the card second from the end nearest to him.

FACE-UP LOCATION

Using any pack, shuffled by a spectator if desired, have a card freely chosen and noted and then returned to the pack. Bring it to the top.

Let any other card be taken and thrust into the middle face upwards. Square the pack, then pretending not to have noticed what this face-up card was, run through the pack to find it, In doing this push the top card (the selected one) off the pack into your right hand, then push the cards that follow on top of it with the left thumb. The selected card rests on the right fingers below the others. When you come to the reversed card, stop for an instant, call its name and square up the pack. The chosen card will slide automatically under the reversed card. Hand the pack at once to the spectator; order the two cards to come together and let him verify the fact for himself.

THE DREAM CARD

Effect. A card is freely chosen from a borrowed pack and without being looked at, is inserted in an envelope which is sealed and put into a spectator's pocket. The pack is riffled face up and a stop made at any point called for by a spectator and the card stopped at it noted. The pack is immediately searched, but the card just seen is no longer in the pack. The envelope is opened and in it is found the card just chosen.

Method. To prepare for this most effective feat, sort a pack of cards into suits with each suit in order from A to K. Put one suit in each of your outside coat pockets and trousers pockets. Place an envelope on the table.

Borrow a pack, have it freely shuffled and any card selected but not looked at. Take it face down and insert it in the envelope but glimpse the index in sealing the flap.

Again have the pack thoroughly shuffled and take this opportunity to find the duplicate of the chosen card from one of the packets in your pockets. Palm it face towards your palm. As you receive the shuffled pack place it face up on the palmed card, thus adding the palmed card in a reversed position to the bottom of the pack. Riffle the ends inviting spectator to call 'Stop'. Stop and secretly reverse the lower packet, so that as you lift the top packet the duplicate of the card in the envelope is seen by everyone. Call particular attention to the card, then replace the top packet, again secretly reversing the lower one. Palm the duplicate from the bottom and hand the pack to spectator. The card cannot be found. The envelope, sealed before the card was chosen, is opened and in it is the very same card.

ELIMINATION
R. M. Jamison
Reprinted by permission from *The Sphinx*, May, 1935

Here is a clever interlude at any card table that has proved to be a real mystifier to all. I do not know the origin. I call it the 'Thirty Card Elimination'.

Effect. Thirty cards are dealt from the pack on to the table, into six packets of five cards each. A spectator now takes any two cards from the remainder of the pack, the pack being discarded. Spectator is asked to remember the cards, and place one of them on any packet and other card on any other heap. Performer now takes up the packets and deals them off into two piles. Spectator selects one packet and again deals them off into two piles. Again one pile is eliminated, until only two packets of two cards each remain. The spectator now finds that he has chosen his two original cards.

Method. The performer places any two packets on the first packet on which is the spectator's card and places the two remaining packets on top of the one with the second chosen card. Then either half of the pack is put on the other half. He then deals the cards into two piles. Both chosen cards will be in heap to which the first card is dealt. If the card is dealt to the left pile first, the selected cards will come out in the left pile. In repeating the trick deal the right card first, so that the cards come out in the right side. Deal snappily and lead audience to believe it's a demonstration of crooked or second dealing or what have you.

Vary your 'magician's choice' line of patter. If the thirty-two cards are returned to the pack before dealing, and a few fake cuts, with pack face out, are given, it adds to the idea that the selected cards are hopelessly lost.

A SUPER-REVERSE PROBLEM   By Judson Brown

Numerous excellent versions exist of the effect in which a chosen card reverses itself in the pack; the particular feature of this version is that any card called for is instantly caused to reverse itself in the pack! To give the effect more in detail: the performer first runs the pack from hand to hand, showing without calling particular attention to it that all cards are face down. The spectator is requested to call the name of any card he thinks of; instantly the magician runs the cards from hand to hand again, and the card whose name was called will be found face up in the face-down pack. A further elaboration can be worked by fanning out the cards and requesting the spectator to insert the Joker face up at any spot he fancies. The pack is then closed up; when the cards are spread again the card required will be found up next to the Joker, it having been caused to appear reversed at that selected spot in the pack.

Let us explain the basic version first, after which we will make clear the working of this variation. The principle upon which the effect is worked was admittedly suggested by some of the feats in Impey's *Original Card Mysteries*; the application is so far as I know original.

The pack is so arranged that every other card is face upward, all the red cards being face upward and the black face downward. The red cards are arranged in sequence, from top of pack downward, running H's

A to K, and D's A to K. Similarly if the pack be turned completely over, the black cards will be face up, and they are also arranged in order from top downward, S's A to K, and C's A to K.

This gives us twenty-six sets of cards, each set consisting of two cards face to face. A spot of wax on the face of each card causes these pairs of cards to stick together, face to face, so that if the cards be run from hand to hand only the backs of cards will be visible, regardless of which side of pack is uppermost, yet a little pressure will cause the separation of any desired pair of cards. With this much explained the method should be fairly obvious.

The performer first runs the cards from hand to hand, showing that all are face down. The cards must be run lightly, and not fanned. Now any card is named. The performer is holding the pack, say, so that all the black cards are face uppermost. If a black card be named he is all ready for the finale. If a red card is named the whole pack must be secretly turned over. Suppose the 10S to be named. The performer begins running the cards slowly from hand to hand, counting to himself. When he knows that he has reached the 10S, a slight pressure of the fingers separates that card from the one above and consequently the 10S appears face up in the face-down pack.

Hard wax, such as beeswax, will work better than the usual soft wax employed by conjurers, as the cards separate more smoothly and with less pressure. Burling Hull's 'Magnetizo' is ideal for this.

Now for the variation. The spectator is handed the Joker, which is ordinary. As before, the cards are run from hand to hand to show that they are all face down, but the performer secretly keeps track, and when he has run thirteen cards (or rather sets of cards) from the left hand into the right, he stops, as he knows he holds half the pack in each hand. Now he requests that any card be named. The two halves of the pack are then placed back together again, but in such position that when the pack is turned right side up the chosen card will be in the top half of the pack. As the performer knows the positions of each suit, this requires no calculation. The performer starts running the cards now from hand to hand again, counting. When he comes to the selected card, it is secretly separated from the one above it, but kept out of sight beneath the spread fan of cards. At the same moment the performer says: 'Place the Joker anywhere you wish in the cards as I run them,' giving the impression that this is the reason for running out the cards. The performer continues to pass the cards from hand to hand, running the selected face-up card secretly along beneath the spread fan, until the Joker is placed in, when in closing up the cards it requires no sleight of hand to slip the selected card into the fan next to the Joker, where it will be found when the cards are once again spread out.

CARD IN THE ORANGE   Cazeneuve

A very effective variation of the torn card and corner trick.

A little preliminary preparation is necessary. You require an orange, two cards alike, say 10S, two small pill-boxes and a rubber band. Remove the small part of the stem remaining on the orange and thrust a skewer into it without piercing the other side. Into the hole thus made insert one of the cards after having torn off a corner and rolled it up tightly. Replace the stem part with a drop of glue. Properly prepared, such an orange will bear close inspection. The torn corner you put in one of the pill-boxes, which you place together with a rubber band in your right-hand outside coat pocket. The remaining 10S goes on the top of the pack.

Thus prepared, begin by showing the orange, toss it to a spectator to examine and put it in his pocket. Force the 10S, have it torn up and the pieces placed in the duplicate pill-box. As this is being done, palm the other pill-box from your pocket in your right hand. Take the box containing the pieces with your finger-tips of the same hand. Throw a handkerchief over this hand and under cover of it switch the boxes. Take the duplicate box and the handkerchief in the left hand, thrust your right hand into the coat pocket, drop the original pill-box and bring out the rubber band. Snap this around the handkerchief just below the pill-box and give it to be held.

Having thus finished the mechanical part of the trick you have only to present the dramatic, magical effect by pretending to pass the card into the orange. In the end the pill-box is unwrapped and opened, the odd piece only of the card being found. Take the orange, cut it in half around the middle, the opposite way to which the card was inserted, so that half the card projects from the lower half. Open it out, show that it is the 10S with a corner missing. Fit the corner to it and garner the applause which this fine effect always evokes if well presented.

THE SLAP TRICK

The trick depends on the double lift. Secretly get a 7 and an 8 of any suit together, pass them to the middle and force the 7. Have it replaced under the 8, slip the tip of the left little finger above the 8 and pass the two cards to the top of the pack. False shuffle, leaving the cards there, then make the double lift and show that the 7 has passed to the top. Turn the pack face down, take off the top card, the 8, and thrust it half-way into the pack, holding it so that the tip of your forefinger covers the index at the top right corner; lift the pack and show the card which will then appear to be the 7.

Turn the pack face down and let the spectator push the card flush with the rest, then put his finger on the top of the pack. Order the card to again mount to the top, slap the pack gently and allow the spectator to remove the top card which he finds to be the 7.

THE CONJURER'S TOUCH

A handkerchief with a pocket on one side large enough to carry three cards is required, also duplicates of three cards. Put the three cards in this secret pocket and then the handkerchief in your pocket in such a way that when it is taken out later, the secret pocket will be towards yourself mouth upwards. On the top of the pack place the three cards corresponding to those in the handkerchief. Better, if you can do it, have them in a pocket and palm them on to the pack after it has been shuffled.

Force the three cards, have them noted and replaced and the pack shuffled by a spectator. Take out your handkerchief, don't say it is un-prepared, just form it into a bag by holding the corners, and have the pack dropped into it. Knowing the order of the cards in the pocket you can bring out the chosen cards (duplicates) in any order called for. After producing two you may vary the proceedings by laying the handkerchief over your right hand pocket, side down and mouth towards yourself. Lay the pack face up on top of the handkerchief and over the card still in the pocket so that they coincide. Lift the outer side of the fabric up and over the cards and gather the edges together with the right hand. The pocket will be at the back and its mouth should coincide with the lower end of the pack. By gently shaking the hand up and down the card will make its appearance gradually as if penetrating the handkerchief, finally fluttering to the floor.

THE CARD THROUGH THE HANDKERCHIEF

A card having been freely selected and replaced is brought to the top of the pack and palmed off. A handkerchief is borrowed and immediately spread over the right hand, thereby concealing the palmed card. The pack is now placed face upwards, on the centre of the handkerchief, by which means it is brought immediately over the concealed card.

The part of the handkerchief lying on the forearm is first brought over the face of the cards, which are then raised, still covered. The sides of the handkerchief are brought around to the back in the act of concluding the operation of folding up the cards. The pack is then screwed up tightly and the position of the whole reversed. Performer holding the screwed-up ends of the handkerchief shakes it slightly and the chosen card is gradually seen to make its appearance and as the shaking continues, the card becomes more and more visible, finally falling to the floor. The effect to the onlookers, being that the card actually penetrated through the handkerchief.

Two cards may be caused to pass through in the same manner, but in the process the second card is pushed back up under the cover of the first card.

THE PENETRATING CARDS

The trick is an improvement on the preceding effect. The cards are placed in their case and a chosen card apparently penetrates the case and the handkerchief.

A pack of cards with a case of the flap variety and a handkerchief are required. After the cards are shuffled, have a card freely chosen, noted and replaced. Pass it to the top and put the pack in its case in such a way that in closing the case the flap goes between the top card and the rest of the pack. Lay the case, flap side down on the table, show the handkerchief and spread it over your left hand. Pick up the case in the right hand with the thumb on the exposed part of the selected card and throw the handkerchief over the case. Under its cover the right-hand fingers pull the card out of the case as far as possible.

With the left hand take the case from under its covering, the selected card is thus drawn completely out of the case and lies face up on the right hand. Put the case on the handkerchief just above the palmed card, throw the front part of the fabric back over the case, twist the sides so that they retain the card outside at the rear, gather up the four corners and hold them in the right hand. The chosen card is then named and ordered to penetrate the case and the fabric. A gentle shake of the hand will gradually bring the card into view.

GET THEE BEHIND ME, SATAN

Spectators always think a trick worked with the cards behind the back is wonderful. In this trick the spectator apparently does the trick himself, and he holds the pack behind his own back, making the result still more remarkable.

Any pack, after being shuffled by a spectator, is cut by him into two packets, of which he chooses one, handing you the other. You instruct him to look over his cards, take out any one, note what it is and place it on the top of the packet. Turn away for the moment as he does this and quickly reverse the bottom card of your packet and also the second card from the top of it.

Turn around, place your packet on top of the spectator's thereby bringing the card you reversed on the bottom of your packet immediately above his card. Square the pack but do not remove it from the spectator's hands, tell him to grasp it tightly and place it behind his back. Instruct him to take off the top card, then hesitate as if changing your mind and continue, 'Better place that card on the bottom. You might have some suspicion if we used that card. Now take the next card, reverse it and thrust it into the middle of the pack. Right? Bring the pack forward and if you have done the trick properly you will find you have located your chosen card with the card you reversed.'

Much to his surprise he finds this is actually the case. With a little care and skill the reversal of the two cards in your own packet can be done quite easily without turning away, in which case the trick becomes one of the most effective impromptu tricks possible.

THE PRINCESS CARD TRICK   Hardin

A most effective feat which can be done with any pack at any time. First have the pack shuffled by a spectator, then holding it spread face up, request four spectators to each select one card, the first taking any C, the next any H then a S and lastly any D. Palm the three top cards of the pack and retain the pack in that hand.

Collect the four cards face down on your left hand beginning with the D, followed by the S, H and C. Lay pack on the table and take the four cards in your right hand adding the three palmed cards. Hold the seven cards facing the audience and well squared between the fingers at the upper ends, thumb at the lower ends. With the left hand slowly separate the four chosen cards, fanning them towards the left, but keeping the three added cards perfectly squared behind the C card. Ask a spectator to mentally select any one of the four selected cards. When he signifies that he has done this, close the fan and turn the packet to face yourself.

Spread the cards with the left hand as before but this time it is the three indifferent cards that you fan, the four selected cards being perfectly squared as one card. Pretending great concentration draw out one of the single cards, hesitate and put it back in a different position in the fan. Repeat with another single card, finally take the four cards as one and place them in your right-hand outside pocket. Count the three remaining cards face down on to the pack and cut them to the middle. Have the mentally chosen card named, thrust your hand into your pocket and bring it out. The arrangement of the suits, C, H, S, D, enables you to do this quickly and without fumbling.

THE CLOCK TRICK

Another excellent trick which can be done with any pack.

Beforehand take an opportunity of placing eleven cards in your lower right waistcoat pocket. Shuffle the pack and lay out on the table a circle of twelve cards saying that they are to be considered as representing the figures on a clock face. Place the card figuring as twelve a little higher in the imaginary circle than the others so that it can be readily distinguished. Count around from this card exactly as on a real clock face, impressing on the spectators that the cards must be associated with the hour figures at which they lie. Turn away and ask a spectator to choose one card, look at it and remember the hour figure at which it lies. This done, turn around and gather up the cards beginning with twelve and putting it face down on your left hand, follow with the card representing eleven, then ten and so on around to the card at one.

On a slip of paper draw a small square and alongside of it a circle. Ask a spectator to write the name of the card selected in the square and the hour at which it stood in the circle. Turn away so that you will have no chance of seeing what is written, telling him to afterwards fold the paper and put it in his pocket. Keeping your elbows close to your sides, palm the twelve cards in your right hand and take out the eleven cards from your waistcoat pocket. Hold these in your right hand. Turn around, take pencil back from the spectator with your left hand, put the eleven cards in the left hand, take the pencil with the right and put it in your right-hand trousers pocket, leaving the palmed cards there.

Turn the packet face up and count the eleven cards as twelve thus: 'Twelve, eleven, ten, nine, eight, seven, and five (spread the last five cards) are twelve.' Square the cards and hand them to the spectator face down. Order the chosen card to vanish. Ask the spectator to count to the hour chosen. With your right hand in your pocket keep count with him with the twelve cards in your pocket. When he stops you have the chosen card. He finds his card has gone, counts the cards and he has eleven only, and the card is named and you produce it from your pocket.

PAINT BRUSH CARD   Merlin

Take from a pack the 2, 3, 4 and 5 of S's. Put the 2S face down on the table, on it the 4S face up, then the 3S face down. Take the three cards and give them a rather sharp bend lengthways so that they are convex when looking at the 2S. Place them on the face of the pack so that the 2S becomes the bottom card. On the top of the pack put the 5S face down.

Show the pack in the left hand face outwards and call attention to the 2S. Turn the pack face down and turn over the top card, the 5S, leaving it face outwards. Hold the pack in the usual colour change position in the left hand, thumb on the upper side, fingers on the lower and the tip of the forefinger at the outer end of the pack. With the forefinger push down the three set-up cards, the bend enabling you to do this as if they were one card only. Take them openly in the right hand, thumb on the face of the 2S, fingers on the backs, and show them as one card, the 2S. Draw them face down over the faced card, the 5S, a couple of times, showing the faces of the 5S and the 2S each time. At the third time release the 2S and the 4S from the right thumb, leave them on the faced 5S and carry away the 3S only.

The effect is that the centre pip has been brushed off the 5S and becomes attached to the 2S. Remove the 4S and 3S and show them freely, the face-down 2S making the pack appear regular. You must remember, however, that the 5S is reversed second from the top and take the first opportunity of righting it.

THE ECLIPSE VANISH

Five cards are laid out in a row and one is chosen by a spectator. The cards are gathered up and again dealt out, there are four only, the chosen card has vanished.

Have the pack shuffled and ask the spectator to deal out five cards on the table in a row, then to signify which one he chooses. As he does this, casually bring your left hand to the mouth and wet the ball of your thumb. Pick up two of the cards and put them face up on your left hand, then put the one chosen on these and rub your left thumb over its face, wetting it. On this place the other two cards also face up. Turn the cards face down and contrive to squeeze them tightly but imperceptibly.

Order the card to vanish. Deal the cards face up. There are apparently four only, the chosen card has gone. Due to the moisture it is stuck to the card placed on top of it and the two appear to be one card only.

THE CARD FROM THE POCKET   C. O. Williams

This is a trick that has stood the test of time and is still one of the best impromptu tricks with cards in existence.

Hand a pack to a spectator and have him shuffle it until he is satisfied you cannot know the position of any card. Tell him to think of any single digit, count down to that number, not reversing the cards, lift the packet, look at the card at the number thought of and remember it, then replace the packet. Turn away as he does this.

When he is ready, turn around and take the pack. Point out that you ask no questions, you simply want him to concentrate on his card and number. Place the pack behind your back. Affect intense mental effort and bring forward the bottom card with its face towards yourself. Hesitate as if not quite sure, then with a confident air place the card in your right-hand trousers pocket, really palm the card and put it on the top of the pack as you take the pack off your left hand. Point out that if you have succeeded his card is in your pocket. Ask him to name the number but not the card.

Suppose he says 'Five'. Deal four cards face down and throw the fifth card a little nearer to him saying, 'Is that your card?' At the same moment the left thumb pushes the next card over the side of the pack and the right hand comes back and palms it and puts this hand into trousers pocket. Bring the card into view at the tips of the fingers holding it by the upper end, 'How could it be?' you continue, 'when I have it here in my pocket.' Hold the card almost out of the pocket and ask the spectator to name it. Turn the card around and show you have that very card.

With proper presentation the trick is perfect.

CARD FROM THE POCKET

S. H. Wimbrough—Another presentation

The trick affords an excellent reply to that oft-asked question, 'Can you hypnotize?' Should you be asked the question, reply on the following lines and do this trick. 'Well I don't know, sometimes I can and sometimes I can't but there is an experiment I have often tried and with it I almost always succeed.' Generally this arouses interest so go ahead. Continue, 'I will make use of a pack of cards and subject. Please take the cards and shuffle them. Right, now hand me any card at all without looking at it. Thank you. I'll put it in my waistcoat pocket (do so). Most likely it will surprise you to know that you are already under my influence. You don't believe it but I'll prove it directly.

'I'll turn my back and you count down to any number you think of, look at and remember the card you find there but don't let anyone else see it. I can only control one person at a time. (Turn away, take card from waistcoat pocket and palm it in your right hand. Don't move your elbows in doing this.) Are you ready? (Turn around, take pack and add palmed card to the top.) Now remember you are under control and are not accountable for what you see or do, and the more you try not to be influenced the easier you make it for me. What number does your card rest at? Twelve? (Deal to that number and throw the twelfth card out face up and palm the top card in the right hand.) What? That's not your card? (Hold pack in right hand.) What was it? The.........of .... ? That proves you've been completely under the influence. That card is not in the pack. (Spread the cards face up.) You gave it to me yourself just now. Here it is in my pocket. (Put the palmed card in and at once bring it out, tips of the fingers on the top end.) I must admit that you have been an excellent subject.'

BANNER CARD DISCOVERY

Jordan

Have the spectator shuffle any pack freely. Ask him to mentally select any number between twelve and twenty, then when your back is turned to count down to that number and note the card lying there, replacing the cards as they were. Turn away while he does this.

Turn around and take the pack, put it behind your back, rapidly count off twelve cards and put them at the bottom. Separate the next seven cards at the top from the rest with your little finger-tip, bring the top card forward, its back to the spectators and put it in your right-hand trousers pocket. Palm the six cards above the left little finger and hand the remainder of the pack to the spectator. As he counts down to see if his card is still in the pack, place your hands in your coat pockets. Watch the spectator's count, if he turns up the thirteenth card you have the right card in your trousers pocket. If not, count from then on with the cards in your coat pocket, taking card for card with him.

When he turns up a card palm the one you have arrived at amongst the six. Thrust your hand into your trousers pocket, drop the card just palmed and palm the one already there. Then hesitate and say, 'It will be more convincing if you remove your card yourself. Please name it first.' As he does this, take the pack in the right hand and add the palmed card to the top. Take the first opportunity of returning the five cards from the coat pocket to the pack.

LIKE SEEKS LIKE   Jordan

A trick which makes use of the back palm as a secret sleight. Four hats are borrowed and placed mouths upwards on a table, in front of each hat place the A, K, Q and J of one suit, faces out. These are placed into their respective hats. At command the four A's congregate in one hat, the four K's in another, and so on.

In putting each set of four cards in front of a hat they must be set in the following order: S's, J, Q, K, A—H's, J, Q, A, K—C's, J, K, A, Q—D's, Q, J, A, K.

Begin by picking up the JS and apparently put it in its hat, really back palm it. Next the JH back palmed, then JC back palmed, next take QD, drop the three J's and back palm the Q, three J's now in the fourth hat. Do the same with the QS and QH, dropping them in the third hat as you back palm the KC.

Treat the three K's in order in the same way, dropping them into the second hat as you take the A. Back palm two more A's, finally dropping all four into the first hat. The last three cards are set in front of the proper hats.

THE MASTER RIDDLE   Jordan

Hand an unprepared pack to a spectator to shuffle and then remove one card, retaining it. Have him pass the pack to a second person who also takes out a card. In similar fashion allow four more cards to be drawn and retained by different spectators. Take the pack and ask one person to collect the cards face down and mix them thoroughly. While this is being done, quietly count down six cards from the top of the pack and hold the break so that they will be ready for the bottom change.

Receive the packet of six chosen cards in your right hand and as you turn to put them on the table, execute the bottom change and put down the six indifferent cards taken from the top. Sight the bottom card and ask someone who has not drawn a card to help you. Cut the six chosen cards from the bottom to the top. Turn your back, fan the pack behind you and ask the spectator to pick up one of the six cards from the table and thrust it into the pack. Call it as being the card you just before sighted, the bottom one of the six selected cards. Bring the pack forward, run through it, remove the card just named, and at the same time memorize the five cards next to it.

Hand the pack to be shuffled, then continue in the same way, but for these five let the spectator remove them from the pack as you call for them one at a time.

If you cannot do the bottom change, secretly bridge the six bottom cards while the chosen cards are being collected. Have them placed on a tray in a packet and put the pack alongside. Turn to your table, lift the pack at the bridge, leaving six cards on the tray and put the pack on top of the six selected cards.

TRANSPOSITION . . . BOX TO ENVELOPE

The trick calls for an ordinary pack, an envelope and a card box without the flap.

Hand the box and the envelope to spectators, sitting some distance apart, to be examined. Have the pack shuffled and allow the person holding the box to draw a card freely. After he has noted it and returned it to the pack, bring it to the top and shuffle one card on top of it.

Order the chosen card to mount to the top and by means of a double lift show that it has obeyed. Turn the card face down and push it off into the box which the spectator holds ready and immediately closes. This is what you appear to do, really an indifferent card goes into the box and the chosen card remains on the top.

Go to the person holding the envelope and force the same card on him but do not allow the card to be looked at, simply slide into the envelope.

The command for the cards to change places is given. The spectator holding the box names his card but finds an entirely different one in the box; this you say is the card the second spectator drew. The envelope is opened and in it the first person's card is found.

MENTAL CARD MYSTERY

If possible borrow both the cards and the envelope for use in this trick. First have the pack shuffled freely and sight the top card. Next borrow an envelope and paper, write down the name of the card just sighted, fold the paper and enclose it in the envelope. Casually lay the envelope on the pack as you return the pencil to your pocket. Take the envelope in your right hand again and secretly carry away the top card with it. Hand the pack to be shuffled and cut.

Receive the pack back in your left hand, the envelope plus the sighted card on it as you reach for your pencil again with your right hand. Give the pencil to the spectator who cut the pack and ask him to write his initials on the envelope. Let him take envelope and cards in his own hands to do this, then put the envelope in his pocket. Have him take off the top card and note it 'as the card at which he cut after he had shuffled the cards'.

If you then recapitulate what has been done, ignoring the fact that you handled the cards at all, the effect left on the minds of the spectators is that the card was taken immediately after the person shuffled and cut the pack himself, and their reaction to the fact that your prediction names that very card will be quite satisfactory. (*Editor's Note.—After spectator has placed the envelope in his pocket, you hold the pack while he stabs a knife into the pack to locate a card. In breaking the pack at the cut slip the sighted card from the top of the pack to the top of the lower packet in the accredited fashion. Let him note this card and then read your prediction.*)

SATAN'S MAIL   Hardin

A simple method of apparently passing a card into an envelope. The whole effect is dependent on the presentation. A small pellet of wax, affixed to a waistcoat button, an unprepared envelope and a pack of cards are all you require.

From the pack, which you have had thoroughly shuffled, any card is freely selected by a spectator, noted, returned and secretly passed by you to the bottom. Secure the pellet of wax and transfer it to the face of the bottom card, the chosen one. Hand the envelope to be examined and taking it back, casually put the pack on it with a little pressure. Approaching your table turn the pack and envelope over and carelessly toss the envelope on the table. The chosen card will have adhered to it by the pellet of wax. Place the pack in another envelope, seal it and have the spectator hold it. Order the chosen card to leave the envelope in his hand and pass to that one on the table.

Pack is examined the card has gone. Pick up the table envelope and hold it before a light, it will appear that a card is inside. Tear off the end of the envelope, blow it open in the usual way, insert thumb and forefinger and apparently extract the card, really drawing it up from the outside.

CARD AND ENVELOPE Sellers

Place the AC face down on the table overlapping the rear edge slightly and over it place an envelope so that both may be picked up together, the card being concealed by the envelope. In the envelope you have placed a slip of paper on which is written, 'The selected card will be the Ace of Clubs.'

Hand a pack of cards out to be shuffled, take it back and hold it in your left hand. Pick up the envelope together with the AC and lay the envelope on the pack in the left hand thus placing the AC on top of the pack. Take a pencil from your pocket, hand it to a spectator asking him to write his initials on the envelope which you then hand to him to hold. Force the AS by means of the knife force or one of the forcing methods, Chapter 19. Have the prediction read and the card shown.

CARD AND ENVELOPE NO. 2 Gravatt

Beforehand bend up the tip of the flap of an envelope creasing it well, then turn it down again. Proceed just as in the preceding trick but when you fasten the flap of the envelope, turn the tip of the flap back where it was creased so that when you put the envelope on the pack the moistened tip of the flap sticks to the top card and carries it away when you toss the envelope on the table.

Finish the effect just as described above.

TUNED MINDS
Albright

Have the pack of cards shuffled and take it back placing it on your left hand. Ask a spectator to think of some prominent person. Hand him a pencil and have him cut the cards taking a card at which he cut while you take back the cut portion in your right hand. Ask him to write the name thought of on the face of his card. As he does this give the inner ends of the packet on your left hand a squeeze, bending the sides upwards, while the outer ends of the cards facing the spectator remain quite straight. Have him return his card on top of the left hand-packet and you drop the right-hand packet on top.

Make a series of cuts finally cutting at the crimp, his card will be the lowest card of this portion. Lift off the cut holding it by the thumb at the inner end, second and third fingers at the outer end and fourth finger resting against the side just at the right corner. Push off the top card of the lower packet with the left thumb, pick it off with the tips of the first and second right fingers at the right-hand corner and hold it up face out towards the spectator. The bottom card of the right-hand portion is facing you and you read the name written on it. Ask for the pencil, re-place the cut with the right hand, place the card just shown face up on the pack and pretending intense concentration write the same name on it. Turn the card face down, cut the pack and hand it to the spectator.

He picks out the two cards and finds you have written the very same name as he did.

TWO-CARD SLATE PROPHECY
Annemann

Required are two slates and a half-flap for each, two packs of cards, one an ordinary one but prearranged in any system you may use, the other a single card forcing pack. In the ordinary pack the duplicate of the force card must be discarded. On one slate write 'The lady will get the..........,' cover it with the half-flap, on the other slate write, 'The gentleman will get the..........,' and cover this with the flap also. Place the slates on the table one above the other with 'gentleman's' slate on top and lay the pack on them. Put the forcing pack in your side coat pocket and you are ready.

Go to a lady, write on the flap of the 'gentleman' slate, 'The lady will get the ....,' draw a line across along the edge of the flap and show the writing freely, turn slate towards yourself and write the name of the force card, then put slate on table writing downwards. Spread stacked pack, lady removes card, pick up pack, starting from point from which card was removed and scoop up the rest. Glimpse bottom card and so get name of card selected, drop pack into pocket.

Take second slate, 'lady' slate, and write, 'The gentleman will select the..........,' on the flap, draw a line as before and show freely. Then write the name of the lady's card just chosen below flap, put slate flap side down beside the other. Take out the forcing pack and give the gentleman a free choice. Drop pack into pocket, pick up the slates and put them together, written sides inwards. Have the cards shown, open the slates and show the predictions. Casually remove the ordinary pack from your pocket and have the two chosen cards replaced. Pack is now quite regular.

THE SPECTATOR FINDS YOUR CARD Kli Ban

After the spectators have shuffled a pack, take it and give the cards a riffle shuffle yourself, seizing the opportunity to sight the top and bottom cards. Ask a spectator to cut the pack about the middle and choose either heap. Whichever one he takes you have a key card in it. You take the other packet.

Take a card from your packet and pretend to name it, really calling the name of the key card in the spectator's packet, and put it face down on top of your heap. Spectator does the same, putting his card on the top or bottom of his packet depending on where the key card is. You each make one complete cut.

Hand your packet to the spectator asking him to shuffle it, then draw one card from it and, without looking at it, to push it into his packet. He does this, squares his packet and cuts it once more. Name your card again and deal your cards face up showing it is no longer there. Spectator searches his packet and finds your card and his together.

WATCH HIS ELBOW

Hand a pack of cards to a spectator to shuffle, ask him then to turn his back, take cards off the top one by one, stop whenever he pleases, look at the next card and drop the cards taken off on the top of it.

All you have to do is to watch his elbows, one or the other, or both will move slightly with every card taken. Keep count and the total gives you the number of cards down that the noted card lies. Take the pack and reveal it as you wish.

By having sighted the bottom card you may allow the spectator to cut the pack before handing it back to you. You can then cut the pack to bring the original card back to position before making the count.

TWO PILE TRICK

A very ingenious twist given to an old trick. Hand the pack to a spectator to shuffle freely, and when your back is turned instruct him to deal two packets of cards face down on the table, the same number of cards in each packet and not more than ten in each. Have him note the next card on the pack, replace it, and put one of the packets back on top of the pack, and the other packet in his pocket. Now you turn around and take the pack and point out that there is an unknown number of cards above his card. Put the pack behind your back and count off, say, fifteen cards, reversing them, then replace them on top of the pack. Bring the pack forward, and in order to make it still more difficult, have the packet from the spectator's pocket placed on top of the pack.

The noted card will then be the fifteenth card from the top. In exactly the same way you can put it at any number you please. The mechanical part of the trick is well covered and it can be made very effective.

THE VOICE OF THE SPIRIT

Effect. Assistant is guarded in another room by a committee. From any pack a card is freely chosen, a spectator takes paper and pen to the assistant who instantly writes the name of the card.

Method. An ingenious code is used as detailed below.

ACE. Send own fountain pen with cap screwed on to be handed to assistant without a word being spoken.

KING. Pen in same condition, but messenger hands a scrap of paper or an old envelope with it.

QUEEN. Take cap off pen, and send it thus without paper.

JACK. Pen in same condition and a piece of paper.

TEN. Cap on back of pen, ink filler even with clip. No paper.

NINE. Same as for ten, with paper.

EIGHT. Cap on back, clip quarter turn to right of ink filler. No paper.

SEVEN. Same as for eight, plus paper.

SIX. Cap on back, clip half-way round barrel. No paper.

FIVE. Same as for six, plus paper.

FOUR. Cap on with quarter turn to left. No paper.

THREE. Same as four, plus paper.

TWO. Cap a trifle only to left. Paper optional.

To denote the suits proceed as follows:

HEARTS. Borrowed pen, woman holding it.

DIAMONDS. Borrowed pen, man holding it.

SPADES. Your own pen, woman holding it.

CLUBS. Same but man holding it.

For an all male audience you would have to use three of your own pens to represent three suits, a borrowed pen indicating the other. When no paper is sent assistant uses his own or borrows some.

THE BUDDHA WHISPERS   Ovette

On the table have a small figure of Buddha, on either side of it put two small glasses and number them mentally from left to right, 1, 2, 3, 4. In No. 1 put midget cards AH, 3H, 5C, 7C, 9D, JD. In No. 2 glass—2C, 3C, 6D, 7D, 10S, JS. In No. 3 glass—4D, 5D, 6S, 7S, QH, 4H. In glass No. 4—8S, 9S, 10H, JH, QC, 8C. To each glass assign a number, No. 1 is 1, No. 2 is 2, No. 3 is 4, No. 4 is 8. In the Buddha's hands place a number of coins or poker chips.

Ask a spectator to shuffle a pack of cards and merely think of one of them. Lay the pack aside. Instruct the spectator to place a coin in any glass in which there is a midget card of the same value as that he is thinking of, and also to put a coin in front of each glass that has a card of the same suit as his thought card.

To determine the value simply add the set values for each glass in which there is a coin. J is value eleven, Q is twelve, K is thirteen. It will be noted that each set of cards has one suit missing, therefore to tell the suit simply note the glass with no coin in front of it.

Compare with Albright's 'Perfect Card Divination'.

TRIPLE CARD MYSTERY

Any pack is thoroughly shuffled by a spectator who then cuts the pack, keeping one half and handing you the other. Tell him to deal three cards face down in a row on the table and on top of each to deal a small number of cards, the same number on each card. Note how many cards go in the first heap then turn away until the heaps are completed. Suppose there are five cards in each. Three spectators each note the top card of a heap and replace it. The three heaps are collected one on top of the other. Drop your half of the pack on the pile, having in the meantime noted its bottom card which thus goes on top of the first chosen card. Any cards left over in the hands of the spectator who dealt the cards are now put on the top or bottom of the pack and this is cut several times.

To find the cards, deal until the key card appears and the next card is the first of the three and is so acknowledged. Place the pack behind your back, count to the fifth card and take it out, leaving the other four on the pack. Bring the card forward and have it acknowledged. Replace this card and the others on the table on to the pack in your hand thus bringing the last card to the tenth position from the top. Let a spectator blindfold you, and have him take the pack and deal the cards slowly one by one. By looking down along your nose you keep track of the deal and when he has the tenth card in his hand stop him and have that card identified by the last spectator.

INFALLIBLE PREDICTION   Page Wright

Two packs with the same backs are used, one ordinary pack you have in your coat pocket, the other you have prepared by writing, 'This is the card you will take,' down one side of every card, except the top and bottom cards. Shuffle this pack without disturbing the top and bottom cards and let spectators see the bottom card after the shuffle. Pretend to write something on one of the middle cards, shuffle again bringing the top card to the bottom and let the spectators get sight of this card also, thus they will have seen two unprepared cards.

Spread the cards on the table and have a spectator draw one out without looking at it. Gather up the remainder and run over the faces exposing the unwritten side to the spectators. Explain that you are looking for the card you wrote on. Finally square the pack and have the card on the table turned over. The writing is on it. Drop the pack into your pocket, then as an afterthought bring out the unprepared pack and hand it to someone to shuffle so that you can show another trick.

More Miscellaneous Tricks

FACES OR BACKS, WHICH?   Jordan

'I have found a rather strange thing with the Bicycle League Back cards in the matter of reverse marks. In any pack of fifty-two cards and the Joker there are twenty-two cards, possibly twenty-three, that can be reversed the same as reversible back design, or one-way card, thus making it possible to tell from the face of the cards which one has been reversed. This is by the placing of the spots on the cards marking a top or bottom. The cards that can be thus distinguished are the A, 3, 5, 6, 7, 8, 9, of C's, H's, and S's and the 7D and possibly the Joker. What is unique with this make of card and back design is that when these cards are all headed one way by the face characteristics, **the wing design on the backs on all the cards is also headed one way.** Thus a reversed card of these twenty-two or twenty-three cards can be told from either face or back. And when a pack has been arranged all the one way by the back design the twenty-two or twenty-three cards have also been automatically ended in the one way.

'I think I have found a way of utilizing this principle. Get twenty of these cards on to the top of the pack. State that you will try a location with twenty cards. Hand the pack to a spectator and have him deal twenty cards. Shuffle these overhand, let him take a card, reverse the packet and have the card replaced. Hand him the packet and shuffle the cards overhand. Turn away and instruct him to deal the cards into four rows of five cards face down, then he is to turn any cards he pleases face up and not to tell you whether his card is face up or face down. Turn round. Look at all the backs and note if one is reversed, if not you have only to look over the faces and apply the old principle. You may detect the card by pulse-reading or adopt any presentation you prefer. The magicians will be puzzled because of the face-up and face-down privilege.'

THE LIFE SAVER   Jordan

From any pack you allow a spectator to remove any card and keep it for the time being. Holding the pack face up, rapidly deal it into two heaps placing in one heap the reversible cards, the A, 3, 5, 6, 7, 8, 9, of C's, H's and S's and the 7D. Do not turn these cards to bring them pointing one way, deal them as they come but count them. At the end of the deal if there are only twenty-one of these cards you know that the

390

chosen card must be one of them and by having it replaced in the other pile you can allow the spectator to shuffle them freely and yet pick the card with ease. In similar fashion if the count of the pointer cards is complete you know the chosen card is one of the other variety so you have it replaced in the twenty-two packet. Of course you apparently give the spectator a free choice of packets.

Note.—By arranging these pointer cards beforehand so that the indicating pips are pointing one way and placing them on the top of the pack you may have a card chosen from amongst them and spread the lower part of the pack for its return, or a card taken from the lower part may be replaced in the pointer cards in the upper half, in either case the stranger in the house locates the chosen card.

Again you may have these cards in the middle, have a card taken from amongst them, secretly turn the pack so that the card will be reversed and so easily found. If a perverse spectator insists on taking a card from near the top or bottom, have it returned amongst the pointer cards in the middle. You then locate it with ease.

THE MAGNETIZED CARDS

Effect. A number of cards are spread on the performer's hand which is then turned over. Instead of falling the cards remain attached to the hand in some mysterious manner but fall from it at command.

Method No. 1. A prepared card and a finger ring are required. Cut off the head of a pin with a small part of the pin, solder this to the middle of a piece of thin tin. Pierce a hole in the middle of a card which will allow the head of the pin to pass through to the back. Glue another face card to the face of this one. The ring has a small slot cut in it into which the head of the pin will fit.

Palm this prepared card on to the pack after the cards have been shuffled by a spectator. Place it face up on the palm of your left hand engaging the head of the pin in the slot of the ring. Push a number of cards all around between the card and your palm. Quite a large number can be thus inserted. Turn the hand over and the cards remain attached and can be safely carried amongst the spectators in this position. Due attention should be paid before attaching the cards to the pretended generation of magnetism by rubbing the hands together and on the coat sleeve.

Method No. 2. Push a fine needle through a small part of the skin of the palm so that the needle projects on either side. Arrange the first two cards under each projecting end of the needle and the other cards under these. After exhibiting the cards, return to your table, hold the cards above it and by a slight pressure of the fingers, free the needle and the cards fall. They can be immediately gathered up and given for examination, the needle remaining unnoticed on the table.

Method No. 3. Devised by Burling Hull, this calls for a prepared card. Choose a card that has a small circle in the middle of its back pattern. Cut this from one card and glue it in place on the back of another card, attaching one half only. This will then form a flap which can be bent up and clipped between the fingers. The trick then proceeds as in the other methods.

THE MAGNETIZED CARDS Sellers

Method No. 4. Take a circular piece of cardboard or thin tin of such a size that you can easily span it between the thumb and little finger of the right hand. On one side glue several cards to completely cover it. Stick them on as irregularly as possible. To the other side glue a piece of cloth of the same material as your table cover.

This fake you have on your table, card side down. Produce or borrow a pack of cards, and deal a number face down and scattered over the back of the fake. Show your hand and put it flat down on top of the cards. Grip the edges of the fake between the thumb and little finger, pressing on the cards with the other fingers. Now lift the hand and wave it in any position you fancy.

Of course it will be easier at first if you use a few cards only; this does not alter the effect in the least. Having shown the magnetic quality of your hand sufficiently, replace it with the cards flat on the table. Sweep the cards together leaving the fake lying unobserved as at first.

TEARING THE PACK

Various methods of preparing the pack in order to duplicate the real feat.
   No. 1. Clip each card slightly, with a pair of scissors, on both sides in the middle.
   No. 2. Have a printer impress the middle of each card with a perforating rule using no ink. If this is not available score each card across the middle with a penknife.

No. 3 Spread the cards in a moderately hot oven and let them bake for a couple of hours.

No. 4. Soak the cards and split them. Wash the glue off the surfaces and let the backs and fronts dry. Stack them together and put them under pressure to dry out thoroughly.

No. 5. Actually tear the cards almost for half their width, making the tears correspond by doing about a quarter of the pack at a time. Replace the pack in its case and replace the tax stamp. The half-packs can be prepared for being torn in half in exactly the same way.

A good idea is to have the face card an AD or 2D and on it have stamped your name and the date the feat was performed. Snap a rubber band around and toss the quarter packs to the spectators.

To tear an unprepared pack in half grip one end tightly between the four fingers and the base of the thumb, the thumb lying over the back, while the other end is gripped with the other hand placed across around the side of the pack. The feat can be made somewhat easier by slightly spreading the cards so that the tear starts in a few cards only.

REVERSED CARDS   Jordan

Borrow a pack, shuffle it and show all the cards are faced one way. Hold the pack face down as for dealing. Deal the cards one by one into the right hand, letting the arms hang down and swing gently to left and right with each card. Both hands hang to the left as the first card is dealt. Then they swing a little to the right of the body as the left thumb starts to slide the next card off. At the same moment turn the left hand over dealing the card face up into the right hand. Swing the arms to the left dealing the next face down, then to the right, the fourth card face up, and so on alternately, left and right, face up and face down. Do this for nine or ten cards.

From then on when the left hand turns over to deal a card face up, the face card's right edge only goes as far as the left edge of the right hand's cards where the right fingers press on its back and causes it to fall face down on the packet. Repeat this for every card supposed to fall face up. The action is undetectable if the right-hand packet is not held towards the spectators except when a card has been fairly dealt face down. Deal rapidly. At the end of the deal turn the pack over and show the first few cards really reversed alternately.

Blow on it, turning the pack face down and squaring it. Fan out the first forty cards showing them all face down. Turn the pack and rapidly push off the first eight or ten cards in one packet then show the faces of all the rest.

SIMPLICITY FOUR ACE TRICK   Stewart James

Place four A's on the table face up, deal three cards face up on each A. Pick up the A's one by one and change their positions from the bottom to the top of each pile. Take the first pile and put it face down on the palm of your left hand. Show that the A is the fourth card by counting and showing the A. Place the other three heaps face down on this pile one by one. Every fourth card is an A.

Deal the four top cards in a row. Take off the next card and using it as a pointer touch the three indifferent cards and then the fourth card saying, 'And the ace is here,' casually replace the pointer card in the left hand but to the *bottom* of the packet and at once turn up the A. Now continue the deal as before, stressing that every fourth card is an A, *really*, owing to the alteration in the position of the one card, the three A's are in the third pile and the last pile has three indifferent cards.

Turn over the first two piles, show the A's to the spectators and drop them on the pack. Pick up the third pile and show the bottom card only, an indifferent one. Turn it face down and slide out the bottom card, placing it face up in front of the pile. In the same way show the A at the bottom of the fourth pile, turn it down and slide out the A, putting it face up in front of that pile. Change the positions of the two cards and then show that birds of a feather always flock together by turning up A's opposite the A and three indifferent cards opposite the other card.

ANOTHER SIMPLICITY FOUR ACE TRICK

This may very well follow the last trick. Pick up the A's and the rest of the cards casually and without remark, but see that the A's go on the top. Execute several riffle shuffles retaining the four top cards in that position. If you can follow this with a false shuffle and several false cuts do so. Anyway you should have the four A's on the top without the audience having the slightest suspicion that they are there. Ask a spectator to cut the pack at about the middle and then each of the two packets in half again. Keep note of the packet with the A's. Pretend that one of the piles has a few cards too many (not the A packet), and ask the spectator to transfer a few cards from it to one of the other indifferent piles. Continue the same manœuvre with the three indifferent piles. Then have him transfer one card from the A pile to one of the others. Next a couple of cards from one of the two indifferent piles to the other, then two from the A pile on to one of these two heaps, finally (after carefully studying the size of the packets), transfer one of the last two cards to the last indifferent heap. After all this apparently indiscriminate jockeying around of the cards of the turning up of the A's, one on each pile, is a baffling effect.

The moves, of course, may be made in any way you please, so long as you keep track of the A's.

Instead of using four A's have four memorized cards on the top of the pack. Have the pack cut into four piles by the spectator and then keeping track of the four cards have the top cards shifted around as above, finishing with one of the memorized cards on each packet. Name them and have the cards turned over. Always use a borrowed pack to avoid suspicion of using marked cards. This is G. G. Gravatt's variation.

INSEPARABLE ACES   Jordan

After having been unmistakably placed in different parts of the pack, the four A's are dealt out together.

Hold the pack face up and remove the four A's, showing that there are four only. Square the pack, still face up and with the left thumb riffle off about eight or ten cards. Note the index of the last card and drop the packet face down on the table. On this put one of the A's, letting about one-third of its length project.

Riffle off a second packet, noting the last card, put the packet face down and an A on top, projecting like the first A. Do exactly the same with the third A, but for the fourth simply riffle off a packet taking no note of its top card. Replace packet four on the face of the pack, and on this packet three, and so on. Now although the A's are well scattered through the pack you know the card which lies next below the first three from the bottom.

Push the A's flush and begin your deal from the bottom placing the cards face up. When the first card you noted appears you know that the next card is an A. Pull it back by the glide sleight and draw out the card above. Deal in the same way until the second noted card appears, draw back the next card and retain it at the bottom with the first A. Do the same with the third A and hold all three back until the last A appears then draw out the other three one by one.

The second and third A's must be pushed back with the right second finger and it is advisable to make the deal rather deliberate so that there will be no perceptible difference when the A's are pushed back.

SLATES AND ACES   Annemann

Effect. The performer has two of the audience step forward. One is handed a slate and the other a pack of cards. Spectator shuffles the cards and removes the A's, the names of which are written on the slate in order by the other one. Performer writes the same thing on his slate, has it initialled and places it in an open paper bag which anyone holds. The four A's are now well mixed, one is selected and shown to all. The spectator with the slate erases the three other A's leaving only the chosen one. Slate is removed from bag and an unseen hand has done the same thing.

Method. Needed are two slates, a bag, one slate flap-backed with paper to match the paper bag, a pack of cards and four duplicate A's. These A's are in your inside coat pocket. Write the name of the AH in the second place on your slate, make a smudge in place of the other three as if they had been rubbed out. Place the flap over it. Have the four A's from the pack in order S, H, D, C, on the top of the pack. The AH should have a pencil dot on the back so you can identify it.

Have the spectator riffle shuffle the pack several times, this only distributes the A's without changing their order. He turns the pack face up, deals through, throwing out the A's as he comes to them calling the names. Spectator with the slate writes them down, so AH is second name on both slates, as performer's slate and it is dropped into the paper bag which has a piece cut out leaving initials visible. Bag is placed in full view. The A's are mixed and apparently placed in performer's breast pocket, really into waistcoat pocket. Spectator has a free choice of the duplicate A's and gets an AH. Performer removes three A's from waistcoat pocket leaving the AH behind, making pack complete. The slate is removed from the bag and the striking result shown. Flap is left in the bag which is laid aside.

THE TREND OF THE TIMES   Guest

Effect. In the course of a little story the four K's are reversed in the pack. At the end of the trick the K's are face down and the Q's face up.

Method. Take out the four Q's and bend them lengthwise so that the faces are concave. Place them face up and under the top card of the pack. All the other cards are face down, the K's at intervals near the bottom.

Begin by saying, 'We will suppose that the pack represents our earth. From the earliest days man has made himself the dominating creature. To represent man we will use the four Kings.' Fan the cards face up and have a spectator remove the K's. Turn the pack and shuffle overhand running off the five top cards as the first movement, the bend in the Q's facilitating the action. At the end of the shuffle the Q's are reversed on the bottom. As you go to the spectator to take the K's drop the left hand with the pack, turn the hand and bring it up backs uppermost. The pack is thus turned over with the Q's face down on the top, and all the other cards are face up. Take the K's and insert them in different places in the pack face up, saying, 'So now we have four rulers each going to his particular domain. To represent the passing of several centuries I'll shuffle the pack.' Turn the pack over as before bringing the reversed Q's to the bottom, the K's being face down with the rest of the cards. Shuffle distributing the Q's throughout the pack. Continue, 'At present we find that the trend of the times has exerted a peculiar influence over the earth. You see that the Kings, no longer the rulers, are back with the common herd and the Queens are the dominant creatures.'

Spread the pack backs up and show the Q's are face up.

THE GREAT PEARL MYSTERY

A good trick of the story variety. An ordinary pack and five glasses are required. A little preparation is necessary. Take from the pack the four Q's, four K's, four A's, and the JC. Put the JC face up on the table, on it put the K's in this order; C, H, D, S, and on top of these place the four A's, in the same order. Lift the A's and K's and give them a rather sharp bend lengthways making the faces convex and the backs concave. Replace the packet on the JC. On these put the four Q's also in the same order; C, H, D, S, with the QS as the face card of the pack. Put the four glasses in a row and the fifth behind them.

The story runs to the effect that four Q's each owned a precious pearl. Show the Q's and drop one in each of the row of four glasses. Take off the A's (representing the pearls) and K's in one packet which is easily done because of the bend. Now put the AC on its side, face out, against the glass which holds the QC. Do the same with the other three A's

More Miscellaneous Tricks

putting them against the glasses with the Q's of the corresponding suits, keeping the four K's perfectly squared behind the AS. Show the JC as representing a notorious robber and drop it, face out like all the others, into the fifth glass. The K's, having to go away on business, leave a guard to protect the Q's pearls. Put out the Joker or another J face down near the glasses.

The robber, JC, sneaked down in the night, stole the pearls—pick the A's up one by one at the back of the JC holding it face to the spectators and taking the AS (backed by the four K's) last. Seeing the guard, he quickly replaced the jewels—turn the packet with its back to the spectators, take off the four cards (K's) and replace them back out against the glasses—and stole back to his hideout. Put the JC (with the four A's behind it as one card) in the fifth glass. The guard woke up—lift the Joker—but seeing everything was all right, turned over and went to sleep again. In the morning the Q's found their pearls gone. The K's arrived by radio—turn the four K's—but the pearls were gone. The clever thief had stolen them after all. Take out the JC and spread the four A's.

PARADE OF THE QUEENS

Use four clear glass tumblers, with straight sides, in which the cards to be used will fit nicely. From any pack take the four Q's by running over the faces of the cards towards yourself, and on coming to the last Q carry away three indifferent cards well squared behind it. Hold that packet of seven cards facing the audience and take off the first three Q's, one by one, and put them in the glasses faces out; do the same with the last Q and the three cards secretly held behind it. Do not drop the first three in carelessly and then handle the last one differently. Patter about a style parade of Q's in cellophane dresses. Lift the first Q and draw it slowly in front of the others to the fourth glass and drop it in front of the Q there which has the three indifferent cards behind it. Do the same with the second and third Q's. Now turn the glasses around bringing the backs of the cards to the front. Repeat the parade bringing out not the three Q's as the audience think but the three indifferent cards and place them, still with the backs to the front in the other three glasses.

Force the glass containing the four Q's, or simply place it to one side. Take one of the supposed Q's from a glass, drop it face down on the table and put the empty glass mouth to mouth over the Q glass. Count off three cards from pack (really take two only), and drop them on to the first supposed Q on the table and add the other two supposed Q's to the pile. Now pick up this pile, shuffle it well and drop it back outwards into one of the empty glasses. Put the last glass on top mouth to mouth.

Patter about the disgust of the Q's at being placed in contact with the common herd and show they have vanished from the packet and joined the first Q. Smoothly done the trick is as effective as many more elaborate sleight-of-hand tricks.

BURIED ALIVE

From any pack take out the four J's and throw them on the table face down. Ask a spectator to mix the four cards in any way he likes as your back is turned. Turn away with the rest of the pack face down in your left hand, then with your right hand give the whole pack a sharp bend downwards over the left forefinger. Next lift half the cards an inch or two with the right hand and turn the lower half face up with the left thumb. Square the pack and you will find that you have a marked division, a bridge, between the two halves of the pack which face one another. The movements take a few seconds only and should be done with the elbows pressed to the sides so that the spectators cannot detect any movement at all.

Turn and face the spectators holding the pack well down in the left hand, the outer end sloping downwards so that the reversed cards will not be exposed. Take the J's, inserting the first one face down in the top half of the pack; the second J face up in the lower half; the third face down in the top half and the last J face up in the lower half. Throw a handkerchief over the pack, as it lies on the left hand, cut at the bridge with the right hand and with the left hand turn the bottom half over, thus bringing all the cards face down. In wrapping the handkerchief tightly around the pack give the pack a bend upwards to straighten the cards and hand them to the spectator to hold. Order the J's to turn all the one way and when the pack is unwrapped this is found to have taken place.

It is more effective to insert the J's in reverse order to that given above, place the two face up in the upper half and two face down in the lower half, then at the finish all four will be found to be face up. In this case, as with all reversed card tricks, cards with white margins should be used. Spread the cards in a line with a quick sweep, the J's show up with fine effect.

READING THE CARDS

Two methods have been handed down through the ages of magic. In the first, the bottom card is noted in taking the shuffled pack from a spectator. The pack is put behind the back, reversed and the bottom card placed face outwards on the top. Thus when the pack is brought forward, the original bottom card still faces the spectators but all the rest face the magician. The bottom card is named and the card facing the performer is noted. Putting the pack behind his back, this noted card is put in front of the original bottom card face out and is named, another card now faces the performer, this is noted and so the trick continues.

The method is so well known that one can hardly find an audience in which someone is not acquainted with the secret. This is precisely what you want, to get someone to show that he can do the trick. Secretly make the half-pass, facing the pack, before you hand him the cards. Your victim puts the cards behind his back, proceeds in the orthodox method, brings the pack forward and finds that instead of a faced card he has the back of a card facing him. He will probably try again but with no greater success. This is a good thing for use on occasion when suffering from the interruptions of the know-it-all.

The second and less well-known method consists in first noting the bottom card and bringing it forward in the right hand, keeping the pack behind the back in the left hand, but you have palmed the top card in your right hand and note it as you read the card brought forward. Your right hand goes back for another card, straighten the card just palmed and palm another, which is noted in due course and so on. It is well to bring the right hand forward empty occasionally, putting it to your forehead as you affect great mental effort and incidentally let everyone see the hand is empty.

The later methods follow.

HINDU MIRACLE   H. Hardin

Hand the pack to be shuffled after you have palmed off eight or nine cards. Turn away while the shuffling is being done, spread the cards in your hand so that you can read the indices and memorize the cards. Take a hat in your right hand and have the pack dropped in. Pretend to stir the cards about with your right hand and leave the palmed cards on the pack. You can now shake the hat quite violently but the cards remain in the same order since there is not sufficient room for them to slide above one another. Name the first card you memorized, dip your hand in and bring it out. Proceed in the same way with the rest. Nine cards, or even less are ample for the effect.

THE BELT TRICK

Secrete nine or ten cards in a known order under your belt at the back. This may be done in the course of some trick in which you leave the room with the pack in hand. After the pack has been shuffled, sight the bottom card; put the pack behind your back and proceed for a couple of cards just as if you were using the old faced-card method. Really you have slipped the arranged packet from under your belt on to the top of the pack. After the second or third card, keep the pack in front of you so that all can see you are actually reading the top cards one by one.

MODERN CARD READING   S. H. Sharpe

Sight the bottom card and place the pack behind back. Slip the bottom card to top, reverse two bottom cards. Name the sighted card, bring pack forward, turn the top card, pull the reversed bottom card out towards body and note the index. Put pack behind back, slip reversed card to top, turning it over. Name this card, bring pack forward, turning it over and noting index of bottom card, and so on. Finally bring pack forward with a known card on top. Have number called. Deal cards to it face down and quietly replace them on top. Hand pack to a spectator and name the card now at the required number.

ANY TIME, ANY DAY, CARD READING   Ivanhoe Trudell

Any pack of cards having been thoroughly shuffled take it back and sight the bottom card. Place the pack behind your back and take the bottom card and put it on the top of the pack. Next bend all the cards towards the bottom with your right hand. Divide the pack in half and turn the under portion face to face with the one above, thus making a bridge. Do this while explaining that you are about to attempt a very difficult test.

Holding the pack in the left hand, thumb at one side and fingers at the other, cards resting flat on the palm, draw the bottom card with the right thumb half an inch from the others. Now name the first card on the pack, the one you sighted on the bottom at the start, bring the pack to the front, turn the top card and show you are right.

While turning this one you can see the index of the bottom one as it projects. Remember it, place the pack behind your back again, reverse pack, draw out the new bottom card half an inch and name the top card. Bring the pack forward and turn the card. Continue naming the cards but do not continue to the extent of dragging the feat overlong.

When you decide to stop, knowing the top cards, cut at the bridge behind your back, turn the lower portion over and square the cards, giving them a slight upward bend to take the crimp out of them. Name the top card, bring the pack forward and turn it over. Lay the pack down, or hand it to be shuffled prior to another experiment.

MYSTERY CARD READING   Annemann

At any time or place, and with any pack of cards, the performer is able to look through them and read them one by one, faces down.

When you first place the shuffled pack behind your back it is necessary that you know the top card. I do it this way. Crimp one corner of the bottom card as you hand the pack to be shuffled, and at the same time sight it. Take the pack back and cut the crimped card to the top and there you are.

With the pack behind your back you slowly name this card and secretly push the two top cards into your right hand, turn the next four or five cards face up on the pack and replace the two cards on top. The right forefinger pulls up the left-hand corners of the two top cards so that when the pack is brought to the front the index of the first reversed card is plainly visible.

The pack is put on the left palm, the break closed and the top card dealt face up. When the pack is again placed behind the back it is only necessary to take out the second card, the one just sighted, place it on the top, turning it over, of course, and again securing the break.

This process is repeated until the cards reversed are exhausted.

READ THEM OFF

Tear a piece off the top left corner of one card, just large enough to allow you to read the index of another card which is turned face up under it,

With the mutilated card in the pack you may safely offer the cards to be shuffled. Take the pack receiving it with your thumb underneath so that by tilting it very slightly you can sight the outer index of the bottom card. Put the pack behind your back, riffle to the cut corner and slip the card out to the top. Turn the card below it face up. Bring the pack forward, face out and holding it between your right thumb at the bottom and the fingers on the top. Cover the cut corner with the tip of your forefinger and you can show the back of the pack freely. Name the bottom card and hold the pack upright to show that you are right. Rest the tip of the right forefinger on the top of the pack and read the index of the reversed card under it.

Put the pack behind your back, slip the reversed card to the bottom, turning it face out and reverse the next card under the top torn corner card. Bring the pack forward, name the bottom card and note the index of the reversed card. Continue the process *ad lib*. At any time you can show the back of the pack by covering the cut corner with your forefinger and more convincing still, you can slowly riffle the cards showing the whole pack faces outwards by merely being careful not to riffle the last three cards.

X-RAY   Williams

Set up a pack of one-way cards thus: first separate the four suits, arrange each one in the 'Eight Kings, etc.' order and put the two red suits together, also the two black suits. Put the two packets together so that the only one-way designs point in opposite directions. Introduce the pack so arranged, cut as near the middle as possible and riffle the two packets together very openly and thoroughly, calling attention to the way the cards are mixed. Each suit will now be distributed thoroughly, calling attention to the way the cards are mixed. Each suit will now be distributed throughout the pack but the individual cards remain in the same order. Note by the design if the card on the top is a black or red card, then to show what you are going to do deal it face up on the table, suppose it is a black card. From it you know the name of each black card as you come to it and you call its name before turning it face up. When a card appears with the design in the reverse direction you know the colour and the suit but simply guess the value, when you turn it over it gives the key to the following red cards. It is only necessary to remember the last card of the same colour and name the next in order according to the formula.

READING CARDS. MIRROR METHODS

You have a small convex mirror, about the size of a shilling, flesh coloured on the back. After the pack has been shuffled hold the mirror at the lower joints of the third and fourth fingers in which position you can see the reflection of the lower index by pulling the top card slightly back. Name the cards hesitatingly and act the part. A blindfold will greatly strengthen the trick and will not interfere with the execution of it since one can see all that is necessary down the sides of the nose.

ANOTHER METHOD

This is a radically different idea. The mirror is a tiny one which can be affixed to the back of the right-hand thumb-nail. Smear the back of the mirror with good adhesive wax, and lay the mirror back up behind the pack on the table so that you can get it on the thumb-nail in picking up the pack. The procedure is then to have the pack held by a spectator before him, upright, the cards facing him.

The cards are supposed to be read by feeling the indices. Reach your hand over the top of the pack and in feeling the index contrive to get the mirror so that you can read the index of the first card, then rub the tips of the first and second fingers on the index. Read the card with apparent difficulty and hesitation.

Separate this card from the next by inserting the tip of the thumb behind it and thus getting the reflection of the next card's index. Continue for as many cards as seems advisable. The tiny reflector can be disposed of without any trouble.

A SUBTLE SET UP

From any pack remove the four A's, or any cards you prefer and lay them out in front of a spectator. Hold the pack face downwards in your left hand as for dealing, then put the tip of left thumb on the top outer left corner of the pack and bend the forefinger underneath. Ask the spectator to hand you an A; whichever one he gives you make some remark about everybody always choosing that particular A and while talking quietly thumb count four cards. Pick up the A and put it in the break below the four cards, but push it only half-way into the pack, saying that the first A goes in near the top. Hold the pack with the outer end pointing downwards so that no one can see just where the card enters the pack. Ask for another A and thumb count four more cards, put the second A in the new break remarking that it goes in a little above the middle of the pack, let it protrude like the first.

In exactly the same way insert the next two A's asserting that one goes in just below the middle and the last near the bottom. If the pack is held pointing downwards the deception cannot be detected. Push the cards flush with the rest.

Proceed with false shuffles and cuts. Finally deal the four A's to yourself as in a five-handed game; or to any chosen player by slipping one, two or more cards, as required to the bottom.

With the proper misdirection the trick is very effective and easy to do.

A MEMORY FEAT   Billy O'Connor

Performer borrows a pack of cards that has been well shuffled and announces that he will memorize the entire pack so that he can immediately name any card at any number in the pack. Performer slowly goes through the pack and then requests that someone name a number between one and fifty-two. Whatever number is given performer names the card at that number in the pack, and to prove he is correct the number is counted down to and there is the same card that performer predicted. Again a number is given and again performer names the card there and may again repeat.

Performer really memorizes every fifth card, making ten in all. To memorize the cards it is advisable to learn the mnemonic system which is explained in the 'Nikola Card System', Chapter 20. Here is a brief summary for this effect:

The Figure 1 made with one stroke	1		Ale
2 ,, ,, two strokes	N		Hen
3 ,, ,, three ,,	M		Emblem
4 represented by FOUR-	R		Arrow
5 ,, FIVE-	V		Ivy
6 ,, Similar shape-	p or b		Bee
7 ,, ,, ,,	to or d		Tea
8 ,, (eight-aitch)	sh or ch		Shoe
9 ,, (similar shape)	k or g		Key
0 ,, (as in zero)	s or z		Lass

By supplying vowels at discretion, numbers can be translated into the names.

15, means L and V, is Loaf. 20, is N and S—Nose. 25, N and V—Knife. 30, M and S—Moss. 35, M and V—Muff. 40, R and S—Rose. 45, M and V—Roof. 50, F and S—Face.

The cards are represented in the same manner:

Clubs	Hearts	Spades	Diamonds
2 Can (C & N)	Hun	Sun	Din
3 Comb (C & M)	Ham	Sum	Dome
4 Car	Hair (H & R)	Sire	Dear
5 Cough	Half	Safe	Dove
6 Cap	Hop	Soup	Dope (D and P)
7 Cat	Hat	Suit	Dot
8 Cash	Hash	Sash	Dish
9 Cog	Hog	Sack	Dagger
10 Kiss	Hiss	Sauce	Dose
Ace—Club	Heart	Spade	Diamond
King—Clubman	Bridegroom	Gardener	Jeweller
Queen—Waitress	Bride	Garden Girl	Jeweller's Asst.
Jack—Porter	Cupid	Garden Boy	Burglar

After the table has been throughly familiarized as a groundwork it is easy to associate them both together.

You have your ten key figures from five to fifty.

Go through the pack slowly and note the card at the fifth position from the top. Say, for instance, the card is the 2C. The 2C is a Can, and Five is Ivy. Bring the two together and picture 'Ivy growing round a Can.'

Again, say the tenth card is a 5S. Ten is Lass, and 5S is a Safe. You get 'A Girl carrying a Safe'.

Although the above seems complicated it is really quite simple after just a little study.

Now with your ten cards memorized. A number is requested. If it be one of your numbers everything is easy. But if the number is for instance twelve—just pass two cards from the bottom of the pack and name your tenth card. Likewise if seventeen is given pass two cards and name your fifteenth card. If nineteen is given pass one card from top and name the twentieth card and so on. The strong feature of this trick is that it is never necessary to pass more than four cards at any time.

THE POKER SHARK   Jordan

Beforehand set up the top seventeen cards thus:
JC, KC, 9C, JH, KH, JS, KS, 9S, 7S, 7C, KD, AH, 7H, 2C, AS, AD, AC. Dealing three poker hands will give the first man J's full, the second man four K's and you a nine full on A's. When dealing you hold a break under the seventeenth card and on the last round deal yourself three cards as one. Pick up your hand, keep the extra two A's squared behind the fifth card and show three 9's, taking them off with the right hand; in replacing them slide the rear 9 behind all the other cards. The second man shows J's full, beating your hand. Fan your hand exactly as before but it now shows A's full on 9's. Take the 9's in the right hand as before and again slide on to the back. Square the cards in your left hand and drop the hand quietly to your side as the next man shows his four K's, and thumb off the two rear 9's into your coat pocket. Throw your hand on the table and maintain that it beats the K hand. Finally turn it up and show four A's and an odd card.

DOUBLE POKER DEAL

Arrange twenty cards on the top of the pack as follows:
3D, 9H, 9C, AS, AD, 10D, 6C, 10C, KC, 8D, 4C, 10S, KD, JC, AC, 10H, KH, 7H, QC, AH.
False shuffle and false cut, and deal out four poker hands. Turn the hands face up and show. No. 1 has three K's; No. 2 a straight; No. 3 a flush and No. 4 a full house.
Pick up the hands by dropping No. 4 face up on No. 3, these two on No. 2 and all on No. 1. Put the packet on top of the pack and again false shuffle and cut. Deal four hands again. This time No. 4 hand gets four A's but No. 3 hand beats it with a K high straight flush.

POKER PLAYER'S DEAL   Jordan

To arrange the pack first sort out all the high cards, 10's to A's. Paying no attention to values, take the S's and the H's and arrange them alternately, then start with a C and alternate with D's. The twenty cards then run from the top down S, H, S, H, etc., then C, D, C, D, etc. Put the packet on the top of the pack.

To begin, give the pack a genuine riffle shuffle. Say that you will use the high cards only and spread the pack out on the table from the left to right. Start at the right-hand end, push the cards to the right carelessly, taking up each high card and putting it face down on your left hand as you come to it, one card only at a time. The cards are now just as they were originally stacked.

Show the cards fanned face up casually, close the fan and turn the packet face down. Say you will mix them still more. Deal two face-down heaps, a card at a time to each heap, and then put the right-hand pile on the left. Ask for a handkerchief and in the meantime count off five cards at the bottom, inserting the little finger, five more inserting the third finger and five more separating them with the second finger. The top five cards are the D's, followed by H's, C's and S's. Any suit being called you bring out the five cards instantly.

POKER DEMONSTRATION
Vernon

Remove the four A's and arrange the following cards on the top of the pack reading downwards:

Two K's and two Q's in any order.

Four 2's.

Five cards of any suit, say H's.

10, J, Q, K, of S's.

Any five cards.

Any single H (supposing H's used for flush).

QH.

On the bottom place a pair of J's and have no other pair amongst the first five bottom cards. Fourth from bottom have a crimped, broken corner, or short card. (See 'Short Cards'.) Distribute the A's throughout the pack.

Thus prepared begin by openly removing the A's and state you will show how gamblers run up hands. Place AS on the bottom, the other three A's on the top. Then overhand shuffle thus—Run eleven cards singly into the left hand and replace them thus reversed on top. Run four into left hand and throw pack on top. Run five and throw pack on top. Run one card and throw on top. Lastly run five and throw pack on them.

Now locate the key card and hold a break. Holding the pack by the sides offer it to spectator to be cut. He must cut by the ends and at the break. Or you may cut the pack yourself. Deal five poker hands, keep the cards in their order. Show you hold four A's. Point out that it is useless without competition. Turn the first hand face up and show it, and then the others in succession dropping each on the first hand and not disturbing the arrangement.

Take your own hand, take out the odd card, a high S and drop it on top of the other face-up cards. Pick these up and put them on the top of the pack. Pick up the four A's, keeping their order, and turning pack face up, find the QH and put the A's immediately underneath with AS the lowest. Bury the top card near the bottom of the pack.

Again deal five poker hands. No. 1 has four-card flush to draw to. Show the hand and leave it face up.

No. 2 has two K's and two Q's.

No. 3. Four 2's.

No. 4. has two J's.

Look at top card of your hand but replace it without showing it or the other cards. Make the draws: No. 1 discards one, draws one, and fills a flush; No. 2 discards one, draws one to a full house; No. 3 stands pat; No. 4 discards three, draws three A's to a full house. You discard one, draw one, showing Royal Flush in S's.

QUADRUPLE POKER TRICK   M. P. Zens

Three sets of cards in the order given are needed:
1. 10H, JH, KS, QH, AS, AH, KH, AD, AC, KC.
2. 10H, JH, KH, QH, AH, AS, KS, AD, AC, KC.
3. 10S, QH, 10C, AD, JH, JC, 10D, JS, QC, KD, KS, AH, QD, AS, KH, AC, QS, 10H, KC, JD.

Lay the cards of No. 1 set face up before you. Notice that the first five make a straight and the last five a full house. From these cards you can produce any hand called for except a flush which is provided for later. Suppose a pair is called for ignore the first card and you have a pair of A's with K, Q, J, the highest hand possible with a single pair. Suppose two pairs called for. Ignore the first two cards and the next five are a pair of A's, a pair of K's and a Q. For three of a kind pass over the first three cards and you have three A's, a K and a Q. For four of a kind ignore the first four cards and the next five are four A's and a K. The hand called for denotes the number of cards to be passed over.

To repeat the effect a duplicate set is required with a different arrangement, No. 2 above. The first five cards make a Royal Flush and the last five a full house. In the same way as before you can produce any hand called for except a straight and this is arranged for in set No. 1.

Place set No. 1 in the lower right waistcoat pocket facing inwards, set No. 2 in your inside coat pocket also facing inwards. Thus prepared come forward shuffling a pack, let a spectator shuffle and cut, then you drop the cards into your inside coat pocket, at once bringing them out again with the ten set-up cards on the top. Have the pocket examined, replace the cards and invite anyone to call for any poker hand. If a Royal Flush is called for at once ask for lower hands at the start to make it easier for you.

Suppose two pairs are called for. The cards are upright in your inside coat pocket so turn the first two down sideways and pull out the next five one by one, faces to you, then spread the five and show them. Close the fan and replace them in their former position, and then turn the first two cards straight up again. In exactly the same way produce any hand called for and try to get as many as possible before going to the Royal Flush. Before producing this, hand the pack out to be shuffled and you can allow the spectator himself to replace the pack in your pocket himself. Carry on now with the cards in the waistcoat pocket and stand with the right side turned a little towards the spectators to shield the action of your left hand.

Set No. 3 should lie face up behind a small stand or easel which you use to display the poker hands. After producing as many hands from the pocket as you think fit, take the pack out and again have it shuffled. Return to the platform, drop pack on the face-up packet as you pick up the easel to show it. Place the easel in position, pick up the cards and begin a stud poker deal, faces up on to the stand. Let the cards of each of the four hands overlap slightly so that each card is quite visible but cannot get out of order. Dealer gets the winning hand.

The deal finished drop the rest of the cards into your left outside coat pocket. In this pocket, on one side of a handkerchief, you have beforehand placed the thirty-two cards of the pack from which the twenty of set No. 3 was made up. Drop the cards now on the other side of the handkerchief. Sweep the cards off the stand in an apparently haphazard way but actually begin with hand No. 1 and push against the last card so that the cards slide one on the other and put the packet face up on your left hand. Pick up No. 2, 3, and 4 in the same way. With them in hand bring out the thirty-two cards from your left coat pocket which made up the complete pack, leaving the other lot on the other side of the handkerchief. You have thus a complete pack with an arranged stack on the top.

If proficient you may false shuffle and have the pack cut, bringing the cards back to the original set-up. Now deal four poker hands in the regular way. Drop the rest of the cards on the table and announce that you have dealt the four highest possible hands in poker. Ask the spectators what these hands are and they will reply, Royal Flush, Straight Flush, Four of a Kind and a Full House. You maintain that they are mistaken and in the end you prove that the four highest hands in poker are four Royal Flushes. Turn the hands face up and show those hands.

POKER SET-UP   Lane

This is a quick set-up for a four-handed game. The four cards you wish to deal to yourself must be at the bottom of the pack and the arranging is done under cover of an overhand shuffle. Begin by drawing off the top and bottom cards with the left thumb and fingers, then run, that is draw off cards one by one with the left thumb, counting eleven and throw the remainder of the cards below those now in the left hand.

Repeat the movements, drawing off the top and bottom cards, run eight, and throw the rest below.

Again draw off the top and bottom cards, run five and throw the remainder below.

Finally, draw off the top and bottom cards and run two, throwing the balance below the cards in the left hand as before.

The four cards are now set to fall to the dealer. If they are to fall to any one of the other players you have only to slip one, two or three cards to the bottom to have them fall to the third, second or first player. The setting-up moves should be followed by a false shuffle of the whole pack and several false cuts.

ANOTHER POKER SET-UP   Lane

The following is probably the easiest and quickest set-up for a four-handed game that is possible by the use of the riffle shuffle.

Have the four required cards on the top. On the first riffle hold back the last three cards of each heap, then let the left hand three drop first and follow with those in the right hand.

For the second riffle hold back three in the left, two in the right, hand, third riffle three in left, one in right hand, and for the last riffle hold back three in the left hand and let them fall on the top last of all. The four cards are set for a four-handed game to fall to the dealer. The count for the cards to be held back requires practically no practice but the riffle should be made with the fingers covering the packets and a series of false cuts follow the riffles.

THE GAMBLER IN PERSON   Annemann

From a borrowed and shuffled pack you first deal five poker hands fairly, turning them up and showing the cards. You gather the hands, shuffle the cards and deal the highest hand to any player chosen.

The first deal is merely a feint to give you an opportunity of selecting the cards for the hand which is to follow. You must locate one card in each hand to make up a good hand and with but little practice you can do this while dealing them face up.

The real secret is in the picking up. The hands are scooped up one at a time and dropped face down on top of the pack, it is only necessary that the desired card from each hand be on top, that is at the back of the hand. Thus in picking up each hand, you take one, two, three or four cards, as the case may be and scoop up the remaining card or cards with these in hand, drop the hand on top of the pack with the wanted card on top.

To allow the choice of the winning hand it is only necessary to add one, two or three cards from the bottom. This can be done in the course of a series of false shuffles and cuts which should be done thoroughly since the trick is supposed to be an exhibition of how gamblers set up hands.

THE GAMBLER IS BACK AGAIN   Annemann

Remove the high cards, 10's, J's, Q's, K's and A's, and say you will have the spectators arrange the cards in any order to prove the dealing of a winning hand can be done by skilful shuffling alone. Have various hands called and lay them out face up on the table putting the last five before yourself. In arranging the hands with the values called for fix the H suit to come out right. Place a H second in one hand, third in another, fourth in another and in the last hand put a H first and last. With the hands face up pick the one with the two H's, drop it on that which has the H in the second place, these two on the one with the H in the third place and these three on the remaining heap. Turn the packet face down and have it cut by spectators, completing each cut until a H again appears at the bottom.

Deal the four hands and you get a Royal Flush in H's.

KLONDYKE POKER   Tom Bowyer

A new pack of cards is opened and seven poker hands are dealt with the dealer drawing four cards to his own hand. Six hands show a full house each, while the dealer lays down a Straight Flush.

Most makes of cards are packed with each suit separate and some makes are in suit order, reading from A to K consecutively from the face of the pack. When such pack is removed from its case it should be false shuffled and then may be genuinely cut by spectators any number of times. Seven poker hands are dealt but every fourteenth card is dealt from the bottom. Each person except the dealer will have a Full House and naturally will not draw any cards. The dealer is thus able to draw from the balance of the pack the top four cards, and this he does retaining only the last card he dealt to himself. He will thus get a Straight Flush.

The deal will not give a higher Straight Flush than a K high.

IMPROMPTU POKER DEAL

Secretly get the four A's to the top of the pack with three indifferent cards above them. False shuffle the pack and have a spectator cut it. Pick up the bottom portion and casually push the top cut a little to your left. Deal two poker hands, one to the spectator, one to yourself. Lay the remainder of the cards near the cut packet and as you both pick up your hands and look at them, quietly pick up the cut packet and put it on top of the other one.

Ask spectator how many he wants to draw, if he says 'Three' deal him the three top cards, but if less or he is undecided, look at his hand and see that he takes three. You discard four and draw the four cold A's.

EFFECTIVE POKER DEAL   Stadelman

Secretly get the cards of a Royal Flush, A, K, Q, J, 10 of any suit but S's to the top of the pack in any order. Riffle shuffle several times, leaving the five cards in position. Make a false cut and hand the pack to a spectator asking him to deal five poker hands face down. This with the object, you say, of showing that when the cards are shuffled and dealt fairly the hands will most likely be of low value. Pick up the hands one by one and show the poker value but covering up the first card in each as much as possible. Drop each hand face down on the remainder of the pack.

The pack is now arranged to give the dealer a Royal Flush. Say that no luck can stand up against skill and give as convincing a display of false shuffling and false cutting as you can. Now deal five hands giving yourself the Royal Flush. It is effective to turn each card of your hand face up so that the spectators see it building up. Do not use the S suit as the AS is too conspicuous a card and its reappearance would cause suspicion.

THE PERPETUAL ALMANAC OR GENTLEMAN SOLDIER'S PRAYER BOOK

The Perpetual Almanac or Gentleman Soldier's Prayer Book, printed in the 'Seven Dials' of London two or three centuries ago. This book relates how 'one Richard Middleton was taken before the Mayor of the city he was in for using cards in church during Divine Service; being a droll, merry and humorous account of an odd affair that happened to a private soldier in the 60th Regiment of Foot,' which, by the way, is known today as the King's Royal Rifles. The story reads thus:

'The sergeant commanded his party to the church, and when the parson had ended his prayer he took his text, and all of them that had a Bible pulled it out to find the text; but this soldier had neither Bible, Almanac or Common Prayer Book but he put his hand in his pocket and pulled out a pack of cards and spread them before him as he sat; and while the parson was preaching he first kept looking at one card and then at another.

'The sergeant of the company saw him, and said, "Richard, put up your cards for this is no place for them." "Never mind that," said the soldier, "you have no business with me here." Now the parson had ended his sermon and all was over; the soldiers repaired to the church-yard, and the commanding officer gave the word to fall in which they did. The sergeant of the city came and took the man prisoner.

' "Man, you are my prisoner," said he. "Sir," said the soldier, what have I done that I am your prisoner?" "You have played a game of cards in the church." "No," said the soldier, "I have not played a game, for I only looked at a pack." "No matter for that, you are my prisoner." "Where must I go?" said the soldier. "You must go before the Mayor," said the sergeant.

'So he took him before the Mayor and when they came to the Mayor's house he was at dinner. When he had dined he came down to them and said, "Well, sergeant, what do you want with me?" "I have brought a soldier before you for playing at cards in church." "What, that soldier?" "Yes." "Well, soldier what have you to say for yourself?" "Much, sir, I hope." "Well and good, but if you have not you shall be punished the worst that ever man was."

' "Sir," said the soldier, "I have been five weeks upon the march and have had but little to subsist on, and am without either Bible, Almanac or Common Prayer Book, or anything but a pack of cards. I hope to satisfy your Honour of the purity of my intentions." Then the soldier pulled out of his pocket the pack of cards, which he spread before the Mayor; he then began with the Ace.

' "When I see the Ace," he said, "it puts me in mind that there is one God only; when I see the Deuce, it puts me in mind of the Father and Son; when I see the Trey, it puts me in mind of the Father, Son and Holy Ghost; when I see the Four it puts me in mind of the four evangelists that penned the Gospels, viz.—Matthew, Mark, Luke and John; when I see the Five it puts me in mind of the five wise virgins who trimmed their lamps—there were ten, but five were foolish and were shut out; when I see the Six it puts me in mind that in six days the Lord made Heaven and Earth; when I see the Seven, it puts me in mind that on the seventh day God rested from all the works which he had created and made, wherefore the Lord blessed the seventh day and hallowed it. When I see the Eight it puts me in mind of the eight righteous persons that were saved when God drowned the world, viz., Noah, his wife, his three sons and their wives; when I see the Nine it puts me in mind of the nine lepers that were cleansed by our Saviour, there were ten but nine never returned God thanks; when I see the Ten it puts me in mind of the Ten Commandments that God gave Moses on Mount Sinai on the tables of stone."

'He took the Knave and laid it aside. "When I see the Queen it puts me in mind of the Queen of Sheba who came from the furthermost parts of the world to hear the wisdom of King Solomon, for she was as wise a woman as he was a man, for she brought 50 boys and 50 girls all clothed in boys' apparel to show before King Solomon for him to tell which were boys and which were girls; he could not until he called for water for them to wash themselves; the girls washed up to their elbows and the boys only up to their wrists, so King Solomon told by that; when I see the King it puts me in mind of the great King of Heaven and Earth, which is God Almighty, and likewise his Majesty King George to pray for him."

' "Well," said the Mayor, "you have a very good description of all the cards except one which is lacking." "Which is that?" said the soldier. "The Knave," said the Mayor. "Oh, I can give your Honour a very good description of that if your Honour won't be angry." "No, I will not," said the Mayor. "If you will not term me to be the Knave." "Well," said the soldier, "the greatest Knave I know is the Sergeant of the city that brought me here." "I don't know", said the Mayor, "that he is the greatest Knave but I am sure he is the greatest fool."

' "When I count", added the soldier, "how many spots there are in a pack of cards I find there are 365, there are just so many days in the year. When I count how many cards there are in a pack I find there are 52, there are so many weeks in a year. When I count how many tricks in a pack I find there are 13, there are so many lunar months in a year. You see, sir, that this pack of cards is a Bible, Almanac, Common Prayer Book and pack of cards to me."

'Then the Mayor called for a loaf of bread, a piece of good cheese and a pot of good beer, and gave the soldier a piece of money, bidding him go about his business saying he was the cleverest man he had ever seen.'

Now you and I, gentle readers, know exactly the useful and comprehensive purpose that our soldiers at the front require packs of cards for. Aye, but it is good to be brought before the Mayor, after he has dined.

19

Indispensable Sleights

INDISPENSABLE SLEIGHTS

Card tricks of any really entertaining value cannot be presented without the aid of a few simple sleights but with them, even a simple trick can be made to look like real magic. The word 'sleight' has a terrifying effect on most people who like to learn a few tricks, and is at once associated with the idea of hours of drudgery practising intricate movements requiring intense application to master them. However, I will guarantee that anybody of ordinary intelligence, with the ability to shuffle a pack of cards by the overhand method fairly neatly, can in a couple of hours' time gain a working knowledge of the simple sleights that follow and in a very short time he will, by using them, have them literally at his fingers' ends. The novice is advised to follow the directions given exactly. Later, as the simple principles underlying the various moves become clear, he will experience the fascination of devising his own methods and putting into practice variations and tricks of his own invention.

1. THE OVERHAND SHUFFLE

This is the term applied to the ordinary shuffle in which the cards are passed singly or in small packets from the right hand to the left, the cards being drawn off by the left thumb. It affords a means of keeping a card or several cards completely under control without arousing the least suspicion on the part of the onlookers. In the following exercises turn the top card face up so that you can follow the processes easily.

A. Take the pack face down in the left hand, holding it at an angle of

417

about 45 degrees towards the right. Lift the pack with the right hand retaining the top card in the left by a slight pressure of the left thumb. Shuffle off all the cards on top of this one. Lift the whole pack with the right hand and shuffle off all the cards into the left to the last card, dropping this on the top. Thus with two perfectly fair shuffles you have the top card back in its original position.

B. With the pack in the left hand lift it with the right but this time press lightly on the bottom card with the left fingers, retaining it and at the same time draw off the top card with the thumb as before. The top cards thus falls on the bottom card in the left hand while the right hand holds all the rest of the pack. Shuffle these cards freely on top of the two in the left hand. The card you are controlling is now second from the bottom and you can turn the pack over and show the bottom is an indifferent one; then turning the cards face down lift off and show several cards from the top, also indifferent cards. Shuffle again, this time retaining the bottom card and lifting all the others with the right hand. The special card will now be the last card of this portion and you have simply to shuffle freely until it alone remains in your hand and you drop it on the top of the pack.

C. To retain a card at the bottom of the pack you will have already noted that it is merely necessary to retain it in your left hand by pressing on it with the left fingers.

D. It is very often necessary to place a definite number of cards on top of another card. This is done by what is termed 'running', and means simply drawing cards off the top of the pack one by one with the left thumb in the course of a shuffle. If the cards are in good condition, and I take it for granted that only such cards will be used by you, a few minutes' practice will enable you to run off any number of cards in this manner with the greatest of ease.

E. To make the best use of the overhand shuffle, it must be combined with a very simple move, so simple that I evolved it from my own inner consciousness as a schoolboy only to find in later years that it had been used by gamblers as far back as records go. It is called the jog, that is, a card pulled back a little over the inner end of the pack so that it becomes a marker indicating its own position or that of the card or cards immediately below it. To apply the idea take a few cards, say the four A's and put them on top of the pack. Hold the pack in the left hand ready for shuffling and lift the rear half with the right hand. In making the first movement of taking the cards off with the left thumb, move the right hand about half an inch inwards towards the body and draw off one card only, then move the right hand forward again and continue the

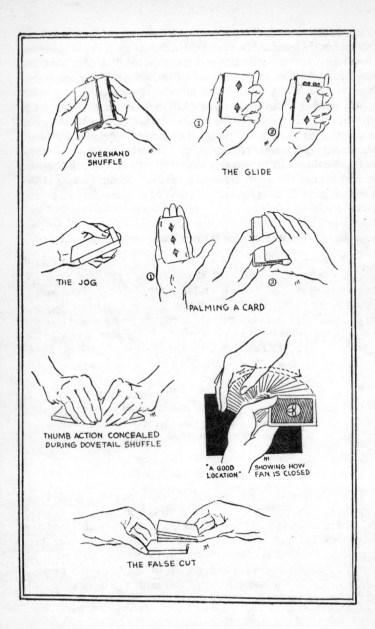

OVERHAND SHUFFLE

THE GLIDE

① ②

THE JOG

PALMING A CARD

① ②

THUMB ACTION CONCEALED
DURING DOVETAIL SHUFFLE

"A GOOD
LOCATION"   SHOWING HOW
FAN IS CLOSED

THE FALSE CUT

shuffle as usual. At the end of the movement one card will protrude from the pack at the inner end marking the location of the four A's. To bring them back to the top seize all the cards below the protruding card, lift them and drop them on the top just as if you were making a simple cut. You have the four A's back on the top. (See illustration.)

Any number of cards, up to about half the pack can be retained undisturbed by this simple expedient. After the first card has been jogged make the shuffle so that the cards fall irregularly and the projection of the jogged card from the rear end of the pack cannot be noticed. I cannot advise the reader too strongly to use this expedient until it becomes second nature. The whole action can be done without looking at the hands and while carrying on an animated conversation with your audience.

To Retain the Whole Pack in Order

F. Take the pack in the left hand as if about to deal, push off a small packet with the left thumb and take them in the right hand. From the bottom of the pack push off a few cards on top of the right-hand packet. Again push a packet off with the left thumb receiving it below the cards in the right hand, and again with the left fingers push a packet taking it on top of the right-hand packet. Continue in the same way until the whole pack is in the right hand. Do not attempt to make the movements quickly, this is the only sleight I know of where a rather rough execution rather enhances the effect.

The shuffle leaves the pack in the condition of having been cut once. If it is necessary to return it to its original order from the top card down, spread the faces to show the cards are well mixed and cut at the original bottom card which you noted before beginning.

The Riffle Shuffle

This is the term applied to the shuffle in which the pack is divided into two packets, the ends put together, the cards being bent upwards and released in such a way that they become interlaced. To retain a card or a small packet of cards on the top, you have simply to release it or them from the right-hand portion last of all. If the bottom cards are to be retained then they are let fall from the left hand in the first movement of the shuffle. It will readily be noted that cards can be retained both at the top and the bottom at the same time.

A False Cut

Hold the pack by the sides near the ends between the thumb and second finger of each hand. Now pull out about one-third of the cards from the bottom and put them on the top but still hold them with the thumb and second finger. With the right third finger lift about half the lower packet, draw the hands quickly apart releasing the top packet which falls on the table resuming its original position. On it drop the packet from the left hand, and on that the right-hand packet. The cards are in their original order. (See illustration.)

2. PALMING A CARD

Contrary to the opinions of most magicians I maintain that palming a card is not a difficult operation. It simply requires confidence and a proper understanding of the right method. To get the right position hold your right hand palm upwards and on it lay a face-up card so that the top index corner touches the top joint of the little finger and the lower index corner presses against the fleshy part at the base of the thumb. Bend the fingers naturally, keeping the thumb near the side of the hand and the fingers close together. Now turn the hand over. The card will be retained in the hand with ease and as long as you keep the palm towards your body it will be safely hidden. (See illustration.)

Now with a thorough understanding of the way the card is to be held in the hand, the next step is to learn how to get it secretly into that position from the top of the pack.

Take the pack face down in the left hand in position for dealing. Place the right hand over it, thumb at the inner end, the first joints of the four fingers resting on and covering the outer end of the pack. Run the fingers and thumb of the right hand over the edges and ends of the cards in the natural way of squaring the pack, and bring them back to the same position with fingers covering the outer ends. Then with the left thumb push the lower end of the top card to the right. The least contraction of the right hand will then secure the card in the exact palming position. Move the fingers and thumb of the right hand to the right-hand corners of the pack and hold it between the forefinger and thumb while the left hand squares the sides. Remove the left hand and hold the pack in the right. (See illustration.)

If these actions are followed exactly, the palming of the card will be imperceptible to the closest observer. Later when you put the pack down to be cut, or hand it to be shuffled by someone on your extreme left, the action is perfectly regular.

Do not hold your right hand and arm stiffly as if paralysed or immediately put it behind your back. Keep your wrist relaxed and natural and forget about the card being in the hand.

To get the card back on the pack, hold out your left hand and have the pack placed on it and cut by the spectator. Pick up the lower portion with your right hand, adding the palmed card to the top, and assemble the pack.

3. THE SIMPLE PASS

A card having been chosen, cut the pack for its return. Have it replaced on the lower portion and replace the cut on top, slipping the tip of your left little finger on the card and between the two packets. Hold the outer ends of the pack tightly closed and riffle the ends of the cards a couple of times. Seize the upper portion between the right thumb at the rear and the fingers at the outer ends. Lift it off, and at the same moment drop the left thumb under the lower packet and turn it face upwards, and immediately shuffle the cards of the right-hand packet on to the faces of the lower packet.

Do not be in a hurry and do not look at your hands. Look at your victim, ask him if he is sure he will know his card again and go straight into the shuffle. Turn the pack over and continue the shuffle. You have the card on the top to do with as you will.

It should be sufficient to say that the greatest of present-day magicians use this pass only.

4. THE DOUBLE LIFT

Many modern card tricks employ this sleight of lifting two cards as one. It is not difficult, the difficulty lies in making it naturally. With the pack well squared in the left hand face down, bring the right hand over it, thumb at the rear, fingers on the outer end. Make a motion of squaring the ends and at the same time press the fingers back a little making the ends of the pack slightly wedge-shaped. With the ball of the thumb lift the rear ends of the two top cards and slip the tip of the left little finger under them.

With the right thumb-tip on the back of the two cards and the tip of the right forefinger on the face, turn the two cards as one and lay them face up on top of the pack, the ends protruding over the inner end of the pack for about half an inch. Exhibit the card in this position, name it, and seize the cards again at the lower outer corner as before and turn them face down on the back of the pack.

The little finger-tip should be inserted before attention is called to the card and the turn made naturally and without hesitation or fumbling. There are many uses for the sleight: for instance, you apparently show the top card, and put in the middle, it immediately returns to the top.

5. THE GLIDE

Hold the pack face up in the left hand between the first joint of the thumb on one side and the second joints of the four fingers on the other. Call attention to the bottom card, say it is the 2D. Turn the pack face downwards and with the tip of the left finger draw the bottom card, 2D, back towards the body about three-quarters of an inch. Now with the tip of the right-hand second finger draw out the next card, say it is the 8H and put it face downwards on the table.

The sleight is easy and deceptive. For instance, you may get a chosen card second from the bottom by means of the overhand shuffle as already explained. Show the bottom card, turn the pack face down and deal the bottom card face up; draw back the next card by the glide and deal cards from above it to a chosen number—then deal the chosen card face down. Have the card named and turn it up.

A GOOD LOCATION

Pack is held in the left hand and any card is freely selected. The selected card is now returned to the pack, but performer pinches the cards tightly so that the selected card will not go all the way into the pack. Immediately the other hand swings the cards around left to right closing the pack as in the illustration. It will be noted that the selected card is now protruding slightly. Right hand now picks up all of the cards underneath the protruding card and shuffles on to top of the pack. Next the protruding card is removed and placed on top of the pack. Thus your selected card is brought to the top of the pack in a simple manner.

With these few simple sleights at his command, it is hoped that the reader will find the pages of this book an open sesame to endless hours of entertainment.

FOR READY REFERENCE:
SEVERAL METHODS OF FORCING CARDS
(from Annemann's *202 Methods of Forcing*)

The pack, having been shuffled by a spectator, is returned to performer who takes it in right hand, at the same time casually pulling up left sleeve followed by the left hand pulling up right sleeve. When right hand with pack pulled up left sleeve, the bottom card of pack was easily spotted. Asking spectator if he is satisfied, a pass is made and card brought to about two-thirds down in pack. A slight break is held at this spot. The thumb of left hand now runs the cards of the upper portion, fanwise over into the right hand, the person being, at the same time, invited to take one. When about half of the upper portion has been passes, a card, NOT THE ONE TO BE FORCED, is pushed temptingly forward. The person may be inclined to take it—whether he is so inclined or not, the performer draws it back, with the remark. 'Oh! not necessarily that one.' This gives him confidence, and the performer continues to pass the cards over to the right hand, spreading them nicely fanwise, until he reaches the one to be forced, which he exposes a little more than usual, then continues, 'Just take any one you please.' It will, of course, be understood that the action must be timed, as near as possible, to meet the hand, as it is raised to draw a card.

The card to be forced is on the bottom of pack. The cards are run from left to right in the usual manner, but the action is started while approaching the audience so as to give time for the following manœuvre: With the second and third fingers of the left and right hand work the bottom card over toward right side. The cards are still run from left to right passing above the chosen card. Ask someone in the audience to indicate his choice by touching the card desired. When it is indicated lift up this card with all the cards above it and as the pack is squared up the forced card slips in from below.

In this method a few top cards are prearranged. Three cards of one number (say five) are placed on the top of the pack and the card to be forced then placed at eight from the top. The pack is false shuffled, keeping the top eight cards in place. The three top cards are then dealt on to table in a row and one selected while face down. This one is turned over and the spectator handed pack to count down and remove the fifth card, which is the right one.

What is known as the 'bridge' makes possible a neat cutting force. The card is on bottom of pack. Cutting same about centre, the lower half, which is to be placed on top, is given a bend (concave) at the ends. Spectator is asked to cut pack somewhere and look at face card of cut. If cut is made at sides, this will work time after time, as the slight break at sides will cause upper half to be lifted off by a quick cut. By bending the sides, the bridge can be placed at ends for an end cut. Previous cutting by the spectator will give you this information. Most cuts are at sides.

Place a short card near centre of the pack. Card to be forced mentally is above it. Hold pack straight up in front of spectator. With first or second right fingers riffle top of pack from face to back, smoothly and without a stop. Ask spectator to note cards and to think of one that he sees. Practise before a mirror to get speed. The short card will click by and the following card will register on the spectator when the rest of the pack is a slow blur. Don't try to stop at the card but let it work itself. It will seem impossible at times that a card will show up in this way but try it before several people before you judge.

THE KNIFE METHOD

In this method the card to be forced is placed about fifteenth from the top. Cards are held in the left hand. The little finger makes a break directly underneath the known card. A flat knife is handed to spectator who is asked to insert it anywhere he may please. Performer slowly riffles the pack. It is only necessary that the knife enter the pack below the chosen card and fairly near it. The top fifteen cards are now pushed forward on to the blade, pack being tilted slightly downward. Performer grips the knife with right hand and the fifteen cards, the lowest of which is the known card, are pushed well forward and slightly raised. The spectator is asked to note this card, which appears to be the one he has cut.

20

The Nikola Card System

The last word in Card Conjuring. A development, on astonishing lines, of the principle of the stacked pack, presenting features unbelievable until demonstrated.

By this system prearrangement seems impossible. The sequence bears close investigation, and is undetectable in counting, displaying, repeating, or even in deliberate examination.

All that has been done by previous systems can be done with this, and more.

The most valuable feature of the system is that the pack can actually be stacked during the performance, which may be entirely impromptu, and given a moment's notice with a borrowed pack of cards.

A complete description of the system, including pictorial chart, with detailed instructions for tricks in conjunction, and valuable subsidiary devices and artifices applicable to this and general purposes of conjuring with cards follows.

ARGUMENT

This thing seems simple and obvious when explained. Yet in practice it is completely baffling to the uninitiated, and productive of effects that are astonishing. Without knowledge of sleight of hand, the possessor of the secret, by easily acquired mental processes alone, may produce a range of effects conveying an impression of the most absolute control of the cards. Allied to skill in the execution of standard sleights commonly used in card conjuring, the system may be fortified and amplified until its results seem almost miraculous.

The idea of using a pack prearranged in a memorized order for the accomplishment of specific tricks is an old one, but has not at any time found great favour, probably because it was a little too much for the casual and not quite enough for the expert.

The reader is recommended at this point to take a good look at the chart, which represents the order of the pack as arranged for use. On any reasonable inspection no peculiarity of arrangement is apparent. Prolonged scrutiny may reveal the fact that the heart suit appears upon every fourth card, but beyond that no regularity is detectable. And this for a very solid reason. **There is none.** The disposition of the cards is not, however, indiscriminate. There is method in the madness.

Every fourth card being the H suit permits of an all-trump hand being dealt for whist or bridge.

On the same deal every second card forms one of a sequence complete as to values but regardless of suits, for the presentation of an elaboration of the trick known as 'The Spelling Bee'. (For the reason that a K is not available, in consequence of more pressing demands, a J has to do duty for such, as will be explained in its proper place.)

The first twenty-one cards are studiously placed for the purpose of a 'game of Poker'—to the advantage of the dealer.

The remaining cards have no special significance. The complete arrangement is not even arbitrary: once the principle has been grasped it may be revised to meet individual requirements or fancy, or for partial disguise.

This is the basis of the system, and the rotation of the cards, with their numerical equivalents, must be memorized until as familiar as the alphabet. This of course, presents a greater immediate difficulty than the 'eight kings threatened to save' achievement, but even so, and purely by an effort of concentration, it is not an insuperable task.

Fortunately, however, there is a system of mnemonics by the aid of which it can be made a mental fixture much more quickly and with greater certainty than without. This is outlined in the next section.

CURRICULUM

To readily distinguish the cards in the mind, every card is symbolized by an object and every number from one to fifty-two is represented by another object. The numbers and their corresponding cards produce combinations of objects which form mental pictures that indelibly imprint the relations upon the memory.

That is it in a nutshell: this is it in detail:

The mnemonic system is built up in stages.

First, let every figure be represented by a consonant, thus—

TABLE 1

Let the figure 1 be represented by	1	(**one** stroke)
,, ,, 2 ,,	n	(**two** strokes)
,, ,, 3 ,,	m	(**three** strokes)
,, ,, 4 ,,	r	(as in four)
,, ,, 5 ,,	f or v	(as in fi **v** e)
,, ,, 6 ,,	p or b	(similar shape)
,, ,, 7 ,,	t or d	(,, ,,)
,, ,, 8 ,,	sh or ch	(eight-aitch)
,, ,, 9 ,,	k or g	(similar shape)
,, ,, 0 ,,	s or z	(as in zero)

(The notes in parenthesis are a further aid to memory in the laying of this simple foundation.)

Now, by supplying vowels at discretion, every number can be translated into a name, thus—

TABLE 2

1. Ale	19. Log	36. Mop
2. Hen	20. Nose	37. Mat
3. Emblem	21. Nail	38. Match
4. Arrow	22. Nun	39. Mug.
5. Ivy	23. Gnome	40. Rose
6. Bee	24. Norway	41. Rail
7. Tea	25. Knife	42. Rain
8. Shoe	26. Nap	43. Room
9. Key	27. Net	44. Rower
10. Lass	28. Niche	45. Roof
11. Lily	29. Neck	46. Rope
12. Lion	30. Moss	47. Rat
13. Lamb	31. Mill	48. Rush
14. Lyre	32. Moon	49. Rack
15. Loaf	33. Mummy	50. Face
16. Lobby	34. Mare	51. File
17. Lad	35. Muff	52. Fan
18. Latch		

And if Table 1 has been thoroughly familiarized as a groundwork, Table 2 can be fixed in less than half an hour. Another half-hour concentrated upon the four columns of Table 3 should absorb them also.

Herein the letters corresponding to the spot values of the cards are combined with the initials of their suits to form other names, so that every card in the pack becomes translated into something pictured in the mind.

A's take simply the name of the object of which they are conventional representations.

The associations applied to the picture cards are obvious.

TABLE 3

	Clubs	Hearts	Spades	Diamonds
Two	Can	Hun	Sun	Din
Three	Comb	Ham	Sum	Dome

Four	Car	Hair	Sire	Dear
Five	Cough	Half	Safe	Dove
Six	Cap	Hop	Soup	Dope
Seven	Cat	Hat	Suit	Dot
Eight	Cash	Hash	Sash	Dish
Nine	Cog	Hog	Sack	Dagger
Ten	Kiss	Hiss	Sauce	Dose
Ace	CLUB	HEART	SPADE	DIAMOND
King	Clubman	Bridegroom	Gardener	Jeweller
Queen	Waitress	Bride	Garden Girl	Jeweller's Asst.
Knave	Porter	Cupid	Garden Boy	Burglar

Table 4 is evolved from the preceding tables, which are merely stages in its construction, and if each development has been properly mastered, this last can be acquired almost in a single reading. It is the systemized code for the arrangement of the pack and the key to its working.

The use of the completed mnemonic should be easily mastered. A mental picture of associated objects (more especially if the association is curious or bizarre) is more easily and securely retained than such similar forms as numerical figures and playing-card designs. It must be emphasized that the objects themselves are to be visualized, and not merely the descriptive words thought of.

For example:

No.	1.	The Ale is Doped.
No.	2.	The Hen has a Cough.
No.	22.	The Nun drinks from a Can.
No.	26.	The King Sleeps.
No.	27.	A Net Suit for summer.

And so on. It is not necessary to go through the list. The slight effort of composing a picture will help in its retention, so I will leave the student to make his own.

To illustrate the use of the table in its elementary application:

Required the position of the 10S. The 10S is represented by Sauce. The Sauce is spilled on the Mat. Mat is thirty-seven. Therefore the 10S is the thirty-seventh card of the sequence.

Required the name of the fifteenth card. No. 15 is a Loaf. The Jeweller is selling a Loaf. Jeweller represents the KD. Therefore the fifteenth card is the KD, and so on.

TABLE 4

1. Ale	Dope	27. Net	Suit
2. Hen	Cough	28. Niche	Hog
3. Emblem	Clubman	29. Neck	Sash
4. Arrow	Cupid	30. Moss	Soup
5. Ivy	Safe	31. Mill	Cap
6. Bee	Dagger	32. Moon	Hun
7. Tea	Sack	33. Mummy	Spade
8. Shoe	Bride	34. Mayor	Garden-boy
9. Key	Comb	35. Muff	Car
10. Lass	Kiss	36. Map	Half
11. Lily	Gardener	37. Mat	Sauce
12. Lion	Heart	38. Match	Diamond
13. Lamb	Dear	39. Mug	Porter
14. Lyre	Burglar	40. Rose	Hair
15. Loaf	Jeweller	41. Rail	Sun
16. Lobby	Bridegroom	42. Rain	Dot
17. Lad	Din	43. Room	Garden-girl
18. Latch	Waitress	44. Rower	Ham
19. Log	Cog	45. Roof	Sum
20. Nose	Hiss	46. Rope	Cash
21. Nail	Dish	47. Rat	Dose
22. Nun	Can	48. Rush	Hop
23. Gnome	Club	49. Rack	Dove
24. Norway	Hat	50. Face	Dome
25. Knife	Cat	51. File	Jeweller's Asst.
26. Nap	Sire	52. Fan	Hash

Having learnt the code the next step is to acquire facility in the use of it.

To this end the learner should take a pack of cards, and proceed to arrange it from memory in the tabulated order. When this has been done, shuffle thoroughly—and repeat again until it can be done without hesitation. The exercise may be alternated by questions as to the numerical position of specified cards, and by naming cards at numbers chosen at random.

In case the process has not already been made quite clear, we will take two more examples:

Question: What is the eighteenth card? Eighteen is l-ch—latch; the Waitress is fastening the Latch; Waitress represents the QC. *Answer ·* The QC.

Question: At what number is the KH? The KH is a Bridegroom; he is waiting in the Lobby; Lobby (l-b) is sixteen. *Answer:* Sixteenth.

We may profitably conclude the section by an analysis of the arrangement. If the pack is stacked and then dealt into four, the heaps will be as follows:

TABLE 5. (For reference only)

Five of D	Three of D	Queen of D	Eight of H
Three of S	Eight of C	Ten of D	Six of H
Two of S	Seven of D	Queen of S	Three of H
Ten of S	Ace of D	Jack of C	Four of H
Ace of S	Jack of S	Four of C	Five of H
Eight of S	Six of S	Six of C	Two of H
Seven of C	Four of S	Seven of S	Nine of H
Eight of D	Two of C	Ace of C	Seven of H
Two of D	Queen of C	Nine of C	Ten of H
Four of D	Jack of D	King of D	King of H
Three of C	Ten of C	King of S	Ace of H
Five of S	Nine of D	Nine of S	Queen of H
Six of D	Five of C	King of C	Jack of H

NOTES ON TABLE 5

The second and fourth hands are available for special purposes, the fourth for play as under, the second for the 'Spelling Bee' trick.

The first and third may be named in order by repeating the sequence with the omission of the intermediate cards.

Whist or Bridge. The fourth hand contains the whole of the H suit. The performer may either deal it to himself and let it go at that, or he may invite the spectators to 'choose' a heap, and force this one upon them. Or, he may trust to luck and accept it if the choice falls upon it. The suit for trumps may be forced by inviting a player to cut for trumps from this heap. If the choice falls upon the second heap he may instead give the 'Spelling Bee' trick. If upon either of the other two he offers to tell the chooser what cards he holds. In either case there is nothing to prevent a further choice being offered.

Spelling Bee. The cards as dealt face down, of course, are in the correct order for this. The performer takes up the cards and spells—o.n.e, one. At each letter he transfers a card from top to bottom of the packet, and on the word 'one' turns up the A and lays it on the table. T.w.o, two, is spelt out in the same way, and so on throughout the packet to the end of the story. No K can be provided, as three have been appropriated to the poker hands, so the JS has been made to do duty for the K. It is very similar, and if shown quickly it will pass.

Poker. The first twenty cards of the pack, dealt as poker hands, are rather artfully disposed.

The first player gets a sequence—2, 3, 4, 5, 6.

The second gets—5, 9, 10, J, Q.

This is one card short of a sequence, and if he exercises his option of 'buying' a card his enterprise is rewarded. He gets the 8D (the twenty-first card) and then holds—8, 9, 10, J, Q.

The third hand gets a 'full house'—K, K, K, 9, 9.

Such a combination of hands in a real game of poker might give rise to some little excitement. Whatever the speculative proclivities of the players, the wizard can stand firm to the last in the triumphant posses-sion of a royal flush—A, K, Q, J, 10 (all H's).

'Nap.' The same hands will ensure the happy security to the dealer.

Finally, Table 6 is given from which to refresh the memory from time to time. The memory tags, once acquired, can easily be recalled, and an occasional reading of the table (if it should fall into disuse) should be sufficient to revive the impressions.

TABLE 6. (The Order of the Pack)

1. Six of D	19. Nine of C	36. Five of H
2. Five of C	20. Ten of H	37. Ten of S
3. King of C	21. Eight of D	38. Ace of D
4. Jack of H	22. Two of C	39. Jack of C
5. Five of S	23. Ace of C	40. Four of H
6. Nine of D	24. Seven of H	41. Two of S
7. Nine of S	25. Seven of C	42. Seven of D
8. Queen of H	26. Four of S	43. Queen of S
9. Three of C	27. Seven of S	44. Three of H
10. Ten of C	28. Nine of H	45. Three of S
11. King of S	29. Eight of S	46. Eight of C
12. Ace of H	30. Six of S	47. Ten of D
13. Four of D	31. Six of C	48. Six of H
14. Jack of D	32. Two of H	49. Five of D
15. King of D	33. Ace of S	50. Three of D
16. King of H	34. Jack of S	51. Queen of D
17. Two of D	35. Four of C	52. Eight of H
18. Queen of C		

UTILITY

The prearranged pack in hand, and the knowledge of it in the head, the possessor may proceed to the execution of marvels.

For the sake of brevity I will allow the words of essential description by the performer to the audience to serve also as description to the reader.

The reader is probably wondering how it can be possible to stack a pack in view of the audience. May I beg his patience for a while. I have reasons.

Methods of false shuffling are given in Chapter 19.

1. 'STOP'

(To apparently count the cards in riffling)

'I will give you an illustration of what may be accomplished by a highly cultivated sense of touch.

'After shuffling these cards, as I riffle the pack somebody say "Stop" —anywhere you like.

'Stop? There are (so many) cards here. (Count and verify.) I'll do it again to show you it wasn't an accident. Stop? There are (so many).' (Count and verify.)

Procedure. The cards are held in the left hand as for dealing. The right thumb rests against the lower end, and the right forefinger riffles. When stopped, the right hand lifts off the upper packet of cards at the break and turns it face up. A glance at this card, and a reference to its number indicates the number of cards in the packet. For instance, if stopped on the 8S, twenty-nine cards are in the packet. If the face card of the packet is 10H there are twenty cards. In counting the cards, of course, proper care must be used not to displace the order.

A variation may be effected by cutting any number of cards demanded. To do this, riffle slowly and stop at the card bearing the equivalent Code number. For instance, if thirty cards are asked for, riffle to the 6S: if thirty-nine, riffle to the JC, and so on.

2. CARDS BY WEIGHT

'Perhaps you think I count the cards. I won't say that I don't but I need not.

'Will you cut, please, at any point you like. Just by weighing these cards in my hand I can tell you that you have cut exactly (so many) cards. Of course, it's easy to **tell** you that. I'll count them or perhaps you would not believe me. . . . Correct.'

In this case the procedure is varied. Presumably the spectator who cuts the cards will deposit the packet face down on the performer's palm, and to turn it over might be conspicuous. Directing public attention unconsciously towards it by a gesture of careful consideration of its weight, he tilts the **left-hand** packet with the left thumb, and with the left-hand finger-tips pushes the top card slightly over the edge of the packet until the index is just readable. Say this is the 4C, which is the thirty-fifth card, then there are thirty-four cards in the right-hand packet.

3. WEIGHING CHOSEN CARDS

'Will somebody take a card, please. Don't let me see what it is.

'It hardly seems credible that the difference in the printing of the faces of the cards—the colour of the ink and the difference in quantity for the different spots and designs would make a perceptible difference in the weight; but perhaps I can distinguish it. "Perhaps not," you may retort, but let me try. Lay that card face down on the palm of my hand, please. . . . That is the 2C. See.

'No. I didn't guess it. I'll do it again. Will you take one, please. I can recommend any of these. Lay it on my right hand as before. . . . That is the 8C.'

Procedure. The cards are spread fan-wise in offering a choice. When a card is removed the performer retains the break with the little finger of the left hand in closing up the pack, and immediately after makes a secret cut ('The Pass' or 'The Shift') or if not proficient in sleight of hand, boldly lifts the cards above the break and puts them at the bottom. He then tilts the pack with the left thumb, and sights the bottom card. The chosen card is the card next in order in the sequence. Thus, in the first instance the bottom card is the 8D (twenty-one) and the chosen card is the 2C (twenty-two) and in the second instance the indicating card is the 3S (forty-five) and the chosen card is the 8C (forty-six).

4. THE SENSE OF TOUCH

'Another card, please. Don't let me see it. Look at it intently, and remember it well. Then, instead of laying upon my hand, lay it on the palm of your own face down. Just for three seconds. One—two—three. Good. Now replace it in the pack. It will not be required any further.

Allow me, please, to place the palm of my hand upon yours. The card leaves an impression behind which can be felt by the super-sensibility of my highly trained touch. It feels like a picture card—a diamond—the KD.'

Procedure. When the card is removed the performer retains the break as before, but he does not cut the cards. When offering the pack for the card to be returned, he divides it at the break, so that the card is replaced in the same position. He also lifts the upper half of the pack in such a way as to enable him to sight the bottom card of that half, in this case the JD (fourteen) and thereby becomes acquainted with the fact that the KD (fifteen) has been chosen.

5. LOCATING

'Again take a card, please. Look at it, remember it, and return it to the pack. Then I will shuffle. Will you please cut. . . . You chose the 4C, and it is the forty-sixth card, counting from the top.

This is accomplished by calculation. First the chosen card is ascertained by means already made use of: viz., a break is held at the point where the card is removed, and in opening the pack to have the card replaced at the same point, the card above is sighted. In this case it is supposed that the JS (thirty-four) is sighted, therefore the 4C (thirty-five) is the chosen card. It is replaced, and the pack plainly squared up. The shuffle is false. The cut, or any number of cuts, is genuine. Now to find the position of the chosen card, note the bottom card (say the 2C, forty-one): if, as in this example, the code number of the bottom card is higher than the code number of the chosen card, subtract the code number of bottom cards from fifty-two, and add the number of the chosen card to the result—thus: $52 - 41 = 11$. $11 + 35 = 46$, and the 4C will be found at that number.

If the code number of bottom card be lower than that of the chosen card, it is only necessary to subtract the former from the latter. For example: Chosen card = 10D (forty-seven), bottom card + 9C (nineteen), $47 - 19 = 28$, and the twenty-eighth card will be found to be the 10D.

If the performer prefers digital to mental activity, he may adopt a different procedure. This is to make a secret cut below the 8H (the normal bottom card of the sequence) to restore the pack to its regular starting point. No calculation is then necessary, it only being necessary to name the numerical equivalent of the ascertained chosen card.

To facilitate the restoration of the pack on occasion, it is necessary that the top or bottom card should be prepared as what I have chosen to term a 'pilot' card. This card may be cut short as explained in Chap. 17.

Or a plan recommended is to bend up the bottom left-hand corner of the **top** card (the 6D) and work it between the thumb and finger until it is soft. Only a small extent is necessary, say to within an eighth of an inch or so of the edge. When the cards are riffled with the right thumb across this corner, the cards will 'break' above the 6D, and the point can be checked by a quick glimpse of the 8H. Increased pressure of the thumb will bend up the upper half of the pack slightly to permit the insertion of the little finger of the left hand, and a secret cut will transpose the two halves of the pack.

6. Spelling

'Sometimes I can find cards by spelling them. For instance—K.I.N.G. S.P.A.D.E.S, and I get the KS. T.E.N.H.E.A.R.T.S, and I get the 10H. S.I.X.S.P.A.D.E.S, and I get the 6S.'

Procedure. This is perfectly straightforward and automatic. It is only necessary to start with the 8H at the bottom. As each letter is spelt, an accompanying card is taken from the top of the pack, and placed at the bottom. After the letter S of the first spelling, the KS turns up, and after showing it is replaced **on the top.** This is the only point to remember. The 10H is then spelt out, and **transferred to the bottom.** The 6S follows. If the 6S be replaced **on top,** the JC can be spelled out. Transfer the JC **to the bottom** and spell out the 6D (including the word 'of' in the spelling) and the original starting point will be reached.

7. To Spell Any Card Called For

If the experimenter cares to go to the trouble he may elaborate the last feat to the extent of inviting the audience to name any card and spell it out in the same way.

To do this, make a rapid calculation of the number of letters in the description of the card, i.e.—start with the value, add five for C's, six for H's or S's, and eight for D's. Subtract the sum from the tabulated number of the card and transpose the pack to bring to the top the card which is the numerical equivalent of the result.

Thus, if the 7C is called for

$5 + 5 = 10$
Seven of Clubs $= 25$
$25 - 10 = 15$
Card No. 15 $=$ KD.

The KD being cut to the top, the 7C is the eleventh card down, the desired position for revelation by spelling.

Another example—

Required, the 8D

$$5 + 8 = 13$$
Eight of Diamonds $= 21$
$$21 - 13 = 8$$
$$8 = QH.$$

Cut the QH to the top of the pack, and the thirteen cards required for spelling are on top of the 8D.

In the event of the number of letters in the name of the card being greater than the code number of the card, subtract the number of letters from fifty-two and add the code number to obtain the indicator.

To divide the pack at the right point to bring the card desired to the top, sight the card preceding by riffling the left-hand bottom corner of the pack with the right thumb. This is not difficult as the sequence is a guide to the approximate position. When the card is sighted, the little finger of the left hand is inserted, and a secret cut made. If the reader cannot execute a secret cut he make make an open cut. Better than either, the false riffle shuffle (see Chapter 19), necessitates the pack being divided into two packets as a preliminary, and it is a perfect cover to the artifice of the break to make it openly in this connection, while the 'shuffle' itself can be so executed as to leave the pack cut or intact at will.

8. THOUGHT ANTICIPATED

'Now, will somebody just **think** of a card. Do you mind? Think of just any card you like, but don't think of more than one card, and once having made a choice, don't change it, but think of it exclusively and intently. And will somebody else please think of a number—a number between one and fifty-two.

'Now, sir, what card did you think of? The JC. And what number did **you** think of? Twenty-four. Very well. Now listen attentively, please. I have not handled these cards at all. They have been out of my hands while the card and the number have been mentally chosen. My object has been, not merely to divine your thoughts but to anticipate them; and if my effort has been successful the JC will be found twenty-fourth in the pack.'

Procedure. Here is an application of 'system' to an older effect whereby a more complete realization of the idea is obtainable than by the elementary process usually associated with it.

Rule 1. If the specified number be lower than the table number of the chosen card, the difference must be transferred from top to bottom. **Therefore,** subtract the required number from the table number of the card, and take the remainder as the indicator of the card to be sighted, and cut to the bottom of the pack.

Example. Required to place the JS fifteenth, $34 - 15 = 19 = 9C$. Cut the 9C to the bottom, and the JS becomes the fifteenth card.

Rule 2. If the specified number be higher than the table number of the chosen card, the difference must be transferred from the bottom to the top. **Therefore,** subtract the table number of the card from the required number and subtract the remainder from fifty-two. This gives the indicator of the card to be sighted and cut to the bottom of the pack.

Example. Required to place the 4D twenty-seventh.

$$27 - 13 = 14$$
$$52 - 14 = 38 = AD.$$

Cut the AD to the bottom of the pack, and the 4D becomes twenty-seventh.

Rule 3 (Applicable to either case). This general rule may, if preferred, take the place of both the preceding rules.

Deduct the required number of appearance from fifty-two, and add the table number of given card. When the sum exceeds fifty-two, deduct fifty-two.

Examples. Required to place the JS fifteenth.

$$52 - 15 = 37$$
$$37 + 34 = 71 - 52 = 19 = 9C, \text{ which cut to bottom of pack.}$$

Required to place the 4D twenty-seventh.

$$52 - 27 = 25$$
$$25 + 13 = 38 = AD, \text{ which cut to bottom of pack.}$$

For the double purpose of emphasizing the effect and facilitating the procedure, the pack at the outset is laid upon the table. After the two participants have been invited to 'think', the performer pauses for a period of masterly inactivity. Then he asks for the card and the number, upon receipt of which he makes the necessary calculation as quickly as possible: he also makes a mental estimate of the approximate position of the card to be cut to the bottom of the pack. Deliberately reaching for the pack he, in process of lifting it, first turns it upon its edge, the backs of the cards towards the spectators. With the thumb he pushes a portion of the pack from left to right in such a way as to reveal the indices round about the required card. The location is completed in gathering up the pack, and the little finger inserted at the break. The few subsequent remarks are framed to give time to make the secret cut. This is a case where technique should be faultless. If the reader will turn back a moment to the performer's remarks, he will note that the audience is invited to 'listen' and not to 'watch', and with experience in control he should be able to divert attention from his hands to his face for just so long as may be necessary.

9. Unconscious Thought Transmission

'I will give you an astonishing example of the effect of unconscious thought transmission. Will somebody take any one card, please—but don't look at it.

'I will at once place it, without looking at it myself, face down in this envelope. I will seal the envelope and place it in sight and out of reach— here. None of you, nor I, know what card is in that envelope.

'Next I will invite you to name any card, but so that there shall be no suspicion of collusion, let it be a joint selection. First name a suit . . . D's. Will you have a court card or a spot card. . . . A spot card: very well, how many spots shall we say? Eight!

'The choice, then, falls on the 8D, and I think you will admit, under the conditions, it could not have been prearranged. It is a strange thing —I would not believe it myself, if I hadn't done it—the 8D is the identical card in that envelope over there.'

The envelope used is preferably of a large size—$5\frac{1}{4}$ in. x $4\frac{1}{4}$ in. and is prepared by neatly slitting the bottom to a little more than the length of a playing card.

When a card is taken, a secret cut is made at the point where it is removed. The pack is retained in the left hand, back upwards, and the envelope is casually laid on top of the pack, and grasped in the same hand. The right hand receives the chosen card and pushes it, face down, into the envelope. It is pushed through the slit in the bottom to the extent of about a quarter of an inch, and in this position is gripped in the fork of the thumb against the top of the pack. When the envelope is withdrawn the card remains behind on the top of the pack, and it is an empty envelope that is erected for the contemplation of an expectant audience. Upon the front of this envelope is stuck a minute pellet of wax, or diachylon.

While a card is being named in stages, the performer holds the pack in front of him edge up, with the faces to the right and the backs to the left, grasped in both hands in such a way that it is completely covered. The thumb of the right hand supports the bottom end, and the four fingers of the same hand cover the opposite end. The side of the pack nearest the spectators rests upon the second, third and fourth fingers of the left hand, the thumb of the same hand rests upon the opposite side (nearest the performer) and the first finger, bent, rests upon the top. The upper corners can therefore easily be riffled by a slight action of the left thumb, and as soon as the required card is known it is sighted (using the sequence as a guide) and a break made above it. It is secretly cut to the top of the pack and in due course the envelope is laid over it while it is ripped open with a knife. The cut is made along the edge already partially severed, and the evidence of faking thereby destroyed. Meanwhile the top card of the pack is pressed against the pellet of wax, and when it has been secured to the envelope, the pack is placed aside, and the fingers inserted into the envelope. The concealed card is drawn up behind as though coming from the interior of the envelope.

10. WIZARD'S WHIST

'I will give you an example of the practical application of thought-reading to card-playing. It is useful sometimes to know what card your opponent thinks of playing.

'Will you please suppose you had these cards in your hand at the card table, and decide upon one of them to play. You need not necessarily choose the highest or a good card, but just think of any one, for the purpose of a test. Only one, please, and don't forget it. Keep it in mind for a little while.

'Will you do the same, please? Think of one of these. And you. Thank you.

'Who else will take a hand? You? Thank you.

'Remember the one card in each case, forget the others, and return them all to me.

'For the purpose of illustration we will imagine the game is whist, so I will deal the cards accordingly.

'Now, as I show you the hands, tell me if you see your particular card amongst them.

'You thought of the........, you have in mind the............, you are going to play the........, and you decided upon the.........'

Procedure. This is entirely independent of the system, and can be done without any prearrangement of cards; but it is introduced here because it happens to make a very appropriate conjunction of effects.

Each of the four spectators taking part is given four cards from the top of the pack. They are taken back in the same order as they were given out, and replaced at the **bottom** of the pack. A false shuffle may be introduced here, but the cards must be left intact at the bottom of the pack. Four whist hands are then dealt, and the process of the deal will distribute the sixteen bottom cards of the pack to the tops of the four heaps and divide each original group of four cards among the same. So that directly the information is obtained that a chosen card is in a particular heap, as it can only be one card of that heap, it is easily discovered. The group of four cards last returned to the pack are the top cards of the newly dealt hands, and when the last 'player' points out the heap that contains the card he thought of, it must be the top card. The four cards next returned are the second cards of the whist hands, and the second card of the hand that contains the thought-of card is it. And so on with the other two groups. It is essential to remember that the cards first returned to the pack are fourth after the deal, the second to be returned are third after the deal, the third the second, and the fourth the last.

When performing this trick with an unprepared pack it is necessary for the performer either to look at the faces of the cards, or secretly glimpse the indices. With the pre-arranged pack this is unnecessary as he can name the cards by mental reference to the Code.

He cannot, with the prepared pack, show the fourth hand without prematurely exposing the fact that it contains all of one suit, but this is not only unnecessary, but the omission adds somewhat to the effect. Any card or cards not revealed in the first three heaps must necessarily be in the fourth, and knowing this and being acquainted with the contents of the heap he can name them without any reference to it.

11. ALL TRUMPS

'Now, gentlemen, if you please, we will play the hands out. Will you cut for trumps?

'H's. . . . Then I think the game is mine!'

Procedure. This has already been explained (see page 427). While astonishment over the last effect is still fresh, and the victims are not in a condition to notice the irregularity of the proceeding, the performer picks up his own and offers it for the cut. The other hands are pushed across to the would-be players, and after due interval they are confronted with the constellation of trumps.

So far it is a smooth-working, rational sequence of effects. It may be extended or varied at discretion. The possibilities are not yet exhausted:

12. THE SPELLING BEE. 13. THE GAME OF POKER, AND 14. THE GAME OF 'NAP' have already been referred to. Here are some others,

15. TO NAME THE POSITION OF ANY CARD CALLED FOR,

16. TO PICK OUT ANY CARD CALLED FOR BEHIND THE BACK

This is merely a disguise of No. 15. All that is necessary is to note the bottom card, and follow the code while counting the cards behind the back until the required one is reached. If the pack has been disarranged it forms a suitable opportunity for an exchange of packs.

17. TO PRODUCE CARDS CALLED FOR FROM THE POCKET

This, a feat usually achieved by the use of a duplicate pack sorted into the divisions of card holders, can be done with the stacked pack.

Cut the 6D to the top, and divide the pack into four equal parts by riffling and sighting the indices. The first packet is cut at the thirteenth card, the 4D, and placed in the left breast pocket; the second is cut at the twenty-sixth card, the 4S, and placed in the right trousers pocket; the third is cut at the thirty-ninth card, the JC, and placed in the left trousers pocket; and the remaining thirteen cards are put in the right breast pocket. The backs of the cards in each case are outwards.

When a card is called for, mentally refer to its Code number, from which it is clear which pack it is in; plunge both hands alternately into various pockets, and with the hand most convenient to the one containing the required card, count in accordance with the Code until it is reached, and bring it out of the pocket, **together with all above it, and show as one,** then return to the pocket. In this way the order of the cards is undisturbed.

For instance, the KS is wanted. KS is the eleventh card, and therefore in the first division, and in the left-hand breast pocket. The right hand counts the cards, in this case conveniently **backwards**—thirteen, twelve, **eleven:** the thumb separates twelve from eleven and the rest, and these are gripped with thumb at one end, second and third fingers at the other end, and the first and fourth fingers one on each side, so that the cards are neatly and securely squared up.

Again. The 3H is asked for. This is the forty-fourth card, and therefore in the fourth heap and in the right-hand breast pocket. Count from the top—forty, forty-one, forty-two, forty-three, **forty-four**, and grip the five cards in the same way.

The 6C would be thirty-one—in the left-hand trousers pocket. The left hand counts, twenty-seven, twenty-eight, twenth-nine, thirty, **thirty-one,** and shows as before.

At the conclusion, the packets are removed from the pockets in the reverse order to their insertion, and stacked one above the other to restore the order.

18. A SUBTLE GAME

Although the system is made use of in this trick, it is not necessary for the pack to be prearranged. To begin with it is therefore handed out for thorough shuffling. Prior to so doing, however, the performer abstracts, and palms, any four cards in Code order. For convenience we will assume the cards to be the four bottom cards of the stack—

> Three of Diamonds
> Five of Diamonds
> Queen of Diamonds
> Eight of Hearts.

After the pack has been shuffled to satisfaction, the palmed cards are returned to the top and subsequently forced upon four spectators.

The four cards are returned and manipulated to the top of the pack by any of the usual processes. A false shuffle of any type that retains the four top cards is given. The cards are then dealt into four hands and one given to each of the four people who chose cards. They are distributed in order so that each gets the hand containing his own card, and in gathering up, it is desirable to displace the bottom, so that the chosen card is not conspicuous.

The parties are then instructed to sort their hands into suits, as for a game, and to hand the performer such cards as he calls for. On this amiable understanding, he proceeds to name the cards according to the Code backwards from the next in order to the four forced cards. In the present example therefore, he will first call for the 6H, then the 10D, next the 8C, and so on. As the cards are handed to him he places them naturally, face down, in the left hand. This he continues until one card only remains in each person's hand, that card being the one originally chosen. The spectators are left with their chosen cards, and the wily wizard is left with—!

I promised my reader that I should show him how to arrange the pack in full view of the audience, and I have now redeemed my promise. I have done more than I promised. He has not even had the trouble of arranging the pack. It is done, and the audience has done it for him, lured into the belief that they are assisting a trick. The four isolated cards are taken in their proper order and added to the stack to complete the chain. If you can beat that for audacity—next please!

This properly precedes the other tricks in order of execution, but I have kept it till the last, partly so that it might come as a surprise and partly because familiarity with the material was necessary, both for its appreciation and for its performance.

It may be used or not, by way of introduction, as circumstances demand, or, commencing with a previously arranged pack, it may be held in reserve against an accidental or antagonistic disarrangement.